Corsica and
North Sardinia

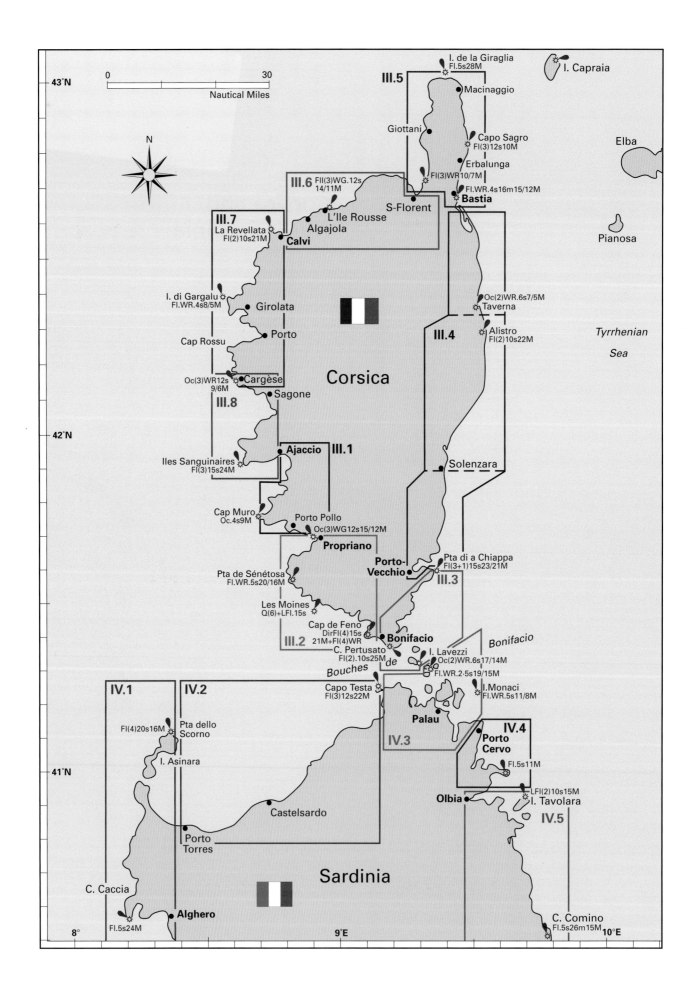

Corsica and North Sardinia

ROYAL CRUISING CLUB
PILOTAGE FOUNDATION

John Marchment

Imray Laurie Norie & Wilson

Published by
Imray Laurie Norie & Wilson Ltd
Wych House The Broadway St Ives
Cambridgeshire PE27 5BT England
☎ +44 (0)1480 462114
Fax +44 (0) 1480 496109
Email ilnw@imray.com
www.imray.com
2007

This work has been based on *South France Pilot -
La Corse*. Robin Brandon 1983

1st edition 2001
2nd edition 2007

ISBN 978 085288 914 5

British Library Cataloguing in Publication Data.
A catalogue record for this title is available from the
British Library.

Printed in Singapore by Star Standard Industrustries Pty

CORRECTIONAL SUPPLEMENTS

This pilot book may be amended at intervals by the issue of
correctional supplements. These are published on the internet at
our website www.imray.com and also via www.rccpf.org.uk and
may be downloaded free of charge. Printed copies are also
available on request from the publishers at the above address.
Like this pilot, supplements are selective. Navigators requiring
the latest definitive information are advised to refer to official
hydrographic office data.

www.rccpf.org.uk may include additional supporting
information including files with updating photographs
received from yachtsmen or the authorities.

CAUTION

Whilst every care has been taken to ensure that the information
contained in this book is accurate, the RCC Pilotage Foundation, the
authors and the publishers hereby formally disclaim any and all
liability for any personal injury, loss and/or damage howsoever
caused, whether by reason of any error, inaccuracy, omission or
ambiguity in relation to the contents and/or information contained
within this book. The book contains selected information and thus is
not definitive. It does not contain all known information on the
subject in hand and should not be relied on alone for navigational
use: it should only be used in conjunction with official hydrographic
data. This is particularly relevant to the plans, which should not be
used for navigation.

The RCC Pilotage Foundation, the authors and publishers believe
that the information which they have included is a useful aid to
prudent navigation, but the safety of a vessel depends ultimately on
the judgment of the skipper, who should assess all information,
published or unpublished.

WAYPOINTS

This edition of the *Corsica and North Sardinia* pilot includes the
introduction of waypoints. The RCC PF consider a waypoint to be a
position likely to be helpful for navigation if entered into some form
of electronic navigation system for use in conjunction with GPS. All
waypoints are given to datum WGS 84 and every effort has been
made to ensure their accuracy. Nevertheless, for each individual
vessel, the standard of onboard equipment, aerial position, datum
setting, correct entry of data and operator skill all play a part in their
effectiveness. In particular it is vital for the navigator to note the
datum of the chart in use and apply the necessary correction if
plotting a GPS position on the chart.

The attention of the navigator is drawn to the Waypoint paragraphs
on page 1 of the text.

We emphasise that we regard waypoints as an aid to navigation for
use as the navigator decides. We hope that the waypoints in this pilot
will help ease that navigational load.

POSITIONS

Positions given in the text and on plans are intended purely as an
aid to locating the place in question on the chart.

PLANS

The plans in this guide are not to be used for navigation – they are
designed to support the text and should always be used together
with navigational charts. Every effort has been made to locate
harbour and anchorage plans adjacent to the relevant text.

All bearings are given from seaward and refer to true north. Scales
are indicated on the plans. Symbols are based on those used by the
British Admiralty – users are referred to *Symbols and
Abbreviations (NP 5011)*.

Contents

THE RCC PILOTAGE FOUNDATION

In 1976 an American member of the Royal Cruising Club, Dr Fred Ellis, indicated that he wished to make a gift to the Club in memory of his father, the late Robert E Ellis, of his friends Peter Pye and John Ives and as a mark of esteem for Roger Pinckney. An independent charity known as the RCC Pilotage Foundation was formed and Dr Ellis added his house to his already generous gift of money to form the Foundation's permanent endowment. The Foundation's charitable objective is 'to advance the education of the public in the science and practice of navigation', which is at present achieved through the writing and updating of pilot books covering many different parts of the world.

The Foundation is extremely grateful and privileged to have been given the copyrights to books written by a number of distinguished authors and yachtsmen including the late Adlard Coles, Robin Brandon and Malcolm Robson. In return the Foundation has willingly accepted the task of keeping the original books up to date and many yachtsmen and women have helped (and are helping) the Foundation fulfil this commitment. In addition to the titles donated to the Foundation, several new books have been created and developed under the auspices of the Foundation. The Foundation works in close collaboration with three publishers – Imray Laurie Norie and Wilson, Adlard Coles Nautical and On Board Publications – and in addition publishes in its own name short run guides and pilot books for areas where limited demand does not justify large print runs. Several of the Foundation's books have been translated into French, German and Italian.

The Foundation runs its own website at www.rccpf.org.uk which not only lists all the publications but also contains free downloadable pilotage information.

The overall management of the Foundation is entrusted to trustees appointed by the Royal Cruising Club, with day-to-day operations being controlled by the Director. All these appointments are unpaid. In line with its charitable status, the Foundation distributes no profits; any surpluses are used to finance new books and developments and to subsidise those covering areas of low demand.

PUBLICATIONS OF THE RCC PILOTAGE FOUNDATION

Imray
The Baltic Sea
Norway
North Brittany and
 the Channel Islands
The Channel Islands
Faroe, Iceland and
 Greenland
Isles of Scilly
South Biscay
North Biscay
Atlantic Islands
Atlantic Spain & Portugal

Mediterranean Spain
 Costas del Sol & Blanca
Mediterranean Spain
 Costas del Azahar,
 Dorada & Brava
Islas Baleares
Corsica and North
 Sardinia
North Africa
Chile

Adlard Coles Nautical
Atlantic Crossing Guide
Pacific Crossing Guide
On Board Publications
South Atlantic Circuit
Havens and Anchorages for the South American Coast
The RCC Pilotage Foundation
RCC PF website www.rccpf.org.uk
Supplement to Falkland Islands Shores
Cruising Guide to West Africa
S. Georgia
Supplements
Passage planning guides

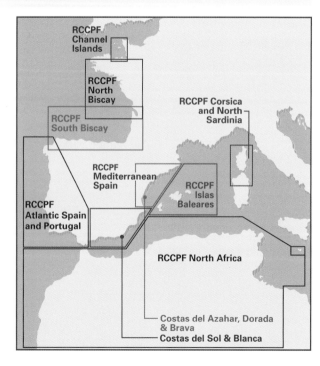

Foreword

Corsica and North Sardinia may be well known to French and Italian yachtsmen but many sailors entering the Mediterranean through the Straits of Gibraltar tend to bypass this area as they head east. They miss a wonderful cruising ground which extends well beyond the Bonifacio Straits. Whilst one must keep a watch on the weather, careful cruise planning can lead to many quiet and remote anchorages and also some stunning coastal scenery, particularly on the northwest coast of Corsica. Those who want a break from the sea can enjoy towns full of history, or gain a closer view of the dramatic mountains by taking the Ajaccio train into the rugged interior.

John Marchment has now built on his knowledge of this area and his earlier revision and extension of Robin Brandon's original pilotage work. The Pilotage Foundation is grateful for his continued support for this book and to Willie Wilson and his team at Imray who have worked hard to present it clearly.

As always, we welcome comments, photographs and updating information from passing yachtsmen and may publish these in supplements available through the Publisher or our own website.

Martin Walker
Director
RCC Pilotage Foundation

Preface and acknowledgements

The author started sailing in 1946 in a Bristol Channel Pilot Cutter, *Christabel*, from Falmouth and has, since then, sailed in most oceans of the world in all sorts of sailing craft. However, his sailing was concentrated on the Channel Isles/Brittany coast areas which were easily accessible from his home in Weymouth. In 1984 he was fortunate to find a job in La Spezia where he spent 8 happy years sailing/motoring in the Mediterranean (when not working!). In 1998 he was asked by the RCC Pilotage Foundation to update the Brandon volume of Corsica. Naturally he had used the volume before and, with much trepidation, he accepted the task of modifying the work of the master. The two main reasons for accepting this work were the Brandon volume was published in 1980 and with only a few updates over the years it was clearly out of date, and he also felt the volume would benefit from the addition of a section on Sardinia. Due to many reasons the gestation period of the first edition was four years and, now, a further five years on it was considered time to introduce another edition, especially as the yearly correction supplement was up to 14 pages which took some time to download. Also there appears to be an upswing in the numbers of pleasure craft visiting the islands again. For some years now very few comments have been received on the problems of the first edition as most yachtsmen have opted for the delights of Greece, Turkey and, more recently, Croatia. However these are now getting crowded and yachtsmen are returning to the superb cruising ground of Corsica and Sardinia, where, so long as one avoids July and August, one can cruise in reasonable weather secure in the knowledge that there are vacant berths in both anchorages and marinas.

This volume has been completely updated and reformatted and again has taken much more work and time than originally thought. The majority of the photographs in this volume were taken at various times by the author but he would like to thank M. Walker, J. Hooper and R. Innes for the use of their material which is attributed on the relevant captions. Thanks must also go to Ros Hogbin for her assistance and suggestions and to the staff at Imray for their patience in the acceptance of my rudimentary sketches and late changes.

John Marchment
Weymouth
February 2007

Early morning looking south to the tower and beach at Porto (see page 116)

Key to symbols used on the plans

	English	French	Italian
⚓	harbour office	bureau du port	capitaneria di porto
⛽	fuel (diesel, petrol)		carburante
⛴ (25T)	travel-lift		travel-lift
⚑	yacht club		circolo nautico/club nautico
⚓	anchorage		ormeggio, ancoraggio

I. Introduction

Using this book

Aim

It is generally agreed that the west coast of Corsica and the northeast coast of Sardinia have some of the finest scenery in the Mediterranean, if not in the northern hemisphere, for the cruising yachtsman. Clear, limpid blue waters, small coves and spectacular cliffs and beaches are scattered along the 1,000 miles of coastline. This book is written with the sole intention of providing a simple and safe guide for yachtsmen who wish to sample the delights of this superb cruising ground. Although crowded in July and August with mainly French and Italian yachts, early and late season visitors will find the waters much less busy than, for example, the Spanish coast or the Greek islands. In the area around the Bonifacio Straits alone there are over 20 harbours and hundreds of anchorages within a 20-miles radius and you can spend a very pleasant month or two here without remaining for more than one night in the same place – although if you cruise at this pace, you are likely to encounter winds of force 6 and higher on occasions!

Layout

Part I of this book is concerned with the general background information necessary to make a cruise in these waters as enjoyable as possible. Technical information on climate and weather, documentation, etc, is included in this section.

Part II describes the routes into the islands, ports of refuge and includes an important section on the marine reserves which have sprung up over the last few years. Planning guides listing harbours, anchorages, headlands and passages, as well as distances between important places and the wind directions that might make the anchorage/port uncomfortable, if not actually dangerous, are found alongside the pilotage data in chapters III (Corsica) and IV (North Sardinia). In this guide, the circumnavigation of Corsica is taken anti-clockwise, starting from Ajaccio on the west coast, and North Sardinia begins with Alghero on the west coast and continues northwards.

The pilotage notes have been written for power or sailing yachts of conventional design between 10 and 20 metres in length with a draft of 2m. Note that small multihulls are relatively rare in the Mediterranean and are certainly not popular in marinas where they can be charged up to three times

the norm in places. Most yacht harbours are equipped with pontoons, jetties, catwalks, landing stages and piers to which yachts can secure. There are many types of design, both floating and fixed, but in this book all have been referred to as 'pontoons', with 'quay' and 'pier' used as appropriate.

Soundings shown on the plans and mentioned in the text are in metres and are based on the local datum which is Lowest Astronomical Tide (LAT). The water level will only fall below this in extreme meteorological conditions.

Plans and data

The plans that are provided for each harbour are simplified for the express use of yachtsmen and they should not be used for navigation. They have been taken from the best information available as well as local visits, but in view of continuing change they should be used with care and prudence.

All bearings in this book are given in degrees true and are from seaward.

All times are local unless specified. Local winter time is UT+0100 and summer time is UT+0200.

Waypoints and positions

The use of the term 'waypoint' does not imply that all vessels can safely sail over these positions at all times or link adjacent waypoints to form routes unless specifically stated. However, skippers should be aware of the risk of collision with another vessel which is plying the exact reciprocal course. Verification by observation or the use of radar to check the accuracy of a waypoint may sometimes be advisable and reassuring.

Note that over the past few years France and Italy have been updating their charts and documents to WGS 84 datum, although many charts in current use may still be European ED50 or even earlier. Although the differences may be 200m or less, care must be taken to work to the datum of the chart in use.

Magnetic variation

In 2006 the lines of magnetic variation ran virtually north/south over the two islands, with the west coasts experiencing 0°25′E variation and the east coasts 0°40′E variation, both increasing by some 6′E per year.

In practice, for the next few years this can virtually be ignored due to the lack of accurate data on the exact current set and rate and the difficulty of steering to better than 2° or 3°. There are also some areas of magnetic perturbations which will be mentioned in the sections where they occur.

Lights

The numbering system for lights shown in lists and on the harbour plans is taken from the Admiralty *List of Lights*, where possible. However, many of the smaller lights and buoys are not covered by the UK light list and in these cases the number is taken from the equivalent French or Italian publication and indicated with a bracketed (F) or (I), as appropriate. Also note that, unlike the lights around the UK coast, all of which are administered by one central authority, Trinity House, there are many privately maintained lights and buoys, especially in Sardinia. These are generally only operated in the summer months and even then may be missing or out of position, making it important to know your position at all times. These 'private' lights and buoys will be indicated (where known) by the symbol (P).

Facilities

Rather than repeat a long list of facilities at every one of the 70 or so main ports and yacht harbours in the book, the exceptions are given. The majority of modern yacht harbours are well equipped and those that are new are making great efforts to reach a good standard. Some of the extremely new ones have very limited facilities at present and these will be mentioned as appropriate.

Where the following facilities are available the text will simply say 'All':

• Fuel available at fuelling berth
• Water on pontoons
• Electricity on majority of pontoons
• Rubbish bins, showers and toilets available ashore
• Telephones available ashore
• Weather forecast available at office
• Repairs can be undertaken
• Crane available
• Restaurants and bars nearby, if not as part of the harbour
• Provisions and chandlery available close by
• Diver available
• Internet café within reasonable distance
• ATM available ashore
• Launderette ashore.

Exceptions will be noted under the facilities heading of each port.

Entrance lights at Cargese (see page 122)

Yacht and equipment

Engines A powerful and reliable engine is essential for motoring through the inevitable calms of the Mediterranean. On other occasions it will be required to motor against strong winds and a short steep sea to get into harbour. A petrol engine can be very dangerous in these waters as in the high temperatures petrol vaporises easily and the risk of explosion or fire is that much greater. Petrol is also not always available at fuelling berths.

Refrigeration A refrigerator is important in these waters and it is recommended that you have one driven off the engine. The engine is used frequently enough to keep a well insulated fridge cool throughout the day. Ice boxes are not recommended as it is getting more and more difficult to obtain blocks of ice, even at commercial fishing harbours.

Ventilation Most British-built yachts have inadequate ventilation for Mediterranean cruising but extra skylights, vents and deck insulation can help mitigate the problem. An awning is essential to keep the hot sun from the deck/cockpit area. It should be well made with side flaps and fitted so that it can be rigged while motoring (and preferably while sailing, although this is less important: if there enough wind to sail, then the draught is enough to cool the deck). An air-scoop to funnel air down the forward hatch is also an excellent investment, especially in marinas, where the surrounding quays and walls seem to maintain a bowl of hot, humid air even during cooler days.

Anchoring Much has been written about the difficulties of anchoring in these waters, and looking at a cross-section of 'decorative trivia' hanging over some bow rollers in marinas one can see why. There is no substitute for weight, and a main anchor of CQR or Danforth type with at least 60m of heavy chain is required. A lighter kedge with 10m of chain and a 50m line (preferably one that sinks!) is useful for lunch stops and when mooring stern-to or bows-to quays (but do make sure there is no holding off line available before dropping your anchor). A common habit in the islands is to dive on the anchor to ensure it is well bedded in – if not, it can be dug in by hand. If caught out in an exposed anchorage, it is useful to have a weight available which can be lowered down the anchor cable to prevent snatching in the steep seas that quickly build up. (In fifteen years of cruising in these waters the author has never had any problem with a dragging anchor.)

Mooring The standard method of mooring in yacht harbours is to back up to the nominated berth and drop a short warp over a bollard or cleat while picking up a small line or chain which is led forward to a larger warp or chain, attached to a sinker *corpo morto*. The boat can then be positioned as required, with 2 stern warps (with chain loops to prevent chafe) and appropriate tension put on the forward warp to keep the craft off the quay. The light line (*pendillo*) is quite often very dirty and in most harbours is covered in small mussels, barnacles, etc., which can inflict nasty cuts to bare skin. Keep a pair of heavy leather gloves in the cockpit lockers for use during mooring operations.

Electricity Electricity is available in most harbours and 220V 50Hz is universal. It is worth having a 25–30m coil of heavy 3-core cable to enable a trickle charger to be run, since the high harbour charges generally include electricity! There are numerous types of sockets and it is advisable to have a male plug on the end of the cable to the yacht and a number of short jumpers which allow connection to any type of shoreside connector.

Water Good-quality water is commonly available at the quay/pontoons in most harbours. There is usually a hose as well but it is advisable to have a 30m length of hose on board just in case. There are numerous connector types but ingenuity (or borrowing the next-door neighbour's hose) can make this unimportant.

Shower A shower fitted to the stern is now common on modern yachts – as are pressurised hot water systems. The sun-shower outfits (a black plastic bag with a short hose and shower rose attached) also work well, but be careful the water does not get too hot.

Gang planks These *passerelles* are most useful if you are spending a fair bit of time in harbours. A plank of wood is adequate but heavy, especially if it is required to project over the modern long sloping stern. An aluminium ladder with rungs covered with marine ply is lighter and easier to stow than a thick plank.

Mosquito nets Some people advocate fitting screens or nets to all openings. Others think this is tedious and inconvenient and use mosquito coils and/or repellents. The editor has never found the need for either (although he has been attacked many times when ashore for a meal). Eating a clove of garlic a day is said to be an effective repellent!

Maritime information

Climate, winds and weather

Although Corsica and Sardinia appear quite large when sailing around their coasts, in meteorological terms they are small . Their weather patterns are similar and, in general, are controlled by the larger land masses that surround them. Local land and sea breeze effects are common in summer and can blow at surprising force, especially off deep valleys that abound round the islands' coasts. The Straits of Bonifacio are another very special area where there can be strong westerly (or easterly) winds blowing, sometimes for days on end, while 20 to 30 miles north or south there is no wind at all!

The Italian (and Corsican) habit of referring to the direction of the wind by name is initially confusing to strangers, as not only do they use names for winds but they use the same names for compass points (see below). Officially the compass point *grecale* is northeast as shown, but of course the *grecale* wind rarely blows from exactly northeast, so there is plenty of scope for error. The *maestrale* (*mistral*) often blows westerly in northern Corsica and it is obviously a *maestrale* from the temperature and strength. A *ponente* pressure wind is quite different and can blow from the west as well. You must be clear whether the person you are speaking to is referring to a direction or the wind itself!

Radio weather forecasts usually use the quadrantal system for wind direction. The first quadrant – I covers winds in the 90 degree quadrant from north to east, with quadrants II, III and IV continuing clockwise from east to south, to west and back to north.

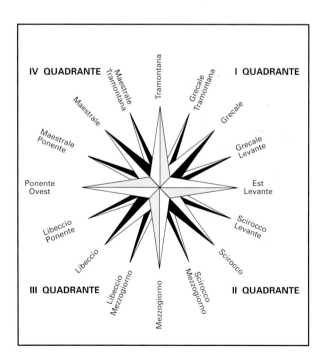

Coast scene near Castelsardo in a *maestrale* (see page 146)

Maestrale

The major wind to affect the islands is the *maestrale*, the cold wind that blows down the Rhône valley and fans out over the Golfe du Lion, arriving at the islands normally as a cool northwesterly air stream, but it can be westerly or even southwesterly at times. It can be very strong (force 6-8) in winter at Cap Corse in the north (usually less in the summer) but rarely reaches more than force 4-5 at the south end of the west coast of Sardinia. This can be a dangerous wind on the west coast of the islands, as the longer fetch can build a much bigger sea than that found near the French coast. The effect of the *maestrale* on the leeward east coast can also be dramatic as the wind is accelerated over the high mountains and sometimes comes down the valleys at force 8 to 9, causing chaos in normally sedate marinas! Weather forecasts are excellent, however, and give up to 12 hours' notice of a strong *maestrale*.

Tramontana

The *tramontana* is the cold northerly air stream that comes from the Alps and the Apuane mountains, generally in the winter or spring. The fetch can build up a large sea but the wind rarely gets above force 5 and is generally a short-lived blow – in fact, the sea may build up without the wind arriving at all.

Libeccio

The *libeccio* is a southwest to west pressure wind which blows fairly frequently throughout the year. It is a warmer and more humid wind than the *maestrale*, but it can blow up to gale force in winter and the fetch allows a nasty sea to build up. It can be dangerous to be in an exposed bay on the west coasts but as this wind originates from a depression moving through the Mediterranean, the forecasts usually give 12 or more hours notice.

Scirocco

The *scirocco* is a very warm south to southeast wind that blows off the deserts of Africa. It can reach gale force in the winter months and blows fairly strongly in the summer, especially on the south and east coasts of Sardinia. It picks up sand from the desert and water from the sea, forming 'red rain' sometimes as far north as Genoa.

Grecale

The *grecale* is a northeast wind which can be dangerous in the central Mediterranean (Malta) but rarely blows above force 6 in the northern part of the islands. However, if in an exposed anchorage, it is wise to move if a *grecale* is forecast.

Ponente and levante

These are normal pressure winds, west and east respectively, but are usually subsumed into one of the other names above.

Clouds and precipitation

The islands are relatively free from cloud cover, with a summer average of 2/8 and a winter average of 4/8. In spite of this lack of cloud cover, the islands do receive 400 to 1200mm of rain each year, except on the north coast of Corsica, which is virtually a desert. When it does rain, it is very heavy (50mm in one hour is not uncommon!) and can seriously reduce the visibility. The main rainy season is around October but rain can occur in any month, with thunder storms prevalent in the summer. These storms normally take place near the coast or over the nearby mountains and can be absolutely spectacular, with almost constant thunder and lightning and torrential rain. The winds can increase from nothing to force 5 to 6 in minutes and blow all round the compass, which makes for excitement in crowded anchorages. The one consolation is that they usually only last for only an hour or so. Generally the locals know what to expect and make sure they are tied up in a secure place.

Fog is rare and any dawn radiation fog quickly clears by mid-morning. Mirages can also form on calm days.

The sea

Water temperature varies considerably due to local wind effects but is about 12°C (54°F) in winter and 24°C (76°F) in summer. Currents around the islands in the Mediterranean are generally weak and tend to flow in a southerly direction at about half a knot or less. However, the sea is much saltier than the Atlantic Ocean, which increases the surface tension and the surface wind effect. If the winds have been blowing in one direction for 2 days or more, there will be a surface current in the direction of that wind. Surface currents of up to 3 knots to the west have been reported in the Straits of Bonifacio after an easterly blow of 3 days and the same in the opposite direction for westerly winds.

This surface tension effect also helps to account for the incredibly swift build-up of seas around the islands. Where there is enough fetch for the sea to develop, in less than two hours a force 5 to 6 wind will build up a one-metre trough-crest sea, with crests only tens of metres apart. These seas should not be underestimated and a powerful engine is required to motor against them. Swell is not such a problem, as the fetches are usually quite short, but the swell that remains after a blow can be uncomfortable for up to a couple of days. Swell seem to get everywhere, including quite sheltered marinas where it can create a nasty surge or *risacca*. For this reason berthing lines should be heavy, preferably with a chain loop around the bollard or ring ashore, and some form of spring or stout rubber snubber is advisable. Needless to say, deck cleats must be capable of taking the extra strains imposed.

Tidal range can be 0.25m at springs, which can be ignored for all practical purposes, as the atmospheric effects of barometric pressure and onshore/offshore wind effects can exceed this range by a factor of 4.

Waterspouts have been witnessed off the north and west coasts of Corsica, but the author has never heard of any damage to yachts being caused by these spectacular occurrences.

Weather forecasts

Both the Italian and French forecasts for the areas around the islands are extremely accurate, considering the complexities of the meteorological situation. The main stations are given below but times and frequencies are prone to change and an up-to-date almanac or the RYA Weather Forecasts handbook (G5) should be carried to ensure details given below are correct. The RYA booklet G5 is updated each year and contains all the information required, together with a very comprehensive multi-language vocabulary.

Weather forecasts in French and English

Monaco (43°43′N 07°43′E)
On 4363kHz SSB (Ch 403) at 0903, 1403 and 1915 LT in French and English for Lion, Provence, Ligure, Corse, Elbe, Baleares, Minorque, Sardaigne, Maddalena and Est Cabrera.
On 8728 and 8806kHz (Ch 804, 830) SSB at 0715 and 1830 UTC in French and English for all western Mediterranean areas.

Weather forecasts in French and Italian

Bulletin Inter-Servicer-Mer on 162kHz Sat, Sun 0654, 2003 LT

Radio France-Internationale 1184kHz at 1140

Radio Bleue from Bastia 1494kHz at 0655 LT

La Garde CROSS on 1696, 2677kHz SSB after call on 2182kHz at 0650, 1433 and 1850 LT for same areas as Monaco (1) above.

However, Radio Italia (Radiouno) broadcasts a Bollettino del Mare at 0554, 1408 and 2249

Monday to Friday, with the 1408 broadcast being omitted during the weekend, in Italian for all Italian sea areas. Porto Cervo gives local waters forecast on VHF Ch 26, 28 or 85 at 0150, 0750, 1350 and 1950 (in English and Italian) as does Ajaccio on VHF Ch 24; also Grasse on VHF Ch 2 at 0733 and 1233 (in French), all with a call on VHF 16 beforehand.

A forecast from the Italian Aeronautical Service is broadcast continuously on VHF Ch 68 in Italian and English at dictation speeds (in a boring monotone!). Gale warnings (burrasca) are broadcast as they are received and the whole message is updated two or three times a day.

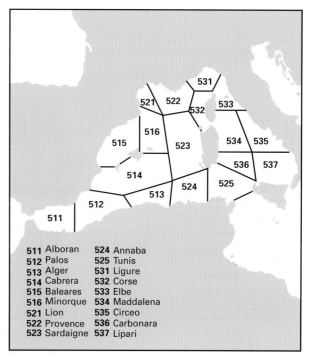

511	Alboran	524	Annaba
512	Palos	525	Tunis
513	Alger	531	Ligure
514	Cabrera	532	Corse
515	Baleares	533	Elbe
516	Minorque	534	Maddalena
521	Lion	535	Circeo
522	Provence	536	Carbonara
523	Sardaigne	537	Lipari

France. Forecast areas

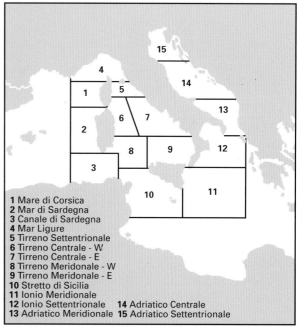

1 Mare di Corsica
2 Mar di Sardegna
3 Canale di Sardegna
4 Mar Ligure
5 Tirreno Settentrionale
6 Tirreno Centrale - W
7 Tirreno Centrale - E
8 Tirreno Meridonale - W
9 Tirreno Meridonale - E
10 Stretto di Sicilia
11 Ionio Meridionale
12 Ionio Settentrionale   14 Adriatico Centrale
13 Adriatico Meridionale   15 Adriatico Settentrionale

Italy. Forecast areas

GMDSS

This has been embraced in a big way by the Mediterranean countries and traffic on both VHF and MF has been markedly reduced. For Corsica the MSI broadcasts are as shown below on the diagram:

In Sardinia the automatic stations for distress and rescue are as shown below:
MSI broadcasts are as shown below:
Note that VHF Ch 68 broadcasts weather information continuously from all stations in Sardinia.

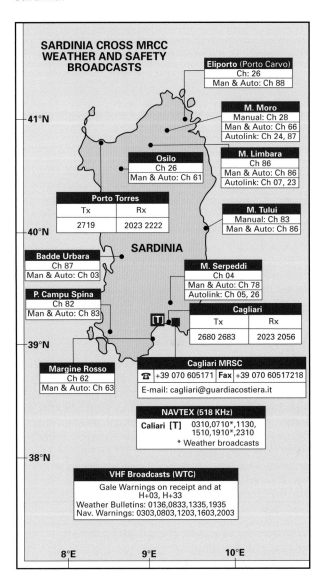

NAVTEX (N4) TRANSMITTERS

Country	Transmitter identification character	Freq kHz	Times	Language used	Range (NM)	Status of implementation
France						
La Garde	(W)	518	0340, 0740, **1140**, 1540, 1940, **2340**	French	250	Operational
(CROSS)	(S)	490	0300, 0700, 1100, 1500, 1900, 2300	French	250	Operational
Italy						
Augusta (Sicilia)	(V)	518	On receipt 0330, **0730**, 1130, 1530, **1930**, 2330	English/Italian	320	Operational
Cagliari (Sardinia)	(T)	518	On receipt 0310, **0710**, 1110, 1510, **1910**, 2310	English and Italian	320	Operational
Roma	(R)	518	On receipt 0250, **0650**, 1050, 1450, **1850**, 2250	English and Italian	320	Operational
Trieste	(U)	518	On receipt 0320, **0720**, 1120, 1520, **1920**, 2320	English and Italian	320	Operational

Times in **bold** are weather broadcasts

Internet

Many sites provide weather information and most, even the official sites, do change from time to time. For a good starting point, the RCCPF recommendes Frank Singleton's site at www.franksingleton. clara.net. (See also www.rccpf.org.uk under technical matters.) Skippers are urged to use the internet as a supplementary source of information and to ensure that GMDSS forecasts can be received on board.

GRIB coded forecasts

GRIB enables arrow diagram forecasts for up to 5 days ahead, and other information, to be obtained in email form (or by Marine HF and HAM radio). The data are highly compressed so that a great deal of information can be acquired quickly and at low cost, even if using a mobile phone connected to a laptop. For details email query@saildocs.com (subject 'any'). There is no charge for this service.

Navigation

Since the previous edition of this, Loran has disappeared from the Mediterranean, all Coastal Radio Stations have closed down and most light intensities have been markedly reduced. Marine Direction Finding stations have been disbanded but, due to the increased air traffic to the islands, there are still a few air beacons operating. The countries around the Mediterranean have embraced GMDSS in a big way and Italy has set up a Maritime Rescue Co-ordination Centre (MRCC) at Rome and a Maritime Rescue Sub-Centre (MRSC) at Cagliari, with 10 remotely controlled stations around Sardinia. France has an MRCC at La Garde and an MRSC at Ajaccio, with 6 remotely controlled stations around Corsica.

GPS receivers are now commonplace and most yachts travel with at least two, on board. A VHF set must still be carried, although in Italy its use has been markedly reduced by the introduction of the mobile phone (*il cellulare* or *il telefonino*) to contact the various marinas. A good SSB set with digital tuning is also useful, and essential if you wish to download weather information onto a laptop. Electronic charts are now becoming popular but it is the author's experience that they are not yet entirely foolproof and it is still advisable to carry adequate large-scale paper charts of the desired cruising area.

Place names

Place names on charts of these islands vary considerably according to the age of the chart and the nationality of the publisher. The official language of Corsica is French, but the Corsican dialect is becoming more prevalent for place names. Sardinia is Italian-speaking but also has its own dialects. This can cause a certain amount of confusion, in addition to which features a few miles apart (or sometimes very close) can have identical names. This book uses the Italian and/or common spelling in all cases, but local variations abound; this makes a GPS almost mandatory, because although most of the navigation is by eyeball, it is often necessary to check your actual position on the ground.

Local habits

For some reason local yachts tend to head home to their moorings or a secure place for the night at around 1700, despite being happy to anchor off a beach or in a bay for a lunch or a swim until then. This need for a more secure berth at night cannot, however, really be explained by changes in the weather: while it is true that conditions do change more rapidly in the Mediterranean than in the Channel, the forecasting is usually as accurate as in the UK and the author has only been caught out once or twice.

Sailing around the coast at night is strongly discouraged by local sailors (although with GPS, an experienced navigator and reasonable crew there should be no real difficulty, and the Mediterranean does not have tides to worry about). Note, however, that there are many unlit rocks; also that some harbours close at night, and one or two prohibit all movement during the hours of darkness.

Cliffs and town walls of Bonifacio (see page 50)

Another custom, very common in Sardinia, is that many yachts leave their berths at about 0900-1100, motor a few miles and anchor off a beach for lunch but return around 1700 or 1800, having reserved their berth with the capitaneria for as long as a week or two. This enables the family to come over from the mainland by car and have a one or two-centre holiday without a long sea cruise each way. This habit does create problems because if you enter a relatively empty harbour at say, midday, and tie up to a berth, you nearly always have to shift when the (temporary) owner returns. A yacht harbour at 1700-1800 on an August day is not a place to be, as the battle for berths can become quite acrimonious.

There is one very useful and friendly facility which is fairly common in Corsican yacht harbours (but less so in Sardinian ones), which is that of allowing a visitor to berth free for 2 or 3 hours. This enables one to shop, fuel and water and then leave for a chosen anchorage without having to check in to the bureau and pay money (which can sometimes be a lengthy procedure).

Like the mobile phone another modern convenience the Italians have taken to in a big way is the – *gommone* (*dinghy* RIB). These are trailed to the islands in their thousands during the summer season and used for fishing, swimming, etc. As they cannot easily be brought ashore this has resulted in a big increase in pontoons in all sorts of shallow water areas, especially around the Maddalena islands. A crowd of RIBs tied to a pontoon should be viewed with extreme caution by a yacht with a normal 2m draught.

Berthing

Due to the vast numbers of yachts and limited space available, berthing stern-to the quays and pontoons is the normal method used throughout the Mediterranean. For greater privacy or because the design of the yacht prevents berthing stern-to, it may be desirable to berth bows-to the quay or pontoon.

Manoeuvring

The manoeuvres to bring a yacht stern first into a narrow berth between two other yachts, sometimes with a cross wind blowing, is a skill which has to be acquired and it is most advisable that some practice at manoeuvring astern should be undertaken in advance. As well as this:

- Have plenty of fenders out especially near the stern
- Approach the berth slowly from some distance off
- If not fully satisfied with the approach draw off and try again
- Warping the yacht or pulling her in by hand when close in is better than using the engine.

It is better to make several attempts in slow time and to berth quietly in a seamanlike manner than to go rushing around with engines roaring and endangering nearby yachts.

Mooring up

The yacht is usually secured to the quay or pontoon by two stern lines leading from the quarters. In order to hold the yacht away from the quay or pontoon, a bow mooring of some kind will have to be picked up. These take several different forms, as follows.

- A small buoy with line or light chain attached to it which leads to a heavier chain which must be pulled in, brought aboard and secured
- A line or light chain that has one end attached to the quay or pontoon and the other to the heavy mooring chain. This light chain is picked up from near the quay or pontoon and followed along to the heavy chain which is pulled in, taken on board and secured
- Mooring posts or piles located either side of the berth which sometimes have chains running out to them from the quay or pontoon. In this case it is necessary to secure the bow lines to the posts.

In many cases the chains are heavy and dirty and gloves are advisable when handling them because they are often covered with small sharp mussels or barnacles. Where no mooring chains are provided, yachts have to use their own anchors. These should be dropped at least 50m from the berth and should have an unbuoyed sinking type of anchor tripline attached, to facilitate recovery should they become foul.

In winter and stormy weather, these securing lines will have to be doubled, and extra lines such as quarter lines, cross-stern lines and bow lines laid out. Extra fenders may be necessary, especially where the stern (or bow) could ride up to and touch the quay or pontoon.

Winds of gale force can arise with great speed and if the yacht has to be left unattended even for a short period it is wise to lay out extra lines. In the few places where it is possible to lie alongside, holding-off lines are usually employed, especially by fishing boats, and can present an unexpected obstruction when approaching a berth. During gales, harbours in the Mediterranean are subject to exceptionally

Tomb Chamber near Alghero (see page 135)

Nuraghe in N Sardinia (see page 135)

strong surges of water, much more powerful than encountered in British harbours, and berthing lines and cleats should be stronger than those usually used at home.

Moorings

Virtually all moorings in harbours are privately owned and if one is used it will have to be vacated should the owner return. There are often no markings to give any indication as to the weight and strength of the mooring, so they should be used with caution. Recently in the Marine Reserve areas numbers of mooring buoys have been laid in popular anchoring areas to minimise damage to the sea bed. These should be used if vacant, as any payment, if collected, has to be paid even if you are at anchor!

Charges

Although there is a law in Italy that states that mooring at a pier for 24 hours is free, in reality, the local Commune (council) rents out sections of the quay to individuals who are allowed to charge (usually a modest sum) for assisting you to moor and will look after the vessel. If you refuse to pay you may occasionally find that a few small items disappear but it is much more likely that the water/fuel charges will be inflated to a point where you pay anyway. Play this one by ear but even if you do not think the man that approaches you is genuine, it is prudent to smile and pay up to keep on the right side of him. In the yacht harbours where you moor to a pontoon there will be charges, and these charges depend on size, season and who you know.

In 2001 a 'tax' which all visiting craft have to pay was instituted in all Italian national parks including Isola Asinara and all the islands of the Maddalena group. Buoys have been laid in many bays and use of these costs € 2 per metre per day, even if one anchors in the area of the park. The fee is collected by official boatmen but note that there is a monthly fee of € 320 or fortnightly fee of € 165 euros (for a 11–14 metre craft) which makes stays of more than 6 days somewhat cheaper. Areas prohibiting the use of anchors, fishing and diving gear have also been set up, see www.parks.it (and in Marine Reserves section II below).

Documentation

Requirements tend to change frequently (in Italy especially), even though we are all in the EU. The RYA handbook *Planning a Foreign Cruise. Volume 2. The Mediterranean and the Black Sea* is worth having as it is kept up to date on a yearly basis. However, as a minimum you should carry the following.

- Ship's registration papers
- Proof of yacht's VAT status
- A certificate of insurance with a translation in Italian.

In Italy there are numerous organisations which have the authority to board any vessel, even at sea, and check the ship's papers, etc. These include the *guardia di finanza* (finance officals); *guardia di costiera* (coastguard); *capitaneria di porto* (harbour officials); *dogana* (customs), and *carabiniere* (police), all of whom have smart high-speed powerboats. They should all be treated politely, and it helps to have a printed list of the following items ready for such an occasion:

Name of yacht	Nome della barca
Country of registration	Paese di registro
Registration number	Numero di matricola
Registered tonnage	Stazza netta di registro
Length (overall)	Lunghezza fuori tutto
Beam	Traverso
Draught	Pescaggio
Type of vessel	Tipo di barca
Owner's name	Nome di armatore
Owner's address	Indirizzo
Passport number	Numero di passaporto
Time and date of arrival in port	Ora e data d'arrivo
Last port of call	Porto precedente
Next port of call	Porto prossimo
Crew list with surname	Cognome
Christian name	(Nome)
Date and place of birth for each crew member	(Data e paese di nascita)
Passport number	Numero di passaporto
Nationality	Nazionalità

However, following a series of complaints from irate (mainly Italian) yachtsmen, some of whom had been boarded up to three times in one day, the government is now looking into ways of reducing this harassment by appointing just one of the above authorities as the boarding authority. Discussions are likely to go on for years, but a yacht flying a foreign ensign, that is obeying the international rules (an inverted cone hoisted when motor sailing, for example), is now unlikely to be boarded.

II. Getting there, Ports of Refuge and Marine Reserves

Corsica and Sardinia span the Mediterranean and are accessible from all directions. The north coast of Corsica is relatively close to the French and Italian rivieras, whereas Southern Sardinia is within easy reach of the African coast. The majority of northern Europeans yachts will arrive in the Mediterranean either through the French canals or via the Straits of Gibraltar. The other main routes inbound are from the Italian Riviera in the north, from further south along the Italian coast, from the Eastern Mediterranean via Sicily, and from Tunisia.

Getting to the islands

A. FROM GIBRALTAR VIA THE BALEARICS

Departing eastwards from Gibraltar, sail up the Spanish coast and over to the Balearic Islands. This allows a departure from Mahon with a journey of about 180 miles (on 077°) to Alghero (⊕60) or 225 miles (on 060°) to Ajaccio (⊕1). These are clearly overnight passages and the weather forecast should be studied before leaving Mahon. If bad weather or the *maestrale* are encountered it is possible to bear away and make for the safe harbours of Alghero, Oristano (or even Carloforte in extremis).

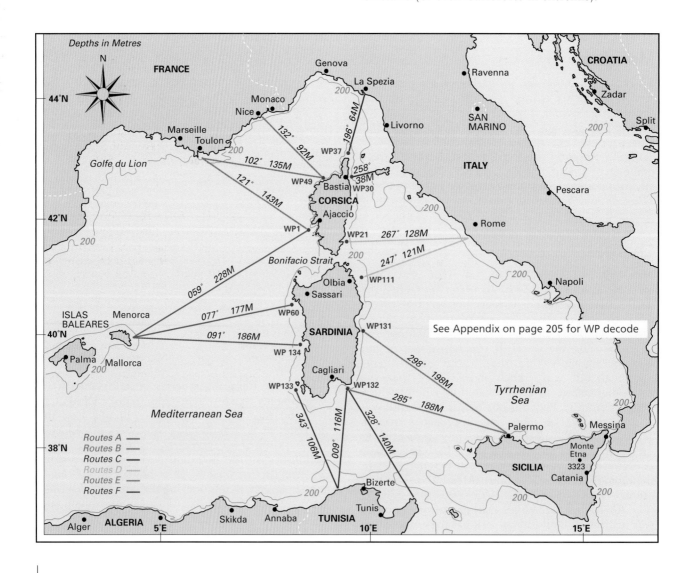

Banchina Dogana (Customs Quay), Alghero (see page 135)

B. FROM MARSEILLE VIA TOULON

After exiting the French canals, sail down the coast to the Toulon region and then make the slightly shorter crossing of about 150 miles (on 131°or 102°) to ⊕1 or ⊕50. If the *maestrale* is blowing, however, the course is virtually dead downwind (and a prudent mariner would not want to spend a night running on a rising wind onto a lee shore!). In this case, sail further up the French coast to somewhere in the Nice region and cross the 92 miles (on 132°) to Calvi (⊕50). There is then the further possibility of bearing away to shelter on the east coast of Corsica if the weather turns inclement.

C. FROM ITALIAN RIVIERA

For yachts coming from the northern Ligurian coast, the distances are much shorter: 65 miles (on 196°) from La Spezia to Giraglia (⊕38), for example, with the choice of continuing on to San Florent (a further 22 miles) if going westabout, or dropping down to Macinaggio if the weather turns nasty. Alternatively, for those wishing to make shorter hops, one can day sail from the north to just south of Castiglioncello before crossing, where a recently completed marina, Cala de Medici (42°24′N 10°25′E), is now a preferable alternative to Livorno, which is mainly a commercial harbour that does not really welcome pleasure craft. If travelling in the opposite direction, make for Punta Ala (42°48′N 10°44′E). From both marinas it is an easy day sail over to Porto Ferraio on Elba. Bastia is then only 40 miles from Porto Ferraio and if this is still considered to be over long, then a break can be made at Capraia, some 25 miles NW of Porto Ferraio and a mere 15 miles from Macinaggio.

D. FROM MID/SOUTH ITALY

From further south in Italy, in the region of Porto Turistico di Roma at Ostia (41°44′N 12°15′E), it is 130 miles (on 267°) to Porto Vecchio (⊕21) or 120 miles (on 247°) to Capo Figari (⊕111). Both overnight passages require study of the forecast before departure. One benefit of this approach is that any strong westerly winds will be blowing offshore and you can simply retreat to the Pontine Islands or even the mainland.

E. FROM SICILY

For yachts coming from the eastern Mediterranean, one possible route is to sail through the Strait of Messina, along the north coast of Sicily and depart from Palermo to Capo Bellavista (⊕131), a distance of 200 miles (on 298°), or Cabo Carbonara (⊕132), 180 miles (on 285°).

F. FROM TUNISIA

Yachts coming from the east may also depart from Kelibia in Tunisia (36°50′N 11°07′E), just south of Cap Bon, and make the 140-mile crossing (on 328°) to Capo Carbonara (⊕132). Alternatively, sail along the coast to Tabarka (36° 57′N 08°46′E) and cross 106 miles (on 343°) to San Antioco (⊕133), where you can always bear away to Cagliari if weather dictates.

Ports of refuge

The following harbours can be entered under storm conditions although in some cases with difficulty.

CORSICA

Bastia Use the commercial port if the gale is from NE or E
Calvi Use the yacht harbour for a NW gale (but there are problems with the swell)
Ajaccio Swell enters when gale is from S
Bonifacio Strong gusts in east or west winds
Porto Vecchio Swell enters during NE gales with a confused sea at entrance

NORTH SARDINIA

Santa Teresa di Gallura Tricky entrance in N or NE gales
Olbia Some swell can enter in E gales
Alghero Difficult approach in W and NW winds.
Note The section of 42 miles of coast from Santa Teresa di Gallura to Olbia has literally hundreds of anchorages, small harbours and marinas and a secure mooring can be found in all weathers with judicious use of large-scale charts. Note that it is a very crowded area in July and August and this may be the time to explore the east and west coasts!

SOUTH SARDINIA

Weather forecasts in this area of the Mediterranean are reasonably accurate, but conditions can change suddenly and catch even the most prudent skipper unawares. With the strongest winds in summer predominantly coming from the NW or NE sectors, this annotated plan of S Sardinia is included to show ports of refuge, when the intended port of arrival is out of reach.

1. **GOLFO DI ORISTANO**
   Area Waypoint
   ⊕134 Oristano 39°46'N 08°11'E
   Watch for Isola Mal di Ventre and Scoglio Il Catalano on the approach as both of these are nature reserves and craft should keep well clear.
   Destinations
   Marina: Porto Turistico atTorre Grande (39°54'N 08°30'E). Good shelter from NW.
   Anchorage: Near Capo San Marco (39°52'N 08°26'.5E) in 5 to 8 m reasonably sheltered from NW.
   Approach
   Porto Turistico Marina: 3M to NE of Capo San Marco, at mouth of Santa Mardini lagoon. Dredged to depth of 2.8m (but possible seaweed/sand build-up). Straightforward entrance between line of lit yellow buoys. Main access between 0600 and 2100
   Capo San Marco anchorage: Just around northern headland of Oristano Harbour, 0.5M N of Tharros, no facilities.
   Note: nature reserve around Capo San Marco and islands above and the prohibited zone around the southern headland (Capo Frasca).
   Contact
   Torre Grande Marina: 400 berths, max LOA 30m, run by Marine Oristanesi srl Contact before entering on VHF 09 ☎ 0783 22189 *Fax* 0783 28800.
   Note: If the wind eases as one proceeds south, either Carloforte E of Isla di San Pietro, or Portoscuso on the mainland can be approached. However if there is still a strong NW wind blowing it is not recommended to attempt the entrance to the Canal di San Pietro as there will be breaking seas and a heavy swell over the shallow rocky bottom.

2. **GOLFO DI TEULADA**
   Area Waypoint
   ⊕135 Capo Teulada 38°51'N 08°39'E
   Destinations
   Marina: Porto Teulada (38°55'N 8°43'.4E) good shelter from NW but open to S–SE.

Anchorage: Porto Zafferano (38°53'.1N 08°39'.3E) very good shelter from NW.
Approach
From Capo Teulada steer to pass well outside Isola Rossa and continue until Torre Budello N of port bears 320°. Then steer to avoid rocky shoals to W.
Porto Zafferano: About 1 mile north of the point there is a large bay where one can anchor in the NW corner in 5–10 m. No facilities.
Contact
Porto Teulada Marina: 150 berths, depths 1–5m, run by Teulada Navigando srl. Contact on VHF 9 ☎ 070 9283705
Email teuladamarina@tiscali.it

3. **GOLFO DI CAGLIARI**
   Area Waypoint
   ⊕136 Cagliari 39°09'N 09°07'.5E
   Destinations
   Cagliari is a large commercial port but there are 3 areas allocated to pleasure craft. Motomar Sarda (NW of harbour), Marina di Bonaria and Marina del Sole (SE). Shelter reasonable for all winds but swell enters after a southerly blow and washes from commercial traffic can cause some discomfort.
   Approach
   From either direction make for the waypoint and the end of the jetty will be seen. Enter the port keeping well clear of any commercial shipping.
   Contact
   Motomar Sarda: 108 berths, depths 1.6–3.5m, maximum LOA 35m. Contact VHF Ch 74 ☎ 070 605 1901
   Fax 070 653 501 *Email* motomarsarda@tiscali.it
   Marina del Sole: 150 berths, depths 7.5–9m, maximum LOA 40m. Contact Cantieri del Sole ☎ 070308 730
   Fax 070 383 7951 *Email* marinadelsole@tiscalinet.it
   www.marinasole-santelmo.com
   Marina di Bonaria: Depths 1.5–7.5m. This area is leased to the *Lega Navale Italiana* (the Italian RNSA) and there may be berths here but try the other two marinas first. ☎ 070 370 380
   Fax 070 300 240.

4. **VILLASIMIUS**
   Area Waypoint
   ⊕132 Capo Carbonara 39°00'N 09°30'E
   ⊕137 Villasimius 39°07'.3N 09°29'.5E
   Destination
   Marina: Villasimius (39°07'N 09°30'E) very good shelter from all directions.
   Excellent facilities for haulout/laying up.
   Approach
   From NE, pass outside Isola Serpentara (unlit) and Isola dei Cavoli. When Cavoli is well past the beam, alter to 315° and leave Secca Santa Caterina well to port. When Molo di Sopraflutto comes into view, steer for the end and round it with 50m berth. Steer south to enter marina.
   Contact
   Villasimius Marina: 750 berths, depths 1.5–6.5m, max LOA 30m, run by Marina Villasimius. Contact before entering on VHF 9 ☎ 070 797 8006 *Fax* 070 797 137,
   Email secretariat@marinavillasimius.it
   www.marinavillasimius.it

5. **ARBATAX**
   Area Waypoint
   ⊕131 39°56'N 09°48'E
   Destination
   Arbatax commercial port (39°56'.6N 09°42'.0E), shelter from all directions.
   Approach
   From ⊕131 steer for the end of the Molo Levante, round the end close to and steer about 150° to enter inner harbour.
   Contacts
   Commercial port with some space for pleasure craft. 80 berths (most taken by local craft), depths 2.5–14m, max LOA 30m. Contact the authorities on VHF 16 or 11.
   Marina di Arbatax: 400 berths, depths 8–15m, max LOA 80m. Contact Turismar snc. VHF Ch 9 ☎ 0782 667405 *Fax* 0782 664359
   Email marinadiarbatax@tiscali.it
   www.marinadiarbatax.it

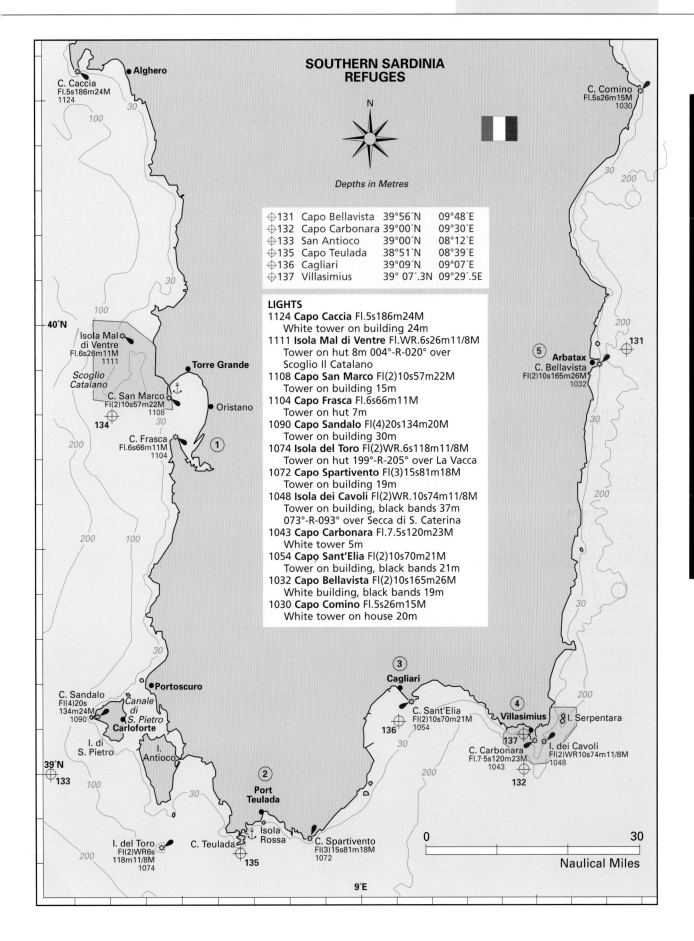

SOUTHERN SARDINIA REFUGES

N

Depths in Metres

⊕ 131 Capo Bellavista 39°56′N 09°48′E
⊕ 132 Capo Carbonara 39°00′N 09°30′E
⊕ 133 San Antioco 39°00′N 08°12′E
⊕ 135 Capo Teulada 38°51′N 08°39′E
⊕ 136 Cagliari 39°09′N 09°07′E
⊕ 137 Villasimius 39° 07′.3N 09°29′.5E

LIGHTS
1124 **Capo Caccia** Fl.5s186m24M
  White tower on building 24m
1111 **Isola Mal di Ventre** Fl.WR.6s26m11/8M
  Tower on hut 8m 004°-R-020° over
  Scoglio Il Catalano
1108 **Capo San Marco** Fl(2)10s57m22M
  Tower on building 15m
1104 **Capo Frasca** Fl.6s66m11M
  Tower on hut 7m
1090 **Capo Sandalo** Fl(4)20s134m20M
  Tower on building 30m
1074 **Isola del Toro** Fl(2)WR.6s118m11/8M
  Tower on hut 199°-R-205° over La Vacca
1072 **Capo Spartivento** Fl(3)15s81m18M
  Tower on building 19m
1048 **Isola dei Cavoli** Fl(2)WR.10s74m11/8M
  Tower on building, black bands 37m
  073°-R-093° over Secca di S. Caterina
1043 **Capo Carbonara** Fl.7.5s120m23M
  White tower 5m
1054 **Capo Sant'Elia** Fl(2)10s70m21M
  Tower on building, black bands 21m
1032 **Capo Bellavista** Fl(2)10s165m26M
  White building, black bands 19m
1030 **Capo Comino** Fl.5s26m15M
  White tower on house 20m

C. Caccia
Fl.5s186m24M
1124

● Alghero

30

100

C. Comino
Fl.5s26m15M
1030

30

200

40°N

Isola Mal
di Ventre
Fl.6s26m11M
1111

100

Scoglio
Catalano

Torre Grande

C. San Marco
Fl(2)10s57m22M
1108

● Oristano

200

134

30

C. Frasca
Fl.6s66m11M
1104

①

200 100

200

⑤ Arbatax
C. Bellavista
Fl(2)10s165m26M
1032

200

131

30

200

30

③ Cagliari

● Portoscuro

C. Sandalo
Fl(4)20s
134m24M
1090

Canale
di
S. Pietro

Carloforte

I. di
S. Pietro

I.
Antioco

C. Sant'Elia
Fl(2)10s70m21M
1054

136

30

④ Villasimius

137

● I. Serpentara

C. Carbonara
Fl.7·5s120m23M
1043

I. dei Cavoli
Fl(2)WR10s74m11/8M
1048

132

39°N

⊕ 133

100

②
Port
Teulada

30

Isola
Rossa

200

I. del Toro
Fl(2)WR6s
118m11/8M
1074

C. Teulada

C. Spartivento
Fl(3)15s81m18M
1072

135

0   30

Naulical Miles

9°E

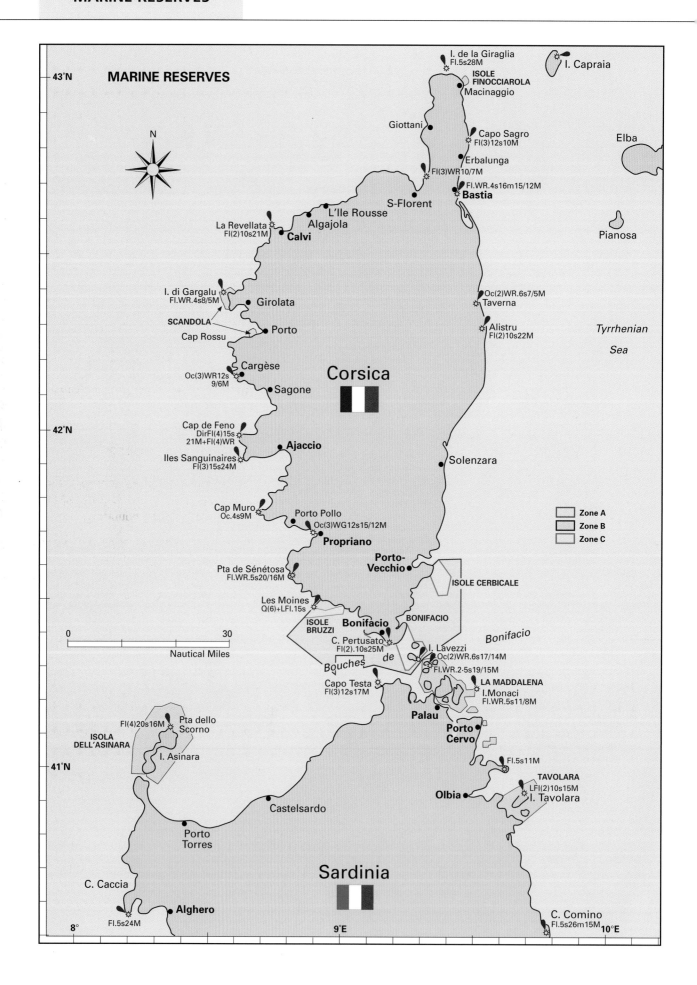

MARINE RESERVES

I. de la Giraglia
Fl.5s28M

I. Capraia

ISOLE
FINOCCIAROLA

Macinaggio

Giottani

Capo Sagro
Fl(3)12s10M

Elba

Erbalunga
Fl(3)WR10/7M

Fl.WR.4s16m15/12M
Bastia

Pianosa

S-Florent

L'Ile Rousse

Algajola

La Revellata
Fl(2)10s21M
Calvi

I. di Gargalu
Fl.WR.4s8/5M

Girolata

Oc(2)WR.6s7/5M
Taverna

SCANDOLA

Porto

Alistru
Fl(2)10s22M

Cap Rossu

Tyrrhenian

Sea

Cargèse

Oc(3)WR12s
9/6M

Sagone

Corsica

Cap de Feno
DirFl(4)15s
21M+Fl(4)WR

Ajaccio

Iles Sanguinaires
Fl(3)15s24M

Solenzara

Cap Muro
Oc.4s9M

Porto Pollo
Oc(3)WG12s15/12M

Zone A
Zone B
Zone C

Propriano

Pta de Sénétosa
Fl.WR.5s20/16M

**Porto-
Vecchio**

ISOLE CERBICALE

Les Moines
Q(6)+LFl.15s

BONIFACIO

**ISOLE
BRUZZI**

Bonifacio

Bonifacio

C. Pertusato
Fl(2).10s25M

I. Lavezzi
Oc(2)WR.6s17/14M

de

Fl.WR.2·5s19/15M

Bouches

Capo Testa
Fl(3)12s17M

LA MADDALENA
I.Monaci
Fl.WR.5s11/8M

Palau

0   30

Nautical Miles

**Porto
Cervo**

Fl(4)20s16M
Pta dello
Scorno

**ISOLA
DELL'ASINARA**

I. Asinara

Fl.5s11M

TAVOLARA
LFl(2)10s15M
I. Tavolara

Olbia

Castelsardo

Porto
Torres

Sardinia

C. Caccia

Alghero
Fl.5s24M

C. Comino
Fl.5s26m15M

8°   9°E   10°E

Marine Reserves

In the late 1990s it was clear that the boom in leisure pursuits around the islands of Corsica and Sardinia was having a serious effect on the environment. Walkers and campers were destroying the delicate flora on the smaller islands, while yachtsmen were not only destroying the seabed flora by anchoring (and dragging) but fouling the waters with their waste discharges. One classic example is that of Spiaggia Rosa (Pink Beach) on Budelli – this was truly pink due to the coral beds just offshore shedding pieces which washed onto the beach. Over the years most, if not all, the coral was removed for the jewellery trade and everyone that visited the beach took home a bag of pink sand. The net result was that by the mid 1990s, the beach had lost all trace of its pink coloration. It was clear to everyone that something had to be done to protect the environment and in 1997, marine reserves were discussed and many ratified by both France and Italy. It was only during the 2001 season, however, that the authorities started to get really serious about them. Buoys were laid in many popular bays and wardens were employed to collect fees (€2 per metre per day in 2005) from visitors who used the buoys or even if they anchored nearby (mainly in the Maddalena areas).

In practice, the yachtsman should sail normally, use the mooring buoys, keep out of the no-go areas and pay the fee when approached by an official warden. Sea toilets should not be used anywhere near the coast because the waters are tideless, crystal clear and there are lots of people who swim. Fishermen and/or sub-aqua enthusiasts should get permission to use their gear at the local park office (ask the harbour authorities for directions).

Marine reserve locations

There are 3 reserve areas in Corsica and 4 in north Sardinia. In broad terms the regulations are similar for all reserves but may differ slightly from reserve to reserve and it is sometimes quite difficult to obtain details about exact zone areas. However, up-to-date information regarding zones and dues can be obtained from the yearly issues of *Livre de Bord* and/or *Pagine Azzurre*. In addition, the websites www.reserves-naturelles.org for Corsican reserves, and www.parks.it for Sardinian reserves are also useful.

Generally all reserves have 3 zones :
Zone A *Riserve Integrale* in Italy or *Zones de non-prélèvement* in France
Zone B *Riserve Generale* or *Zones de protection renforcée*
Zone C *Riserve Parziale* or *Réserve naturelle*

Within these broad categories there may be different regulations between countries and between reserves in the same country.

Marine reserves in Corsica

R1 Réserve naturelle des Bouches de Bonifacio

This is the largest reserve, taking up most of the straits north of the French/Italian boundary.

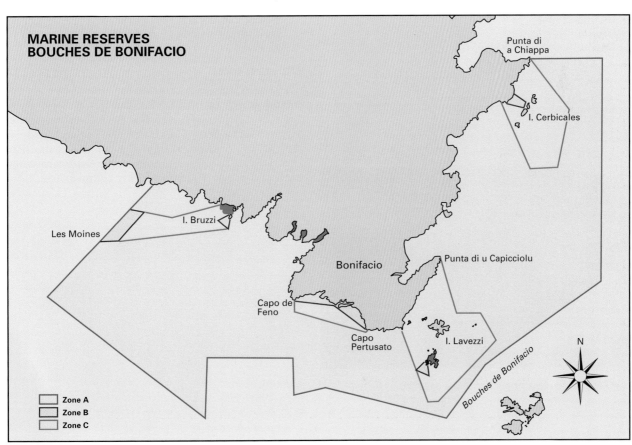

**MARINE RESERVES
BOUCHES DE BONIFACIO**

Punta di a Chiappa

I. Cerbicales

Les Moines

I. Bruzzi

Bonifacio

Punta di u Capicciolu

Capo de Feno

Capo Pertusato

I. Lavezzi

Bouches de Bonifacio

N

Zone A
Zone B
Zone C

A leaflet describing the regulations in detail can be found at most local marina offices and bordering harbourmasters' offices. In summary they are as follows:

Inside the blue line of the Périmètre de la réserve naturelle

Forbidden

Introduction of foreign species

Hunting

Underwater fishing.

Permitted

Free use as long as the tranquillity of the place is not disturbed

Approved public and private works

Approved professional or rod fishing.

Inside the green lines of the Zones de protection renforcée

Forbidden

Underwater fishing

Dogs or camping.

Permitted

Landing of persons on the Lavazzi archipelago

Landing of persons on the Cerbicale archipelago between 1 September and 31 March

Trips ashore, keeping to the paths

Pleasure fishing

Maritime traffic entry and anchoring (but it can be regulated by the local authorities)

Scuba diving.

Inside the red lines of the Zones de non-prélèvement

Forbidden

All forms of fishing

Scuba diving

Permitted

Bathing and snorkelling.

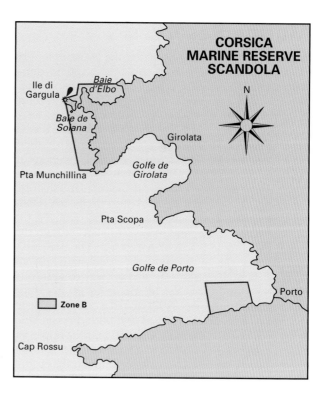

R2 La Réserve Naturelle de Scandola

Forbidden

Fishing and diving in the Baie d'Elbo

Fishing and diving in the Baie de Solana

Anchoring between sunset and sunrise

Fishing, diving and anchoring at all times around Gargalu and in passage between Gargalu and the mainland

Fishing and diving west of Porto

Anchoring between sunset and sunrise west of Porto.

Other reserves

There are three other reserves in Corsica; two are on inland *étangs*/lakes and the third is a very small reserve (3 hectares) at the Iles Finocchiarola, where you are forbidden to land between 1 March and 31 August or to swim within 50m of the islets. (All these are really out of the normal areas for cruising craft and are only mentioned for completeness.)

Cliff formations east of Bonifacio (see page 50)

Marine reserves in Sardinia

In Sardinia there are no less than seven reserves, of which four are in the area of this pilot. The largest and most complex, as it deals with land as well as sea, is the Parco Nazionale dell'arcipelago di La Maddalena.

R3 La Maddalena

Details are obtainable from the park offices at Maddalena and Cannigione or at the website www.lamaddalenapark.it

Inside the blue lines (MB)
Forbidden
> Jetski
> Water skiing outside designated areas
> Pumping bilge water, washing water or anything containing detergents into the sea.

Permitted
> Sailing or motoring in the two zones at no more than 7 knots inside 300 metres from the coast and 15 knots outside 300m from the coast.

Inside the red lines (MA)
Forbidden
> Sport fishing by any method
> Scuba diving unless authorised
> Navigating and anchoring any type of craft (except to save life)

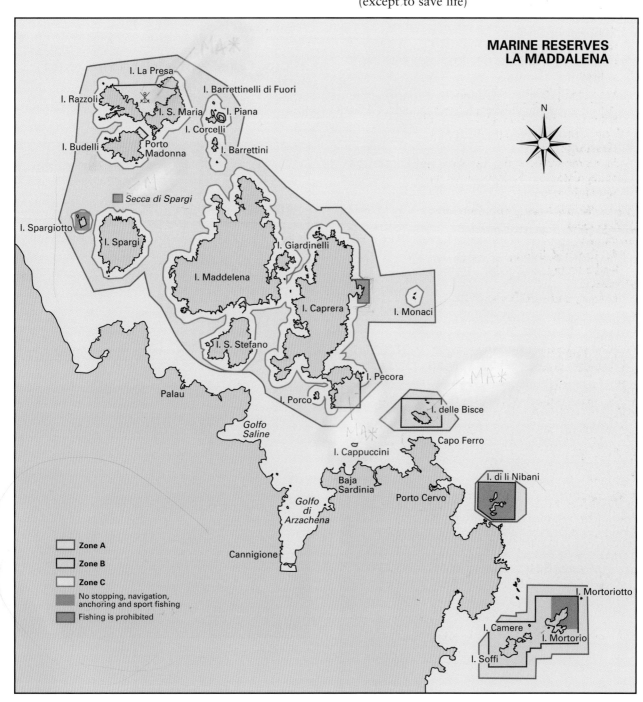

MARINE RESERVES
LA MADDALENA

GETTING THERE, PORTS OF REFUGE AND MARINE RESERVES

Discharging any substances which may affect the environment
Removing any marine formations
Approaching any nesting area
Discharging any arms or explosives
Throwing any object overboard.

In the northern group (effective from 2003)
Forbidden
Entering, bathing or even walking on the beach at Spiaggia Rosa
Entering Porto Madonna except with a rowing boat (without engine)
Permitted
Bathing.

All the southern islands are effectively in the red zone (MA)
Forbidden
All forms of fishing
Navigating or anchoring from 1 March to 30 October all round the I. Nibani and in the NE corner of I. Mortorio.

Further details of the regulations and zones can be found on www.lamaddalena.it

R4 Tavolara
A small handout for the Tavolara and Punta Coda Cavallo reserve just south of Olbia is available at local marina offices.

The regulations for the above reserve are as follows.

Blue zone C (Riserva Parziale)
Permitted
Navigating all types of vessel
Mooring as prescribed by the authorities
Scuba diving
Fishing with rod and line (stationary).

Yellow zone B (Riserva Generale)
Forbidden
Fishing with net or trawl
Fishing for pleasure by any means.

Permitted
Navigating vessels at less than 10 knots
Visiting and scuba diving with the park authorities' approval
Bathing
Mooring to appropriate places laid out by the park authorities.

Red zone A (Riserva Integrale)
Forbidden
Bathing
Any type of fishing
Entering the zone with any vessel other than those of the authority.
Permitted
Access is allowed to personnel of the Park authority.
Guided subaqua visits authorised by the authorities

R5 Capo Caccia, west of Alghero (protected area)

Further details can be obtained at:
www.comune. alghero.ss.it

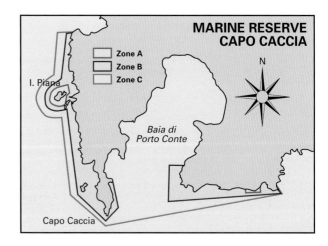

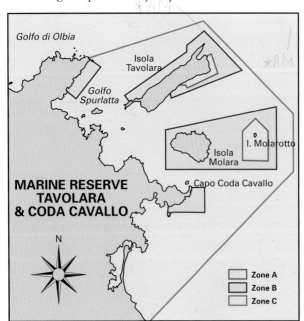

Isola Mortorio looking NE (see page 186)

R6 Asinara

This reserve is different in detail from the others above. Since 1885 Asinara has been a penal colony, a quarantine station, a POW camp in the first world war and a high security prison in the seventies housing the mafia and terrorist prisoners. It was not until 1997 that the island became a national park. Access is still strictly controlled and tickets must be booked well ahead on www.parcoasinara.it Note that the park office for the Asinara reserve is located at Porto Torres. Very recently a 'field of buoys' has been laid in Cala Reale as a sort of marina for yachts only (no engines allowed to be used) and details of these buoys and the quite stringent regulations for their use can be found on www.cormorano.com

The southern boundary has been modified to allow passages to be made through the Passage dei Fornelli. There are 3 zones:

Inside 1,000 metres from the coast (the green dotted line in above diagram)
Forbidden
   All navigation, anchoring, scuba diving, any alteration to the environment, and all activities that might cause damage, including swimming (except on two beaches made available for the day trippers carried by official ferries).

Inside 1 mile from the coast
Forbidden
   All fishing.

Inside 3 miles from the coast
Forbidden
   Fishing with trawl or dragnets.

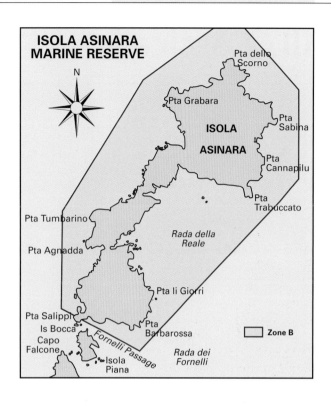

Pointe Sperono looking NE (see page 55)

III. Corsica

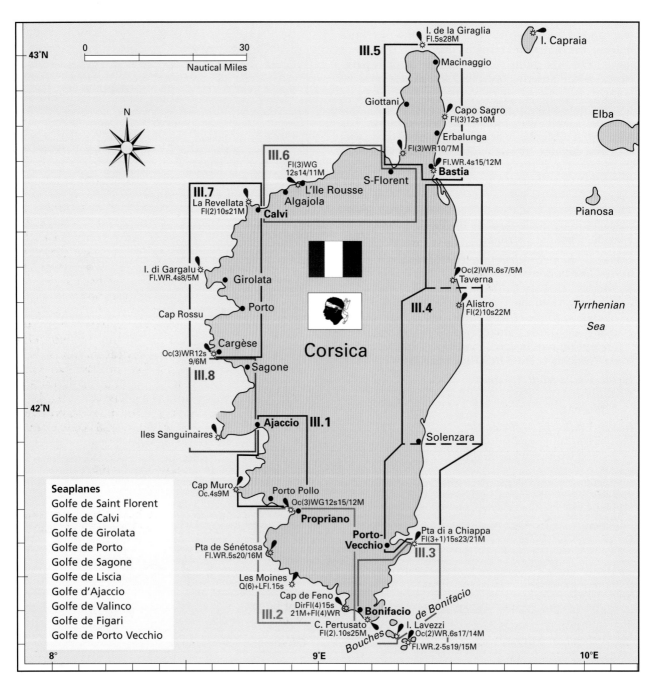

Courtesy Flags

Corsicans feel strongly about their country and appreciate visiting yachts displaying their Corsican Bandana (readily available on arrival) as well as the French national Flag.

Major lights

Full characteristics are given in each section and at Appendix 1.

Waypoints

The positions of waypoints are given in each section and at Appendix 1

Seaplanes

The French authorities use large seaplanes to fight forest fires which plague the islands during the summer season. These Canadair planes scoop up water into body tanks while taxiing at high speed on the water. They then take off, drop the water on the fire and come back for more. Depending on the size of the fire there may be up to 10 or so planes involved in the exercise. The first plane to arrive flies down the flight path at low level and all yachts must leave the area as quickly as possible and stay well clear. Areas commonly used are marked above and on section plans. On the east coast the planes may use the open sea if calm.

Introduction

The island of Corsica lies 100 miles off the French Riviera and from 50 to 120 miles from the Italian coast. To the north is the Gulf of Genoa and the Ligurian Sea. To the east are the Tuscan Archipelago islands and the Tyrrhenian Sea, to the south only 7 miles away, is Sardinia, while some 220 miles away to the west lie the Balearic Islands and Spain.

The island itself is 100 miles long and a maximum of 45 miles wide, with a coastline of nearly 600 miles, because of its many bays and peninsulas. Many illustrious writers have tried to describe this island in a concise way. From a yachtsman's point of view, Corsica could be said to be 'a scented granite mountain surrounded by anchorages' and it is certainly one of the finest cruising areas in the western Mediterranean. The island is sparsely populated with only some 300,000 people, nearly half of whom live in the two largest towns of Bastia and Ajaccio. The rest of the island has not suffered too badly at the hands of the developers. Except for the bare mountain peaks (highest is Mt Cinto at 2,710m (8,900ft)) and a few cultivated areas, the island is covered in Mediterranean maquis: a mixture of low, aromatic shrubs, which in spring gives off a characteristic scent, detectable many miles offshore.

History

It is impossible to give more than a bare outline of the long and complex history of Corsica, but those interested in the subject should refer to *History of Corsica* by Paul Arighi (1966), or *The tragic history of the Corsicans* by Dom JB Gai (1951).

Around 3000BC the first megalithic civilisation inhabited the SW of the island and left many dolmens and menhirs; by 1600BC these people were building statue-menhirs to honour the dead. Another group, the Toreens, was established in the SE around 2000BC and left a series of large domed buildings called Torris, not unlike the Nuraghs of Sardinia. The Toreens vanished about 1200BC and may have moved to Sardinia.

The Phoenicians with the Greeks founded Alalia (Aliera on the east coast) in 560BC and, in spite of invasions and occupations by the Carthaginians and Etruscans around 280 to 260BC, they remained at Alalia until driven out by the Romans when they invaded in 259BC. The Romans colonised the island, established several towns (including Mariana) and ruled for 700 years. They were driven out by the Vandals in AD450, followed by the Ostrogoths, Byzantines, Lombards and the Saracens. In 1077 the Pope, who had been given titular control by the Saracen, (Pippen the Short) in 758 when he drove the Lombards out, assigned the administration of the island to the Bishop of Pisa. This was disputed by the Genoese who seized Bonifacio (1187) and Calvi (1278) and finally defeated the Pisans in the naval battle of Meloria. Anarchy still reigned, however, and another pope assigned the islands to the Dukes of Aragon. Unrest continued as the people supported Genoa while the nobles supported Aragon. In 1420,

a large force from Aragon seized the island and ruled it until 1434 when the Viceroy was captured and executed by the Genoese. The Genoese then gave the island to the Bank of St George to look after until 1553 when the French took it, but they gave it back in 1559 and the Genoese ruled it until 1729. During this period they built the fortified citadels of Calvi and Bonifacio, imposing forts at Aleria, Girolata and Tizzano and a series of watch towers around the island.

In 1729 a rebellion broke out against the Genoese but it was Paoli in 1755 who proclaimed himself General of the Corsican Nation. In 1768 Genoa sold the rights of the island to France, defeating Paoli, who took refuge in England. Napoleon Bonaparte was born in Ajaccio in August 1769. In 1790, after the French Revolution and Paoli's amnesty, he returned and occupied a controlling post in the island's government. In 1792 an expedition to take Sardinia failed, Paoli was blamed and he appealed to England for assistance while his partisans drove the Bonapartes from the island. The British put Sir Gilbert Eliot in as Viceroy of the Anglo-Corsican kingdom (Nelson lost his eye in the battle for Calvi in 1794). In 1796 the British evacuated the island and France repossessed it and it has remained with France ever since. The Germans and Italians held it during the Second World War and the Corsicans liberated themselves in 1943. Tourism is on the increase and the depopulation of the island has been halted. However, although France has given them more autonomy, the Corsicans still believe they should govern their own island.

Warnings and restricted areas

Underwater cables

There are a number of cables linking the islands and anchoring and fishing is prohibited in the following areas (shown on the appropriate plans):

S of Bastia
N of Saint Florent
W of Ile Rousse
S of Bonifacio
N and S of Iles Lavezzi

Offshore oil terminals

These are present in the following areas, where fishing and anchoring is forbidden:

S of Bastia
Near Bastia-Poretta Airfield
Near Solenzara Airfield

Underwater and air training area

This area east of Ajaccio harbour near Pointe d'Aspretto must not be entered if a blue flag is flying on the point. There is also a large area south of Taverna (Campoloro) which is a bombing range.

There are several marine reserves around the island and these are described in detail in Section II above.

1 AJACCIO TO PORTO POLLO

The wide and deep Golfe d'Ajaccio is bounded by
Pointe de la Parata to the north with a long chain of
islands, Iles Sanguinaires, lying southwestwards
from it and Cap Muro, a very prominent headland,
to the south. Ajaccio is a major harbour and popular
port of arrival. The sides of the gulf are broken and
rugged and the coast at its head is low with a long
sandy beach. Ajaccio, the capital of the island, lies in
the NE corner of the gulf and is a major harbour. It
caters for commercial, ferry, yacht and naval traffic
and is the main arrival port for those coming from
the Balearics and western Mediterranean. A road
follows the coast and there is an increasing number
of housing estates and some campsites, especially
near the heads of the many small bays where there
are beaches. South of Cap Muro there is another
deep gulf, the Golfe de Valinco, again offering
anchorages, although there are several unmarked
off-lying dangers where care is needed. Some of the
anchorages are deserted; the main centres of
population being near the two harbours of Porto
Pollo and Propriano, although housing development
is increasing around the north shore of this gulf.

La Grande Sanguinaire from SW

PLANNING GUIDE

Headlands	Ports & anchorages	Open to winds
Pointe de la Parata		
Iles Sanguinaires and passages		
	⚓ La Grande Sanguinaires page 25	E-SE-S
La Botte de Canicciu		
Ecueil de la Guardiola		
	⚓ Anse Maestrellu	E-S-SW
Rocher Citadelle		
	C1 ⛵ Ajaccio page 24	
	Port Tino Rossi page 27	
	Port Charles Ornano page 28	
Pointe d'Aspretto		
Pointe de Porticcio		
Écueil Dorbera		
	⚓ Pointe de Porticcio	SW-W-NW
	⚓ Anse de Ste Barbe	W-NW-N
Pointe de Sette Nave		
La Campanina beacon		
	⚓ Anse Medea	S-SW
	⚓ Anse Ottioni	SW-W-NW
	⚓ Port de Chiavari	W-NW-N
	⚓ Ile Piana	NE or SW
	⚓ Anse de Portigliolo	W-NW-N
	⚓ Pointe de la Castagna NE	NW-N-NE
Pointe de la Castagna		
	⚓ Pointe de la Castagna SE	S-SW-W
	⚓ Anse de Cacalu	N-NE-E
Pointe Guardiola and passage		
Cap Muro		
	⚓ Cala di Muru	SE-S-SW
	⚓ Cala d'Orzu	S-SW-W
Capu Neru		
	⚓ Baie de Cupabia	S-SW-W
Pointe de Porto Pollo		
	C2 ⛵ Port de Porto Pollo page 33	E-SE-S

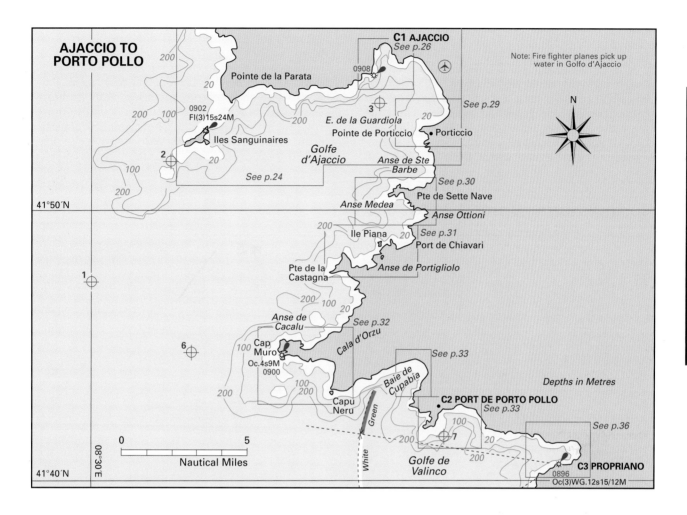

AJACCIO TO PORTO POLLO

Note: Fire fighter planes pick up water in Golfo d'Ajaccio

C1 AJACCIO See p.26

0908

200
200
20
100
200
100
200

Pointe de la Parata

0902 Fl(3)15s24M

Iles Sanguinaires

E. de la Guardiola

Pointe de Porticcio

Porticcio

See p.29

Golfe d'Ajaccio

Anse de Ste Barbe

See p.24

See p.30

Pte de Sette Nave

Anse Medea

Anse Ottioni

41°50'N

Ile Piana

See p.31

Port de Chiavari

Pte de la Castagna

Anse de Portigliolo

Anse de Cacalu

See p.32

Cala d'Orzu

Cap Muro

Oc.4s9M

0900

Baie de Cupabia

See p.33

Depths in Metres

Capu Neru

C2 PORT DE PORTO POLLO See p.33

7

See p.36

Golfe de Valinco

C3 PROPRIANO

0896 Oc(3)WG.12s15/12M

White   Green

08°30'E

0   5

Nautical Miles

41°40'N

N

Typical fire fighting seaplane scooping water

R. Innes

⊕1	**Ajaccio**	41°47'.5N 08°30'.0E
⊕2	**Iles Sanguinaires**	41°52'.0N 08°33'.0E
⊕3	**Ajaccio approach**	41°54'N 08°45'E
⊕6	**Cap Muro**	41°44'.5N 08°38'.5E
⊕7	**C2 Porto Pollo**	41°42'.41N 08°48'.0E

0902 **Iles Sanguinaires** Fl(3)15s98m24M
   White tower, black top on building 18m
0908 **La Citadelle** Fl(2)WR.10s19m20/16M
   White tower, red top13m
   057°-W-045°-R-057° (red over La Guardiola)
0900 **Cap Muro** Oc.4s57m9M
   White square tower, black top 11m
0896 **Scogliu Longu** Oc(3)WG.12s16m15/12M
   White tower, green top 17m
   070°-W-097°-G-137°-W-002°

C1 Ajaccio

Capital of Corsica with two yacht harbours

A large commercial, fishing, naval and yachting port, the second largest city and port in Corsica and the capital of the island. It is an attractive city in a pleasant setting and has good facilities. There are two yacht harbours which can be approached and entered under almost any conditions and shelter found, but with strong winds from the south or southeast, the swell enters the main harbour and is reflected by the Quai Napoleon into Port Tino Rossi, making it very uncomfortable and occasionally dangerous. In the season both yacht harbours become very crowded. The old port (Port Tino Rossi) is to the south and a modern yacht harbour (Port Charles Ornano) is to the north, with a large ferry and commercial harbour between them. Port Tino Rossi has better facilities and is more convenient for the town but is usually more crowded. There is a naval harbour a mile to the east of the town on Pointe d'Aspretto into which yacht entry is totally prohibited.

Northwestern approaches to Ajaccio

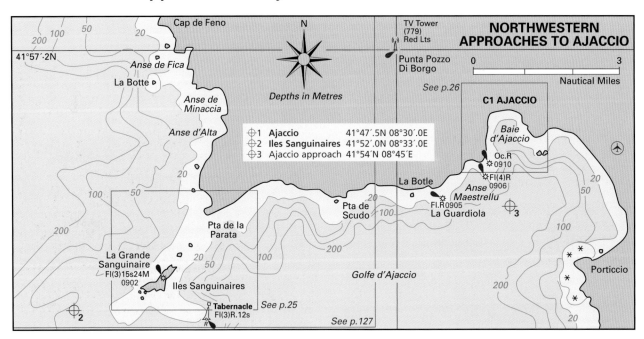

⊕1	Ajaccio	41°47′.5N 08°30′.0E
⊕2	Iles Sanguinaires	41°52′.0N 08°33′.0E
⊕3	Ajaccio approach	41°54′N 08°45′E

POINTE DE LA PARATA 41°53′.7N 08°36′.45E AND ILES SANGUINAIRES

An attractive headland and islands lying in a SW–NE direction which is similar to the Raz du Sein in Brittany but without the strong tidal streams. From the northeast the high (283m) hills slope down to the Presqu'île de la Parata which consists of two distinctive parts, a low flat isthmus connected to a rounded feature with a small house and radio beacon mast on the top (86m). There is a road on the southeastern side leading to a restaurant. A second very low isthmus connects the first part to the second feature which is of a pyramid shape (58m) with a conspicuous tower on top. It is essential to identify this feature if attempting the Passe des Sanguinaires, as from a distance it simply looks like two more islands.

Southwest of this pass lies Ile de Porri (two islets, Iles de l'Oga and Iles Cala d'Alga). Between these four islets it is shallow and foul with rocky heads. The largest island; Ile de la Grande Sanguinaire, is the outer island, it has a white lighthouse, black top and white dwelling (Fl(3)15s98m24M) on the crest near the northeastern end. A signal station is located near the centre of the island and a tower stands near the southwestern end. There are rocks and shallows extending 500m southwestwards from this point. The Écueil du Tabernacle, an isolated rock 3m deep, is 1,300m to southeast of the centre of this island and it is marked by a red pillar light buoy with a can topmark (Fl(3)R.12s4m3M).

Passages des Sanguinaires

The main passage is the Passe des Sanguinaires between the Pointe de la Parata and Ile de Porri. It is 200m long and 200m wide, with a minimum depth of 7m. Take the passage in E–W directions about 50m from the Pointe de la Parata and 150m from Ile de Porri. For yachts drawing 2m or less, the passage is 400m wide with a minimum depth of 2.8m. Currents of up to 3 knots can be experienced in the area and these frequently set across the passage. Under conditions of heavy seas and strong winds the use of this passage is not recommended. Instead proceed south and round the end of La Grande Sanguinaire keeping over ½M to the southwest and pass outside the Écueil du Tabernacle light buoy.

⚓ LA GRANDE SANGUINAIRE 41°52'.6N 08°35'.5E

There are three small anchorages on the SE side of this island.

1. A very small anchorage in a little bay between the Ile Cala d'Alga and the northeastern end of La Grande Sanguinaire, anchor in 3m, sand and rock, open to NE–E–SE–S.
2. A large anchorage just north of the Pointe du Tabernacle which projects in a southeasterly direction from the middle of the island. There are two 3m-deep rocks and also small rocks close in along the coast. Anchor in 2m, rock, open to NE–E–SE. There is a small landing stage used by ferries bringing day tourists from Ajaccio.
3. A very small anchorage just below and to the southeast of the tower on southwestern end of La Grande Sanguinaire in 4m, rock, open to E–SE–S–SW. There is a small stony beach ashore.

POINTE DE SCUDO 41°54'.25N 08°41'.5E

This is an insignificant point with many rocky offliers but with a possible anchorage in 3m, rock, just to the east of the point. In the bay to the west of this point is an ⚓ cardinal BYB buoy (Q(3)5s) indicating a fish farm. Keep well clear of this area.

La Botte de Canicciu

An awash rock marked by a red pole beacon with a square topmark.

Écueil de la Guardiola

A red tower with a square topmark and light (Fl.R.2.5s6m2M) erected on a small group of rocks just over 1M to SW of Ajaccio citadel and 500m offshore, covered by the red sector of the citadel light. Give it a 200m berth to the south. Note that although it is possible to pass between it and the shore, it is not recommended without local knowledge.

⚓ ANSE MAESTRELLU 41°54'.7N 08°44'E

This bay is open to E–SE–S–SW with a road and many houses and apartment blocks behind. Anchor off the sandy beach in 3m, sand.

Ecueil de la Citadelle

A red tower with a square topmark and light (Fl(4)R.15s10m6M) lies 400m south of the citadel, marking a rock and with shallows (3m) 100m to the north and another patch (3.5m) 200m to the west. Pass well south of this beacon.

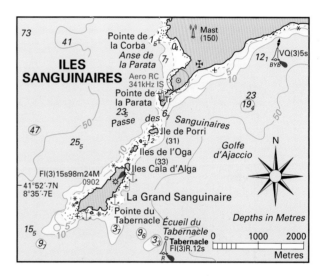

Iles Sanguinaires from the N. Also see photos on pages 22 and 129

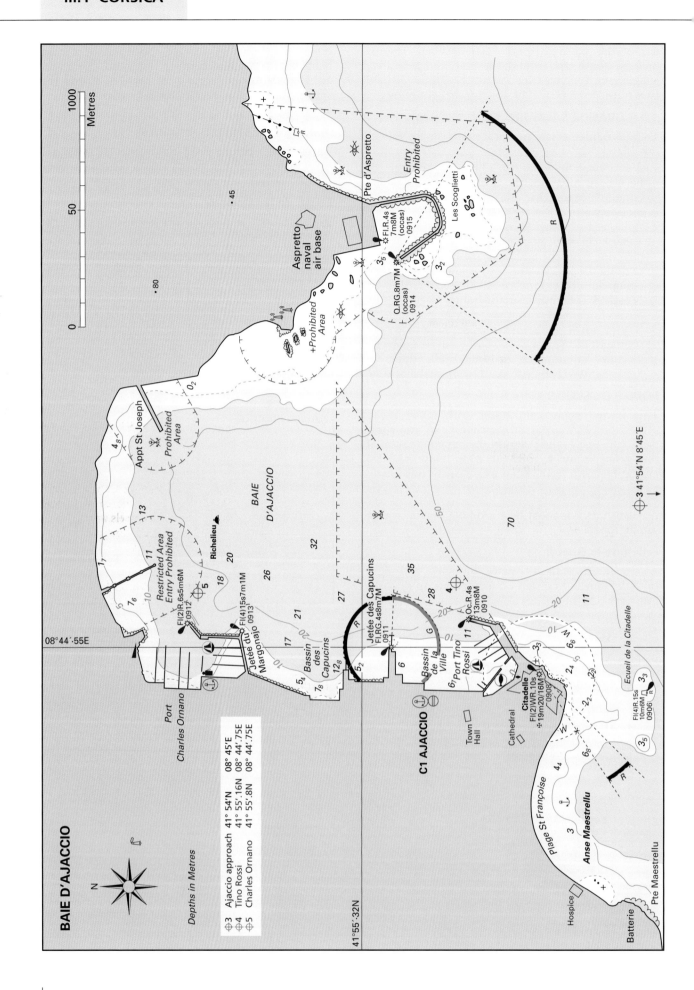

BAIE D'AJACCIO

Metres
1000 · 50 · 0

Depths in Metres

	Ajaccio approach	41° 54'N	08° 45'E
3	Tino Rossi	41° 55'.16N	08° 44'.75E
4 5	Charles Ornano	41° 55'.8N	08° 44'.75E

08°44'.55E

Port
Charles Ornano

Appt St Joseph
Prohibited Area

Aspretto naval air base

+Prohibited Area

Pte d'Aspretto

Entry Prohibited

Fl.R.4s 7m8M (occas) 0915

Les Scoglietti

Q.RG.8m7M (occas) 0914

BAIE D'AJACCIO

Richelieu

Fl(2)R.6s5m6M 0912

Fl(4)15s7m1M 0913

Jetée du Margonajo

Bassin des Capucins

Jetée des Capucins
Fl.RG.4s8m7M 0911

Bassin de la Ville

Oc.R.4s 13m8M 0910

Port Tino Rossi

Restricted Area Entry Prohibited

C1 AJACCIO

Town Hall

Cathedral

Citadelle
Fl(2)WR.10s
19m20/16M
0908

Fl(4)R.15s 10m6M 0906

Ecueil de la Citadelle

Plage St Françoise

Anse Maestrellu

Hospice

Batterie

Pte Maestrellu

3 41°54'N 8°45'E

41°55'.32N

Port Tino Rossi, Ajaccio

⊕4 41°55′.16N 08°44′.73E

Depth
2–7metres

Number of berths
260 berths with 80 places for visitors

Maximum length
60m

Charts
Admiralty *1424*
French *6851, 6942, 7280*

Lights
0906 Écueil de la Citadelle 41°54′.8N 08°44′.5E
Fl(4)R.15s10m6M Red tower 13m
0908 La Citadelle 41°55′.0N 08°44′.5E
Fl(2)WR.10s19m20/16M 057°-W-045°-R-057° White
tower red top 13m
0910 Jetée de la Citadelle Oc.R.4s13m8M White tower,
red column
0911 Jetée des Capucins head Fl.RG.4s8m7/7M
110°-R-271°-G-065°-obscd-110° White column,7m
0912 Port Charles Ornano Quai Est head Fl(2)R.6s5m6M
White tower red top 3m
0913 Jetée de Margonajo head Fl(4)15s7m1M
White post 6m

Beacons
La Campanina 41°50′.3N 08°45′E BRB beacon tower,
⁑ topmark 5M to S of harbour marking 0.3m deep rock
off Pointe de Sette Nave
La Botte de Canicciu 41°54′.3N 08°42′.4E R beacon post,
■ topmark 2M SW of harbour
0905 Écueil de la Guardiola Fl.R.2.5s6m2M stands on a
rock 1.25M to SW of the harbour covered by the R
sector
of the Citadelle lighthouse. R beacon tower, ■ topmark

Buoys
0957(I) Écueil de Tabernacle 41°52′.0N 08°36′.5E
Fl(3)R.12s4m3M Red buoy, ■ topmark
0959.2(I) Buoy W 41°54′.5N 08°47′.6E Q(9)15s1m3M
Ⅹ card
0959.3(I) Buoy E 41°54′.5N 08°47′.7E Q(3)10s1m3M ♦
card

Port communications
VHF Ch 9 ☎ 04 95 51 55 43, *Fax* 04 95 21 93 28
(S 0800–2100; OoS 0800–1200 1400–1800)

Warnings
The Golfe d'Ajaccio has several shallow patches of foul
ground extending up to 500m from the shore in places.
There are some large unlit buoys in the Baie d'Ajaccio.
The wash from manoeuvring commercial craft can
affect yachts in the Vieux Port. Ferries, commercial
vessels and naval vessels have priority over yachts in the
port area and approaches

Fire-fighting planes
Large flying boats may land in the Golfe d'Ajaccio to
pick up water for fire-fighting

0906 **Ecueil de la Citadelle** Fl(4)R.15s10m6M
Red tower 13m
0908 **La Citadelle** Fl(2)WR.10s19m20/16M
White tower, red top 13m
0910 **Jetee de la Citadelle** Oc.R.4s13m8M
White column, red top 13m
0911 **Mole des Capucins** Fl.RG.4s8m7M
White column 7m
0913 **Jetee du Margonajo** Fl(4).15s7m1M
White column 6m
0912 **Marina breakwater** Fl(2)R.6s5m6M
White tower, red top 3m
0914 **Aspretto breakwater** Q.RG.8m7M
White column, green top 5m (occas)

PILOTAGE

Approach

By day
From the north round the Iles Sanguinaires and the
Tabernacle buoy to port (or take the Passe di
Sanguinaires if calm) and steer along the coast,
keeping La Botte, La Guardiola and La Citadelle
beacons to port.

From the south leave Cap Muro to starboard and
steer a NNE course, leaving Pointe de la Castagna,
La Campanina and Pointe de Sette Nave well to
starboard. The houses of Ajaccio will now be
obvious. Steer for the Citadelle.

The jetty should now be visible, steer for the end.

By night
The approaches are well lit, but keep more to the
centre of the gulf until the jetty lights have been
positively identified.

By GPS
From ⊕1 or the centre of the gulf (between ⊕2 and
⊕6) steer for ⊕3. At this position the jetties will be
visible. Alter course and steer a northerly course for
⊕4 or ⊕5, depending on which marina is required.

Entrance

By day
Approach the head of the Jetée de la Citadelle on a
northwesterly course and round it at 25m, having
first checked that no commercial vessels are entering
or leaving. Secure to the small pontoon at the head
of this jetty for berthing instructions.

By night
Leave the Fl(4)R.15s and Fl(2)WR.10s to port;
approach Oc.R.4s on a northwesterly course. Round
it, leaving it 50m to port and then secure to the small
pontoon at the head of the Jetée de la Citadelle for
berthing instructions.

Berths
Berth where instructed – normally at the end of the
Jetée de la Citadelle. Note that anchoring is
forbidden in the harbour.

Facilities
All.

A Corsican 'bandana' courtesy flag may
be bought in marina chandleries

I. AJACCIO TO PORTO POLLO

Port Charles Ornano, Ajaccio

⊕5 41°55′.7N 08°44′.75W

Depth
2–15m

Number of berths
800 with 200 for visitors

Maximum length
35m

Lights
0913 Jetée de Margonajo Fl(4)15s7m1M White column, 6m
0912 Head of east jetty Fl(2)R.6s5m6M White tower, red top 3m

Port communications
VHF Ch 9, ☎ 04 95 22 31 98, *Fax* 04 95 20 98 08 (S 0700–2100, OoS 0800–1730).

PILOTAGE

Approach

As for port Tino Rossi but proceed further north, keeping clear of all commercial traffic.

Entrance

By day

Approach the northwest corner of the Baie d'Ajaccio and leave the head of the Jetée du Margonajo with a white tower to port. Follow along the Jetée Est on a northerly course for 150m and then round its head at 25m, entering the harbour. Secure to the first pontoon to port and report to the *capitainerie* at the root of the jetty.

By night

Approach the northwest corner of the Baie d'Ajaccio, leaving Fl.RG.4s 400m to port and then Fl(4)15s, 25m to port. Follow along the Jetée Est on a northerly course for 150m and round Fl(2)R.6s at 25m, entering the harbour. Secure to first pontoon to port on entering. The lights listed above are difficult to pick out against the lights of the town.

Berths

As instructed but this will normally be at the visitor berths at the end of Jetee Est immediately to port on entering the marina.

Formalities

All authorities are available.

Facilities

All.

History

The name of this old fishing village probably originated from the Latin *adjacium* meaning 'a resting place' and it was sited to the north of the citadel. In the 10th century it was destroyed by the Saracens and later reconstructed by the Genoese. The citadel dates from 1554 as does the Cathedral. The birth of Napoleon Bonaparte on 15th August 1769 in the Casa Bonaparte, a few hundred yards northwest of the citadel, is the local event of importance. The fact that Pascal Paoli's partisans chased him out of his house and forced him to flee to Calvi is not so well known. They confiscated his house and used it as an arms depot.

Ajaccio, which has a pleasant temperate climate, became one of the first towns to be visited by the Victorians seeking to escape the horrors of the English winter and was developed as a resort along with Cannes, Nice and Palma de Mallorca, all of which have similar architecture.

Ajaccio. Port Charles Ornano looking NW

The next port after Ajaccio is 20 miles down coast at Porto Pollo. This harbour lies to the N and E of Pte Porto Pollo – note the offlying rocks and see page 33

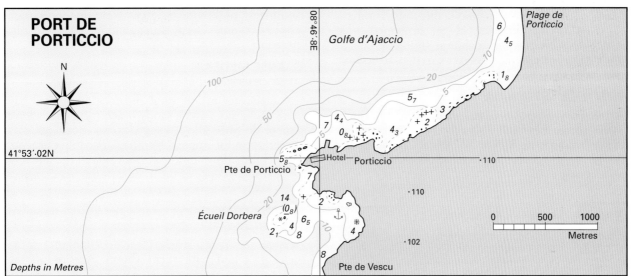

Pointe d'Aspretto 41°55′.2N 08°45′.8E

A low, flat, wide promontory extending south with naval air base buildings on the top where it slopes up to 50m. A spur of shallow water extends 600m south of the buildings, and around this spur there is an enclosing breakwater of a small harbour. The entrance is at the northwestern corner with depths of 3.2m to 1.5m inside. This is a naval harbour and entry is prohibited. The whole of this point, including the islands Les Scuglietti, which are a mass of small islets and rocks lying to the south of this harbour, is bounded by a 200m wide band which is forbidden to all except naval personnel.

Pointe de Porticcio 41°53′N 08°46′.7E

A small low (36m) headland with rocky dangers extending 200m to W. Three large white buildings on the point, which is tree covered with houses inland.

Écueil Dorbera

An area of rocky heads awash and some 3.4m deep 500m to SSW of Pointe de Porticcio.

⚓ PORTICCIO 41°52′.6N 08°46′.9E

Anchor in the small bay off a sandy beach to the southeast of this point in 5m, sand, open to SW–W–NW. Pay attention to some rocky islets close inshore, and to Écueil Dorbera 700m offshore.

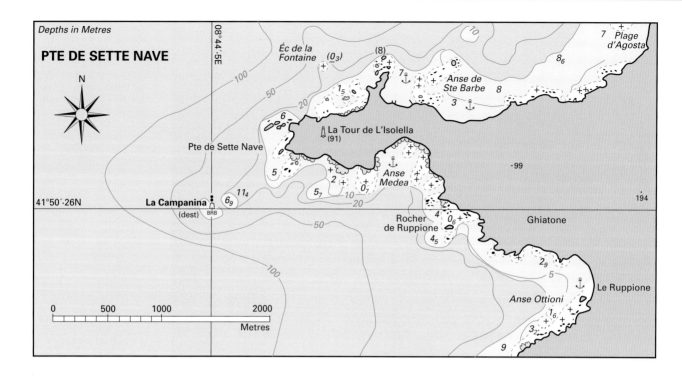

Anse Ste Barbe and Anse Medea looking E

⚓ ANSE DE STE BARBE 41°51′N 08°46′E

Anchorage either side of a shoal area with rocky heads that jut out in a N–NE direction from the coast 400m to the east of an unnamed islet. Approach with care and anchor in 4m, sand, outside moorings, open to W–NW–N. Coast road ashore, two large slips, beach huts, houses in trees.

POINTE DE SETTE NAVE 41°50′.7N 08°45′E

A tree-covered point with outlying rocky dangers 300m to the west and 400m to the north. Tour de l'Isolella stands on a 66m hill behind the point and can be seen from afar. There are many private houses and a coast road.

La Campanina beacon

A BRB tower with ⁝ topmark, located 0.5M southwest of Pointe de Sette Nave marks a rock covered 0.3m. Deep water within 100m of the beacon.

⚓ ANSE MEDEA
41°50′.4N 08°45′.7E

An anchorage in 5m, sand and rock, in a small bay with rocky sides and a sandy beach tucked in behind Pointe de Sette Nave; keep clear of moorings. Pay attention in the approach to La Campanina beacon, to rocky shallows on the eastern side of the bay and to two small rocks in the middle of the beach. Open to S–SW.

⚓ ANSE OTTIONI
41°49′.8N 08°46′.7E

A small and stony beach (Plage de Ruppione) at the head of a gulf with rocky shores. Anchor off the beach in 4m, sand, open to SW–W–NW. There are rocks at both ends of the beach. Coast road, trees and many houses and beach huts behind the beach.

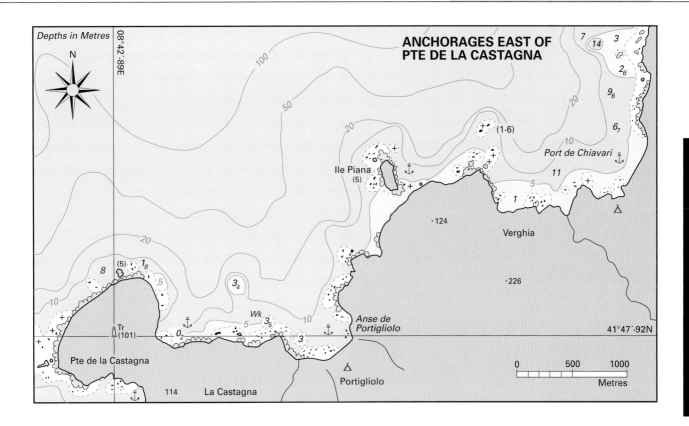

⚓ PORT DE CHIAVARI 41°48′.8N 08°46′E

An anchorage, not a port, in a wide bay open to
W–NW–N. Anchor off a beach in 4m, sand. Keep to
the northern half of the beach as there are rocks off
the southern half. Enter the bay on a southeasterly
heading as there is foul ground off the enclosing
points. Main road and camps behind the beach.
Small jetty, a small quay and a beach café.

⚓ ILE PIANA 41°48′.8N 08°44′.8E

A beautiful little anchorage on the eastern side of the
Ile Piana in 5m sand open to NW–N–NE, rocky cliff
and small sandy beach ashore. An isolated rock lies
50m to the northeast of the north end of this islet.
Very popular in the season and at weekends.

Ile Piana with Portigliolo beyond

⚓ ANSE DE PORTIGLIOLO 41°48′.1N 08°44′.1E

A fine sandy bay open to W–NW–N with a camping
site ashore and a road leading to a small village.
Anchor in 3–5m on sand about 200m offshore, due
to rocks near the beach.

Pointe de la Castagna 41°47.8N 08°42′.6E

A conspicuous promontory with a 91m hill behind
the point with a conspicuous tower and an Aero RC
mast on the next hill inland. Rocky dangers and
shallows extend 500m to the west and southwest.

⚓ POINTE DE LA CASTAGNA NE 41°48′.1N 08°43′.4E

A small bay behind the Pointe de la Castagna, rocky
cliffs and trees ashore with some houses, a track to
the road, a small sandy beach and huts on the beach.
An 0.2m shallow area inshore and rocky heads close
in. Anchor in 5m, sand and rock, clear of moorings,
open to NW–N–NE. Small village inland.

⚓ POINTE DE LA CASTAGNA SE 41°47′.5N 08°42′.9E

A similar anchorage to that on the NE side of the
point except yachts should anchor in 8m, rock, on
the eastern side of the bay to avoid offlying rocky
dangers. This anchorage is open to S–SW–W.

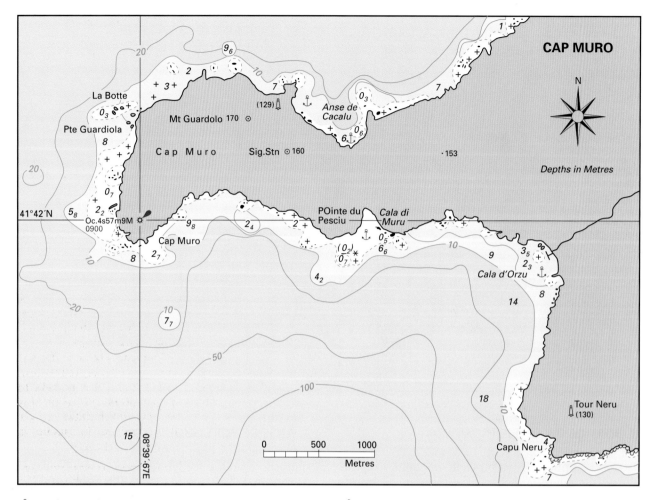

ANSE DE CACALU 41°45′.2N 08°41′E

A pleasant and useful anchorage northeast of Cap Muro which is open to NW–N–NE. Anchor in 5m, sand, in the southern corner off a small sandy and stone beach or in the northwestern corner in 7m, rock. A ruined tower stands to the west of the bay. Offlying rock at each side of the bay. Deserted.

Cap Muro 41°44′.5N 08°39′.5E

An imposing headland rising to 167m. There is a tower on the northeastern side and on the southwestern point is a lighthouse, a white square tower, black top (Oc.4s57m9M). A statue of the Madonna is carved into the cliffs on the southern point.

POINTE GUARDIOLA AND PASSAGE
41°45′N 08°39′.6E

The northwest part of Cap Muro is called Pointe Guardiola. It has offlying rocky dangers including the islet La Botte (the third one in the last 20 miles!) A 100m wide passage 4m deep and 200m long exists between La Botte and the point if taken in NE-SW direction. However, when at the northeastern end of the passage, N–S directions must be taken to pass west of three isolated rocks which have only 2m depths between them and the shore.

CALA DI MURU 41°44′.4N 08°41′.2E

A small anchorage on the opposite side of the peninsula to Anse de Cacalu, with rocky-cliffed sides and a small stone and sand beach. Approach with care because there are 0.7m and 0.2m shallows 400m SSW of the entrance and two islets 300m to the SE. Approach the Cala on NNW course and with a good lookout. Near the entrance there are two ball-shaped rocks. Anchor in 3m sand off the beach, open to SE–S–SW. Track along coast. Deserted.

CALA D'ORZU 41°44′.2N 08°42′.2E

A wide bay with rocky sides and a sand and stone beach. Scrub, covered hills behind with signs of housing development and tracks inland. Camping and beach cafés behind beach. Anchor in 3m sand in the northeastern side of the bay, open to S–SW–W. Pay attention to two lone rocks about 100m offshore.

CAPU NERU 41°43′.3N 08°42′.4E

A rounded blackish rocky-cliffed point and rocky dangers extending 300m, Tour Neru stands on a ridge close to the point amongst green scrub. There are tracks around the headland.

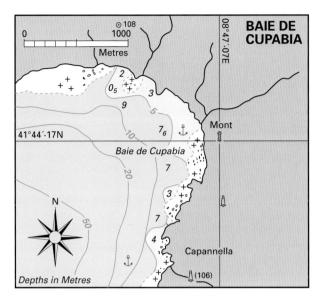

BAIE DE CUPABIA

Depths in Metres

⚓ BAIE DE CUPABIA 41°44′.1N 08°46′.7E

A large bay open to S–SW–W which has good space for anchorage. There is a long sandy beach on the northeastern side of the bay with a monument standing behind it. Anchorage is available along the beach in 3m, sand. To the south of this area an anchorage in 10m sand clear of the rocky shallows can be used. Anchorage is also possible in 17m further out. A track runs inland from the beach; some houses and a road have been built.

POINTE DE PORTO POLLO 41°42′N 08°46′.9E

Care is needed when rounding this point due to extensive offlying rocky reefs and islets. One reef extends 500m southwest from the southwestern corner of the point and another extends 1,000m to the southeast from the southeastern corner of the point. This latter reef, known as Rochers du Taravu, has two islets (6m and 2m) near its southern extremity. Give the outer islet a wide berth of 200m and steer a course east or west to clear the other reef. Two ruined towers stand on the crest inland but are partially hidden in the trees.

C2 Port de Porto Pollo

⊕7 41°42′.41N 08°48′.0E (See photo on page 29)

A small yacht harbour with excellent shelter from any III or IV quadrant winds. It has a 75m-long breakwater with pontoons on the inside. It is quite shallow but a 2m-draught craft can moor to the outside pontoon. Identify Pointe di Porto Pollo with its offlying dangers of Rochers du Taravu and leave the latter well to port. If there is no room at the pontoons, it is possible to anchor off the beach to the north but avoid any swinging moorings. There are no facilities at the harbour but fuel and everyday needs can be supplied in the village. Propriano is only 5 miles away.

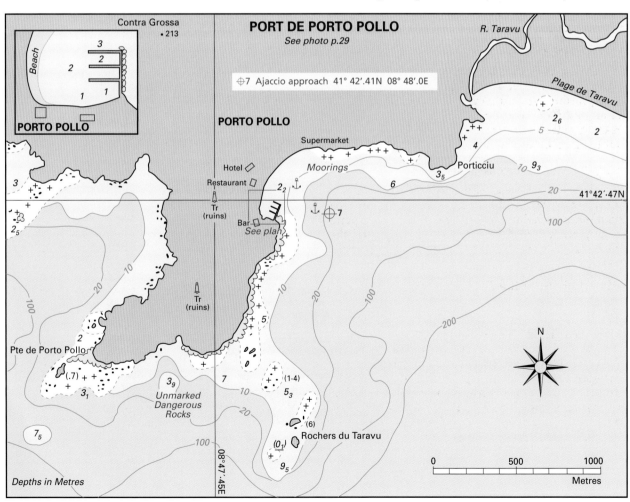

PORT DE PORTO POLLO
See photo p.29

⊕7 Ajaccio approach 41° 42′.41N 08° 48′.0E

Depths in Metres

2 PROPRIANO TO ILES DE FAZZIOLU

The coast running SW from Propriano is generally low-lying with housing developments and a few quiet anchorages. South of Punta de Campomoro the coast is practically deserted until Cap de Feno is reached. Although these headlands are only 12 miles apart, the coast contains dozens of bays and inlets which make delightful isolated anchorages. In general the holding is poor and there are no facilities. It is normally only feasible to explore this coast in settled weather. There are a number of offlying dangerous rocks in this section, notably Les Moines, which is marked with a beacon and covered by special light sectors from two lighthouses. If there are any winds forecast from the westerly direction it is recommended that you pass outside Les Moines and go directly to Bonifacio (or just possibly to Baie de Figari). From Cap de Feno to Bonifacio (and beyond), this coast consists of high chalk cliffs, a feature unique to the area.

Cala di Conca looking E (see page 38)

PLANNING GUIDE

Headlands		Ports & anchorages	Open to winds
	⚓	Plage de Baraci	
	C3 ⚓	**Port de Propriano page 36**	W–NW
	⚓	Portigliolo	W–NW–N
	⚓	Campomoro	NW–N–NE
Pointe de Campomoro			
	⚓	Cala d'Agulia	W–NW
Punta d'Eccica			
Ile d'Eccica reef and passage			
	⚓	Anse de Ferru	S–SW–W
	⚓	Anse d'Arana	S–SW–W
	⚓	Cala di Conca	SW–W–NW
Pointe de Sénétosa and Pointe d'Acula			
	⚓	Cala Longa	S–SW–W
	⚓	Port de Tizzano	S–SW
Pointe de Lattoniccia			
La Botte de Tizzano and passage			
	⚓	Cala di Brija	E–S–SW
	⚓	Golfe de Murtoli	SE–S–W
Pointe de Murtoli			
	⚓	Golfe de Roccapina	SE–S–W
Pointe de Roccapina			
	⚓	Anse de Roccapina	SE–S–SW
Les Moines (islets and reefs and passage)			
Punta di Caniscione			
Écueils d'Olmeto and Le Prêtre and passages			
	⚓	Cala di Furnellu	SE–S–SW
Iles Bruzzi	⚓	Anse d'Arbitru	S–SW
	⚓	Anse de Chevanu	SE–S–SW
Punta di Capuneru			
	⚓	Baie de Figari	SE–S–SW
	C4 ⚓	**Port de Pianottoli-Caldarello page 45**	SW
Punta di Ventilegne			
	⚓	Anse de Pesciucane	S–SW
	⚓	Golfe de Ventilegne	SW–W
	⚓	Iles de la Tonnara	NW–W
	⚓	Port de Stagnolu	SW–W–NW
	⚓	Cala Grande	S–SW
Cap de Feno			
	⚓	Cala de Paraganu	S–SW
	⚓	Iles and Anse de Fazziolu	S–SW

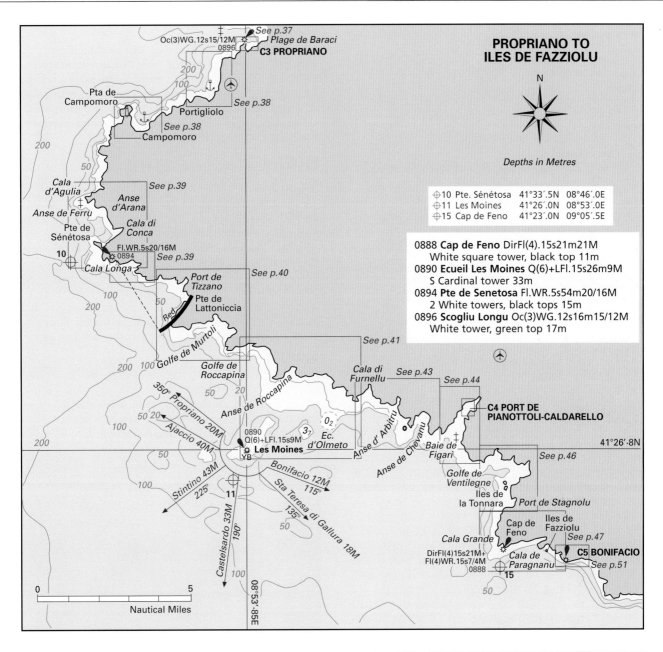

PROPRIANO TO ILES DE FAZZIOLU

N

Depths in Metres

⊕10 Pte. Sénétosa 41°33′.5N 08°46′.0E
⊕11 Les Moines 41°26′.0N 08°53′.0E
⊕15 Cap de Feno 41°23′.0N 09°05′.5E

0888 **Cap de Feno** DirFl(4).15s21m21M
White square tower, black top 11m
0890 **Ecueil Les Moines** Q(6)+LFl.15s26m9M
S Cardinal tower 33m
0894 **Pte de Senetosa** Fl.WR.5s54m20/16M
2 White towers, black tops 15m
0896 **Scogliu Longu** Oc(3)WG.12s16m15/12M
White tower, green top 17m

Oc(3)WG.12s15/12M
0896
C3 PROPRIANO
Plage de Baraci
See p.37

Pta de Campomoro
See p.38
Portigliolo
Campomoro
See p.38

Cala d'Agulia
See p.39
Anse d'Arana
Anse de Ferru
Cala di Conca
Pte de Sénétosa
10
Fl.WR.5s20/16M
0894
See p.39
Cala Longa

Port de Tizzano
See p.40
Pte de Lattoniccia
Red
Golfe de Murtoli
Golfe de Roccapina

See p.41
Cala di Furnellu
See p.43
See p.44

C4 PORT DE PIANOTTOLI-CALDARELLO

41°26′·8N

350° Propriano 20M
Ajaccio 40M
Anse de Roccapina
Ec. d'Olmeto
0890
Q(6)+LFl.15s9M
Les Moines
YB
Anse d' Arbitru
Anse de Chevanu
Baie de Figari
Golfe de Ventilegne
Iles de la Tonnara
Port de Stagnolu
See p.46

Stintino 43M
225°
11
Castelsardo 33M
190°
Bonifacio 12M
115°
Sta Teresa di Gallura 18M
135°
Cala Grande
DirFl(4)15s21M
Fl(4)WR.15s7/4M
0888
Cap de Feno
Cala de Paragnanu
15
Iles de Fazziolu
See p.47
C5 BONIFACIO
See p.51

0
5
Nautical Miles

08°53′.85E

2. PROPRIANO TO ILES DE FAZZIOLU

Elegant yachts off Port de Stagnolu (see page 46) *Martin Walker*

C3 Port de Propriano

⊕8 41°40′.9N 08°53′.8E
⊕9 41°40.7N 08°54′.4E

Charts
Admiralty *1424*
SHOM *6851, 7162*

Depth
3m minimum

Number of berths
429 with 59 for visitors (2hrs free except in July and August)
Maximum LOA 32m

Lights
0896 Scogliu Longu Oc(3)WG.12s16m15/12M White tower, green top 17m
0898 Jetée Nord head Iso.G 4s11m10M White post, green top 7m
0899 Marina Breakwater W head Fl(2)6s2m Red structure 1m
0899.2 E head Fl(3)G.12s5m6M White tower, green top 3m

Port communications
VHF Ch 9
☎ 04 95 76 10 40 *Fax* 04 95 70 26 72 (S 0600–2000; OoS 0800–1200, 1400–1700)
Email yachtclub.valinco@wanadoo.fr
url www.portvalinco.fr

Tourist town

This small commercial, fishing and yacht harbour lies in attractive surroundings near the head of of the deep Golfe di Valinco. The main port is not fully enclosed and with strong NW–SW winds the swell can be unpleasant, but the new yacht harbour to the east offers excellent protection. The small town can provide everyday requirements, it caters for thousands of tourists who pack the area in season. The yacht harbour also becomes very crowded There has recently been a RoRo terminal built in the SW corner of the harbour and while dredging and piling was going on the yacht club extended its moorings to the west and reorganised the entire marina. Work is still ongoing but there are many more berths available now and the port will be a first-class marina with all facilities when completed in 2006.

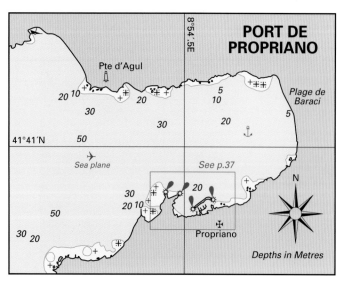

Warnings

To avoid the Scogliu Longu rocks to the east of the west jetty, keep well to the north of the light tower, especially at night when approaching in the white sector of the light. Remember this is mainly a commercial harbour and all ferry and commercial traffic have right of way. Anchoring is prohibited in the main commercial port.

PILOTAGE

Approach

By day

Keeping well clear of Pointe de Porto Pollo and its offlying Rochers du Tavaru (from the north) or Pointe de Campomoro (from the south), steer for the head of the Golfe de Valinco and the town of Propriano will come into sight. It is important to identify the north jetty with its white tower so the Roches de Scogliu Longu can be avoided. Keep at least 200m north of the tower to clear all dangers.

By night

From the entrance of the gulf, keep in the white sector (070° to 097°) of the north jetty light until about 1 mile from the light, then move north to get into the green sector. When the tower is some 400m away, steer to leave it 200m to starboard.

General view of Propriano looking SE

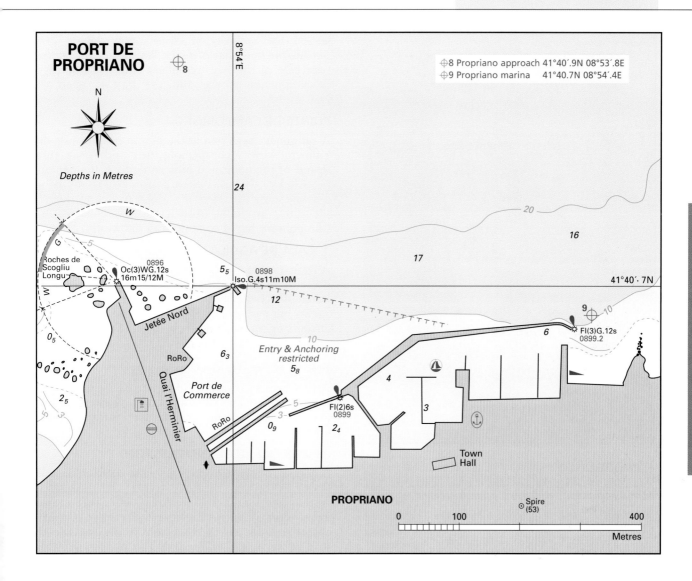

PORT DE PROPRIANO

⊕8

N

Depths in Metres

⊕8 Propriano approach 41°40′.9N 08°53′.8E
⊕9 Propriano marina   41°40.7N 08°54′.4E

8°54′E

24

W

20

16

5

17

Roches de
Scogliu
Longu

0896
Oc(3)WG.12s
16m15/12M

5₅

0898
Iso.G.4s11m10M

12

41°40′.7N

9 ⊕ 10

6

Fl(3)G.12s
0899.2

Jetée Nord

6₃

10

Entry & Anchoring
restricted
5₈

4

0₅

RoRo

2₅

Quai l'Herminier

Port de
Commerce

5

3

Fl(2)6s
0899

0₉

2₄

3

Town
Hall

0
,
0
,
0
0
0
,

RoRo

3

PROPRIANO

Spire
(53)

0   100   400

Metres

2. PROPRIANO TO ILES FAZZIOLU

By GPS

From the entrance of the gulf steer to ⊕8. Then proceed to ⊕9 to enter the yacht marina.

⚓ **PLAGE DE BARACI** 41°41′.1N 08°54′.7E

A long sandy beach at the head of the Golfe de Valinco, usually crowded in the summer. Beach cafés and coast road behind. The mouth of Rivière Baraci lies at the northern end of the beach. Anchor in 4m, sand, off the beach, open to W–NW.

Entrance

Call ahead to the *capitainerie* for berthing instructions before entering. From a position north of the white lighthouse or ⊕8, steer to ⊕9 and round the head of the jetty to enter the yacht marina on a westerly course.

Berths

Stern-to pontoons, with moorings connected to the pontoon by *pendillos* as instructed by the *capitainerie*. Contact must be made with the authorities before entering marina to check on availability of space.

Formalities

All authorities available

Facilities

All

History

A small fishing settlement, which the Turks destroyed in 1583, 1590 and again in 1660. Most of the town is of recent origin created when tourism came to the area.

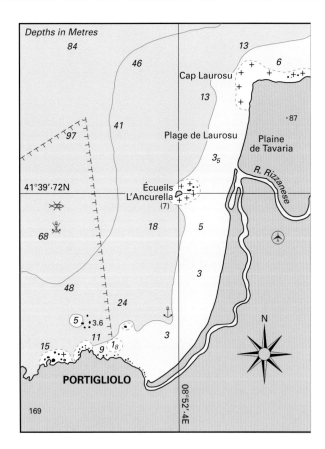

⚓ PORTIGLIOLO 41°39′N 08°52′.3E

A protected anchorage a mile south of the Ecueils l'Ancurella, off the mouth of the river Rizzansa and the small airfield that serves Propriano. Approach on a southerly heading parallel to the beach to avoid offlying dangers to the west. Anchor in 3 to 5m off the village, open to W–NW–N.

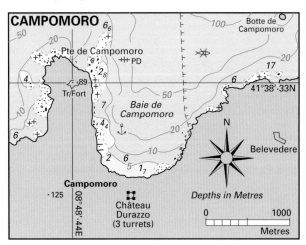

⚓ CAMPOMORO 41°38′N 08°48′.9E

A very popular anchorage in a large bay surrounded by tree and scrub-covered hills. It has a long sandy beach with rocks at each end and a village behind. On the Pointe de Campomoro, which has many offlying dangers, there is a conspicuous tower. There is a line of yellow buoys across the bay which includes a fish farm, many moorings and the jetties. There is a channel marked through the line to the

jetties. The majority of visitors now anchor just outside the buoy line near the 7m spot depth on the west side of the bay (see plan). There are holiday developments ashore and the bay is open to NW–N–NE.

POINTE DE CAMPOMORO 41°38′.5N 08°48′.3E

A prominent headland at the mouth of the Golfe de Valinco, with a conspicuous fort and tower just inland of the point and hills rising to 120m behind it. Rocky dangers extend some 250m in a northwesterly direction and 500m to the northeast, the latter partially obstructing the entrance to Campomoro bay if coming from the west.

⚓ CALA DE'AGUILA 41°35′.9N 08°47′E

A remarkable anchorage, 0.5M ENE of Punta d'Eccica, in a narrow rocky-sided cove with a sandy beach at its head. There is only room for a couple of yachts but enter on an ESE course and moor with 2 anchors in 3m sand and rock, open to W–NW. Track inland. Deserted.

Punta d'Eccica 41°35′.5N 08°46′.5E

A very broken rocky point sloping down from 71m to cliffs and many offlying rocks, exposed, awash and covered, including the low rocky isle Ile d'Eccica.

ILE D'ECCICA REEF AND PASSAGES

A number of complex passages exist between Ile and Punta d'Eccica which should be carefully investigated by dinghy in calm weather before use. There is one simple and relatively safe passage which can be used by passing very close to the east side of Ile d'Eccica on a N or S course. This passage is 150m wide and 400m long with a 12m minimum depth. A 300m clearance is necessary from the west side of the isle on a N or S course when passing outside all the dangers.

⚓ ANSE DE FERRU 41°35′.3N 08°46′.8E

A small bay tucked away behind Punta d'Eccica on its south side with high, rocky, tree-covered hills around it. Enter on a northeasterly course to avoid rocky dangers. Anchor off head in 5m, rock and weed, paying attention to rocks close inshore. Open to S–SW–W. Deserted.

⚓ ANSE D'ARANA 41°35′N 08°47′.25E

A bay surrounded on two sides by tree and scrub-covered rocky hills with a sandy beach and a housing estate at its head. Approach on a northeasterly course, anchor in 3m, sand, rock and weed, off the head of the bay. Open to S–SW–W.

⚓ CALA DI CONCA 41°34′.4N 08°48′E

An attractive anchorage in a narrow V-shaped cove at the mouth of a small river, it has rocky sides with coastal rocks and a sandy beach at its head. Approach on an easterly course and anchor near the bend in the channel in 4m, sand, open to SW–W–NW. Track inland. Deserted except for campers. (See photo page 34)

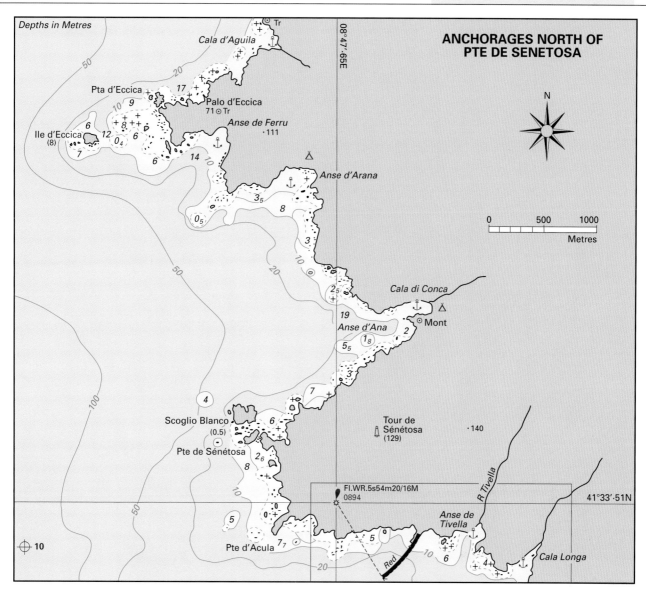

Depths in Metres

ANCHORAGES NORTH OF PTE DE SENETOSA

Cala d'Aguila
Pta d'Eccica
Palo d'Eccica
71 ⊙ Tr
Anse de Ferru
·111
Ile d'Eccica
(8)
Anse d'Arana
08°47'·65E
N
0   500   1000
Metres
Cala di Conca
19
⊙ Mont
Anse d'Ana
Scoglio Blanco
(0.5)
Pte de Sénétosa
Tour de
Sénétosa
(129)
·140
R Tivella
41°33'·51N
Fl.WR.5s54m20/16M
0894
Anse de
Tivella
Pte d'Acula
Cala Longa
⊕ 10

2. PROPRIANO TO ILES FAZZIOLU

POINTE DE SÉNÉTOSA AND POINTE D'ACULA
41°33'.7N 08°47'E

The Massif de Sénétosa has a grey tower on its peak (129m). It slopes downwards westwards to Pointe de Sénétosa and southwestwards to Pointe d'Acula.

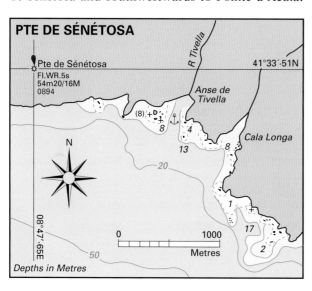

PTE DE SÉNÉTOSA

Pte de Sénétosa
Fl.WR.5s
54m20/16M
0894
R Tivella
41°33'·51N
Anse de
Tivella
(8)
Cala Longa
N
13
08°47'·65E
0   1000
Metres
Depths in Metres

Pointe de Sénétosa has two longish islets off its point. Scoglio Blanco is the larger of the two and furthest to the northwest; between this islet and the point are a mass of rocky dangers. Pointe d'Acula is a long thin promontory. There is a conspicuous lighthouse consisting of a white house with two white towers (Fl.WR.5s54m20/16M). The red sector (306° to 328°) of this light covers Les Moines (see below) and the long banks of rocks stretching north. The point has rocky dangers extending 500m to the west. Give the whole headland a 1,000m berth when rounding these two points.

⚓ **ANSE DE TIVELLA** 41°33'.2N 08°48'.45E

A shallow bay with rocks on both sides of the approach. Use this anchorage only in calm weather and anchor in 5m sand and rock. Open to the SW.

⚓ **CALA LONGA** 41°33'.1N 08°48'.8E

A long narrow cove with rocky sides and a small sandy beach at its head, surrounded by scrub-covered rock, deserted. Anchor in 3m, sand, off the beach, open to S–SW–W.

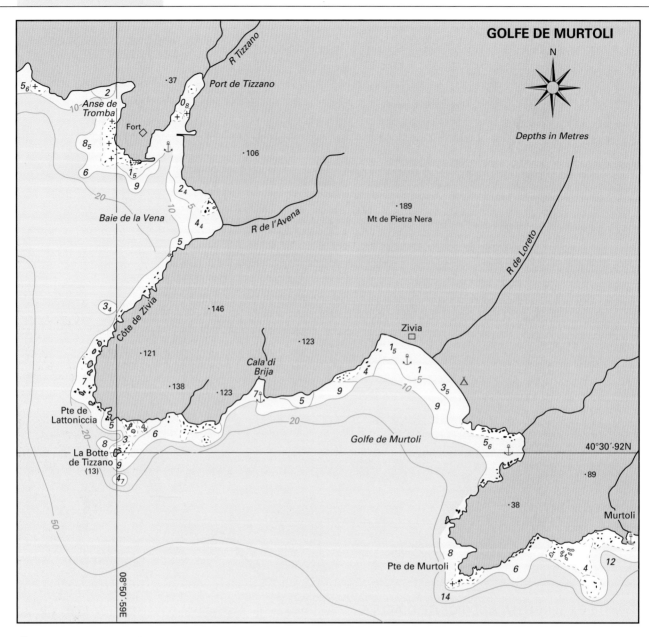

GOLFE DE MURTOLI

Depths in Metres

⚓ **PORT DE TIZZANO** 41°32'.3N 08°50'.9E

Not a port but an attractive and useful anchorage in a narrow estuary which has silted up near its head. There is a 40m-long jetty on the east side. There are many buildings surrounding its rocky shores and a road to the main coast road. The houses and old fort can be seen from afar. Enter on a northerly course and leave the breakwater to port, anchor in 2m sand off the quay, open to S–SW. There is a small village with restaurant, café and a mobile food shop.

POINTE DE LATONICCIA 41°31'.2N 08°50'.4E

A large promontory with hills of 146m a short distance inland. It has rocky dangers close inshore. On the south-facing point there are three patches of rocky heads which extend 100m.

LA BOTTE DE TIZZANO AND PASSAGE
41°30'.92N 08°50.59E

La Botte de Tizzano (13m) lies 300m offshore and has rocky dangers to the north. A passage 100m wide, 200m long with a minimum depth of 3m can

be taken E or W halfway between the Corsican shore and La Botte detailed above. Use with care.

⚓ **CALA DI BRIJA** 41°31'.1N 08°51'.5E

A small bay on the eastern side of the Massif de Latoniccia. Surrounded by scrub-covered rocky hills. Approach on a northerly course, anchor in 3m, sand, off the rock and stone beach, open to E–SE–S–SW. Tracks ashore but otherwise deserted.

⚓ **GOLFE DE MURTOLI** 41°31'.2N 08°52'.6E

A large bay with anchorages off the beaches to the northwest and southeast. The sides are very broken rocky cliffs with one long sandy beach and one short sandy beach. A very small village, Zivia, has a few houses and a road inland. Summer campsites. Anchor in 3m, sand, off the beaches, open to SE–S–SW–W.

POINTE DE MURTOLI 41°30'.3N 08°52'.9E

A point with a hill 38m high, rising inland to 89m. It has a broken rocky-cliffed coastline with rocky dangers projecting 200m towards the SW.

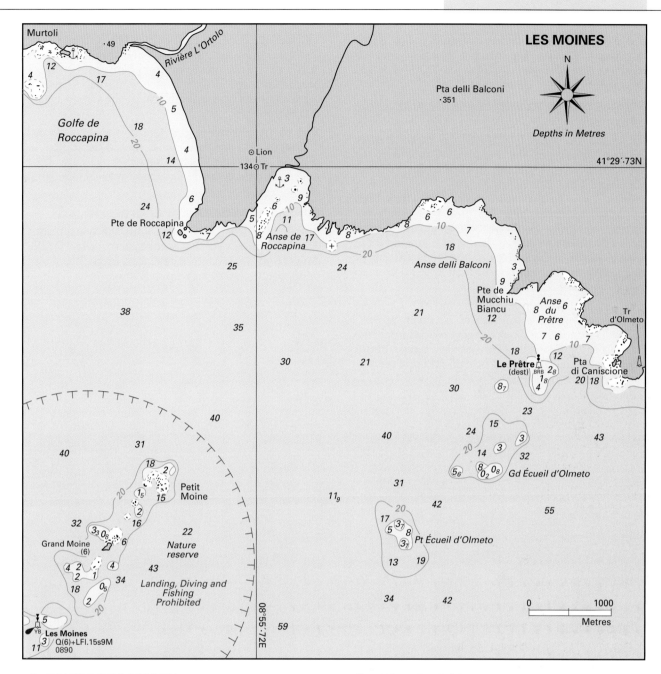

⚓ **GOLFE DE ROCCAPINA** 41°30′.2N 08°54′.8E

A large open bay at the foot of a wide valley of the Rivière l'Ortolo. There is a group of rocks 1M east of Pointe de Murtoli and the coast in the western part of this bay has rocky dangers close in. The eastern half consists of a long sandy beach. Anchorage is available off this beach in 3m, sand, open to SE–S–SW–W. There is a beautiful one- or two-yacht anchorage (for use by very experienced navigators) by the village of Murtoli behind a small rocky projection. There is a track to the main coast road from here.

POINTE DE ROCCAPINA 41°29′.4N 08°55′.1E

A high (134m) narrow promontory with a forked point and rocky dangers extending 200m to the southwest. The crest of the hill behind the point has the appearance of a lion from some directions and in certain lights. There is also a tower on the crest.

⚓ **ANSE DE ROCCAPINA** 41°29′.3N 08°55′.6E

A popular anchorage in a square-shaped bay, the sides of which are rocky, scrub-covered hills. There are many rocks exposed, awash and covered near the eastern side of the entrance and three more isolated islets further up the bay. The recommended entrance is to keep very close to the western side of the bay, inside all rocky shallows and anchor in the north corner as shown on the plan. The head of the bay consists of a sandy beach. Anchor off it in 3m, sand, open to SE–S–SW. There is a track to the main road, holiday buildings and campsites ashore.

LES MOINES (ISLETS, REEFS AND PASSAGE)

A very dangerous area of islets, exposed, awash and covered rocks lying between 1.5M and 3M to the SSW of Pointe de Roccapina. It lies halfway and on the direct line between Pointe de Sénétosa and Cap de Feno. Grand Moine (6m) lies near the centre of the group. There are many exposed rocks at the northern end and Les Moines beacon tower S cardinal, black tower, yellow top (Q(6)+LFl.15s 26m9M) marks the southern end.

ÉCUEILS D'OLMETO AND LE PRÊTRE AND PASSAGES

Three shallow areas lying in a line approximately south-southwest of the Punta di Caniscione. Le Prêtre lies 800m from this point with shallows of 1.7m and 1.8m and an awash rock. This rock was marked by a BRB beacon tower but it has been partially destroyed and has not been replaced. Further out from Le Prêtre beacon lies the Grand Écueil d'Olmeto which has depths of 0.2m and 0.8m with shallows of 3m and 5m on the landward side of them. 1¼M still further out the Petit Écueil d'Olmeto has shallows of 3.7m.

The passage between Le Prêtre and the Corsican shore is 600m wide and should be taken in SSE-NNW directions to avoid dangers extending 250m from the Punta di Caniscione. Keep about equidistant from the ruined beacon and this point.

The passage between Le Prêtre and the Grand Écueil d'Olmeto is about 900m wide and should be taken in NW–SE directions equidistant between the ruined beacon and the broken water over the 0.2m and 0.8m shallows at the south end of the Grand Écueil d'Olmeto.

The passage between the Grand and Petit Écueil d'Olmeto is 1¼M wide and should be taken in NW–SE directions. Except in heavy seas the Petit Écueil d'Olmeto can be ignored by yachts drawing less than 3m.

PUNTA DI CANISCIONE 41°28´.4N 08°59´E

A low rounded rocky point with the conspicuous Tour d'Olmeto on its southeastern side. Rocky dangers on the western side extend up to 150m and on its southwestern side up to 250m.

Port de Pianottoli-Caldarello at the head of Baie de Figari looking ENE
(Note fish farm at the bottom of photo.) (See pages 44 and 45)

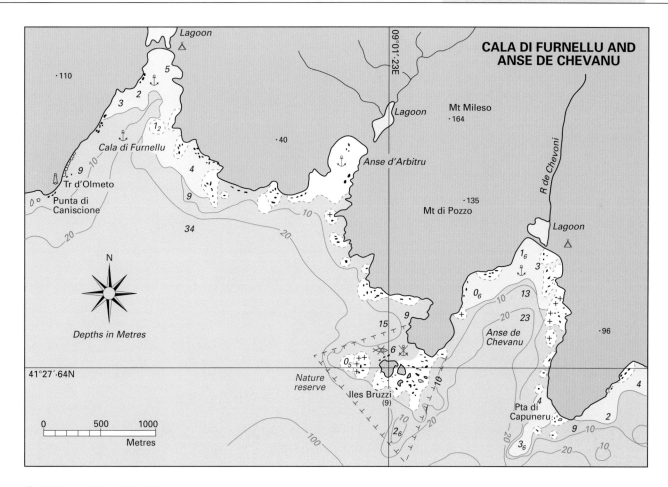

CALA DI FURNELLU AND ANSE DE CHEVANU

Depths in Metres

41°27'·64N

0   500   1000
Metres

⚓ **CALA DI FURNELLU** 41°28'.7N 08°59'.5E

A large pleasant V-shaped bay with rocky low hills, tree and scrub-covered. The Tour d'Olmeto on Punta di Caniscione on the western side of the entrance is conspicuous. There is a 1.2m deep rock near the centre of the bay halfway in. The eastern shore has rocky outliers extending 50m. Anchor in 3m, sand and weed, off a sandy beach at the head of the bay, open to SE–S–SW. Summer campsites, track to main road, otherwise deserted.

⚓ **ANSE D'ARBITRU** 41°28'.35N 09°00'.7E

A small bay with a low rocky coastline and a large sandy beach at its head but with some rocks extending 150m out from the centre of the beach. Anchor in 3m, sand and rock, but the holding is not good, open to S–SW. There is a large red house on the western side of the bay and some smaller apartment blocks and houses behind the beach. Tracks leading inland. Usually deserted. Behind the beach is a lake and marshes fed by the Rivière Agninaccio.

ILES BRUZZI 41°27'.6N 09°01'.2E

A group of one large and eight small rocky islets with many rocky heads and shallows covering a dog-leg shape 1,000m NW–E and 1,000m N–S. Located 200m off the unnamed headland that lies between

the anchorages at Anse d'Abitru and Anse de Chevanu, as detailed above and below. Yachts should keep at least 1,000m from the headland and preferably 1,500m off in bad weather.

⚓ **ANSE DE CHEVANU** 41°27'.5N 09°01'.8E

A large bay with low rocky sides and a big sandy beach at its head. There are many offlying rocks close inshore on the eastern side of the bay and another group extends 150m from the centre of the beach. Two isolated rocks lie 300m to the south and southwest of Punta di Capuneru. The Iles Bruzzi (see above) obstruct direct entrance to this anchorage from SW–W. Enter on a northerly course and anchor in 3m, sand and weed (poor holding), off the beach, open to SE–S–SW. Summer campsite and track inland, otherwise deserted.

PUNTA DI CAPUNERU 41°27'.4N 09°02'.4E

A rocky headland with two islets and many rocky heads extending 300m to south and southwest.

⚓ **BAIE DI FIGARI** 41°27′.1N 09°03′.3E

This is a two-mile-long inlet relatively deserted at its outer end with many rocky patches and shallows on the approach. In strong south to southwest winds the entrance would be dangerous. For pilotage details, see Port de Pianottoli-Caldarello below.

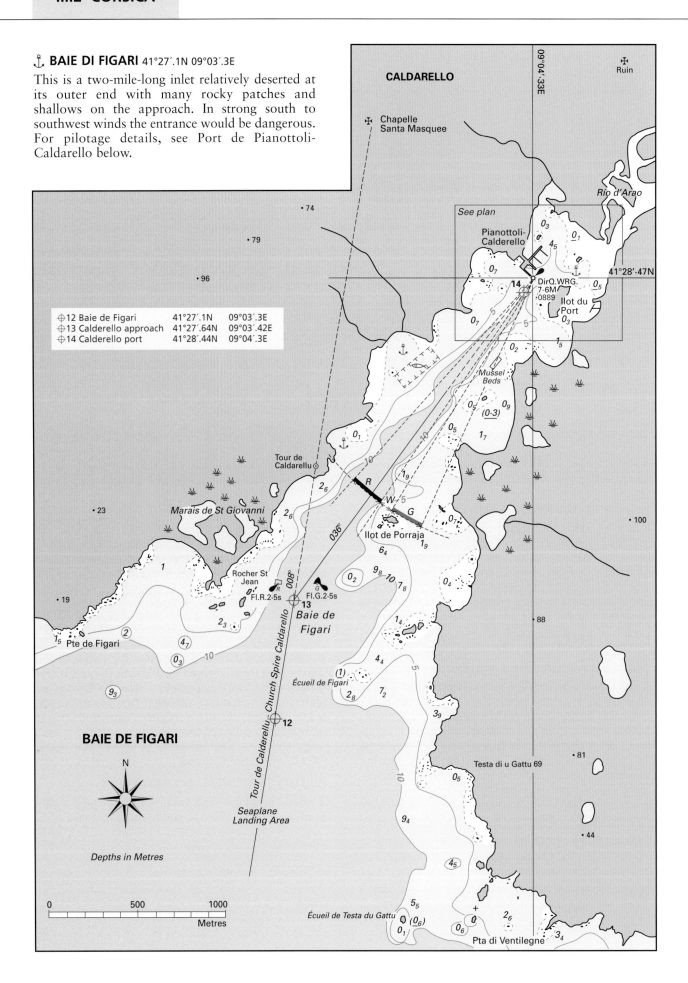

⊕12 Baie de Figari	41°27′.1N	09°03′.3E
⊕13 Calderello approach	41°27′.64N	09°03′.42E
⊕14 Calderello port	41°28′.44N	09°04′.3E

BAIE DE FIGARI

N

Depths in Metres

| 0 | 500 | 1000 |

Metres

C4 Port de Pianottoli-Caldarello

41°28′.5N 09°04′.34E

⊕12 41°27′.1N 09°03′.3E
⊕13 41°27′.6N 09°03′.41E
⊕14 41°28′.44N 09°04′.3E

Charts
Admiralty *1424*
SHOM *7096*

Depths
1.5 to 5m

Number of berths
160 with 80 for visitors

Maximum LOA
27m

Lights
0946(I) Buoy Fl.R.2.5s2M Port hand buoy
0946.3(I) Buoy Fl.G.2.5s2M Starboard hand buoy
0889 Jetty head Dir Q.WRG.7-6M White tower 6m,
026°-G-035°-W-037.5°-R-obscd-026°

Port communications
VHF Ch 9, ☎ 04 95 71 83 57; *Fax* 04 95 71 80 21 (S
0800-1200, 1400-2000; OoS 0900-1200, 1400-1700)

A pleasant but remote marina

This is a relatively new marina at the head of the
inlet running inland from the Baie di Figari. It lies on
the west side of the inlet, opposite the Ilot du Port.
There are reasonable facilities here, electricity and
water on the pontoons, head moorings attached to
the pontoons, showers and WC. There is, however,
no fuel and most supplies have to be obtained in the
village some 3km away, although there may be a few
simple supplies available near the marina in high
season. There is a series of large yellow buoys to the
SW of the seaward pier, which are only used when
the SW wind blows straight up the inlet. It is not
recommended to leave or arrive at this marina if the
wind is strong southwesterly as the entrance to the
inlet itself could be dangerous. (See photo page 42)

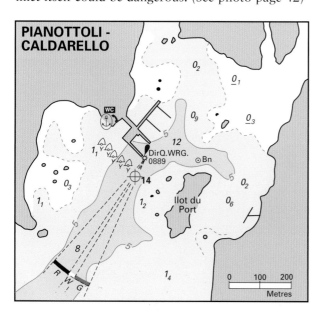

PILOTAGE

Approach

By day

Take a position midway between Punta di Capuneru
and Punta de Ventilegne and steer north towards a
conspicuous tower, Tour de Calderello, bringing the
tower into line with the church tower in Calderellu
on the skyline, a transit of 008°. As Rocher St Jean
comes abeam to port, two small lightbuoys should
be seen. Pass between them and steer 036° which
takes you up the main channel. The sides are steep-
to and 8m can be carried up to the yacht harbour.
Anchor to the NE of the tower or proceed further up
the channel to the marina. There are several fish
farms and mussel beds in the area and these must be
given a wide berth.

At night

Although the lights of the buoys have a nominal 2M
range, they are small and will be difficult to see in any
swell at all. The entrance to the bay is strewn with
rocky outcrops and as the initial leading line is unlit,
it is not recommended to enter this harbour at night
without previous local knowledge. In calm weather
with full sight of the buoys, steer on a course of
008°towards them and alter to 036° when the white
sector of the jetty light is seen. Keep in the white
sector and proceed up the channel to the marina.

By GPS

Steer towards ⊕12 on a northeasterly course, then
alter to 008°and steer to ⊕13. Keep a lookout for the
2 buoys and at ⊕13 alter course to 036° towards ⊕14.

Anchorages in the approach

It is possible to anchor in the small bays just to the
SW and NE of the Tour de Caldarellu in 3m and
above the Ilot du Port, opposite the marina. Do not
anchor in the main channel or anywhere near the
fish farms or mussel beds.

Berths

All berths have headropes attached to the pontoons.
Call ahead to the *capitainerie* to request a berth.
Staff are available to assist. When strong SW to W
winds are forecast, the buoys to seaward of the SW
pier are used as holding-off buoys.

Facilities

Usual water and electricity on pontoons
Showers & WCs
Weather forecasts from *capitainerie*
No fuel
Some supplies in season but otherwise it is a long
(3km) walk to the village.

PUNTA DI VENTILEGNE 41°26′.5N 09°04′.4E

An inconspicuous headland with foul ground
extending 700m from the shore in a southwesterly
direction, to the Écueil de Testa di u Gattu, an
unmarked awash rock, and 500m in a southerly
direction!

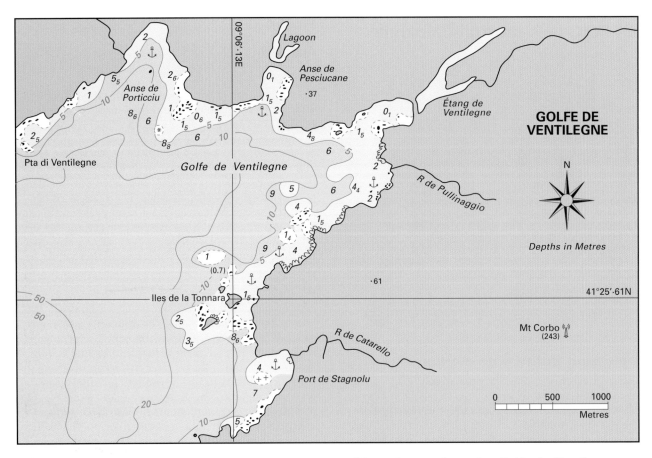

Depths in Metres

41°25'·61N

GOLFE DE VENTILEGNE

⚓ **GOLFE DE VENTILEGNE** 41°26'.2N 09°05'.5E

A large gulf which has several anchorages around its head for use with care due to shallows and several areas foul with rocky heads. The bay is open to SW–W. The coast road runs behind this gulf.

⚓ **ILES DE LA TONNARA** 41°25'.5N 09°06'E

A group of three rocky islets extending up to 600m from the coast with outlying rocky dangers. A small anchorage lies between the northeasternmost island (which is the largest), and the coast where there are several ruined houses and a sandy beach. Approach this anchorage from the Golfe de Ventilegne on a southerly course with care. Anchor in 3m, rock and sand, open to NW–N. Usually deserted. Road to main coast road.

⚓ **PORT DE STAGNOLU** 41°25'.2N 09°06'.1E

This is not a port but a deserted anchorage – a bay with rocky coast and sandy beach at its head. There is a small islet in the entrance of the bay. Pass north or south of this islet and anchor off the beach in 3m, sand, open to SW–W–NW. Track to main road.

Sunset at Cala di Stagnolu

Martin Walker

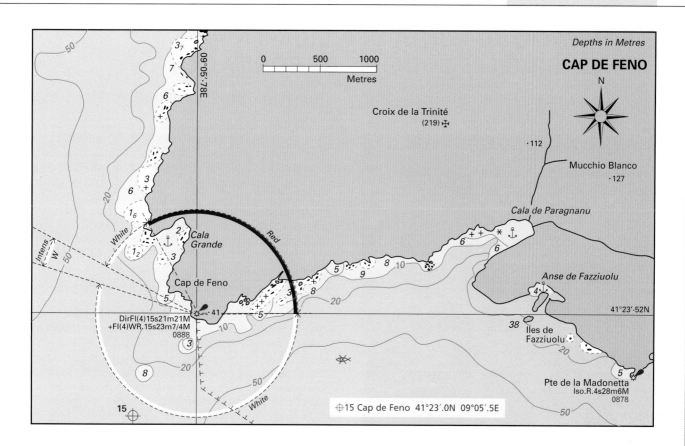

⚓ CALA GRANDE 41°23′.8N 09°05′.4E

In spite of its name, this fantastic anchorage is very small and situated on the west side of Cap de Feno in a rocky-sided bay. The eastern side of the bay has some rocky heads close in and there is an exposed rock in the centre. Enter on a NNE course close to the west side of the bay with a good lookout forward. Anchor in 3m, rock and sand, short of the head of the bay where there is a sand and rocky beach. Open to S–SW. It may be necessary to take a line ashore. Footpath.Deserted.

CAP DE FENO 41°23′.5N 09°05′.8E

A broken rocky promontory sloping up to 114m inland with irregular cliffs. Two small rocky dangers exist 200m to the west of the lighthouse and a 3m shallow patch 200m to the south. The lighthouse is a white square squat tower with a black top marked Feno (DirFl(4)15s21m21M). This intense white sector covers the Les Moines beacon tower (109.4°–111.4°). The white sector of the upper light in the same tower (Fl(4)WR.15s23m7/4M) covers the safe approach to Cap de Feno (270°-150°).

⚓ CALA DE PARAGNANU 41°23′.7N 09°07′.5E

A long, thin bay, with high broken hills and two towers to the west, light grey cliffs to the east and a white sandy beach at the head of the bay. It is popular with summer visitors and tourist boats. A patch of rocky heads extends 100m on the west side of the entrance. Anchor off the beach in 3m, rock and sand, open to S–SW. Road to main road.

⚓ ILES AND ANSE DE FAZZIUOLU
41°23′.53N 09°07′.9E

A fantastic small creek and bay with two islets almost blocking the entrance, providing two entrances/exits, the western entrance being the wider and deeper of the two. The sides are of layered whitish-grey cliffs and there is a small beach at the head of the bay. There is a Glénans Sailing Centre here. Yachts should use the west entrance and smaller day boats can use the east entrance. Anchor to the north of the islet in 2.5m, sand, open to S–SW. There is a path to Bonifacio and in summer there are many visitors who come by land or by tourist boats.

3 BONIFACIO TO PUNTA DI A CHIAPPA (INCLUDING LES BOUCHES DE BONIFACIO)

The channels between Corsica and Sardinia, Les Bouches de Bonifacio and the two Corsican islands Lavezzi and Cavallo, are included in this section. The section of white cliffs from Cap de Feno to Cap Pertusato is unique in this area and includes the port of Bonifacio and two anchorages. The Corsican islands are lower, very rocky and have many offlying dangers, while the Sardinian islands, to the south, are higher and are described in detail in the next chapter.

From Cap Pertusato to Punta di a Chiappa, on the south side of the Golfe de Porto Vecchio, the coast is interspersed with large gulfs and bays. The hills have a more rounded tree-covered appearance, in contrast to the markedly jagged mountains of the W and SW coasts. The Iles Cerbicale and some isolated rocks and shallows lie offshore and are marked by buoys. The main road runs well inland along this section of coast and there are campsites, holiday centres and sailing schools at the head of many bays and few, if any, of the anchorages will be deserted.

Bonifacio looking east

PLANNING GUIDE

Headlands	Ports & anchorages	Open to winds
Cap de Feno	**C5** ⛵ **Port de Bonifacio page 50**	
Cap Pertusato		
Ile St Antoine and passage		
Le Prêtre beacon		
Punta de Sperono		
	⚓ *Anse Piantarella*	NE–E–S
	⚓ *Cala Longa*	ESE–S
	Les Bouches de Bonifacio page 53	
	Iles Lavezzi page 57	
	Ile Cavallo page 58	
Punta di u Capicciolu		
	C6 ⛵ **Port de Cavallo page 59**	
	⚓ *Golfe de Sant'Amanza*	NE–E
	⚓ *Anse de Balistra*	NE–E–SE
	⚓ *Punta di Rondinara*	
	⚓ *Golfe de Rondinara*	NE–E–SE
Pointe de Sponsaglia		
	⚓ *Golfe de Porto Novo*	N–NE–E
	⚓ *Golfe de Santa Giulia*	NE–E–SE
Ile du Toro		
Pointe Cerbicale	⚓ *Plage de Palombaggia*	NE–E–S
Iles Cerbicales		
	⚓ *Anse de Carataggio*	NE–E–S
Punta di a Chiappa		
Roches de Chiappino (and beacon)		

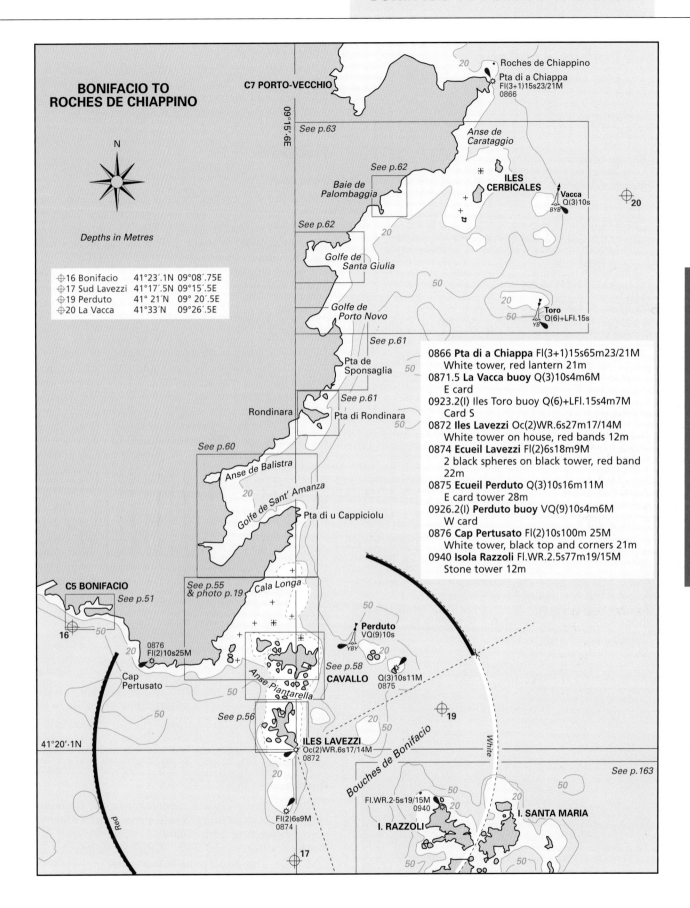

BONIFACIO TO ROCHES DE CHIAPPINO

N

Depths in Metres

⊕16 Bonifacio   41°23'.1N 09°08'.75E
⊕17 Sud Lavezzi 41°17'.5N 09°15'.5E
⊕19 Perduto   41° 21'N   09° 20'.5E
⊕20 La Vacca   41°33'N   09°26'.5E

C7 PORTO-VECCHIO

09°15'·6E

See p.63

See p.62

Baie de Palombaggia

See p.62

Golfe de Santa Giulia

Golfe de Porto Novo

See p.61

Pta de Sponsaglia

See p.61

Rondinara

Pta di Rondinara

See p.60

Anse de Balistra

Golfe de Sant' Amanza

Pta di u Cappiciolu

Roches de Chiappino
Pta di a Chiappa
Fl(3+1)15s23/21M
0866

Anse de Carataggio

ILES CERBICALES

Vacca
Q(3)10s
BYB

Toro
Q(6)+LFl.15s
YB

0866 **Pta di a Chiappa** Fl(3+1)15s65m23/21M
White tower, red lantern 21m
0871.5 **La Vacca buoy** Q(3)10s4m6M
E card
0923.2(I) Iles Toro buoy Q(6)+LFl.15s4m7M
Card S
0872 **Iles Lavezzi** Oc(2)WR.6s27m17/14M
White tower on house, red bands 12m
0874 **Ecueil Lavezzi** Fl(2)6s18m9M
2 black spheres on black tower, red band
22m
0875 **Ecueil Perduto** Q(3)10s16m11M
E card tower 28m
0926.2(I) **Perduto buoy** VQ(9)10s4m6M
W card
0876 **Cap Pertusato** Fl(2)10s100m 25M
White tower, black top and corners 21m
0940 **Isola Razzoli** Fl.WR.2.5s77m19/15M
Stone tower 12m

C5 BONIFACIO

See p.51

16

0876
Fl(2)10s25M

Cap Pertusato

See p.55
& photo p.19

Cala Longa

See p.58
CAVALLO

Perduto
VQ(9)10s
YBY

Q(3)10s11M
0875

See p.56

Anse Piantarella

41°20'·1N

ILES LAVEZZI
Oc(2)WR.6s17/14M
0872

Bouches de Bonifacio

White

See p.163

Fl(2)6s9M
0874

17

Fl.WR.2·5s19/15M
0940

I. RAZZOLI

I. SANTA MARIA

Red

19

C5 Port de Bonifacio

⊕16 41°23´.1N 09°08´.9E

Charts
Admiralty *1213, 1424*
French *7024, 7096*

Depth
1 to 6m

Number of berths
400 berths with 220 for visitors

Maximum length
55m

Lights
0878 Pointe de la Madonetta 41°23´.1N 9°08´.8E
Iso.R.4s28m6M Red square tower, grey corners 12m
0882 Pointe Cacavento Fl.G.4s6m5M White pyramid,
dark green top 4m
0886 Pointe de l'Arinella Oc(2)R.6s9m3M Red tower on
grey base 9m 035°-R-059°.

Port communications
0033 VHF Ch 9 ☎ 04 95 73 10 07 *Fax* 04 95 73 18 73
S 0700–21030, OoS 0800–1200, 1400–1700
Email port.bonifacio@wanadoo.fr.

Warnings
Large commercial craft use this harbour and yachts
must keep out of the way.

A unique port of refuge

This commercial, fishing and yachting harbour,
which is the only harbour on the south coast of
Corsica, almost defies description. It is certainly the
most spectacular and attractive natural harbour in
Corsica and probably in the Mediterranean. The
narrow, deep, fjord-like inlet with high, almost
vertical sides of white rock crowned by a medieval
walled town and citadel is certainly unique. The
approach and entrance are easy and almost complete
shelter is available once inside. The facilities for
yachtsmen are good but unfortunately the harbour
becomes very crowded in the season. The Port de
Plaisance office at the head of the inlet administers
all the mooring and berthing in the harbour. (See
photos pages 7 and 16.)

Bastion de l'Etendard from the harbour

Restricted area

A huge Marine Reserve of some 80,000 hectares lies
along the coast from Cap de Feno to Punta de la
Chiappa. Full details of restrictions can be found at
local marina offices and the main points are outlined
in Section II above.

PILOTAGE

Approach

Although the actual entrance is difficult to make out
from a distance, the two conspicuous headlands of
Cap de Feno and Cap Pertusato should be easily
seen, by day or by night, and a course set towards
the distinctive Pointe de la Madonetta light. The
town and citadel can be seen high up and well to the
east of the entrance.

Entrance

By day

Enter on a northeasterly course, leaving the steep-to
white-cliffed Pointe de la Madonetta with a red
square lighthouse tower on its top 100m to port and
the similar steep-to white-cliffed Pointe du Timon,
which has a large cave, 100m to starboard. Follow
the inlet around to starboard in mid-channel. Using
the engine is advisable because of the vicious
downdraughts that exist in the entrance in certain
winds and (b) the possible need to avoid commercial
traffic, which has right of way in the harbour.

By night

Approach Pointe de la Madonetta light (Iso.R.4s) on
a northeasterly course and then alter towards Pointe
de l'Aranella light (Oc(2)R.6s). When about 50m
short of the light, proceed on an easterly course up
the inlet, leaving Pointe Cacavento light (Fl.G.4s) to
starboard.

By GPS

Approach ⊕16 on a northerly course and then
follow the directions above.

Berths

Yachts berth near the head of the harbour. In the
northern section, yachts secure stern-to the quay or
pontoons with bows-to small buoys. In the southern
section, yachts secure stern-to the quay or pontoon
with moorings from the bow. Pontoons have fingers
for berthing. The use of anchors is forbidden.

Anchorages

There are two secluded anchorages in the harbour,
both with poor holding. The Calanque de la Catena
a mud bottom of 15m sloping to 0.5m has and the
much shallower and less sheltered Calanque de
l'Arenella 10m rapidly shelves to 0.5m.

Formalities

All authorities available.

Facilities

All.

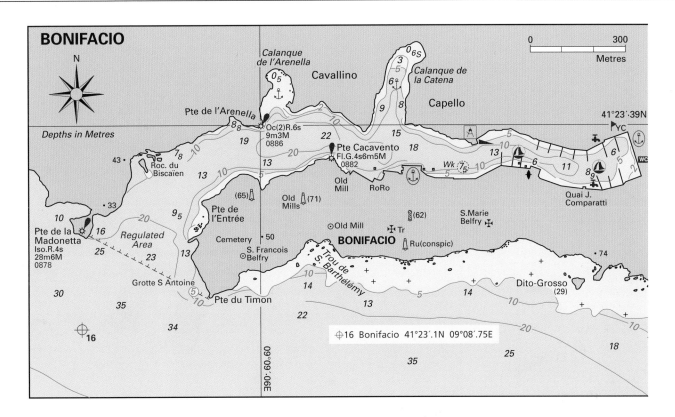

History

This superb natural harbour must have been used by local fishermen since time immemorial, but the real foundation of the town dates from AD 828 when Bonifacio, Marquis de Toscane, arrived here on his return from an expedition against the Saracens. In 1195, during celebrations after a marriage ceremony, a force of Genoese seized and occupied the town, driving out all of the inhabitants. They have been in the town virtually ever since and even today many of the inhabitants still speak a Genoese dialect. In 1420, Alfonso of Aragon arrived with a strong force at the request of the local Corsican lords who had succeeded elsewhere in driving the Genoese off the island, but their attacks on Bonifacio failed. The population of the town was decimated by the plague in 1528 and in 1554 a combined French and Turkish force captured the town, but it was returned to Genoa by a treaty a short time afterwards.

In 1963 the French Foreign Legion took over the barracks in the citadel and in subsequent years development of the tourist industry has slowly taken place.

View of harbour looking just N of west

Belfry of Sainte Maria Majeure

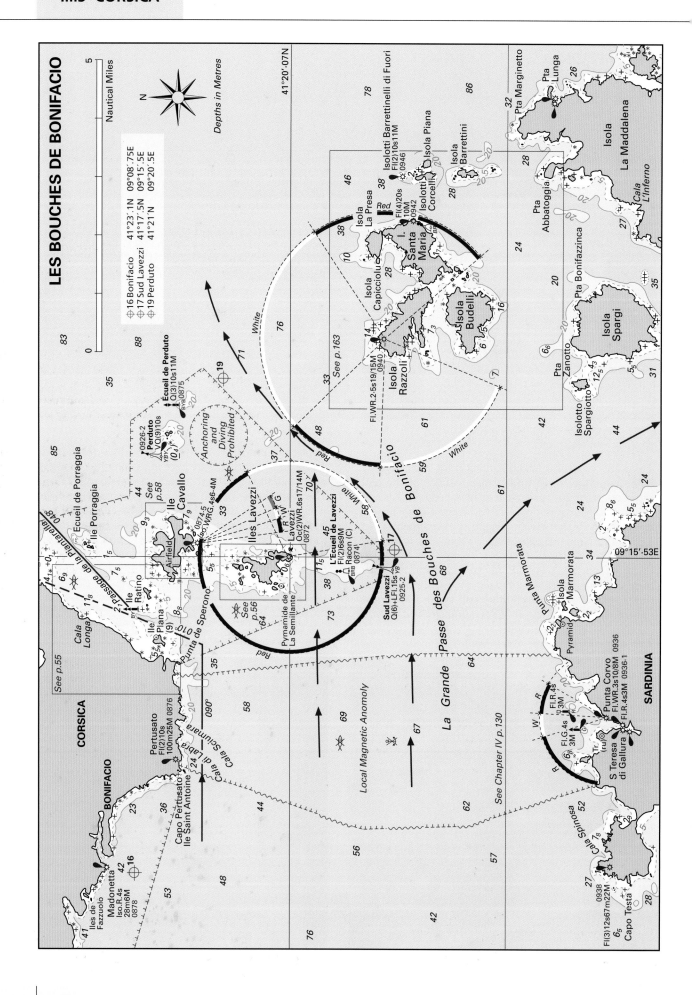

LES BOUCHES DE BONIFACIO

Nautical Miles

Depths in Metres

⊕16 Bonifacio 41°23′.1N 09°08′.75E
⊕17 Sud Lavezzi 41°17′.5N 09°15′.5E
⊕19 Perduto 41°21′N 09°20′.5E

View looking SE towards Cap Pertusato

CAP PERTUSATO 41°22′N 09°10′.8E

A major headland of whitish-grey rock 86m high with an offlying islet, St Antoine, which has a chapel on its top lies 2M SE of the entrance to Bonifacio harbour. The outer rock of this cape is shaped like a French marine's cap. There is foul ground west of the cape extending 100m. The lighthouse stands 400m to the east of the cape and is housed in a white square tower with black top and corners (Fl(2)10s100m25M). A conspicuous signal station stands 800m northwest of the cape. Contact by flag, light or VHF Ch 10 or 16 and ☎ 94 73 00 32, permanent watch.

ILE ST ANTOINE AND PASSAGE

This islet of layered whitish-grey rock is 150m long, 80m wide and 30m high. There is a 30m-wide passage between the islet and the cape with about 1.5m minimum depth, it is most spectacular. Proceed in a NE–SW direction when the sea is calm and with great care. Boats with tall masts cannot get through due to over-hanging rocks.

Le Prêtre beacon

A pole beacon painted black, red and black 6m high with ⦂ topmark, is located on a 4–6m shoal 500m southwest of Punta de Sperono.

PUNTA DE SPERONO 41°22′N 09°13′.2E

This is a low headland which can easily be recognised, because the rear mark (a wall) of the transit for the Passage de la Piantarella stands on the point.

⚓ ANSE PIANTARELLA 41°22′.2N 09°13′.3E
(See plan on page 55)

A small shallow cove with white sandy beach and small river at its head. Caution is necessary when approaching due to shallows between Ile Piana and the Corsican coast. Depths can also change during storms; the deeper water is usually near the Corsican coast. Anchor in 2.5m sand near the mouth of the cove, open to NE–E–SE–S. Track ashore. Very popular with summer visitors.

⚓ CALA LONGA 41°23′.6N 09°14′.4E
(See plan on page 55)

A small bay on the high rocky coast that stands out towards Pointe Cappiciolo. Anchor in 2.5m sand off the centre of the bay, open to E–SE–S. A few houses ashore and a road inland. A group of rocks extend 150m from the shore from the southwest corner of the bay.

Note

In the following sections in particular, there may be a number of different names applied to any particular place. Differences occur not only between similar charts of different countries but also between different issues of charts by the same country. This volume uses the names given in the 2005 editions of French and Italian pilots which, for the most part, agree with one another and use the original dialect names of older charts.

Les Bouches de Bonifacio

The 3.5M passage between the Corsican and Sardinian islands has numerous offlying dangers and adverse weather from time to time. Experienced navigators, especially those used to a similar coasts in North Brittany and around the Channel Islands, should experience no difficulty. The less experienced should take extra care and avoid the area in poor weather conditions. The passages between the Italian islands off Sardinia are described in Section IV below. The large-scale French chart 7024 or the Italian charts 2142 or 3350 are advised for those exploring this most attractive and challenging area.

The passages

Although technically there are six passages between the islands on the north or Corsican side of the straits, only three are advisable in view of local weather and current patterns:

1. Grande Passe des Bouches, which is the main deep-water commercial route running between Sardinia and the Écueil de Lavezzi. 3M wide, 3M long, 19m deep.

2. The pass between the Écueil de Lavezzi and Iles Lavezzi, a route useful for yachts. 1M wide, 1M long, 5m deep.
3. The Passage de la Piantarella, a daytime-only passage in reasonable weather for small craft, between Ile Ratino and Ile Piana. 300m wide, 2M long, 3.5m deep.

Important note

Both Ile Lavezzi and Isola Razzoli light sectors and characteristics were radically altered in 2001 and this has made the use of the pass between Iles Lavezzi and the Écueil de Lavezzi by night more difficult, especially after strong winds, when unknown surface currents can be flowing. Newcomers to the area should not use this pass at night.

Currents

During and after a NW–W gale, east-going currents of up to 3 knots can be experienced. Strong winds from NE–E create weaker west-going currents. In winter this west-going current is semi-permanent.

LIGHTS
0876 Cap Pertusato 41°22′.0N 09°11′.2E Fl(2)10s100m25M 239°-vis-113° White square tower with black top and corners 21m
0938 Capo Testa 41°14′.6N 09°08′.7E Fl(3)12s67m22M 017°-vis-256° White tower on 2-storey house 23m
0872 Lavezzi (Capu di u Beccu) 41°20′.1N 09°15′.6E Oc(2)WR.6s27m17/14M 243°-W-351°-R-243°-partially obscd-138°-obscd-218° Square tower, red band on white house 12m
0874 Écueil de Lavezzi 41°19′.0N 09°15′.3E Fl(2)6s18m9M Black tower, red band ♣ topmark
0875 Écueil de Perduto 41°22′.0N 09°19′.0E Q(3)10s16m11M ♦ card beacon tower BYB 28m
0940 Isola Razzoli 41°18′.4N 9°20′.4E Fl.WR.2.5s77m19/15M 022°-W-092°-R-137°-W-237°-R-320° Stone tower 12m

Buoys
0925.2(I) Sud Lavezzi 41°18′.6N 09°15′.3E Q(6)+LFl.15s7m4M ♥ card YB
0926.2(I) Perduto 41°22′.4N 09°17′.9E VQ(9)10s4m6M ♣ card YBY

Beacons
Pyramide de la Sémillante Pyramid tower on rock SW of Iles Lavezzi commemorating the sinking of the frigate *La Sémillante* in 1854
La Prêtre BRB post with ♣ topmark marking a 4m rocky patch 0.3M SW of Punta de Sperono
Tignosa di Ratino ♣ post BY, ¼M NW of Ile Ratino
Passage de La Piantarella leading marks
Front Beacon on Ile Piana (white wall on SE side)
Rear White wall on Punta de Sperono bearing 228.5°

1. GRANDE PASSE DES BOUCHES

This passage is a 3M wide deep-water passage for commercial shipping, the easiest and safest route by day and the recommended passage at night. There is a local magnetic anomaly 2M to the south of Cap Pertusato with a maximum deflection of up to 3°.

Pilotage

Approach

By day

From the west Approach the pass on an easterly heading approximately 2M north of the Sardinian coast and at least 1M to the south of the Écueil de Lavezzi, marked by a beacon tower, with ♣ topmark. Leave the Sud Lavezzi ♥ cardinal buoy well to port and when this buoy has been passed round onto a northeasterly course and pass between Iles Lavezzi and Isola Razzoli and then leave the Écueil de Perduto (marked by ♦ cardinal light buoy) 1M to port.

From the east The directions given above are taken in reverse order but it is essential to make a positive identification of Iles Lavezzi and Isola Razzoli before entering the area.

By night

From a position some 2M north of Capo Testa, approach Isola Razzoli (Fl.WR.2.5s) on a course between 080° and 085° in its white sector, leaving Sud Lavezzi ♥ cardinal buoy (Q(6)+LFl.15s) well to port. When Iles Lavezzi light (Oc(2) WR.6s) changes from red to white (351°) alter course to 045°. When Écueil de Perduto ♦ cardinal buoy (Q(3)10s) is abeam the passage has been completed.

From the east enter the pass on a southwesterly course with the Capo Testa light (Fl(3)12s) on 235° showing halfway between Isola Razzoli (Fl.WR.2.5s) and Iles Lavezzi (Oc(2)WR.6s), both in their white sectors, leaving Écueil de Perduto (Q(3)10s) over 2M to starboard. When Iles Lavezzi (Oc(2)WR.6s) changes from white to red (351°) change to a westerly course leaving Sud Lavezzi (Q(6)+LFl.15s) to starboard, marking the end of the passage.

By GPS

Approach ⊕17 on an easterly heading and then alter course to ⊕19. In reverse, approach WP19 from the northeasterly quadrant and then steer on a westerly course for ⊕17

2. ILES LAVEZZI – ÉCUEIL DE LAVEZZI PASS

This pass is very suitable for yachts, though in bad weather it will be rougher than the Grande Passe due to the shallower water. The pass is 1M wide, minimum depth 5m.

Approach

By day

From the west Enter the pass on an easterly course halfway between the Iles Lavezzi and the Écueil de Lavezzi beacon tower, BRB, ♣ topmark. When the lighthouse on Lavezzi bears NW change course to northeast and leave the Écueil de Perduto East cardinal buoy 1M to port.

From the east The reverse course holds good provided positive identification of Iles Lavezzi has first been made.

By night

From a position some 1½M south of Cap Pertusato, enter the pass by approaching the light on Isola Razzoli (Fl.WR.2.5s), in the red sector, on a course of 106°. When the red sector of the Iles Lavezzi light (Oc(2)WR.6s) turns white (351°) alter to a course of 080° and remain in the white sector of this light

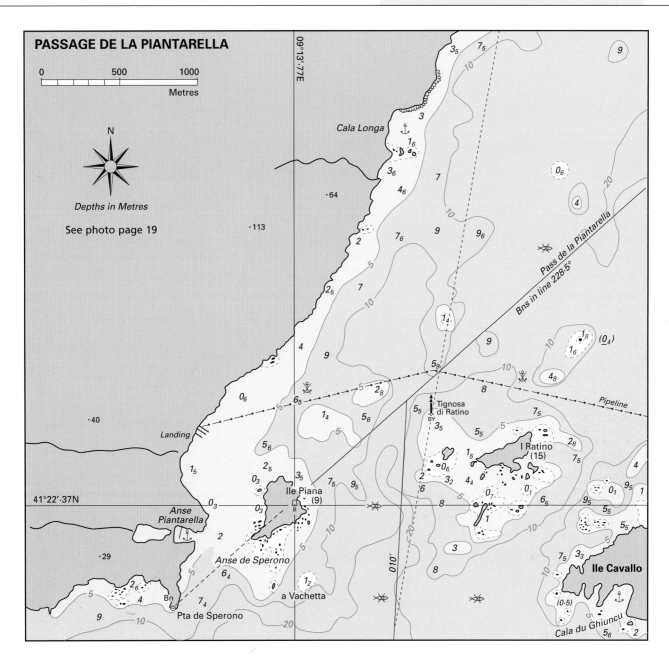

PASSAGE DE LA PIANTARELLA

0   500   1000
Metres

N

Depths in Metres

See photo page 19

09°13'·77E

·64

·113

Cala Longa

·40

·113

Landing

·40

Anse
Piantarella

41°22'·37N

·29

Anse de Sperono

Ile Piana
(9)

a Vachetta

Pta de Sperono

Pass de la Piantarella

Bns in line 228·5°

Tignosa
di Ratino
BY

Pipeline

I Ratino
(15)

010°

Ile Cavallo

Cala du Ghiuncu

---

passing 1M southeast of Écueil de Perduto ⚓ cardinal buoy (Q(3)10s).

From the east approach Écueil de Lavezzi (Fl(2)6s) on a WSW course until the light on Isola Razzoli (Fl.WR.2}5s) bears 106° (in its red sector!), turn onto a course of 286° and keep the stern bearing of Isola Razzoli on 106°.

3. PASSAGE DE LA PIANTARELLA

This is the usual inshore passage for yachts by day and in normal weather. It cannot be used at night or in bad weather.

From the west Steer towards the south point of Ile Cavallo on a course of 090° passing some ¼M off the coast of Corsica and outside Le Prêtre beacon, BRB with ⦙ topmark. When the high land of Sant'Amanza peninsula to the north is in line with the Tignosa di Ratino, alter to a course of 010° and pass equidistant between these islets and Ile Piana.

When the white wall (front) leading mark on Ile Piana bears 225° and nearly abeam of the Tignosa to starboard, alter to a course of 048° leaving Tignosa di Ratino beacon (⟡ cardinal BY) 150m to starboard. The rear leading mark, also a white wall, on Punta de Sperono will soon appear. Keep these in line astern. When Ile Porraggia is abeam you can make a little to NW of the leading line which passes very close to this group of rocks and islands.

From the north Navigate to a position where the Ile Porraggia group of islands lie 300m to the southeast and proceed on a course of 228°. Bring the two stone beacon leading marks in line and follow them. This course passes some 150m to N of the Tignosa di Ratino ⟡ cardinal BY beacon. When this beacon is 200m to the east, turn onto a course of 190°, passing equidistant between Ile Piana and the offlying rocks of Ile Ratino. When the lighthouse on Cap Pertusato appears, alter course towards the west.

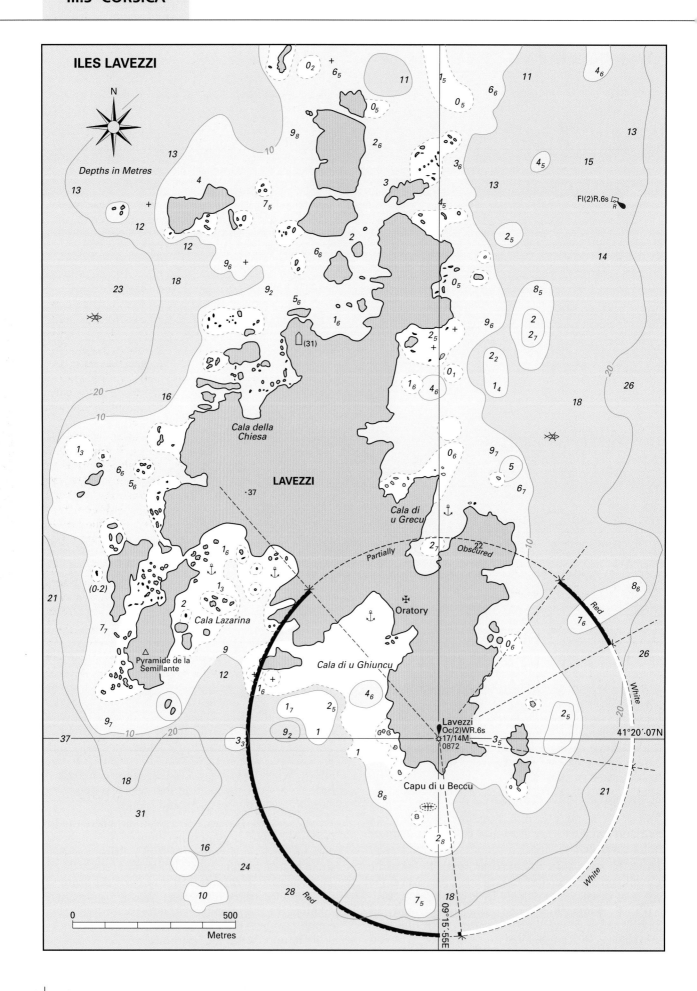

ILES LAVEZZI

N

Depths in Metres

Cala della Chiesa

LAVEZZI

Cala di
u Grecu

Partially   Obscured

Cala Lazarina

△ Pyramide de la
Semillante

Cala di u Ghiuncu

✠ Oratory

Red

White

Fl(2)R.6s

Lavezzi
Oc(2)WR.6s
17/14M
0872

Capu di u Beccu

Red

White

41°20′·07N

09°15′·55E

0   500

Metres

Iles Lavezzi

41°20´.5N 09°15´.5E
See plan page 52 and 56

Delightful island with very tricky approach

A delightful, almost bare, group of rocky islands which offers three beautiful anchorages with crystal clear water over a white sandy bottom. The islands are deserted, though in the season tourists are brought over by motor boat from Corsica in their hundreds and many yachts use the anchorages. The approach and entrance require some care due to offlying rocks and shallows. The various anchorages offer good protection from wind and sea though it may be necessary to change anchorage if the wind direction alters. The island is part of the national park and it is forbidden to land without authorisation. Navigation and anchoring is allowed but this can be revoked by the authorities, if necessary.

Currents

An E-going current of up to 2 to 3 knots may be experienced during and after a west to northwest gale. Weaker west-going currents may be encountered after strong winds from northeast or east, especially during winter months when there is a west-going current of a semi-permanent nature.

Lights
0872 Lavezzi (Capu di u Beccu) 41°20´.1N 09°15´.6E
  Oc(2)WR.6s27m17/14M 243°-W-351°-R-243° 138°-partially
  obscd-218° Square tower, red band, on white house 12m
0874 Écueil de Lavezzi 41°19´.0N 09°15´.3E Fl(2)6s18m9M
  Black tower, red band ‡ topmark
Buoys
0925.2(I) Sud Lavezzi 41°18´.6N 09°15´.3E Q(6)+LFl.15s7m4M
  ⚏ card YB
Beacons
Pyramide de la Sémillante Pyramid tower on rock SW of Iles
  Lavezzi

Warning

In bad weather, especially from the northwest, the seas and winds can considerably increase due to the funnel effect between the high hills of Corsica and Sardinia.

Restrictions

A large part of the area around these islands is a Marine Reserve and all forms of sport which destroy animals, fish, birds and vegetation, etc. are forbidden.

PILOTAGE

Approach

By day

From the west, round the high white cliffs of Cap Pertusato with its conspicuous lighthouse and signal station and set an ESE course towards the SW point of Iles Lavezzi, which has a pyramid-shaped tower La Sémillante on the point, seen in the closer approach.

From the wide and deep Golfe de Sant'Amanza, round the prominent Punta di Capicciolu and steer a SSE course. Leave the small group of rocks Ile Poraggia 0.5M to starboard and pass between Ile Cavallo and Ile Perduto, leaving a ⚐ cardinal light buoy, YBY VQ(9)10s, just to east. Then steer a SSW course towards the lighthouse on the southern tip of the Iles Lavezzi, which should be rounded at no closer than 400m.

By night

Though there are numerous navigational lights for a night approach to the area, a close approach to this island would be hazardous due to the number of offlying rocks and shallows and is not recommended.

Entrances to the three anchorages

1. **Cala Lazarina** Take up a position where the memorial pyramid La Sémillante is some 300m to the northwest and proceed on a NNE course, leaving a series of small above-water rocks 75m to port. There is an anchorage about 220m NNW of the large islet to starboard in 5 to 8m but the venturesome can work their way, with care, deeper into the bay. A bow lookout is advised. This anchorage is open to the south.
2. **Cala di u Ghiuncu** From a position where the Lavezzi lighthouse bears northeast 300m, make a northerly course leaving the shore 50m to starboard to the head of the *cala* where the anchorage lies. Anchor in 2m of sand at the head of the *cala* with the white-walled cemetery bearing northeast and some 25m from the beach. Anchorage is open to S–SW and take care when anchoring as cables run ashore here.
3. **Cala di u Grecu** Approach the north half of the island on a westerly course and in the close approach identify the small white building and wall around the cemetery. Approach it on a SSW course, leaving a small isolated rock 30m to port. With a bow lookout, proceed with care to the anchorage at the head of the *cala*. Anchor in 2m on sand, 30m from the beach. Anchorage open to NE.

Moorings

There are some private moorings in these *calas* which could be used if not required by their owners, but note that some are used by the ferry boats.

Formalities

Customs officers may make random inspections of yachts.

Facilities

None.

Ile Cavallo

⊕18 41°21.25N 09°16′.06E
See plan page 52 and below

A totally private island

This rocky island has a certain amount of low scrub and small trees and has been developed as a high-class holiday area by an Italian consortium. It has four possible anchorages which need some care in the approach and entrance. Shelter from winds from all directions is possible. Facilities ashore are very limited and the house owners do not like visitors, in fact one is not permitted to land on the island. An airfield has been built for small private planes. A small private harbour and hotel complex have been built to the south of Cala di Palma.

Approach

By day

The island is best approached from the SW or NE as these directions minimise the offlying dangers. However, close approach to all the anchorages described below needs care and a lookout forward. It is not recommended to approach Cavallo at night except from the southeast, where lights are available to enter Port de Cavallo, but note entry is only permitted between 0600 and 2200 from June to September.

Anchorages

1. **Cala di Palma** Entrance to this anchorage requires considerable care for the first visit and slow speed with a bow lookout is essential. Enter on a northwesterly heading towards the centre of the *cala*. An alternative approach may be made on a westerly course from a position 100m to south of the southeastern extremity of the island, keeping close to the north shore. Open from E–S. Sand beach, several small landing pontoons and a slip. Anchor off mouth of southern sub-bay in 4m, sand.

2. **Cala di Zeri** Enter on a southwesterly course towards the western corner of the *cala*. The centre and eastern side is rock-filled. Open to NE. A large and a small beach at head of *cala* with a small pontoon (2m) between them. Anchor 100m from the head of the *cala* close to the northwest shore in 3m, sand.

3. **Cala di u Grecu** Anchoring or mooring in this *cala* is forbidden.

4. **Cala di u Ghiuncu** Enter on a northeasterly course. Open S–SW. Several small sandy beaches. Anchor in 3m, sand.

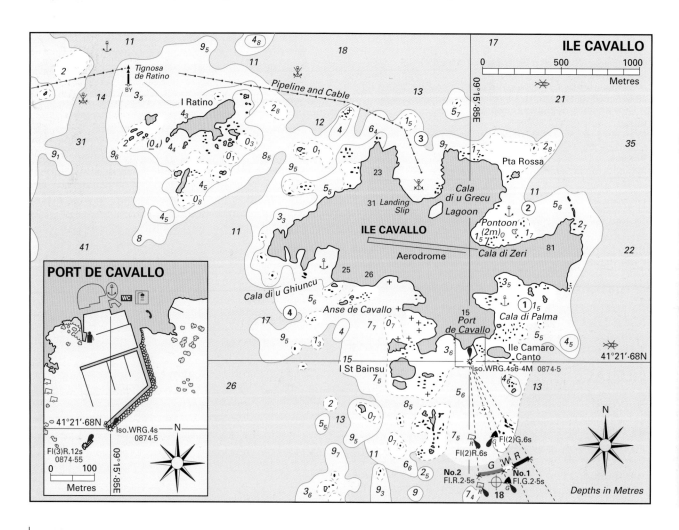

C6 Port de Cavallo

⊕18 41°21.25N 09°16'.06E

Charts
Admiralty *1213*
SHOM *7096, 7024*

Depth
2 to 5m

Number of berths
230 berths with 37 for visitors

Maximum length
30m

Lights
0874.5 Jetty head 41°21'.7N 09°15'.9E Iso.WRG.4s7m6-4M 328°-G-337°-W-344°-R-353° White tower, 3m
0874.51 in same structure as 0874.5 Fl(3)G.12s5m2M
0874.55 on left of entrance Fl(3)R.12s4m2M

Buoys
800m south of above lights there are Boa 1 Fl.G.2.5s2M (stbd) and Boa 2 Fl.R.2.5s2M (port)
250m south there are Boa 3 Fl(2)G.6s2M (stbd) and Boa 4 Fl(2)R.6s2M (port)

Port communications
It is obligatory to call *capitainerie* on VHF Ch 9 or ☎ 04 95 70 10 09 *Fax* 04 95 70 03 74 before entering. Note that the VHF channel operates from 15 June to 15 September only!

Warnings
Many rocks and shallow patches exist outside the approach channel.

An unwelcoming marina

A relatively new, privately-owned yacht harbour built as part of a holiday complex on the south end of Cavallo. Visiting yachtsmen are not encouraged to make use of the facilities ashore here and the security guards patrol with fierce-looking guard dogs!

Approach

Pick up the outside pair of buoys and steer a course of 340° towards the jetty head. Note that although there are lights, entrance is only allowed between 0600 and 2200 (June to September). On reaching the jetty, turn to starboard and take up the berth that has already been allocated.

By GPS

Steer for ⊕18 on a westerly course and then alter course to steer between the buoys (about 340°) for the entrance.

Formalities

Report to *capitainerie* when berthed.

Facilities

All in season, basic out of season.

Ile Cavallo, looking just west of N, with Ile Poraggia beyond in line with Punta di u Capicciolu and Port de Cavallo in centre of photo

Continuing along the Corsican coast

(See plan page 49)

PUNTA DI U CAPPICIOLU 41°25′.7N 09°15′.8E

A prominent point with high cliffs sloping up to a hill (105m). Just under a mile southwest of the point stands the Tour Sant'Amanza (127m). There are a few close inshore rocks to the south of the point, otherwise it is steep-to.

⚓ GOLFE DE SANT'AMANZA 41°25′N 09°13′.9E

A large deep gulf with yellow-white cliffs, which offers excellent protection but is open to NE–E. It is very easy to enter and the channel is in the centre of the gulf, with rocks extending from both shores. Pay attention to the many oyster beds which occupy an area 2,500m by 500m to the southwest of Punta di

u Capicciolu. The best and most sheltered anchorage is in the southern corner near the village of Gurgazo where there is a landing and where provisions may be obtained. There is also a road here. An alternative anchorage is at the head of the gulf. Both anchorages are in 3m, sand and weed. Sailing clubs, houses, hotels and summer camps occupy much of the shore along the beach, which has caught a lot of flotsam. The very beautiful Cala di Stentinu should be visited by dinghy, while craft with less than 1.3m draught can anchor inside. Another anchorage lies just south of Capu Biancu.

⚓ ANSE DE BALISTRA 41°26′.3N 09°13′.7E

An anchorage which is in the northwest corner of a bay, in front of a sandy beach behind which is a lagoon. Anchor in 3m, sand and weed, but the anchorage is subject to more swell than further up the gulf as it is open to NE–E–SE. Main road 1M inland.

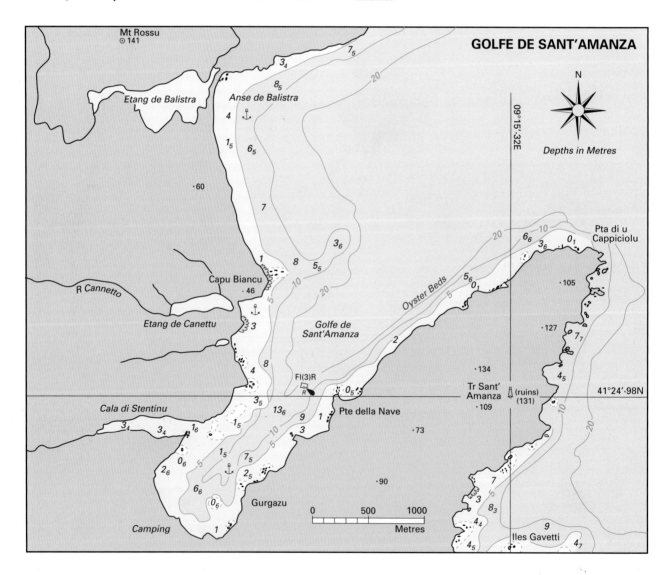

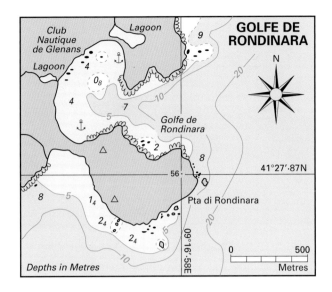

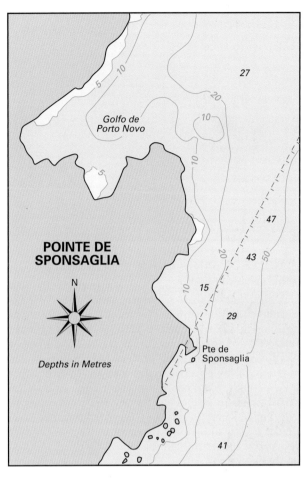

Punta di Rondinara 41°27'.9N 09°16'.7E

A large round headland of reddish rock with a narrow isthmus connecting it to the Corsican shore. The top is scrub-covered, there is a small islet on the point and an isolated rock 200m to the southeast. The point has many close-in rocky dangers on its north side.

⚓ GOLFE DE RONDINARA 41°28'.13N 09°16'.37E

An excellent anchorage in an almost landlocked sandy bay. There is a 0.8m shallow patch in the middle of the bay (occasionally buoyed). A white sandy beach lines the sides of the bay. Anchor in 3m, sand, to suit wind direction. The bay is open to NE–E–SE. The Club Nautique de Glénans has a base here. There is a track inland to the main road.

Pointe de Sponsaglia 41°29'N 09°17'.3E

A small hooked headland of whitish rocky cliffs with a conspicuous ruined tower on its summit. A small islet lies 50m east and an isolated rock lies 90m to the south of this point, otherwise steep-to. A track runs inland to the coast road.

Port de Rondinara looking W

⚓ GOLFE DE PORTO NOVO 41°30'.2N 09°16'.8E

A large deep bay with two areas for anchoring. Entrance is easy, but note a 0.8m rocky shallow patch 150m north of the point on the south side of the gulf. Anchor in 3m, sand off the sandy beach at the western end of the bay, open to N–NE–E. Sand dunes and a lagoon lie behind the beach. Track inland. The Bocca d'Alesia is a sub-bay on the southern side of Porto Novo with rocky sides and close inshore rocky dangers. It is shallow on the western side. Enter with care, anchor off sandy beach in 3m, sand, shell and weed, open to N–NE–E. Deserted.

3. BONIFACIO TO PUNTA DI A CHIAPPA

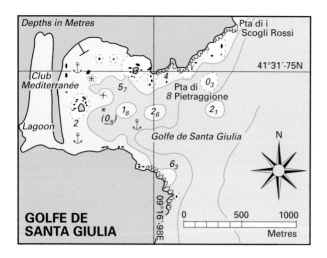

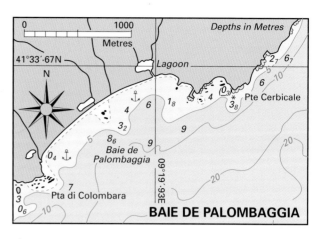

⚓ GOLFE DE SANTA GIULIA 41°31´.5N 09°17´E

A large semi-landlocked bay surrounded by low scrub-covered hills. A white sandy beach runs around the shore with a river mouth in the southern corner. It is a beautiful setting but is always overcrowded in the season. There are a number of shallows and several groups of rocky islets surrounded by covered rocks. Enter with care using a bow lookout and continuous sounding. Anchor on north or south side of the bay in 3m, sand, open to NE–E–SE. There is a large Club Méditerranée base on the N side of the bay, also a jetty which is used by numerous ferries in high season. A road runs inland to the main road.

Ile du Toro 41°30´.5N 09°23´E

This is a 40m-high rock, lying 4½M off the coast, surrounded by three rocks, islets and some awash and covered rocks. ½M to the east of the Ile du Toro lies a 2.6m shallow, the Haut-fond du Toro, which has a ⚑ cardinal light buoy, YB Q(6)+LFl.15s, on its southeast side.

Golfe de Santa Giulia looking W

⚓ PLAGE DE PALOMBAGGIA 41°33´.2N 09°19´.7E

A long shallow bay with a popular sandy beach. The points at each end of the beach have offlying rocks extending 200m. There are also a few rocks extending 250m from the centre of the bay. Anchor off beach at either end of the bay in 3m, sand, open to NE–E–SE–S–SW. Some houses ashore, also a road.

Pointe Cerbicale 41°33´.5N 09°20´.5E

A headland which is not conspicuous unless coasting close in. It slopes up to a 145m hill which is scrub-covered. There is a good view from here of the coast and islands. The coast is free from obstructions with the exception of a rocky projection to the southwest.

Iles Cerbicales 41°33´.2N 09°21´.8E

Four of these islands lie in a 2M long NE-SW line about 1M southeast of Pointe Cerbicale. The fifth island lies 0.5M further to the east. At the northeast end Ile Forana (34m) is sloping with one peak, Ile Maestro Maria (7m) is flat and has good beaches. Ile Piana is the largest with 34m and 31m peaks, Ile Pietricaggiosa (10m) lies at the south end. Rocher de la Vacca (21m) which is 0.5M to the east is high and

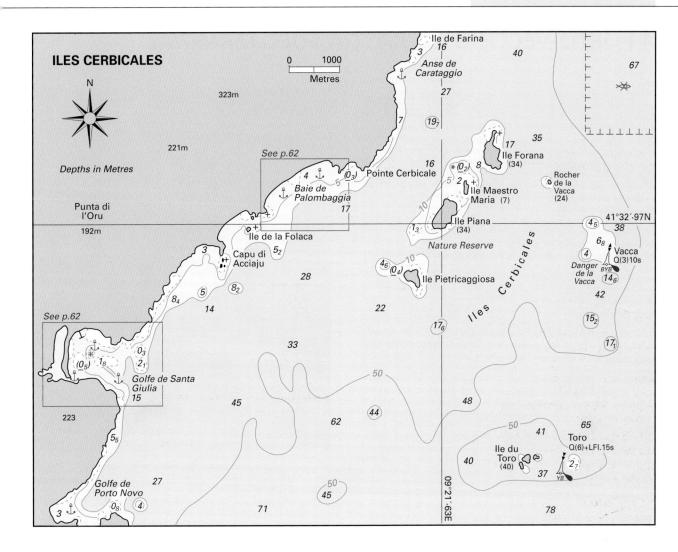

pointed. The Danger de la Vacca with 4.0 and 4.5m shallows lies 1.5M to the east of Ile Piana and is marked by an ♦ cardinal light buoy, BYB Q(3)10s. Passages are available between all the islands with minimum depth of 9m except for the passage north of Ile Piana where there is a 1.4m submerged rock. There are several shallow patches and an isolated rock on the western side of the islands, which are shown best on the chart.

NOTE

All the islands are a nature reserve and landing without permission is forbidden between 1 April and 31 August.

Rocher de la Vacca is sometimes used as a target for naval firing practice. Should this occur, close the Corsican coast and keep within 0.25M of it.

⚓ ANSE DE CARATAGGIO 41°34′.5N 09°21′.1E

A small sandy bay with white sandy beach and rocky sides. Anchor in 3m sand and weed near the centre of the bay, open to NE-E-SE-S. Track to road inland, deserted.

PUNTA DI A CHIAPPA 41°35.8N 09°22′.1E
(See plan on page 49)

A major headland on the south side of the mouth of the Golfe de Porto Vecchio, it has steep whitish-grey rocky cliffs and a scrub-covered top 44m high. There is a conspicuous lighthouse on the summit with white square tower, red lantern on white building (Fl(3+1)15s65m23M) and also a red and white banded radio mast. A signal station stands 250m to the west of the light. The point is steep-to except for some rocky dangers which extend 100m to the south of the point.

ROCHES DE CHIAPPINO (AND TOURELLE)

300m to the north of Punta di a Chiappa lies this group of rocks which was marked with a BRB beacon tower, Tourelle Chiappino, until it was destroyed in 1989. It has not been rebuilt since and now only the old base is just visible in calm weather. The passage inshore of the beacon has a minimum depth of 11m but is not recommended in anything but calm weather.

4 PORTO-VECCHIO TO BASTIA FUEL TERMINAL

The sixty-five mile section of coast northwards from Porto-Vecchio to Bastia covers the larger part of the east coast of Corsica and is in general quite different from the rest of the island's coasts.

The high ranges of hills and mountains draw further and further back from the coast as progress is made north and even the foothills cease near Solenzara, where a flat sandy plain commences and continues as far as Bastia. From Campoloro northwards, the foothills are again in evidence but stand back from the coast.

As would be expected on a flat sandy coast, good sheltered anchorages are not to be found.

From Porto Vecchio to Solenzara, some 14M to the north, there are six anchorages which are described in the text. These are situated in various bays where the foothills come down to the coast. The remaining 41M up to Bastia has only the artificial harbour of Campoloro, where yachts can seek shelter.

The coast is not deserted and there are many holiday houses. Inland, vast areas of fruit, cereal and vines are cultivated. A main road runs parallel to the coast at approximately 2M inland. Between Porto-Vecchio and the lighthouse at Alistro, local magnetic deviations of the order of up to 5° may be encountered.

View SSE from Solenzara Pier Elbow (see page 72)

PLANNING GUIDE

Headlands		Ports & anchorages	Open to winds
	C7 ⚓	Porto-Vecchio page 67	NE
	C7 ⚓	Port de Plaisance page 67	
Tourelle Pecorella and beacon Punta d'Arasu	⚓	Baie de San Ciprianu	E–S
	⚓	Punta Capicciola W	SE–S
Punta Capicciola Ile de Pinarellu			
	⚓	Golfe de Pinarellu	NE–E–SE
	⚓	Pointe de Fautéa SW	E–SE–S
Ile et Pointe de Fautéa	⚓	Anse de Fautéa	NE–E–SE
	⚓	Anse de Tarcu	NE–E–SE
	⚓	Anse de Favone	N–NE–E
	⚓	Anse de Cannella	NE–E–SE
	⚓	Marine de Cala d'Oru	NE–E–SE
	C8 ⚓	Port de Solenzara page 72	E–SE
Aérodrome de Solenzara Offshore Fuel Terminal Solenzara Foce di u Fium Orbu (mouth of the river Orbu) (Calzarello) and wreck Foce de Tavignano Fleuve (mouth of river Tavignano) Phare d'Alistro (lighthouse)			
	C9 ⚓	Port de Taverna page 74	NE–E
Résidence des Iles, Dome and Aero RC Lucciana Offshore Fuel Terminal Aérodrome de Bastia-Poretta Offshore Fuel Terminal – Bastia			
	⚓	Anse de Porto-Vecchio	

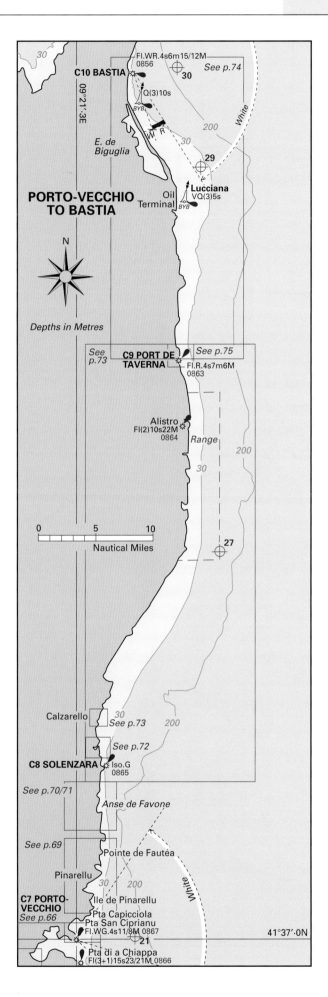

PORTO-VECCHIO
TO BASTIA

N

Depths in Metres

0   5   10
Nautical Miles

⊕21 Porto Vecchio   41°37'N 09°27'.5E
⊕27 Tavignano   42°06'N 09°36'E
⊕29 Lucciana Terminal 42°34'N 09°35'E
⊕30 Bastia   42°42'N 09°32'E

0856 **Jetée du Dragon** Fl.WR.4s16m15/12M
   Grey tower, red lantern 13m
0863 **Campoloro** Fl.R.4s7m6M
   White column, red top 5m
0864 **Alistro** Fl(2)10s93m22M
   Grey tower, black top on red house 27m
0865 **Solenzara** Iso.G.4s3M
   White tower, green top 3m
0867 **Pta San Ciprianu** Fl.WG.4s26m11/8M
   White tower, black lantern 13m
0866 **Pta di a Chiappa** Fl(3+1)15s65m23/21M
   White tower, red lantern 21m

New communications mast at Solenzara entrance
(see page 72)

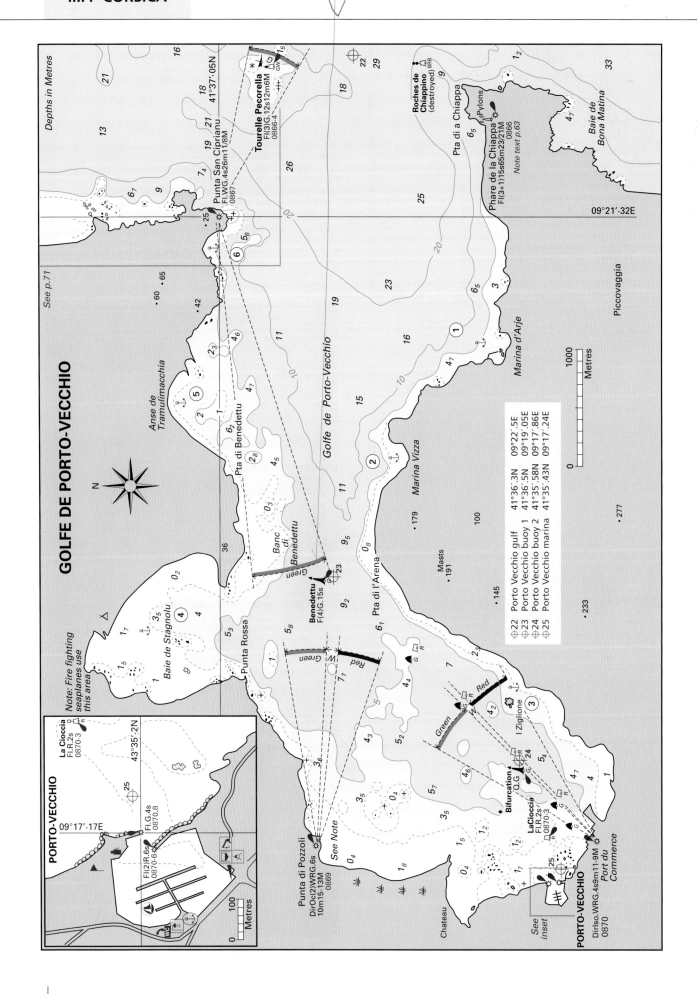

GOLFE DE PORTO-VECCHIO

Depths in Metres

See p.71

Note: Fire fighting seaplanes use this area

PORTO-VECCHIO

09°17'·17E

43°35'·2N

La Cioccia
Fl.R.2s
0870·3

Fl.G.4s
0870.8

Fl(2)R.6s
0870·6

100
Metres
0

Anse de Tramulimacchia

Pta di Benedettu

Banc di Benedettu

Benedettu
Fl(4)G.15s

Baie de Stagnolu

Punta Rossa

Golfe de Porto-Vecchio

Tourelle Pecorella
Fl(3)G.12s12m6M
0866·4

Punta San Ciprianu
Fl.WG.4s26m11/8M
0867

Roches de Chiappino
(destroyed)
0866

Pta di a Chiappa

Phare de la Chiappa
Fl(3+1)15s65m23/21M
Note text p.63

Pylons

09°21'·32E

Baie de Bona Matina

Piccovaggia

Marina d'Arje

Marina Vizza

Pta di l'Arena

Punta di Pozzoli
DirOc(2)WRG.6s
10m15–13M
0869

See Note

Masts

Chateau

I Ziglione

Bifurcation
Q.G

LaCiocciá
Fl.R.2s
0870·3

PORTO-VECCHIO
DirIso.WRG.4s9m11·9M
0870
Port du Commerce

See inset

⊕			
⊕ 22	Porto Vecchio gulf	41°36'·3N	09°22'·5E
⊕ 23	Porto Vecchio buoy 1	41°36'·5N	09°19'·05E
⊕ 24	Porto Vecchio buoy 2	41°35'·58N	09°17'·86E
⊕ 25	Porto Vecchio marina	41°35'·43N	09°17'·24E

1000
Metres
0

C7 Porto-Vecchio

⊕22 41°36′.30N 09°22′.50E (at gulf entrance)
⊕23 41°36′.5N 09°19′.05E (at channel bend)
⊕24 41°35′.58N 09°17′.86E (at bifurcation buoy)
⊕25 41°35′.48N 09°17′.35E (at entrance of Port de Plaisance)

Charts
Admiralty *1425, 1992*
French *6911, 6929*

Depth
1.3 to 3.5m in basin, 3.5m in entrance channel

Number of berths
540 berths with 150 for visitors

Maximum length
40m

Lights
0866 Punta di a Chiappa 41°35′.7N 09°22′.0E
Fl(3+1)15s65m23/21M 198°-vis-027° White square tower, red lantern, 21m
0866.4 Rocher Pecorella 41°36′.7N 09°22′.3E
Fl(3)G.12s12m6M White tower green top 14m
0867 Punta San Ciprianu 41°37′.0N 09°21′.4E
Fl.WG.4s26m11/8M 220°-W-281°-G-299°-W-072°-G-084°-obscd-220° White square tower black lantern 13m
0869 Punta di Pozzoli 41°36′.6N 09°17′.5E
Dir.Oc(2)WRG.6s10m15-13M 258.7°-G-271.7°-W-275.2°-R-288.2°-obscd-258.7° White tower, black top 5m
0870 Commercial port 41°35′.2N 09°17′.5E
Dir.Iso.WRG.4s9m11-9M 208.5°-G-223.5°-W-225.5°-R-240.5°-obscd-208.5° Rectangular stone tower, 12m

Marina
0870.6 Digue Est head Fl(2)R.6s5m6M 212°-vis-302° White tower, red top 4m
0870.8 Digue NE head Fl.G.4s4m5M 200°-vis-290° White tower, green top 2m

Beacons
0866.4 Tourella Pecorella (see above)
Tourella Chiappino – destroyed 1989 – base still visible
0870.3 Écueil de la Cioccia 41°35′.4N 09°17′.5E
Fl.R.2s3m2M Red tower 5m

Buoys
0923.2(I) Haut-fond de Toro 41°30′.4N 09°23′.6E
Q(6)+LFl.15s4m7M ⚓ card, YB
0871.5 Danger de la Vacca 41°32′.7N 09°24′.0E
Q(3)10s4m6M ⚓ card, BYB
0921.4(I) Benedettu 41°36′.6N 09°19′.1E
Fl(4)G.15s4m4M
G pillar buoy, ▲ top off Punta de l'Arena where leading lines change
0922.2(I) Bifurcation 41°35′.6N 09°17′.9E Q.G.3m4M
Green buoy, ▲ top marking the stbd turn into the channel to the marina
Four G buoys, ▲ topmarks and green reflecting strips mark the stbd side of the main entrance channel to the commercial port
Four R buoys with cylindrical topmarks and red reflecting strip, mark the port side of the channel

Port communications
VHF Ch 9, ☎ 04 95 70 17 93 *Fax* 04 95 70 27 68
(S 0800-2100, OoS 0830-1200, 1400-1730)
Email port@porto-vecchio.fr

Warning
The shallow sandy area north of Pointe de l'Arena is slowly extending (see plan page 66). Do not attempt to cut this corner. For a first visit, follow the marked channels carefully. Do not attempt to follow local yachts which are making use of large areas of deep water with unmarked dangers.

Fire-fighting planes
Large flying boats may use the Golfe de Porto Vecchio to load water to fight fires.

A pleasant, well sheltered harbour

A modern yacht harbour and commercial harbour at the head of a large and beautiful gulf, easy to enter in most weather conditions and offering complete shelter in the harbour. Adequate facilities for yachtsmen and everyday requirements can be obtained from an attractive walled town close by. There are several very attractive anchorages around the gulf and many places including a river to explore. Yachts are not to enter the commercial harbour unless they are longer than 40m (the maximum size in the Port de Plaisance). This is a very popular harbour and during the season it becomes very overcrowded.

Restricted areas

A Marine Reserve is established 2½M to the east of Punta di a Chiappa which is 3M long in a north-south direction and 1M wide in an east-west direction. Fishing, subaqua diving and anchoring in the area are forbidden.

The whole of the area around the Iles Cerbicales including the outlying islets and shallows are also a nature reserve and the same restrictions apply between 1 April and 31 August and include landing on any island or islet. For further details see Part II.

Approach

By day

Take up a position midway between the Tourelle Pecorella, (W tower, G top), and Roches de Chiappino and set a westerly course down the centre of the outer part of the Golfe de Porto-Vecchio to a point halfway between Punta di l'Arena, a rounded rocky tree-covered promontory, and Punta di Benedettu, a lower tree-covered headland to the north. In this area Benedettu, G pillar light buoy ▲ topmark (Fl(4)G.15s) will be found. Now set a southwest course between a series of G buoys with up-pointed cones and R buoys with cylinder topmarks towards a group of large metal sheds painted white at the RoRo terminal. When the small conical tree-covered Ilot Ziglione (13m) is abeam to port, a small G light buoy (Q.G) will be seen ahead. Round this buoy onto a course of 254°, leaving it to starboard. ¾M ahead there is a small red beacon tower, Fl.R.2s, Écueil de la Cioccia. Leave this tower close to port and the two light towers at the yacht harbour entrance will be seen ahead.

By night

Enter the outer part of the Golfe de Porto-Vecchio and make for a point near its centre. Course should be set to avoid the dangers around the beacon towers of Chiappino off Punta di a Chiappa and Pecorella (Fl(3)G.12s) off the Punta San Ciprianu (Fl.WG.4s). The directional light Pozzoli (DirOc(2)WRG.6s) will then be seen. Navigate into the white sector and follow it on a course of 273° until the commercial harbour light (DirIso.WRG.4s) is seen. When in the white sector of this light turn to 225° and follow it. After 1¼M a small buoy (Q.G)

4. PORTO VECCHIO TO BASTIA FUEL TERMINAL

Porto-Vecchio, Port de Plaisance looking SW

must be rounded onto a course of 254° leaving it to starboard. The course is now towards a Fl.R which is left to port then towards a Fl(2)R.6s and Fl.G.4s at the entrance to the yacht harbour.

By GPS

Approach ⊕21 from the east and steer for ⊕23. At the buoy alter to steer for ⊕24. Here alter to starboard and steer for ⊕25.

Entrance

By day

Approach the entrance on 254° from Écueil de la Cioccia red beacon tower and round the head of Digue Nord-Est at 15m, to avoid shallows to the south, onto a northwest course entering between the two heads.

By night

Approach the Fl.G.4s light on 254° and when close, divert onto a northwest course to round it at a distance of 15m, leaving Fl(2)R.6s to port.

Warning

Roches de Pecorella and beacon

Near the centre of the mouth of the Golfe de Porto-Vecchio lies a shallow area 500m long by 200m wide with awash and covered rocks 2.0 to 2.6m deep. A tower, Tourelle de Pecorella, a masonry beacon G over W, stands near the middle of the dangers. There are four wrecks on the west and north sides of the beacon.

Berths

Secure close to the fuelling berth and report to the bureau de port on the west side of the harbour for the allocation of a berth. Then secure stern-to quay or pontoon with mooring chain from the bow. This chain is attached to a line which is connected to the pontoon or quay.

Formalities

All authorities available.

Facilities

All.

History

This ancient Genoese walled town with its small fishing harbour below was probably built on the site of a prehistoric settlement, because the area has been in occupation since 3000BC and the town is located on the best natural defensive site. Porto Vecchio means 'old port' in Italian.

The town never expanded greatly due to the unhealthy marshy salines at the mouth of the Stabiacciu river where malarial mosquitoes used to breed.

The Golfe de Porto-Vecchio has been praised since Roman times. Diodorus Siculus called it a most beautiful port and even Boswell said that it may vie with the most distinguished harbours in Europe. In recent times, due to the extermination of the mosquito and to the tourist trade, the area is expanding and becoming more prosperous.

Anchorages in the Gulf

There are numerous anchorages around the Gulf. Details of some are given below, travelling clockwise from the SE. (Numbers refer to plan on page 66.)

1. Marine d'Arji A small sandy bay open to N–NE–N with an anchorage 200m off the beach in 3m, sand. There are a few houses, a large salt pan and a road behind the beach. There is an uncompleted harbour for dinghies and small fishing boats on the west side of the bay.

2. Marine Vizza A deserted anchorage 150m off the small beach in 3m, sand, open to the NW–N–NE but otherwise well protected.

3. Ilot Ziglione An anchorage between the island and the coast in 3m, sand, well protected but open to N. There are some private moorings in the area, a landing stage and houses on the shore. Sound carefully.

4. Baie de Stagnolu Anchor in 3m, sand, off the east side of the bay, well protected but strong winds from SW send in short waves. There is a Touring Club de France base here and summer camps.

5. Anse de Tramulimacchia A shallow bay open to SE-S-SW. Anchor 100m off the beach at the north side of the bay in 3m, sand. Due to shallows, approach this anchorage on a NW course sounding carefully.

6. Bay to W of Punta San Ciprianu A very small bay open to S–SW. Anchor near the moorings sounding carefully at the head of the bay. There are houses around the bay, which has rocks in the southeast corner.

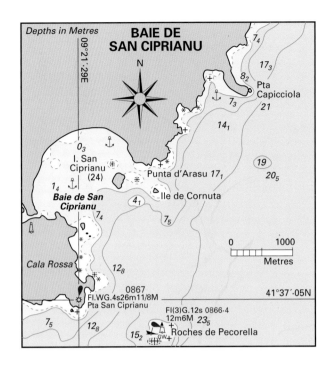

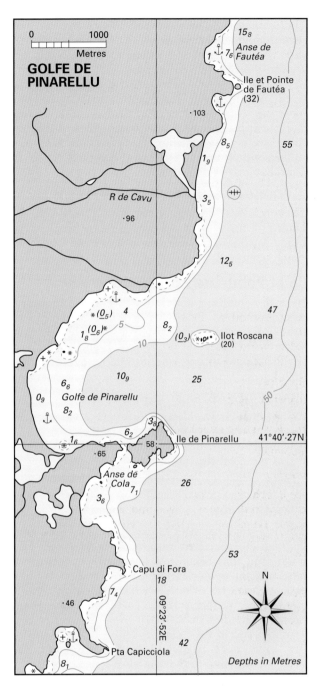

⚓ **BAIE DE SAN CIPRIANU** 41°37′.8N 09°21′.5E

A superb sandy bay which is being spoilt by developments around the shores. Enter on a northwesterly course and anchor off the beach NNW of the island. Take care to avoid an isolated rock 200m NNW of the island.

Punta d'Arasu 41°38′.2N 09°22′.2E

A rounded headland at the north side of the entrance to the Golfe de Porto Vecchio. There are two islets of red rock, Ile de Cornuta (11m) 500m south of the point and Ile de San Ciprianu (23m) 400m southwest. These islands have foul ground extending 150m north. A passage with 4m minimum depth exists equidistant between the islands and the point but care is needed to avoid a lone awash rock in the passage lying north of Ile de San Ciprianu.

⚓ **PUNTA CAPICCIOLA W** 41°38′.7N 09°22′.7E

A pleasant deserted anchorage exists behind the Punta Capicciola, which has rocky cliff sides leading up to high scrub-covered hills. There is a small sandy bay with rocks at northeast end at head of bay. Anchor in 3m, sand and weed off this beach, open to E–SE–S.

Punta Capicciola 41°38′.7N 09°23′E

A 46m hill which slopes to the coast, where a reddish tongue of rock 30m high projects 500m out. One small rock stands close to the point.

Ile de Pinarellu 41°40′.3N 09°23′.6E

A very conspicuous and prominent rocky-cliffed island 500m by 400m and 51m high, lying off the southern point of the Golfe de Pinarellu. There is a small detached islet on its north side and a group of rocks extending 100m south from its south side. A conspicuous square tower stands on the scrub-covered top.

⚓ **GOLFE DE PINARELLU** 41°40′.7N 09°23′.5E

This is a large gulf with a white sandy beach 1.5M long at its head. Ilot Roscana, a bare reddish rocky islet 20m high, is located near the centre of the entrance to the gulf At certain angles and light this island looks like a face with long hair. Rocky dangers extend 100m to east and west of this islet.

4. PORTO VECCHIO TO BASTIA FUEL TERMINAL

The whole of the northwestern side of the bay has rocky dangers which extend up to 500m from the shore but with a good lookout these rocks can be seen in the clear waters, making careful navigation in the area possible. Anchor in 3.5m, sand with some weed, off the sandy beach, open to NE–E–SE–S. Near the centre of the head of the bay are large red apartment blocks and many houses. There are more to the north side of the bay. There is a launching slip to the south of the red apartment buildings. There is a mechanic at Lecci 3M inland.

⚓ POINTE DE FAUTÉA SW 41°42′.7N 09°24′.3E

There is a small anchorage just behind the Pointe de Fautéa on the western side with a sandy beach at its head. Anchor off the beach in 2.5m on sand and weed, open to E–SE–S.

Ile et Pointe de Fautéa 41°42′.8N 09°24′.4E

A small roundish rocky scrub-covered promontory slopes uphill to 79m with a conspicuous round tower on its point. The coast road runs behind this feature. Off the point and almost joined to it is a small pyramid-shaped islet, the Ile de Fautéa, 32m high.

⚓ ANSE DE FAUTÉA 41°43′.1N 09°24′.4E

An open bay between rocky cliffs with a white sandy beach at its head behind which runs the coast road. A conspicuous road bridge with three round tunnels lies at the northern end of the beach, and there is a housing estate on the west side of the bay. Anchor off the beach in 3m, sand, open to NE–E–SE.

⚓ ANSE DE TARCU 41°45′N 09°24′.4E

This is a small bay with sandy beach at its head and landing slip protected by a small breakwater. The coast road runs behind the beach, where there is a large apartment block and a group of houses at each end of the beach. There is a housing estate up the river valley further inland. There is a high road bridge which has three arches over the river at the southern end of the beach. Anchor off the beach in 3m, sand, open to NE–E–SE. The PTT and TV towers 1M inland to the south are conspicuous.

⚓ ANSE DE FAVONE 41°46′.6N 09°24′.2E

A bay with a 800m-long sand beach at its head and the coast road running behind it. There are many houses scattered around the area. Beach restaurants/cafés, a hotel and some shops. Anchor in in 3m, sand, off the beach, open to N–NE–E.

⚓ ANSE DE CANNELLA 41°47′.9N 09°23′.8E

This small bay has a stony beach and reddish cliffs, with the coast road running behind. There are some houses and a beach café. Anchor in 3m, sand in the north corner, open to NE–E–SE.

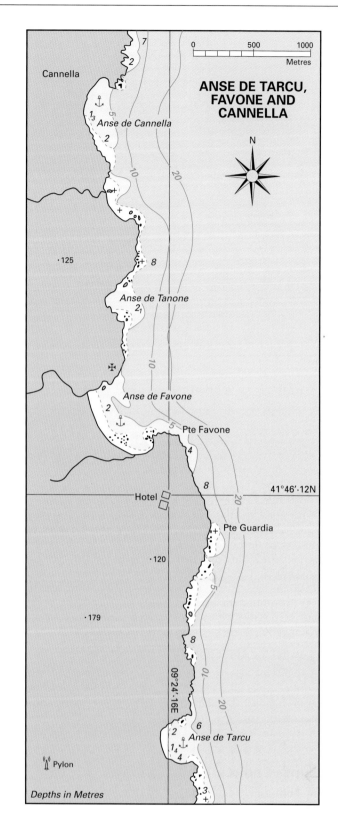

ANSE DE TARCU, FAVONE AND CANNELLA

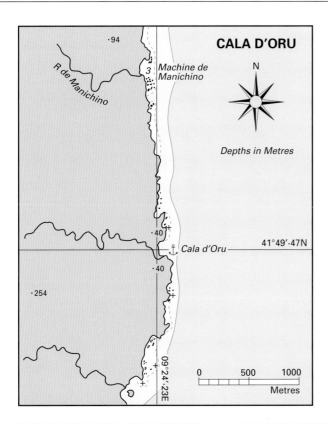

CALA D'ORU

N

Depths in Metres

41°49′·47N

⚓ Cala d'Oru

·94

·3 Machine de Manichino

R de Manichino

·40

·40

·254

0   500   1000

Metres

09°24′·23E

⚓ **MARINE DE CALA D'ORU** 41°49′.45N 09°24′.4E

This is a very small bay with a white stony beach and coast road behind. There is a house on the southern side of the bay and a housing development behind. The bridge over a river is conspicuous. Anchor in 3m, sand and weed. Open to NE–E–SE.

Port de Solenzara looking NNW (see page 72)

4. PORTO VECCHIO TO BASTIA FUEL TERMINAL

C8 Port de Solenzara

⊕26 41°51′.36N 09°24′.3E
(Photos page 64, 65 and 71)

Charts
Admiralty *1999*
French *6855*

Depth
2.4m

Number of berths
450 berths with 150 for visitors

Maximum length
30m

Lights
0865 Jetée Est head 41°51′.4N 9°24′.3E Iso.G.4s3M
0865.2 Quai d'Armement Oc(2)R.6s3M

Port communications
VHF Ch 9, ☎ 04 95 57 46 42 *Fax* 04 95 57 44 66 (S0700-2100, OoS 0800-1200, 1400-1700)
Email capitainerie@mairie-sari-solenzara.fr

To the north
0917(I) Oléoduc 41°55′.2N 9°25′.6E Q(3)10s4m6M ⊛ card BYB buoy 4 miles north marking the inshore fuelling berth

Warnings
Note that access to the port is restricted to 0700–2100 in summer and 0800-1200, 1400-1800 in winter.

It is also recommended that craft proceeding north from Solenzara should keep at least 1M from the coast to avoid military areas, bombing ranges and shallow sandy patches. Certainly off Foce de Tavignano the depths are much less than those given on even modern charts.

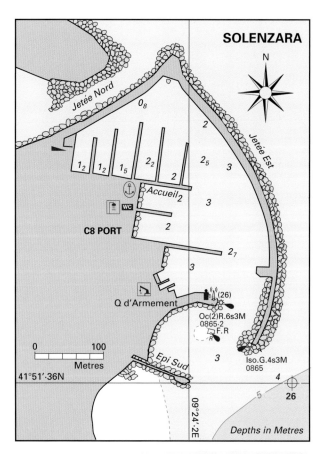

⊕26 Solenzara 41°51′.36N 09°24′.3E

A well run marina

A superb little yacht harbour situated just south of the Solenzara river mouth close to the pleasant village of Solenzara. The village and surroundings (and the harbour) tend to become very crowded in season. Recently France Telecom has erected a 26m high mast at the end of the Quai d'Armement which makes the recognition of the port easier in daylight. Also note the violet light at the north end of the port has been removed and a new toilet block built there. On the Epi Sud there is a 10m pole with what looks like a street lamp on the top, but there is no mention of this being lit in any list of lights to date.

Approach

By day

From the south and the wide and deep Golfe de Porto-Vecchio, the coast has two large gulfs, those of San Ciprianu and Pinarellu, and a number of smaller bays. Look out for the conspicuous tower on the Ile and Pointe de Fautéa and the wide Anse de Favone which has some houses around the bay. In the closer approach, the large blocks of flats located just inland of the harbour will be seen.

From the north The coast has few easily identifiable features. The lighthouse Alistro on a hill inland is one. A very tall water tower some 2M inland from the mouth of the Tavignano river and the airfield at Solenzara with its offlying buoys may also be recognised. In the closer approach, the houses and blocks of flats at Solenzara will be seen. Keep at least 500m from the coast near the airfield. It is foul, with rocks inshore.

By night

The lights of the harbour are not bright and a night approach is not recommended (see warnings above).

By GPS

Steer for ⊕26 from the easterly quadrant.

Entrance

Approach the east jetty head on a westerly course, follow it round 20m off to a NNE course and enter the harbour. Keep close to the starboard side of the entrance channel as there is a shallow patch halfway between the two eastern breakwaters which may be marked with a red buoy. The entrance is dangerous in strong SE winds and should be avoided if at all possible.

Berths

Secure to the pontoon 'I' near the *capitainerie* in the south basin and await berthing instructions, or obtain them from the marina office.

Formalities

Just the bureau staff; customs and other authorities are at Porto-Vecchio.

Facilities

All.

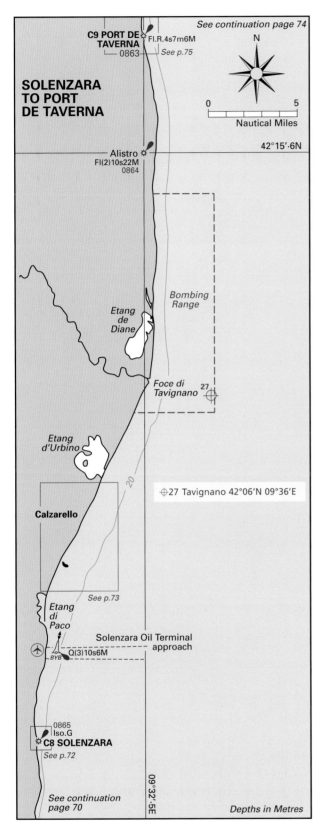

See continuation page 74

C9 PORT DE TAVERNA
☆ Fl.R.4s7m6M
0863
See p.75

N

SOLENZARA
TO PORT
DE TAVERNA

0 — 5
Nautical Miles

42°15'·6N

Alistro ☆
Fl(2)10s22M
0864

Bombing
Range

Etang
de
Diane

Foce di
Tavignano 27

Etang
d'Urbino

⊕27 Tavignano 42°06'N 09°36'E

Calzarello

20

See p.73

Etang
di
Paco

Solenzara Oil Terminal
approach

Q(3)10s6M
BYB

0865
Iso.G
☆ C8 SOLENZARA
See p.72

See continuation
page 70

09°32'·5E

Depths in Metres

Aérodrome de Solenzara 41°55'.5N 09°24'E

A military airfield located 4M to the north of Solenzara. A forbidden area runs for 2M to the north of the river and extends 500m from the coast. This area is shallow and has many dangerous covered rocks. Give it a wide berth. There is a line of trees between the runways and the coast and only a radio beacon tower, the control tower, some hangars and a water tower can be seen from the sea.

Offshore fuel terminal Solenzara
41°55'.2N 09°25'.3E

This terminal is located 700m from the shore near the centre of the runways. There may be a number of buoys inshore but on the seaward side is a ⧫ cardinal light buoy, Oléoduc, Q(3)10s6M. Keep well clear and to seaward of this area.

Foce di u Fium Orbu (Calzarello)
41°59'.3N 09°26'.7E

This river mouth has a conspicuous white house with a tower, Tour de Calzarello, just to the south. ½M further south is a conspicuous wreck – it is forbidden to approach within 200m of this wreck. Just over 1M to the north of the mouth of the river a 0.5m submerged rock lies 200m from the shore.

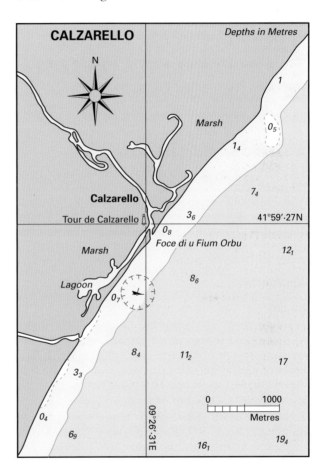

CALZARELLO

Depths in Metres

N

Marsh

Marsh

Calzarello

Tour de Calzarello

41°59'·27N

Foce di u Fium Orbu

Lagoon

09°26'·31E

0 — 1000
Metres

Foce de Tavignano Fleuve 42°06'.2N 09°33'.3E

Dark green trees mark the south side of the entrance and a group of huts the north. It is a large river with a complex sand bar across its mouth. Shallows extend well offshore and there is an extensive area of 3 by 9 miles off the coast to the north, where bombing practice takes place.

Phare d'Alistro
42°15'.6N 9°32'.5E Fl(2)10s 93m22M

An important light situated ¾M inland on a hillock, it has a grey 8-sided tower, black lantern and red house and is surrounded by dark green trees and other houses.

4. PORTO VECCHIO TO BASTIA FUEL TERMINAL

C9 Port de Taverna

⊕28 42°20′.5N 09°32′.6E

Charts
Admiralty *1999*
French *6823, 6713*

Depth
1.3 to 5m

Number of berths
460 with 100 for visitors

Maximum length
25m

Lights
0863 Jetée Est head 42°20′.5N 09°32′.5E Fl.R4s7m6M
White column, red top 5m
0863.4 Jetée Nord head Fl.G4s4m2M White tower,
green top, 2m

Port communications
VHF Ch 9 (24 hrs) ☎ 04 95 38 07 61 *Fax* 04 95 38 07 46
(S 0700-2100, OoS 0800-1200, 1400-1700)
Email porttaverna@mic.fr *url* www.porttaverna.com

Warnings
Due to silting, the depths may not be as shown on the
charts, especially in the Avant-port. The entrance can be
dangerous in strong NE or E winds. No anchoring is
allowed in the harbour

A totally artificial harbour

This modern yacht harbour has been built out from
the coast some distance from any town or village.
Approach and entrance are easy but would become
difficult and dangerous with heavy swell and strong
winds from NE or E. The immediate area around the
harbour is flat and rather dull, but the hinterland is
attractive with mountains, old villages and forests.

Approach

By day

From the south The lighthouse on a small hill inland
at Alistro and the town of Cervione on a mountain
spur are conspicuous some 5M from Taverna. The
harbour itself is not conspicuous and will not be seen
until close-in, but the workshop and the masts of the
yachts already there will be seen.

From the north There is a large white domed
building (Aero RC Poretta) with some other
buildings 6 miles to the north of Taverna. The
harbour itself is difficult to see from a distance but
the workshop and masts are conspicuous.

By night

The light at Alistro Fl(2)10s93m22M is a guide but
the east jetty light should be positively identified
before approaching the coast to closely.

By GPS

From the NE to SE quadrant steer for ⊕28 when the
breakwater lights should be clearly visible.

Entrance

Approach the head of the east jetty and leave it 20m
to port, coming round to a course of east of south
and leaving the north mole to starboard. Do not be

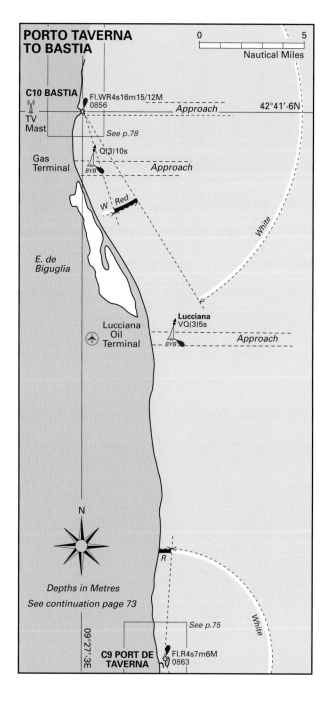

tempted to enter the Avant-port which is badly
silted. The shallows may be marked with a small
buoy.

Berths

Secure to the reception berth immediately ahead on
entry and report to the bureau for berthing
instructions. Berth as instructed with stern to the
pontoon and mooring chain forward secured to the
pontoon by a light chain/rope.

Formalities

All authorities available.

Facilities

All.

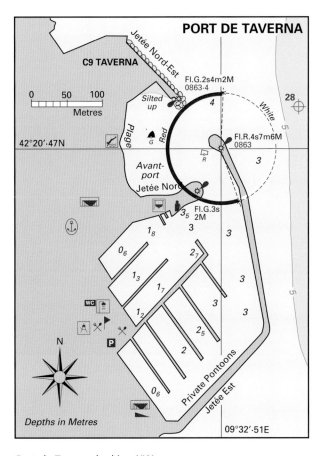

PORT DE TAVERNA

C9 TAVERNA

Jetée Nord-Est

0   50   100
Metres

42°20′·47N

Silted up

Plage

FI.G.2s4m2M
0863·4

4

28

White

Red

G

FI.R.4s7m6M
0863

3

Avant-port

Jetée Nord

R

FI.G.3s
2M

1₈

3₅

3

3

0₆

2₇

3

1₃

1₇

3

wc

1₂

3

2₅

N

P

2

0₆

Private Pontoons

Jetée Est

Depths in Metres

09°32′·51E

Port de Taverna looking NW

Résidence des Iles, Dome and Aero RC beacon

A group of apartment blocks and very distinctive and conspicuous dome with an Aero RC Beacon No. 1069 Bastia. BP (·−··/·−−·) 369kHz located here. In summer a T-shaped floating pontoon is installed in front of the buildings.

Lucciana Offshore Fuel Terminal – Aérodrome de Bastia-Poretta 42°32′.9N 09°32′.9E

A number of buoys are moored off the coast and an ♦ cardinal light buoy, Q(3)5s is moored further offshore. Keep well to seaward of this area.

Offshore Fuel Terminal – Bastia 42°32′.6N 09°27′.7E

A fuel terminal lies 500m offshore and 2M south of Bastia. There are a number of buoys close inshore and an ♦ cardinal light buoy, BYB (Q(3)10s), moored on the seaward side. Note that underwater cables come ashore 600m north of this terminal where there are four yellow beacons. Anchoring is prohibited in the area.

⚓ ANSE DE PORTO-VECCHIO 42°42′.4N 09°27′E

There is an anchorage in a small bay with a popular beach of sand and stone, just south of Bastia itself (see plan on page 78). Behind the beach are roads and the buildings of Bastia, anchor in 2.5m sand and mud, open to NE–S–E–S. A deeper open anchorage is found 400m southeast in 20m, sand and mud. For facilities see Vieux Port, Bastia (page 79).

5 BASTIA TO PUNTA VECCHIAIA

This section covers a peninsula 20M long by only 5M wide lying in a N–S direction, with a high mountain range as its backbone reaching to 1,305m (4,280ft) at its highest point. There are several natural harbours and many anchorages in the bays and creeks around the peninsula. At the heads of the many bays and estuaries lie beaches, most of which are of stone and sand. The coast is steep-to, leading up to the mountains behind and except for the Ile Finocchiarola, a shallow area just to NW of it and the large Ile de la Giraglia, there are no offlying dangers. In general the W side is more rugged than the E and the slope of the hills much steeper.

A corniche-type road follows the coast around the peninsula and there are several roads that cross the mountains. There are no towns and only a few small villages in this area and between these villages the country is almost deserted.

Particular attention should be paid to the dangers of the strong westerly winds which cause heavy gusts of wind to sweep down the valleys on the eastern side.

Winds from an easterly or *levante* direction bring in heavy seas and they make all anchorages on the east coast dangerous and even entry to ports and harbours becomes difficult if not impossible.

Giraglia from the NW (see page 86)

PLANNING GUIDE

Headlands		Ports & anchorages	Open to winds
	C10 ⚓	**Bastia page 78**	NE
	C10 ⚓	**Vieux Port page 79**	NE
	C10 ⚓	**Port de Toga page 80**	NE
Pointe de la Vasina			
	⚓	*Marine de Erbalunga*	NE–E–SE
	⚓	*Port de Erbalunga*	E
Capo Sagro			
	⚓	*Marine de Sisco*	NE–E–SE
Ancien Couvent de Ste Catalina			
	⚓	*Marine de Pietracorbara*	NE–E–SE
Punta a i Ghiunchi			
	⚓	*Marine de Portocciolo*	NE–E–SE
	C11 ⚓	**Port de Luri page 82**	E–SE
	C12 ⚓	**Port de Macinaggio page 83**	NE
	⚓	*Baie de Macinaggio*	NE–E–SE
Punta di a Coscia			
Iles Finocchiarola			
	⚓	*Rade de Santa Maria*	NW–N–E
Pointe d'Agnello			
⚓		*Pointe d'Agnello NW*	N–NE
	⚓	*Marine de Barcaggio*	NW–N–NE
Ile de la Giraglia			
Cap Corse			
Capo Grosso			
	C13 ⚓	**Port de Centuri page 87**	W–NW–N
Ile de Centuri			
		Baie de Centuri	SW–W–NW
	⚓	*Marine de Morsiglia*	SW–W–NW
Punta di Stintinu			
	⚓	*Marine de Giottani*	SW–W–NW
Punta di Canelle			
Amiato asbestos mine and works			
	⚓	*Marine d'Albo*	SW–W–N
Punta Vecchiaia			

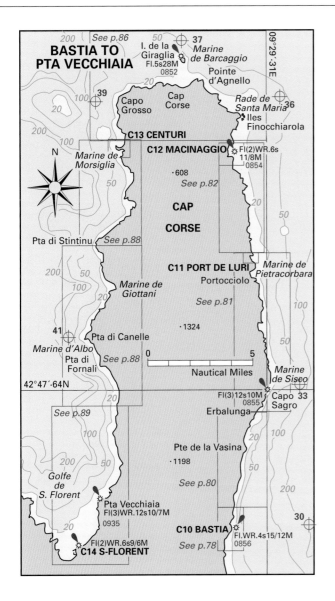

BASTIA TO
PTA VECCHIAIA

See p.86

I. de la
Giraglia
Fl.5s28M
0852

37
Marine
de Barcaggio

Pointe
d'Agnello

09°29'.31E

39

Capo
Grosso

Cap
Corse

Rade de
Santa Maria

36

Iles
Finocchiarola

C13 CENTURI

C12 MACINAGGIO   Fl(2)WR.6s
11/8M
0854

N

Marine de
Morsiglia

·608

See p.82

CAP

CORSE

Pta di Stintinu   See p.88

C11 PORT DE LURI   Marine de
Pietracorbara

Marine de
Giottani

Portocciolo

See p.81

·1324

41

Pta di Canelle

Marine d'Albo

Pta di
Fornali   See p.88

0   5

42°47'·64N

Nautical Miles

Marine
de Siseo

Fl(3)12s10M
0855

Capo 33
Sagro

See p.89

Erbalunga

Pte de la Vasina
·1198

See p.80

Golfe
de
S. Florent

Pta Vecchiaia
Fl(3)WR.12s10/7M
0935

C10 BASTIA   Fl.WR.4s15/12M
0856

30

Fl(2)WR.6s9/6M   See p.78

C14 S-FLORENT

⊕30 Bastia	42°42'N	09°32'E
⊕33 Cap Sagro	42°48'N	09°31'E
⊕36 Finocchiarola	43°00'N	09°30'E
⊕37 Giraglia N	43°02'.3N	09°24'.2E
⊕39 Capo Grosso	43°00'N	09°19'.4E
⊕41 Pta di Canelle	42°50'N	09°17'.5E

0856 **Jetèe du Dragon** Fl.WR.4s16m15/12M
Grey tower, red lantern 13m
0855 **Capo Sagro** Fl(3)12s10M
White tower, green top 4m
0854 **Macinaggio** Fl(2)WR.6s8m11/8M
White tower, red top 8m 120°-R-218°-W-331°-R-000-
R(unintens)-120°
0852 **I. de la Giraglia** Fl.5s85m28M
White tower, black top 26m
0935 **Pta Vecchiaia** Fl(3)WR.12s35m10/7M
White tower, red top 5m 035°-W-174°-R-035°

Vieux Port, Bastia looking SW

Vieux port   Port Toga

Bastia harbours looking SW

5. BASTIA TO PUNTA VECCHIAIA

C10 Bastia

Although Ajaccio is the capital of Corsica, Bastia is by far the largest town due to its position on the east of the island, nearer to mainland Europe. Bastia is very similar to Ajaccio in that it has three ports:

- The delightfully picturesque old fishing harbour, the Vieux Port at the south end of the town, which has good facilities but only limited space for yachts and becomes very crowded in the season.
- The commercial and ferry harbour, Port St Nicolas which is in the centre. Pleasure craft are only allowed to use it with prior permission or in the event of an emergency.
- The modern yacht harbour Port Toga, with 350 berths, at the north of the town. This has all the facilities but is further away from the old town.

The attractive old town surrounds the Vieux Port in the true Mediterranean style. Approach and entrance are easy and protection is offered once inside, though heavy swell from the NE–E makes the old harbour very uncomfortable and sometimes untenable. The town has very smart and excellent shops which can supply most requirements. Port Saint Nicolas, the commercial ferry port and the airfield to the south provide excellent communications for the exchange of crews. A road tunnel passes under the harbour.

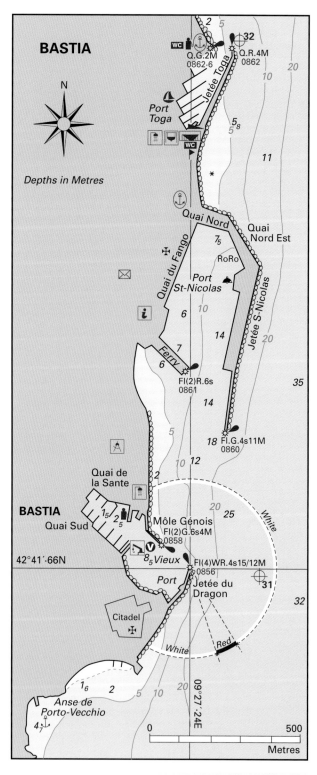

⊕31 Vieux Port 42°41′.7N 09°27′.5E
⊕32 Port Toga 42°42′.65N 09°27′.5E

Vieux Port, Bastia   *Martin Walker*

Vieux Port (Port du Plaisance) (Bastia)

⊕31 42°41′.7N 09°27′.5E

Charts
Admiralty *1425, 1999*
French *6822, 6823, 6856*

Depth
7.1m

Number of berths
267

Maximum LOA
12m on pontoons, 30m in basin

Lights
0856 Jetée du Dragon head 42°41′.6N 9°27′.3E
Fl.WR.4s16m15/12M Grey tower red lantern, 13m
040°-unintens-130°-R-215°-W-325°-R-040°
0858 Môle Génois head Fl(2)G.6s13m4M Light grey
tower, dark green top 9m
0860 Jetée Saint Nicolas head Fl.G.4s9m11M White
tower, green top 5m
0861 Car ferry berth head Fl(2)R.6s2m4M White tower,
red top 1m
TV tower Pigno 2.45M to west F.Rs

Port communications
VHF Ch 9 ☎ 04 95 31 31 10 *Fax* 04 95 31 77 95
(S 0800–2000, OoS 0830–1200, 1400–1700)

Warnings
If there is a strong gale from NE or E it may be
necessary to seek shelter in Port St Nicolas due to the
swell. Heavy gusts of wind can also be experienced
when the wind is blowing from the SW (*libeccio*). If an
anchor has to be used in the Vieux Port it is essential to
set a tripping line because the bottom is foul. Pay
attention to rocks at the foot of the quays. Commercial
craft and ferries have right of way in the port area and
must not be obstructed.

Approach

Due mainly to the physical properties of the site
(mountains behind, sea in front) Bastia has
developed into a classic 'ribbon development' town
with buildings lining the main north/south road for
up to 10 miles or more, especially to the south. At
night it is extremely difficult to make out the
harbour lights against the background of street,
shop and house lights.

By day

From the south The coast is low, flat and sandy with
only a few recognisable features. Identify the
building with a large white dome and some other
large buildings near the mouth of the Fiume Altu
where there are some training walls, and the
Lucciana ⬦ cardinal light buoy (VQ(3)5s), located
outside a series of mooring buoys at the oil pipe
terminal for the airport. There are some black
painted tanks on shore here. The houses of Bastia
will be seen from afar and in the closer approach, the
walled citadel is also visible, which has a tall square
church tower rising above the buildings. The
harbour is situated just to the north of this citadel.
The red and white TV tower on Pigno (961m)
2.45M to the west of Bastia (F.Rs) is conspicuous, as
are the ferries, if in harbour.

From the north The coast consists of rocky cliffs,
with many small indentations and bays mostly with
sandy beaches. The following may be recognised:

- The breakwater at Luri (see page 82)
- The village of Porticciolo which has two small
  breakwaters (see page 81)
- Sisco village which has a training wall at the
  mouth of a river and a statue ¼M to the north
  standing on the cliff by a convent (see page 81)
- The tower and village of Erbalunga (page 81)
  with a small harbour are unmistakable. The TV
  tower (see directions *From the south*) is also
  conspicuous from this direction
- The houses of Bastia will be seen from afar and in
  the closer approach the Jetée St Nicolas will be
  seen, usually with ferry ships behind it.

By night

The following lights allow a night approach, though
in the close approach only the lights from Bastia will
be seen:
0852 Cap Corse, Ile de la Giraglia 43°01′.6N 9°24′.4E
Fl.5s85m28M White tower, black top, signal station
0854 Macinaggio, Jetée Est head Fl(2)WR.6s8m11/8M White
tower, red top
Radio tower F.Rs, 2.45M to west of Bastia
0864 Alistro 42°15′.6N 9°32′.5E Fl(2)10s93m22M
Grey 8-sided tower, red house, black lantern, 27m

By GPS

Steer for ⊕31 from the easterly quadrant, keeping
clear of any commercial traffic.

Entrance

By day

Approach the entrance on a W–SW course and enter
between the head of Jetée du Dragon to port and the
head of the Môle Génois to starboard. Do not
obstruct commercial vessels entering and leaving
Port St Nicolas which lies to the north of the Vieux
Port.

By night

Approach the Fl(4)WR.12s on a W–SW course in
the white sector. Leave it 20m to port and then the
Oc(2)G.6s 20m to starboard. The many lights along
the shore are confusing at night.

Berths

There are 30 places for visitors, 20 on Môle Génois,
10 on Jetée du Dragon stern to the quays. It is
essential to have a trip line on the anchor as the
bottom is foul but only use the anchor in emergency
as anchoring is prohibited in the port area.

Formalities

All authorities available.

Facilities

All.

Port Toga (Bastia)

⊕32 42°42′.65N 09°27′.5E

Charts
Admiralty *1425, 1999*
French *6822, 6823, 6856*

Depth
5m at entrance, 2.5–4m inside

Number of berths
357 of which 60 are for visitors

Maximum LOA
25–35m

Lights
0862 Jetée Est Q.R.10m4M White tower, red top, 6m
0862.6 Contre-jetée head Q.G.2M (not visible until in entrance channel)

Port communications
VHF Ch 9, ☎ 04 95 32 79 79, *Fax* 04 95 32 55 61
(S 0800-2200, OoS 0800-1200, 1400-1800)

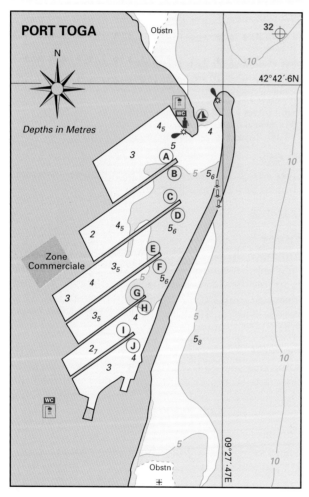

A modern marina

Port Toga is a modern marina with all facilities, but it is quite some way to the old town. It is difficult to make out from seaward but it is situated some 500m to the north of the commercial harbour.

Approach

It is difficult to make out the entrance by day or night (see *By GPS* for waypoint to assist) but identify the commercial harbour with its ferries and move 500m north.

By day

Identify a white 10m high tower, with a red band at the top with Port Toga written on it. This is situated at the end of Jetée Est with a square 3-storey block behind it (the *capitianerie*).

By night

It is difficult to identify the occulting red light until very close – make for the commercial harbour and track north until the red light is obvious. Keep close (20m) around the end of the jetty and the green light will become visible.

By GPS

Steer for ⊕32 from the east quadrant, keeping clear of any commercial traffic.

Entrance

Only 30m wide – try and keep to the middle of the channel in some 4m of water, steering just east of south.

Berth

Turn sharply to starboard at the entrance channel end and moor alongside the *capitainerie*, where berthing instructions will be given.

Formalities

All authorities available.

Facilities

All.

⚓ MARINE DE ERBALUNGA 42°46′.35N 09°28′.5E

A pleasant anchorage just south of the most attractive little harbour of Erbalunga. Open to NE–E–SE. Some inshore rocks, small rocky beach. Anchor in 3.4m, shingle and sand. Supplies from the small village.

Erbalunga

⚓ PORT DE ERBALUNGA 42°46′.45N 09°28′.65E

This is a beautiful little harbour for small fishing boats and dinghies drawing less than 1.5m. There are about 60 berths for small local craft. Open to the

PORT DE ERBALUNGA

east. A useful landing place for yachts' tenders. A shingle hard and concrete slip are at the west end of the harbour. Cafés and restaurants, an unclassified hotel, some shops and an engineer can be found in the village. The ruined tower at the entrance is conspicuous.

CAPO SAGRO 42°47′.7N 09°29′.5E

This headland, with light Fl(3)12s10M, has a conspicuous signal station on top, with rocky cliffs and a coast road at the bottom.

⚓ MARINE DE SISCO 42°48′.55N 09°29′.6E

This wide open bay has a wide deep valley behind with a few houses around it and a small boat harbour at the mouth of the river for craft drawing less than 1m. Anchor off the harbour in 3m sand. The bay is open to NE–E–SE and entrance to the harbour is not possible in strong easterly winds. There is a slip and hard in the harbour, a 3-tonne crane, water point, petrol pump and the Club Nautique de Sisco (CNS) which has showers at the clubhouse. A motor mechanic, a garage, some shops, an unclassified hotel and a shingle beach can be found ashore. There is a conspicuous TV tower to the south.

Ancien Couvent de Ste Catalina

Has a statue close to the rocky cliffs with a large church behind it, which has a tower like a clover leaf.

⚓ MARINE DE PIETRACORBARA 42°50′.3N 09°29′E

A wide bay with the road running behind the sand and stone beach and a few houses scattered around.

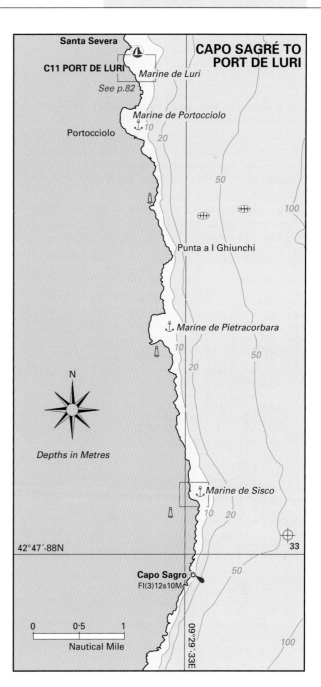

CAPO SAGRÉ TO PORT DE LURI

Santa Severa

C11 PORT DE LURI
Marine de Luri
See p.82

Marine de Portocciolo
⚓ 10
Portocciolo
20

50

100

Punta a I Ghiunchi

⚓ Marine de Pietracorbara
10
50
20

N

Depths in Metres

⚓ Marine de Sisco
10 20

42°47′.88N
33

Capo Sagro
Fl(3)12s10M
50

0   0·5   1
Nautical Mile

09°29′·33E
100

There is a one-star hotel and a restaurant in the small village. Anchor near the moorings at the south side of the bay in 3m, sand and shingle. Open to NE–E–SE. The village has a small jetty where landing is possible. A few dinghies are kept in the river mouth in the south side of the bay. The river has a training wall. A ruined square fort Tour d'Aquila on top of a peaked hill (134m) to the south of this area is conspicuous.

⚓ MARINE DE PORTOCCIOLO 42°52′.5N 09°28.5E

A very small fishing harbour and anchorage open to NE–E–SE with a T-shaped breakwater. Anchor off in 4m stone and sand. The village has a three-star hotel and a small shingle beach at head of cove with the coast road behind.

5. BASTIA TO PUNTA VECCHIAIA

C11 Port de Luri

⊕34 42°53′.2N 09°28′.6E

A harbour built for small yachts and dinghies. There are 130 berths with 20 for visitors up to 12m in overall length. The basin has depths of 2.3m on the east side, is shallower on the west side and is open to E–SE. The entrance is on the southwestern side. Secure and report to the harbour officer for allocation of a berth. Water and electricity on pontoons, and fuel is available on the road nearby. There is a slip on the north side of the harbour. It is possible to anchor in 3m of sand in the bay south of the entrance.

Port de Luri

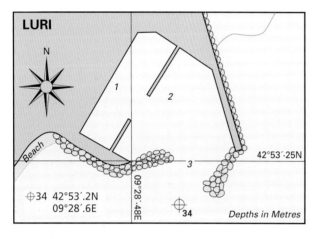

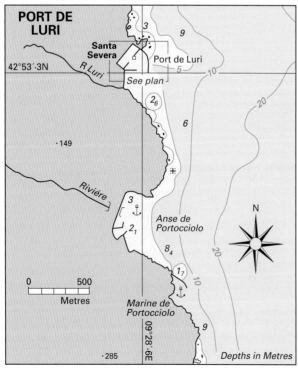

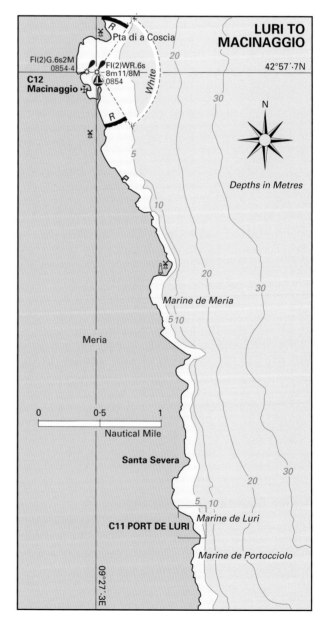

C12 Port de Macinaggio

⊕35 42°57′.8N 09°27′.4E

Charts
Admiralty *1425*
French *6822, 6850*

Depth
1.5m to 3.5m

Number of berths
585 with 200 for visitors

Maximum length
30m

Lights
0854 Jetée Est head 42°57′.7N 9°27′.3E
Fl(2)WR.6s8m11/8M White tower, red top 8m 120°-R-218°-W-331°-R-120°
0854.4 Jetée Nord head Fl(2)G.6s4m2M White tower, green top 2m
0903(l) Finocchiarola 49°59′.5N 9°28′.7E Q(3)5s4m6M ⚓ card BYB light buoy located 2M NNE of port and ½M NE of Iles Finocchiarola

From the south
0855 Capo Sagro 42°47′.7N 09°29′.5E Fl(3).12s10M White tower, green top 4m

Port radio
VHF Ch 9 ☎ 04 95 35 42 57 *Fax* 04 95 35 47 00 (S0700-2100, OoS 0800-1200,1400-1800)
Email portu.paul-luigi.macinaggio@wanadoo.fr

Warnings
Heavy swell from the NE–E will break near the entrance and make it dangerous to enter. Strong gusts of wind from SW–W sometimes occur. Depths in the harbour may be different to the plan due to periodic dredging. No anchoring is allowed in the port.

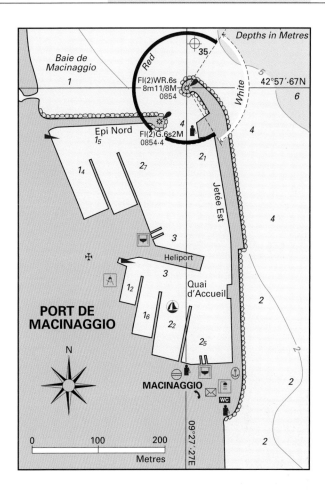

A very popular harbour

This yacht harbour, which was constructed in 1971, is based on an old fishing harbour and has managed to maintain some of the attractiveness of the original. The surrounding area is beautiful and the small village pleasant in an unsophisticated way but inevitably the tourist industry development is spoiling the old charm. Approach and entry are easy but would be hazardous in heavy seas from NE–E. Protection within is good, though a heavy swell from the NE–E makes it uncomfortable. Facilities are reasonable and everyday requirements can be met. The harbour becomes very crowded in the summer as it is usually the first stop of Italians coming from the Ligurian or Tuscan coasts.

Approach

By day

From the south The coastline is broken by many small bays but it lacks any conspicuous landmarks. The houses, tower and small harbour at Erbalunga, the villages of Sisco and Portocciolo, both of which have training walls at the mouths of their rivers, and the small harbour at Luri may be identified. In the closer approach, the village of Macinaggio will be seen but not until the bay opens up. A conspicuous radar and TV tower and dome are located 3M to the west on the skyline.

From the north Directly or via Cap Corse, heading either inside or outside the Ile de la Giraglia (conspicuous with a lighthouse and signal station on top). Follow the coast round and in bad weather give it a 1½M berth to avoid the Banc de Santa Maria (9.5m). Pass outside the light buoy listed above and round the Iles Finocchiarola, which extends ½M from the coast and has a tower on the top of the outer island. The houses of Macinaggio will be seen from here.

By night

Approach using the following lights:
0852 Cap Corse, Ile de la Giraglia 43°01′.6N 9°24′.4E
Fl.5s85m28M White tower, black top, 26m
1404 Punta del Trattoio 43°1′.3N 9°47′.5E Fl.8s150m9M
White house (this is on Capraia, an island 15M west of Giraglia)
Then use the Jetée Est light to approach the entrance.

By GPS

Steer for ⊕35 from the eastern quadrant.

Entrance

By day

Approach the head of the Jetée Est which has a conspicuous white light tower, red top, on a course between NW and SW and round it onto a southerly course, leaving it 20m to port.

5. BASTIA TO PUNTA VECCHIAIA

Macinaggio looking SW

By night

Approach the Fl(2)WR.6s light on course between NW and SW in the white sector. Divert in the close approach towards N into the red sector and round the light onto a southerly course, leaving it 20m to port. Leave Fl.G.2s 20m to starboard.

Berth

On arrival, secure to the holding berth well inside the entrance on the port hand and report to the bureau de port for berthing instructions. Secure stern-to the pontoon or quay berth allocated with the mooring chain from the bow. This chain is connected to the pontoon by a lighter chain or rope.

Formalities

The bureau de port (☎ 04 95 35 42 57) is at the SE corner of the harbour open in summer 0700–2100, 1300–2030, in winter 0700–1200, 1400–1800. The customs office (☎ 04 95 35 43 03) is on the S side of the small square.

Facilities

All.

⚓ BAIE DE MACINAGGIO 42°57′.85N 09°27′.3E

This is a wide bay with the Port of Macinaggio at the south end and the conspicuous Pointe de Coscia at the other. A long sandy beach stretches along the coast with gently sloping ground behind. Open to NE–E–SE. Anchor in 3m sand.

PUNTA DI A COSCIA 42°57′.9N 09°27′.45E

A conspicuous pyramid-shaped point (60m), with a TV tower and the round stone base of an old windmill on top, is situated at the north end of Baie de Macinaggio. The point is steep-to.

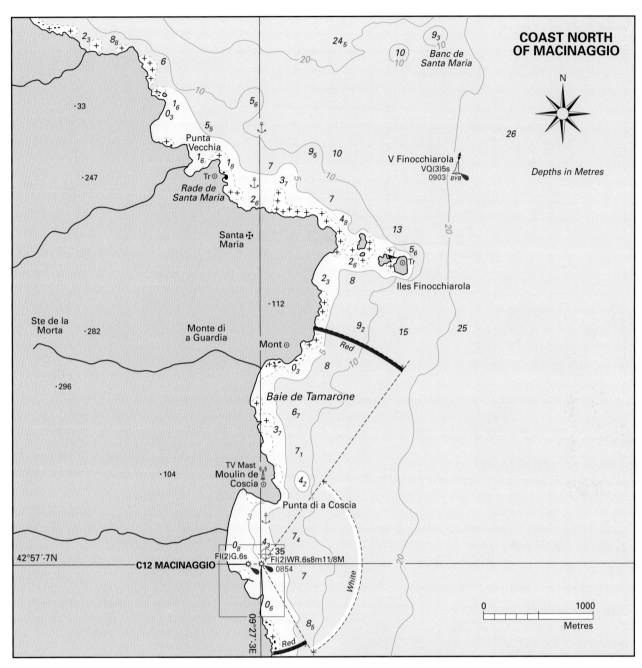

COAST NORTH OF MACINAGGIO

Depths in Metres

Banc de Santa Maria

V Finocchiarola
VQ(3)5s
0903 BYB

Iles Finocchiarola

Red

Baie de Tamarone

TV Mast
Moulin de Coscia

Punta di a Coscia

C12 MACINAGGIO
Fl(2)G.6s
35 Fl(2)WR.6s8m11/8M
0854

White

Red

Santa Maria

Rade de Santa Maria

Punta Vecchia

Ste de la Morta

Monte di a Guardia

Mont

42°57´·7N

09°27´·3E

0   1000
Metres

Iles Finocchiarola 42°59´N 09°28´.3E

There are three rocky islands with some islets and rocky heads extending 700m offshore. These islands are a nature reserve and landing is not permitted. The outer island (27m) is the largest and has a conspicuous ruined tower and small hut. The middle island (12m) is separated from the outer island by a narrow gap partially blocked by two rocks and a wreck of a small coaster. The inner island (5m) is an irregular shape and has many rocks to SE–S–SW, including a small islet. There are also rocks along the Corsican coast to the west. Note the ♦ cardinal BYB buoy Finocchiarola Q(3)5s lying 0.5M NE of this group of islands.

It is not recommended to pass through any of the narrow passages between the islands or the inner island and the shore.

Iles Finocchiarola

Cap Corse

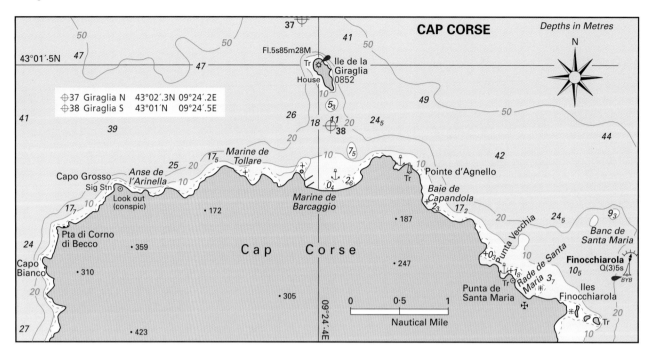

Cap Corse is the general term for the whole of the N section of Haute-Corse and it covers the coast from Iles Finocchiarola to Capo Bianco including the Ile de la Giraglia.

⚓ RADE DE SANTA MARIA 42°59′.5N 09°27′.3E

An open bay with a conspicuous ruined tower on its NW point and Chapelle Ste Maria standing inland. Open to NW–N–NE–E. It has several shingle beaches with rocks between. Track to beach but otherwise deserted. Anchor in 4m on rock and sand in the centre of the bay, paying attention to offlying rocks to SE. Another anchorage is available in 10m, sand and weed, 350m NNE of the tower.

POINTE D'AGNELLO 43°00.6N 09°25′.6E

A conspicuous promontory of green-grey rocks in two parts. It has a ruined tower on its NE point. The land behind the point is round and high (141m). Rocky dangers extend 100m towards the northeast. The point is split into two parts by a narrow creek. The northwestern part of the promontory is lower with whitish coloured cliffs.

⚓ POINTE D'AGNELLO NW 43°00′.65N 09°25′.5E

An attractive small anchorage open to N–NE and deserted. It has three small coves with rocky sides. Anchor in 4m, sand. The Tour d'Agnello is a good landmark.

⚓ MARINE DE BARCAGGIO 43°00′.6N 09°24′.3E

A large bay open to NW–N–NE with a small harbour for fishing boats and dinghies in the western corner, where there is a small fishing village with church, shop and road inland. There is a long sand and shingle beach divided by a group of rocks often used by nudists. Anchor in 3m sand to the north of the harbour. A deep-water (16m) anchorage is available 300m to the north of the village on sand and weed. Another smaller bay to the west, Marine de Tollare, can also be used as a reasonable anchorage in calm weather. Anchor off the beach but watch for an awash rock just offshore NE of the tower.

Ile de la Giraglia 43°01′.5N 09°24′.4E

1M to the north of Barcaggio lies the Ile de la Giraglia which is 1200m long, 300m wide and 65m high with whitish rocky cliffs. There is an old square stone fort at the NW end of the island, with a white lighthouse tower with black top (22m) alongside (Fl.5s85m28M). A low flat white house is near the centre of the island. There are landings on the NE side of the island, where there is a small hut and a road cut into the rock. (See photo page 76)

CAPO GROSSO 43°00′.4N 09°21′.45E

This is a pointed headland with a conspicuous signal station on its top. Steep cliffs and one small rock lie close to the point, which is otherwise steep-to. The land slopes up to 364m inland.

Centuri looking NE

C13 Port de Centuri

⊕40 42°58´.1N 09°20´.8E

Charts
Admiralty *1425*
SHOM *6969, 6850*

Depth
4m at entrance, 2m to 0.8m inside

Number of berths
125

Maximum LOA
10m

Note
There are no lights at Centuri and access to the port is only allowed from dawn to dusk.

Port communications
☎ and *Fax* 04 95 35 60 06

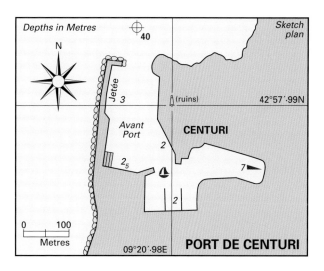

A very small marina

Some 2½ miles south of Capo Grosso is the Baie de Centuri with a small yacht harbour at its south end. It is well protected from the SW by the Ile de Centuri but it is open to the NW which makes it of doubtful tenure during strong northwesterlies. There are 2 to 3m depths in the harbour with space for 125 craft (25 for visitors). Approach the head of the jetty on an ESE course or steer for ⊕35 and pass close to the end of the jetty, coming round to a southerly course inside the jetty.

Formalities

None

Facilities

Water and electricity / WC / Refuse bins
Everyday stores and ice in the village.

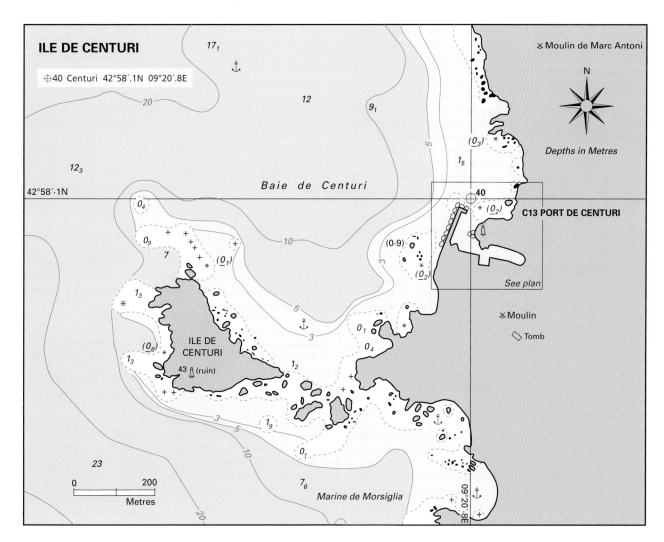

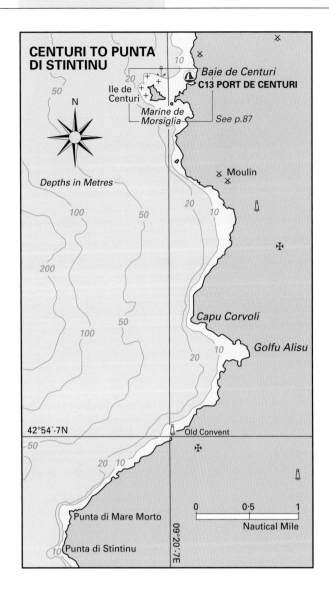

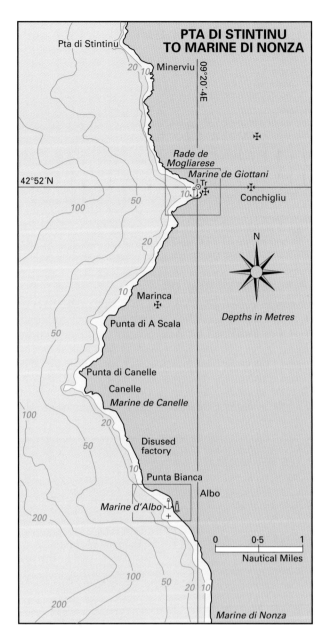

⚓ **BAIE DE CENTURI** 42°58′.1N 09°20′.8E

This large bay, open to W–NW–N, has the Port de Centuri in the SE corner and the Ile de Centuri in the SW corner. Anchor in the southern part in 5m, rock and sand, but note that the holding is not good.

Ile de Centuri 42°57′.8N 09°20′.5E

The island is 300m by 200m and is 43m high. It has foul ground to the east and to the northwest extending to 200m. A dangerous unmarked rock (covered 0.4m) lies 200m north of the island.

⚓ **MARINE DE MORSIGLIA N** 42°57′.65N 09°20′.7E

This is a fairweather anchorage off a stony beach in a small bay with offlying rocks, open to SW–W–NW. It lies about 200m to the north of the village of Mute. Anchor with care in 3m, rock and weed, near to the centre of the bay, between a group of four islets and a single islet. There is a road ashore.

⚓ **MARINE DE MORSIGLIA S** 42°57′.54N 09°20′.75E

A bay more open than that described above, with rocks confined to the sides, open to the SW–W–NW. A small group of houses lie behind a stony beach and a road. Anchor in 3m, rock, stone and weed, near the centre of the bay.

Between Centuri and the next reasonable harbour of Saint Florent there are 19 miles of high rocky coastline with a few small villages on the winding coast road. A good offing should be maintained in all but the most settled weather. In ideal conditions it is possible to anchor for lunch or a swim at a couple of places. Just south of Capu Corvoli there is the small inlet of Golfu Alisu and further south again is Marine de Giottani.

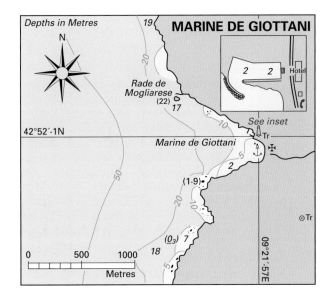

⚓ MARINE DE GIOTTANI 42°52′N 09°20′.1E

This is a deep bay with white rocky cliffs and a rocky beach at its head, where there is also a small fishing boat and dinghy harbour with 2m depth. A tower stands on the hill behind the harbour and the bay is open to SW–W–NW. Anchor near the centre of the bay in 6m, sand. A few houses and a hotel/restaurant stand behind the beach, while the coast road runs further inland. There is a conspicuous church with a tall steeple up the valley behind, and a village further inland.

Amianto asbestos mine and works

The hills above the Roches d'Albo and Punta Bianca have been extensively mined for asbestos and the white scar that has been left on the sloping hillside can be seen from afar. In the closer approach the huge processing buildings will be seen. The works were closed in 1965 but the debris which was discharged into the sea is still washing along the coast, partially filling the bays and indentations.

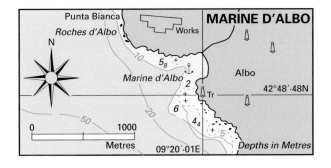

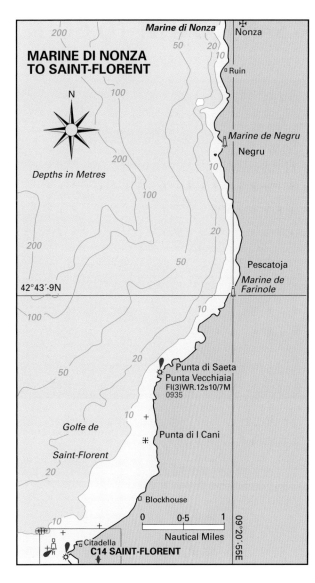

⚓ MARINE D'ALBO 42°48′.55N 09°19′.8E

A wide bay partially filled by the grey debris from the asbestos works; in fact the original pier, together with the old beach, has been totally covered by the debris. The northwest side has a few rocks close inshore. A small village and restaurant stand behind the beach of grey stones and a conspicuous tower marks the south side of the bay. The coast road loops behind the head of the beach. Anchor in 4m, sand and stone, in the middle of the bay, open to the SW–W–NW–N.

PUNTA VECCHIAIA 42°43′N 09°19′.3E

A low headland with a white tower with a red top lit with 0935 Fl(3)WR.12s35m10/7M.

6 SAN FLORENT TO GOLFE DE CALVI

The first part of the coast, running west from the wide and indented Golfe de Saint Florent, follows the mainly low-lying shore of the Désert des Agriates. It is a totally uninhabited section of bare rock and scrub with many deserted anchorages off delightful sandy beaches. Westwards from Punte de Lozari the coast includes the harbours of Ile Rousse and Sant'Ambrogio and is rather more rocky with some offlying dangers. The coast here is backed by a relatively flat, fertile region, La Balagne, and is well populated. This entire section is very open to the prevailing NW winds and shelter should be sought in either Saint Florent or Calvi if a *maestrale* is forecast.

Plage du Loto looking W (see page 95)

PLANNING GUIDE

Headlands	Ports & anchorages		Open to winds
Punta Vecchiaia	C14 ⚓	**Saint Florent page 92**	
Cap Fornali			
	⚓	*Anse de Fornali*	N–E–SE
	⚓	*Anse de Fiume Santu*	N–E–SE
Punta Mortella			
Punta Cavallata			
	⚓	*Plage du Loto*	N–NE–E
Punta di Curza			
	⚓	*Plage de Saleccia*	NW–N–NE
	⚓	*Anse de Malfalcu*	NW–N
Punta di Solche			
	⚓	*Baie de l'Acciolu*	NW–N–NE
Punta di l'Acciolu			
	⚓	*Anse de Peraiola*	SW–W–N
	⚓	*Anse de Lozari*	W–N–NE
Punta Saleccia			
Passage between Grande	C15 ⚓	**Port de L'Ile Rousse page 98**	NE–E
Ile Rousse and Isula dei Brucciu			
Punta di Vallitone			
	⚓	*Anse d'Algajola*	W–NW–N
	⚓	*Port d'Algajola*	N–NE
Punta San Damiano			
Danger d'Algajola	C16 ⚓	**Port de Sant'Ambrogio page 102**	E
Punta Spano(with Ile de Spano off)			
	⚓	*Baie Agajo*	NW–W–SW
	⚓	*Portu Agajo*	W–NW–N
	⚓	*Golfe de Calvi*	N–NW

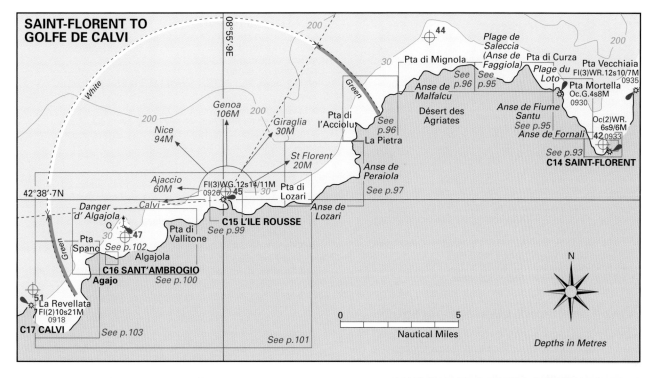

SAINT-FLORENT TO GOLFE DE CALVI

⊕42	Saint-Florent gulf	42°40′.93N	09°17′.4E
⊕44	Pta di Mignola	42°45′N	09°07′.5E
⊕45	Ile Rousse approach	42°39′N	08°56′.5E
⊕47	Danger d'Algajola	42°37′N	08°50′.7E
⊕51	Pta Revellata	42°36′N	08°43′E

0935 Pta Vecchiaia Fl(3)WR.12s35m10/7M
White tower, red top 5m
0933 Saint-Florent Fl(2)WR.6s6m9/6M
White column, red top 5m 116°-R-227°-W-116°
0930 Pta Mortella Oc.G.4s43m8M
White tower, green top 14m
0926 Ile Rousse Fl(3)WG.12s64m14/11M
White tower on house, green top 13m
shore-G-079°-W-234°-G-Coast
0918 La Revellata Fl(2)10s97m21M
White tower, black top and corners 19m

Danger d'Algajola with Pte di Valletone in the left foreground, Pte Spano and Calvi beyond

C14 Saint Florent

⊕42 (west of Écueil de Tignosu) 42°40′.93N 09°17′.4E
⊕43 (entrance to marina) 42°40′.78N 09°17′.78E

Charts
Admiralty *1999*
French *6850, 6969*

Depth
5m to 1.5m

Number of berths
790 with 270 for visitors

Maximum LOA
40m

Lights
0935 Pointe Vecchiaia 42°42′.9N 9°19′.5E
Fl(3)WR.12s35m10/7M Round white tower, red top 5m
035°-W-174°-R-035°
0932 Cap de Fornali 42°41′.3N 9°16′.9E Fl.G.4s14m6M
White square tower, green top 11m
0930 Punta Mortella 42°43′.0N 9°15′.4E Oc.G.4s43m8M
White square tower, green top 14m

0934 Écueil de Tignosu 42°40′.9N 9°17′.7E Fl.R.4s6m3M Red
tower 9m on rocks 350m NW of port
0933 Jetée Nord 42°40′.8N 9°17′.9E Fl(2)WR.6s6m9/6M
White column red top 5m
080°-W-116°-R-080°
0933.2 Jetée Sud Fl(2)G.6s4m3M White tower, green top
3m

Port communications
VHF Ch 9 ☎ 04 95 37 00 79 *Fax* 04 95 37 11 37, (S0700-
2100, OoS 0800-1200, 1500-1800)
Email capitanerie.santflo@wanadoo.fr

Warnings
The shores of the Golfe de Saint Florent are fronted by
shallow banks and rocky patches. Two isolated rocky
patches lie near the entrance of the harbour: the Écueil de
Tignosu, 0.1m deep, some 400m to NW of the entrance
and another rocky patch, 1.7m deep, some 600m to N of
the entrance. The area S of the harbour entrance shelves
quickly.

Important warning
Fire fighting flying boats frequently use the Golfe de Saint

A well sheltered, pleasant harbour

This fishing and yacht harbour is situated on the
eastern side of the wide Golfe de Saint Florent, at the
edge of a flat delta of the Rivière Aliso, with high
ranges of mountains in the background. Approach
and entrance are easy but in heavy weather from the
northwest this could become difficult and perhaps

dangerous. There is good shelter once inside the
harbour, though heavy gusts of wind off the
mountains can be experienced from an E-SE
direction. The old and attractive town has a number
of shops supplying everyday requirements. The town
and harbour are very crowded in the season.

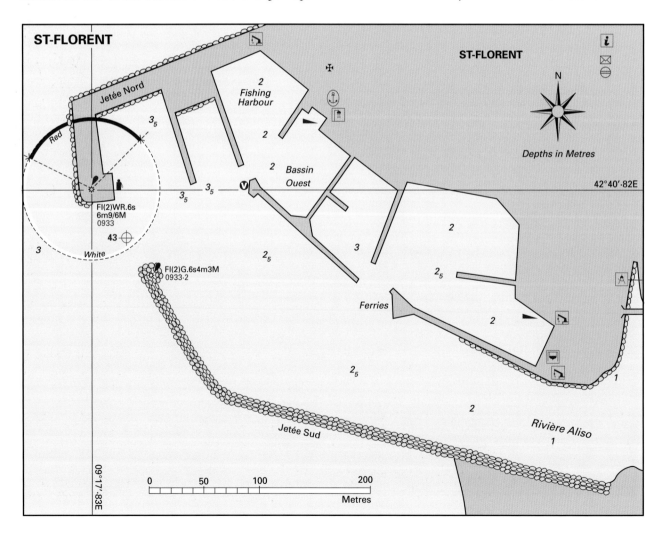

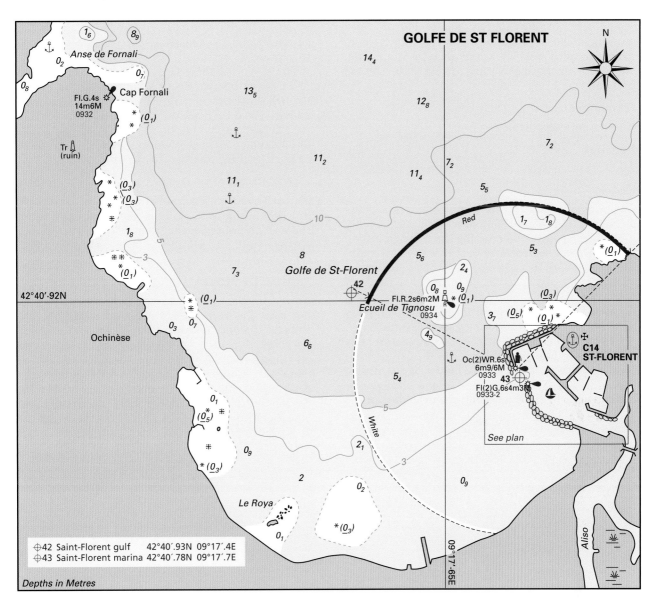

GOLFE DE ST FLORENT

⊕42 Saint-Florent gulf 42°40′.93N 09°17′.4E
⊕43 Saint-Florent marina 42°40′.78N 09°17′.7E

Depths in Metres

Approach

By day

From the north Follow the rocky, mountainous and broken coast southwards. The white cliffs and disused quarry and asbestos factory at Marine d'Albo, the town of Nonza perched on a steep rocky hill and the lower rounded Punta Vecchiaia with a very small lighthouse will all be easily identified. The town of Saint Florent will be seen in the closer approach. Proceed down the centre of the gulf on a southerly course leaving the beacon tower La Tignosu 200m to port. When this beacon is in line with Saint Florent church tower, course may be altered towards the harbour entrance.

From the west Follow the broken rocky coast with white sandy beaches of the Désert des Agriates around into the Golfe de Saint Florent. Punta Mortella, which has a disused signal station and lighthouse, Pointe de Cepo which has an old fort, and Cap Fornali with its small lighthouse are all easily recognised. Keep to the centre of the gulf on a southerly course and proceed as detailed in the approach above.

By night

Using the lights on Punta Vecchiaia, Cap Fornali and Punta Mortella it is easy to arrive off the Écueil de Tignosu. Leave the beacon 200m to port and approach the entrance in the white sector of the light on an east-southeasterly course and steer to go between the red and green lights on the pier ends.

By GPS

From the north quadrant, steer for ⊕42 keeping well clear of Ecueil de Tignosu. At ⊕42, course can be set to steer for ⊕43, off the harbour mouth.

Entrance

The entrance is 30m wide and is simple by day or night.

Berths

Secure to the holding berth immediately ahead of you on entering and obtain berthing instructions.

Secure stern-to pontoon or quay allotted, with mooring chain from the bow. This is connected to the pontoon or quay by a light pick-up rope/chain. Note that anchoring is not permitted inside the harbour.

Formalities

All authorities available

Facilities

All.

History

The original village, dating from Roman times, was at Nebbio 1M inland. This developed considerably in the 12th century on becoming the seat of a bishop and when the cathedral of Sainte Marie was built. The village with its cathedral was abandoned in the 16th century owing to an outbreak of malaria. A new town, Saint Florent, was built beside the round Genoese fort which had been erected some 100 years earlier on a low hill overlooking the harbour.

General Gentile, (one of Paoli's companions) was born in Saint Florent and buried in the cathedral at Nebbio. In 1794 when Lord Hood and the British fleet attempted to reduce the town and nearby fortifications by bombardment, the defenders of the tower on Punta Mortella, now in ruins, refused to surrender and a strong shore party had to be landed to capture it.

The ability of these Genoese towers and forts to resist heavy bombardment so impressed the British that the design and details were sent back to England and used as a basis for the 100 Martello towers that were subsequently built on the south and east coasts of England as a defence against the threatened attack of the Corsican, Napoleon Bonaparte.

CAP FORNALI 42°41′.3N 09°17′.8E

An easily recognised headland with an old square fort on the top of the hill behind the point, a white square lighthouse on the point with green top and corners and a white house alongside 0932 (Fl.G.4s14m6M).

⚓ ANSE DE FORNALI 42°41′.4N 09°16′.65E

An old harbour once used by large sailing vessels, but over the years it has silted up. Old guns are embedded along the coast for mooring and warping purposes. A private landing stage and house stand on the south side of the Anse. Sound carefully as there is a 1.6m shallow patch in the mouth of the Anse and a lone rock in mid-channel further in. Anchor north of the landing stage in 2m sand and mud open to N–NE–E–SE. Road on the southeast coast. (See photo page 97)

St Florent looking S

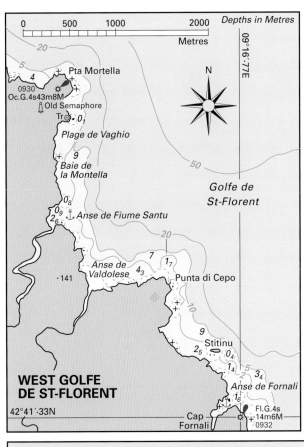

⚓ ANSE DE FIUME SANTU 42°42´.4N 09°15´.4E

A good anchorage open to N–NE–E in 3m sand in a bay at the mouth of a river which once had a large sand and shingle beach to the northwest of its mouth. One hut and track on both sides of the bay. Deserted. Some years ago, the beach was swept away after a cloudburst in the hills behind.

PUNTA MORTELLA 42°43´.1N 09°15´.45E

This very prominent point, with rocky dangers extending 200m eastwards, has a lighthouse on a higher hill behind. There is a coast road. A conspicuous ruined tower stands on a small point 300m to the south. This is the famous tower that Lord Hood's force failed to destroy in the 1794.

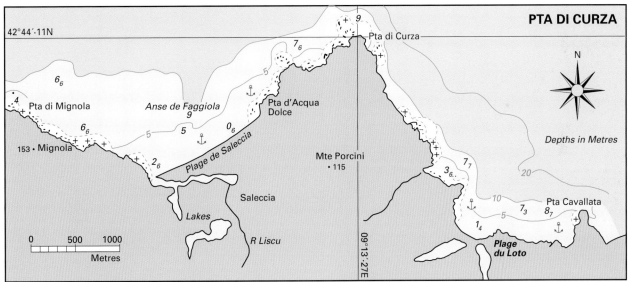

PUNTA CAVALLATA 42°43´.3N 09°14´.8E

A narrow pointed headland, which slopes up inland and then falls away. It is sheer-to with a small anchorage on its W side.

⚓ PLAGE DU LOTO 42°43´.3N 09°14´.1E

This wide white sandy bay is open to N–NE–E. Anchor in 3m sand off sandy beach. Low ground with lagoons behind beach. It is deserted, with a wreck at the west end of the bay.

PUNTA DI CURZA 42°44´.1N 09°13´.3E

A prominent headland of whitish rock sloping up to 115m, with a stony pyramid on top. Rocky offliers extend 200m to the NW.

⚓ PLAGE DE SALECCIA 42°43´.8N 09°12´.3E

A very large bay backed by a long white sandy beach. Anchor in 3m sand off the beach, open to NW–N–NE. Sand dunes and track along back of the beach. There is a camping ground behind the beach in season and a river at southwest end of beach. This is a very popular spot for lunching and swimming during the season as it is only an hour trip from Saint Florent, and it gets very crowded.

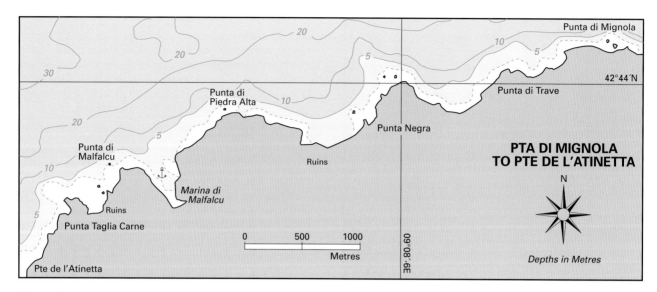

PTA DI MIGNOLA TO PTE DE L'ATINETTA

N

Depths in Metres

⚓ **ANSE DE MALFALCU** 42°43′.65N 09°06′.94E

An attractive narrow *calanque*-type anchorage lies to the east of a point of the same name, with hills around it and low cliffs with some close inshore rocks. Sound carefully while approaching due to shallows. Anchor and moor with 2nd anchor in 3m, sand inside the entrance, open to NW–N. Small white sand and shingle beach at head. There is a ruined house to SW with tracks along coast and inland. Deserted.

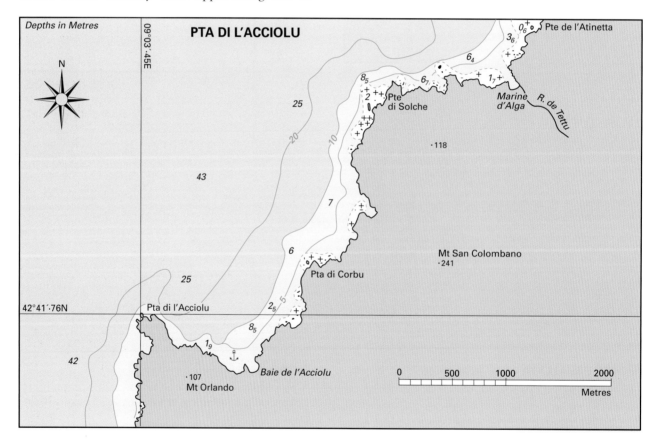

⚓ **BAIE DE L'ACCIOLU** 42°41′.7N 09°04′.1E

A small white sand and shingle beach in the centre of a wide bay with Mont Orlando (107m) towering over it. The sides of the bay are rocky. Enter on a southerly course and anchor off the beach in 3m, sand, open to NW–N–NE. Track inland. Deserted.

PUNTA DI L'ACCIOLU 42°41′.77N 09°03′.45E

This is a conspicuous headland with a narrow jutting rocky point, sheer-to. The W side resembles a beak. Mont Orlando (107m) stands behind this point.

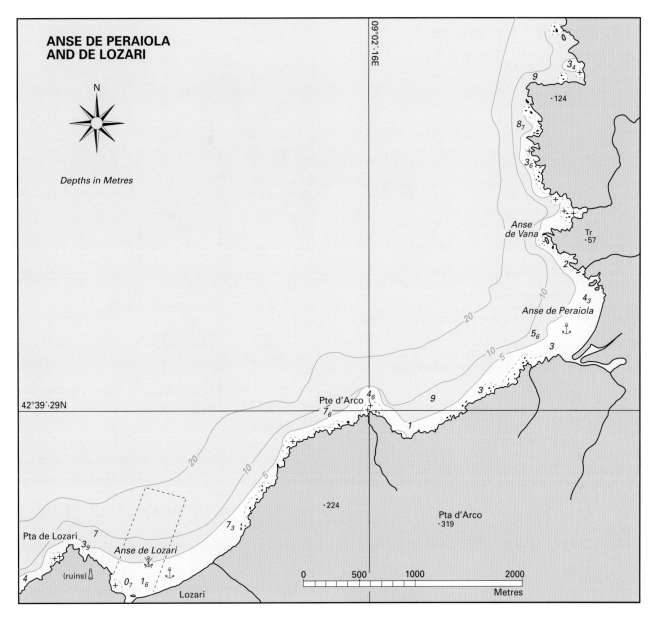

ANSE DE PERAIOLA
AND DE LOZARI

N

Depths in Metres

42°39′.29N

09°02′.16E

Anse de Vana

· 124

Anse de Peraiola

Pte d'Arco

· 224

Pta d'Arco
· 319

Pta de Lozari

(ruins)

Anse de Lozari

Lozari

Tr
· 57

0   500   1000   2000

Metres

⚓ **ANSE DE PERAIOLA** 42°39′.77N 09°03′.4E

A wide bay open to SW–W–NW–N with a long white sandy beach with dunes behind. It has a river mouth at the south end. Some houses and a café are on the road above the river. There is a tower 500m to the north of the north end of the beach. Anchor in 3m, sand, off the beach.

⚓ **ANSE DE LOZARI** 42°38′.55N 09°00′.75E

A wide bay open to W–NW–N–NE with a long sand and shingle beach. Camping site and houses lie behind the northeast end of the beach, with a large apartment block in the middle and the village of Lozari at the southwest end. There are some beach cafés ashore and a small river mouth at the west end of the beach. Note that there is a 750 x 300-metre area off the river mouth, in a 010° direction, where fishing and anchoring are prohibited. Anchor to the east of this area in 3 to 5m on sand.

Anse de Fornali (see page 94)

6. SAN FLORENT TO GOLFE DE CALVI

C15 Port de L'Ile Rousse

⊕45 Ile Rousse approach 42°39'.0N 08°56'.5E
⊕46 Ile Rousse marina 42°38'.5N 08°56'.5E

Charts
Admiralty
SHOM *6980, 6970*

Depth
9m

Number of berths
215 with a few for visitors

Maximum LOA
14m

Lights
0926 Phare de la Pietra 42°38'.6N 8°56'.0E
Fl(3)WG.12s64m14/11M White tower, green top and
white house 13m 000°-G-079°-W-234°-G-000°
0928 Jetée head 42°38'.5N 8°56'.4E Iso.G.4s12m8M
White tower, green top 12m
0927 Quai du Commerce Q(3)10s2m4M Red
pedestal 1m
0926.5 Jetée du Large head Fl.G.4s2M
On hut (300°-vis-218°)
0927.2 Beacon 42°38'.4N 8°56'.3E VQ(3)5s5m3M ↓ card
BYB post in centre of harbour some 250m east of
0926.5.

Port communications
VHF Ch 9 ☎04 95 63 01 80 *Fax* 04 95 60 31 79 (S
0700–2200, OoS 0700–1800)

A ferry port

This harbour had been classified as a commercial
harbour but it has recently been extended with a
new marina, Port Abri, with 250 berths (85 for
visitors) and a fishing port. It is clear the marina will
offer reasonable protection from the prevailing
southwest to northwest winds but the strong
northeasterlies (*tramontana*) may still make the
berths somewhat uncomfortable, and the approach
to the harbour itself difficult.

Approach

Ile Pietra is an unmistakable large reddish island
connected to the mainland by a causeway.
Approaching from any direction, steer to arrive
about 1 mile north of the jetty, keeping well clear of
the island and its outliers. Then steer a course
between 160°and 180° towards the end of the jetty,
passing between the Haut-fond de Naso and the
Danger de l'Ile Rousse. Leave the jetty well to
starboard, taking care to keep well clear of any
commercial traffic that may be manoeuvring in the
harbour, and proceed to the marina entrance on a
westerly course. Keep well to the north of the BYB
beacon and white buoy (if laid). There may be a
number of small white buoys running in an arc from
the end of the Jetée Sud which must be left to port.
Again watch for fishing boats entering and leaving
the entrance and proceed on a northerly course
through the pier heads. Turn immediately to port to
enter the marina.

By GPS

Steer towards ⊕45 from the northerly quadrant. On
reaching the waypoint, steer south towards ⊕46,
passing between the Danger and Haut-fond de Naso

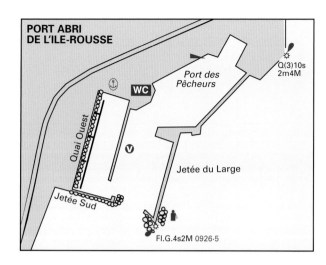

and well to starboard of the pier end. On arriving at
⊕46, turn to starboard and make for the head of the
Jetée du Large (see approach above).

Berths

It is essential to call ahead to the *capitainerie* on Ch
9 or ☎ 04 95 60 00 68, when berthing instructions
will be given. Note that anchoring in the harbour
area is still under the jurisdiction of the *capitainerie*,
who must be contacted before dropping an anchor.

Facilities

Most facilities for yachts are available at the port,
but for stores go to the attractive town some approx.
half a mile to the south of the marina, where there is
a good range of shops.

PASSAGE BETWEEN GRANDE ILE ROUSSE AND
ISULA DEI BRUCCIU

A passage exists between Isula dei Brucciu and
Grande Ile Rousse 50m wide, 250m long and 2.5m
deep, which can be used by an experienced navigator
in good weather. It is spectacular, because the red
rocky sides are high and steep and the water is a
dark blue colour.

From the west There is no problem because depths
are in excess of 18m and the entrance wide. Enter on
an ESE course and cross the mouth of the Crique de
Fontanacci close in.

Ile Rousse

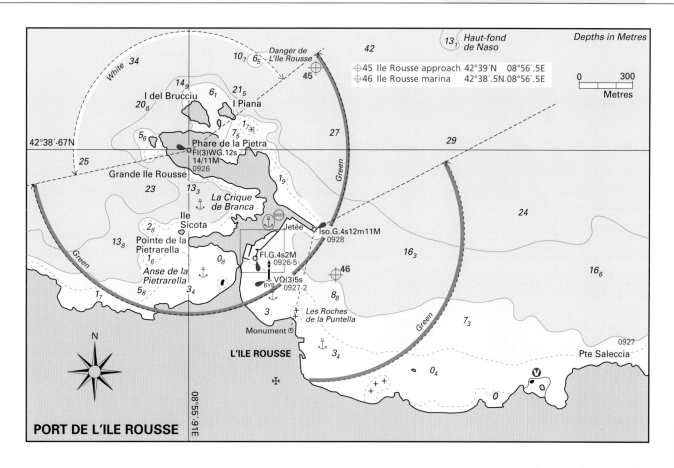

PORT DE L'ILE ROUSSE

From the east More care is necessary, as there is a small isolated rock 120m southeast of the small Isula Piana. Keep close in to the Grande Ile, cross the Crique de Fontanacci and enter the channel on a WNW course.

Passage

The actual passage is 8 to 18m deep and is steep-to, the only problem being a 2.5m rock lying in the approach from the eastern side.

L'Ile Rousse looking SE showing the passage between Grande Ile Rousse and Insula dei Brucciu

6. SAN FLORENT TO GOLFE DE CALVI

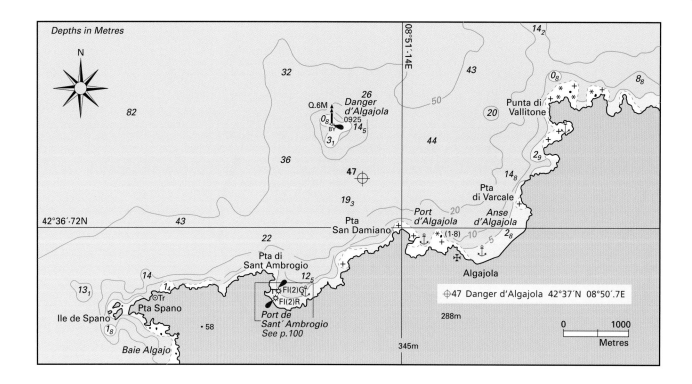

PUNTA DI VALLITONE 42°37′.78N 08°52′.9E

This prominent point has offlying dangers extending 300m to northwest and north. It is low and has a tower near the point, and houses have been built over this area.

⚓ ANSE D'ALGAJOLA 42°36′.5N 08°52′E

This is a wide bay with a long white sand beach. Punta di Varcale is at the north end of this beach and the town of Algajola, which has a conspicuous church tower and fortress, is on a point at the southwest end. There are sand dunes behind the beach, a railway line and a road. A number of apartment blocks and houses have been built and there are several beach cafés. Anchor in 3m, sand, off the beach open to W–NW–N. Everyday supplies are obtainable from the town, where there is a mechanic and chandlers.

⚓ PORT D'ALGAJOLA 42°36′.58N 08°51′.3E

About 800m to the west of the beach, a small harbour for fishing boats and dinghies has been built. There is 6m in the entrance and 3m in the centre of the harbour but the sides are very shallow. On the northwest side there is a slip and a small jetty. A road leading to the main road lies behind the jetty. The area is surrounded by a housing estate and the railway passes behind. A small islet (1.8m) lies 300m to the northwest of the town. Anchor in 3m, sand and rock, just inside the harbour, open to N–NE.

Port D'Algajola looking SW

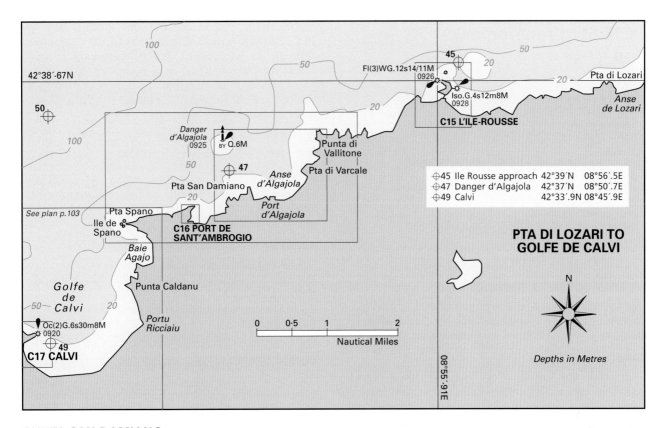

Chart labels:
- 100
- 42°38′·67N
- 50
- 100
- See plan p.103
- Danger d'Algajola 0925 BY Q.6M
- 50
- 47
- Pta San Damiano
- Anse d'Algajola
- Punta di Vallitone
- Pta di Varcale
- Port d'Algajola
- 20
- Pta Spano
- Ile de Spano
- C16 PORT DE SANT'AMBROGIO
- Baie Agajo
- Punta Caldanu
- Golfe de Calvi
- 50
- 20
- Portu Ricciaiu
- Oc(2)G.6s30m8M 0920
- 49
- C17 CALVI
- 45
- Fl(3)WG.12s14/11M 0926
- 20
- 50
- 20
- Pta di Lozari
- Anse de Lozari
- Iso.G.4s12m8M 0928
- C15 L'ILE-ROUSSE

⊕45 Ile Rousse approach	42°39′N	08°56′.5E
⊕47 Danger d'Algajola	42°37′N	08°50′.7E
⊕49 Calvi	42°33′.9N	08°45′.9E

PTA DI LOZARI TO GOLFE DE CALVI

N

Depths in Metres

0   0·5   1   2
Nautical Miles

08°55′·91E

PUNTA SAN DAMIANO 42°36′.7N 08°51′.1E

This is a small point west of the Port d'Algajola which slopes gently inland and is covered by a housing estate. This point is steep-to.

Danger d'Algajola

⊕47 42° 37′N 08°50′.7E

A shallow group of rocks submerged and awash, minimum depth 0.8m, lies 1M NNW of Pointe St Damiano and 2M west of Pointe Vallitone. Note that ⊕47 lies midway between the Danger and the coast. Originally a beacon consisting of a BRB iron pole with two balls topmark was located at the centre of this shoal, which extends for about 250m around it. As the balls were usually missing and the pole was very difficult to see, especially in poor conditions, a buoy which is Danger d'Algajola 42°37′.8N 8°50′.4E Q.6M ⚑ cardinal buoy was laid some 500 metres to the north.

A 1500m passage exists between this danger and the shore. The lighthouse on Grande Ile Rousse bearing 068° leads through the inner passage. Note that the white sector of this lighthouse leads outside this danger and, unfortunately, the green sector covers it. In rough weather the seas break over the shallows. (See photo page 91)

Mediterranean *maquis* in the foothills S of Ile Rousse

C16 Sant'Ambrogio

⊕48 42°36'.2N 08°49'.8E

Depth
2.5m in entrance reducing to 1m near shore
Number of berths
150 with 20 for visitors
Maximum LOA
15m
Lights
0924 Jetée NE head Fl(2)G.6s7m3M White pole, green top,6m
0924.2 Jetée SW head Fl(2)R.6s7m3M White pole, red top, 6m
Port communications
☎ 04 95 60 70 88 (S 0800-2000, OoS 0900-1200)

A small private harbour

Sant'Ambrogio is a modern, private yacht harbour which is part of a large holiday housing complex, and therefore it becomes very crowded in season.

Approach

Approach and entrance are not difficult in good weather but as the entrance lies in shallow water close to the beach, it is potentially dangerous in heavy weather from the N or NE, as you have to turn beam-on to the swell to effect an entrance. The shelter inside the harbour is good, though some swell enters with strong NE–E winds. In season, adequate supplies of provisions are available from shops around the port, but out of season the nearest shops are at Algajola over 1M away. Notice that the entrance tends to silt up during and after storms.

Although the ends of the jetties are lit Fl.G.2s7m2M and Fl.R.2s7m2M, the lights are difficult to see against the background of shop, house and street lights, so a night approach is not recommended for the first visit. In fact, the local pilots have the interesting phrase, 'Night access to Sant'Ambrogio is delicate!'

By GPS

Steer for ⊕48 from the NE sector.

Berths

Once inside berth near the fuelling point and await instructions. However, it is recommended to ring ahead to arrange a berth.

Facilities

Water and electricity on the quays
WC and showers were not available out of season
Public telephone
25-tonne crane and launching slip
Launderette
Some stores at site but all shops 1M away in village.

PUNTA SPANO 42°36'.07N 08°48'.09E

This is a low but prominent point (29m) sloping gently upward and inland, with several islets and covered and exposed rocks off its point. A ruined tower stands 400m to the northeast.

Ile de Spano

The large islet 200m long 90m wide and 14m high is called Ile de Spano, but there is another smaller islet 5.9m high and many small exposed rocks. Fishing craft and dinghies can use the passage between these islets with care in calm weather.

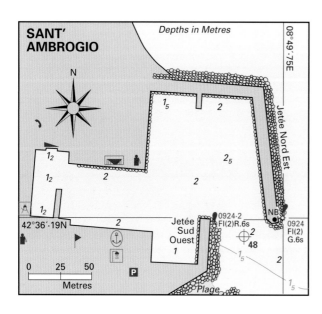

Sant'Ambrogio looking SW

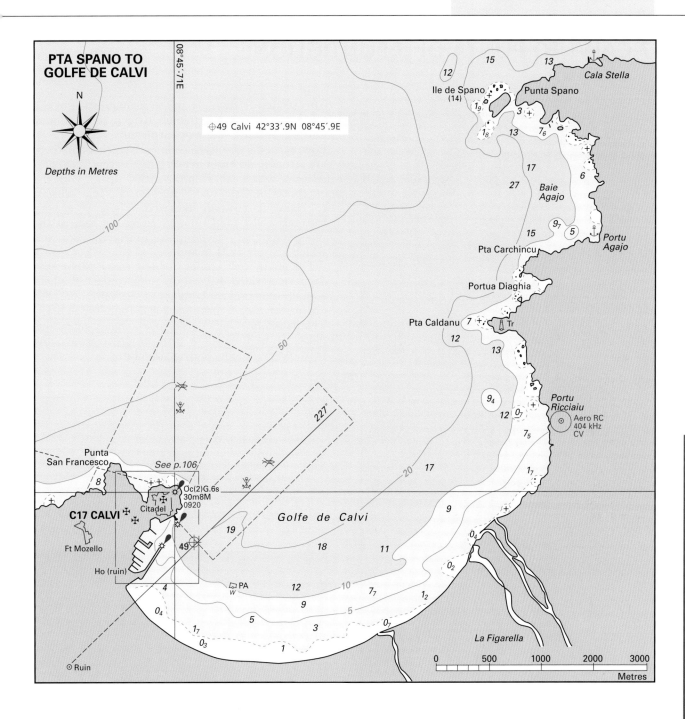

PTA SPANO TO GOLFE DE CALVI

N

Depths in Metres

08°45′·71E

⊕49 Calvi 42°33′·9N 08°45′·9E

100

50

227°

See p.106

Punta San Francesco

8

Oc(2)G.6s 30m8M 0920

Citadel

C17 CALVI

Ft Mozello

Ho (ruin)

19

49

4

Golfe de Calvi

18

11

⊙ Ruin

0₄

1₇

0₃

PA W

12

9

5

3

1

10

5

0₇

7₇

1₂

La Figarella

17

9

0₄

0₂

1₇

1₇

Cala Stella

15   13

12

Ile de Spano (14)   Punta Spano

1₉   3

1₈   13   7₆

17   6

27   *Baie Agajo*

15   9₇   5   *Portu Agajo*

Pta Carchincu

Portua Diaghia

Pta Caldanu   7

12   Tr

13

9₄   *Portu Ricciaiu*

12   0₇   Aero RC 404 kHz CV

7₅

0   500   1000   2000   3000
Metres

⚓ **BAIE AGAJO** 42°35′·8N 08°48′·4E

This open bay, south of Punta Spano, has a rocky shore and some small sandy beaches. There is a camping site on shore, with houses in the northeast corner and a road. Anchor in 5m, sand, open to SW–W–NW–N.

⚓ **PORTU AGAJO** 42°35′·45N 08°48′·54E

This small creek in the southeast corner of the Baie Agajo has white sandy beaches. Sound carefully because it is shallow. Anchor in sand off beach, open to W–NW–N.

⚓ **GOLFE DE CALVI** 42°33′·7N 08°46′·4E

A 2M-wide gulf which has depths of up to 36m. It is backed by a very long sandy beach and pine woods. La Figarella and Fiume Seccu Rau rivers enter the gulf on the southeast side. The bottom is mostly of sand and weed with a few patches of mud and one of rocks. It is open to NW–N–NE but somewhat protected from NW and NE by Punta Revellata and Punta Spano. The usual anchorage is situated to the south and southeast of Calvi's citadel in 5.6m, sand and weed, well clear of the harbour entrance but the holding is reported to be poor and the space much reduced in season by the 200 moorings laid in the bay!

7 CALVI TO PUNTA DI U PUNTIGLIONE

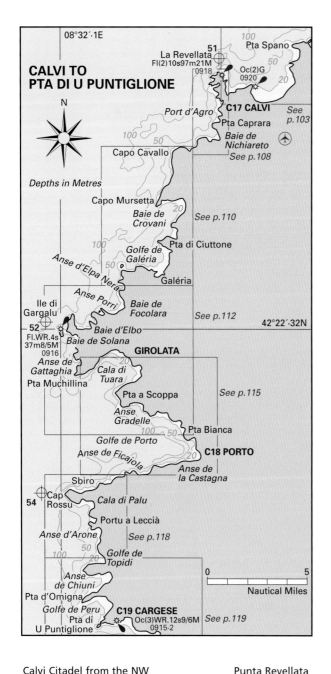

CALVI TO PTA DI U PUNTIGLIONE

08°32'.1E

N

Depths in Metres

42°22'.32N

- La Revellata Fl(2)10s97m21M — 0918
- Pta Spano — 100, 51, 50, 20
- Oc(2)G 0920
- Port d'Agro
- C17 CALVI — *See p.103*
- Pta Caprara
- Baie de Nichiareto — *See p.108*
- Capo Cavallo — 100, 50
- Capo Mursetta — 20
- Baie de Crovani — *See p.110*
- Pta di Ciuttone
- Golfe de Galéria — 100, 50
- Galéria
- Anse d'Elpa Nera
- Anse Porri
- Baie de Focolara — *See p.112*
- Ile di Gargalu — 52, Fl.WR.4s 37m8/5M 0916
- Baie d'Elbo
- Baie de Solana
- **GIROLATA**
- Anse de Gattaghia
- Pta Muchillina
- Cala di Tuara — 20
- Pta a Scoppa — *See p.115*
- Anse Gradelle
- Pta Bianca — 100, 50
- Golfe de Porto
- Anse de Ficajola — 20
- **C18 PORTO**
- Anse de la Castagna
- Sbiro
- Cap Rossu — 54
- Cala di Palu
- Portu a Leccià
- Anse d'Arone — *See p.118*
- Golfe de Topidi — 100, 50, 20
- Anse de Chiuni
- Pta d'Omigna
- Golfe de Peru
- Pta di U Puntiglione
- **C19 CARGESE** Oc(3)WR.12s9/6M 0915.2 — *See p.119*

0 — Nautical Miles — 5

Calvi Citadel from the NW | Punta Revellata

This section is certainly the most impressive of the whole island as it is extremely rugged, mountainous and, in places, of awe-inspiring beauty. It is, however, a dangerous coast in bad weather and there are virtually no harbours of refuge except Calvi and Ajaccio, which are 58 miles apart. Again, with the exception of Calvi and Cargese and a few villages, the land is virtually deserted. There is a very tortuous coast road running along the foot of the mountains that reach up to nearly 3,000m and which lie only 22M inland.

The coast itself consists of red rocky cliffs, with deep steep-sided bays and gulfs, some of which contain anchorages. Girolata is the only one with any pretence of security for a small number of craft. The incredible Golfe de Porto, though a dangerous place, is well worth a visit in order to see the fantastic mountains that surround it.

⊕51 Pta Revellata   42°36'N   08°43'E
⊕52 Gargalu   42°22'.5N   08°31'E
⊕54 Cap Rossu   42°14'N   08°31'.5E

0920 **Calvi Citadelle** Oc(2)G.6s30m8M
   White pylon on house, green top 6m
0918 **La Revellata** Fl(2)10s97m21M
   White tower, black top and corners 19m
0916 **Ile de Gargalu** Fl.WR.4s37m8/5M
   White column, black top 7m 348°-W-214°-R-348°
0915.2 **Cargese S jetty** Oc(3).WR.12s7m9/6M
   White tower, red top 7m 025°-R-325°-W-025°'

PLANNING GUIDE

Headlands	Ports & anchorages	Open to winds
	C17 ⚓ **Port de Calvi page 106**	NE
Punta San Francesco		
	⚓ *Golfe de la Revellata*	N–NE
Station de Recherches Océanographique		
Passage Ile de la Revallata		
Punta Revellata		
	⚓ *Porto Vecchiu*	S–SW–W
	⚓ *Port d'Agro*	S–W–NW
Punta Caprara		
	⚓ *Baie de Nichiareto*	W–NW
Capo Cavallo		
Capo Mursetta		
L'Ile Mursetta and passage		
	⚓ *Baie de Crovani*	SW–W–NW
Punta di Ciuttone		
	⚓ *Golfe de Galéria*	W–NW–N
Iles Scuglietti and passage		
Punta Rossa		
Punta Bianca		
	⚓ *Anse d'Elpa Nera (de la Foata)*	SW–W–NW
	⚓ *Anse de Focolara*	W–NW–N
Punta Scandola		
Écueils de Porri and passage		
	⚓ *Anse Pori*	W–NW–N
Punta Nera		
	⚓ *Baie d'Elbo*	NW–N–NE
Punta Palazzu		
Ilôt Palazzu and passage		
Ile di Gargalu and passage		
	⚓ *Baie di Solana*	S–SW–W
'Dog Leg' Passage		
	⚓ *Anse de Gattaghia*	S–SW–W
Punta Muchillina		
	⚓ *Cala Muretta*	SE–SW
	⚓ *La Girolata*	S–SW
	⚓ *Cala di Tuara*	S–SW–W
Capo Senino		
Punta a Scoppa		
Golfe de Porto		
	⚓ *Anse Gradelle*	S–SW–W
Punta Bianca		
	⚓ *Marine de Bussagghia*	S–SW–W
	C18 ⚓ **Porto Marina page 116**	SW–W–NW
	⚓ *Anse de la Castagna*	N–NE
	⚓ *Anse de Ficajola*	NW–N–NE
Punta di Ficajola		
Ilôt Vardiola		
	⚓ *Sbiro*	N
Cap Rossu		
Cap Rossu Passage		
	⚓ *Cala Genovese*	S–W
	⚓ *Cala di Palu*	S–SW
	⚓ *Portu a Leccia*	SW–W–NW
Punta a i Tuselli		
	⚓ *Porto d'Arone*	S–SW–W
	⚓ *Golfe de Topidi*	W–NW–N
Punta d'Orchina		
	⚓ *Anse de Chiuni*	SW–W–NW
Punta d'Omigna		
	⚓ *Golfe de Peru*	S–SW–W
Punta di u Puntiglione		

7. CALVI TO PUNTA DI U PUNTIGLIONE

C17 Port de Calvi

⊕49 42°33′.9N 08°45′.9E

Charts
Admiralty *1425*
French *6980, 6970*

Depth
5.5m to 1.5m

Number of berths
380 with 160 for visitors

Maximum LOA
50m

Lights
0918 Punta Revellata 42°35′.0N 8°43′.5E
Fl(2)10s97m21M White square tower, black top 19m
0920 Citadelle NE side 42°34′.2N 8°45′.8E
Oc(2)G.6s30m8M White metal tower, green top 6m
0922 Pier head Q.G.10m8M White metal column, green top 10m
0923 Digue du Large head Fl.R.4s6m7M White structure, red top,4m
0981.02(I) Porte de Pêche left side Fl(2)R.6s2M
0981.03(I) Porte de Pêche right side Fl(2)G.6s2M
0981.2(I) From 1 June to 30 September there may be a buoy at 42°33′.9N 8°45′.9E marking the anchorage area with a Q light

Port communication
VHF Ch 9 ☎ 04 95 65 10 60 *Fax* 04 95 65 15 13 (S 0700–2100, OoS 0800–1200, 1400–1730)
Email port-calvi@wanadoo.fr

Warnings
Anchoring is prohibited within 300m of the harbour but there is a mooring area for some 230 yachts laid from June through September about 300m ESE of the breakwater. The commercial harbour including Quai Landry is forbidden to yachts without prior permission of the *capitainerie*

Fire-fighting planes
Large Canadair flying boats may use the Golfe de Calvi to load water for nearby fires

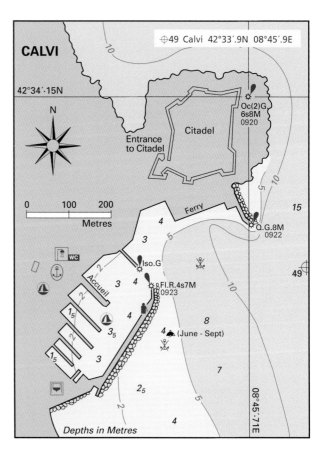

A beautiful harbour

This must be one of the most beautiful harbours on the island. It is easy to enter under almost any conditions and provides adequate shelter, though with strong winds from NW–N–NE the anchorage can become uncomfortable from the swell. Berths in the yacht harbour are well protected but there is still some swell from NE gales. The harbour is very crowded in the season, as yachts from the French mainland usually make this harbour their first port of call. The citadel and the town are most picturesque and everyday requirements can be obtained from the shops. Parts of the harbour are reserved for commercial and fishing vessels.

Approach (See also plan page 103)

The approach is easy by day or night, simply make for the high land in the centre of the gulf and the citadel (and/or its light) becomes obvious. Keep the citadel to starboard and pass outside the pier head, keeping well clear of any commercial traffic. Make for the entrance of the yacht harbour.

By GPS

Steer for ⊕49 from the northern quadrant and at the waypoint, steer south of west for the marina entrance or SW if making for the mooring buoys.

Entrance

It is simple to enter the marina through the 50-metre wide unobstructed entrance, but watch out for and keep well clear of ferry and fishing traffic.

Berths

On arrival, yachts moor to the visitors' pontoon opposite the fuel berth, at the fuel berth or in any vacant berth. Then report to the bureau for berth allocation. All berths are stern-to with chain/rope forward with a *pendillo* from the pontoon.

Anchorage and moorings

From 1 June to 30 September a private company lays some 200 mooring buoys in the bay SE of the port, which, unfortunately, take up most of the space originally used by yachts wishing to anchor. Anchoring is forbidden between the mooring buoys and the port itself, which reduces the space even more. There is a charge of €2 per metre for picking up a buoy and the firm can be contacted on VHF Ch 8 or ☎ 04 95 65 42 22.

Formalities

All authorities available.

Facilities

All.

Calvi moorings   *Martin Walker*

History

Calvi has been a small fishing harbour since before recorded history. The Romans had a small garrison here. In 1268 the little village on the site of the Lower Town was rebuilt and the Genoese colonised it, building the citadelle to defend the place.

Calvi remained faithful to Genoa and the citadelle held, despite the two attacks by the French and Turks in 1553. This is recalled by a plaque over the gateway with the inscription 'Civitas Calvi semper

fidelis'. In 1795 the English fleet under Lord Nelson attacked and, after its surrender, entered Calvi. Over 4,000 shells were fired into the town and the marks of them can still be seen on the dome of the church of St Jean-Baptiste. Nelson lost an eye during an opposed landing, and a tablet to commemorate this event, inscribed '*Ici Nelson dirigeant le feu des batteries contre Calvi perdit un oeil, 12 Juillet 1794*' is to be found on a large rock at Macarona about 1M to the west. His battery of two 26-pounders and a 12-inch mortar from HMS *Agamemnon* were landed at Port Agro 3M to the southwest. Even the patriot Pascal Paoli was unable to shake the inhabitants' faith in Genoa and he was forced to found and develop l'Ile Rousse in 1795 as an alternative to the 'citadelle of the north'.

Christopher Columbus is reputed to have been born in this town and in 1793 Napoleon took refuge in the citadel when he was obliged to flee from Ajaccio. Plaques in the citadel commemorate these events.

In more recent years there has been a steady development of the tourist industry. Holiday camps and hostels are to be found all around the bay, while at the same time cultivation and farming of the fertile area inland, the Balagne, has decreased. Since 1963, the French Foreign Legion has occupied the barracks in the citadel.

Calvi looking SW

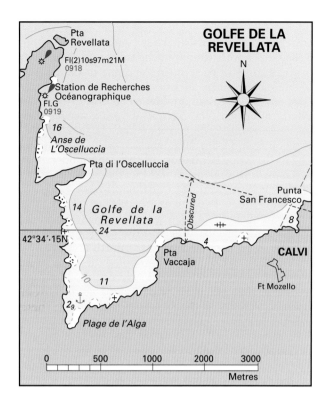

GOLFE DE LA REVELLATA

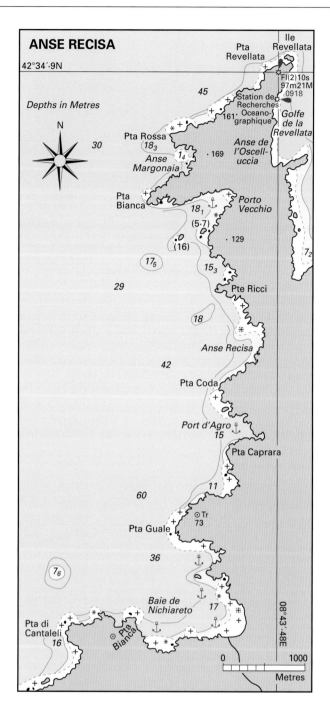

ANSE RECISA

42°34′·9N

Depths in Metres

⚓ **GOLFE DE LA REVELLATA** 42°34′N 08°44′E

This small deep gulf lies just to the west of Calvi, with a bottom of sand, shell and weed. A small stony beach, Plage de l'Alga, is situated in the SW corner of this gulf. Anchor off this beach in 3m, sand and weed, open to N–NE. Track to road inland.

Station de Recherches Océanographique
42°34′.8N 08°43′.5E

A very small harbour with light tower (white and green Fl.G.4s5m6M) on the head of the jetty. A road leads inland. Entrance into and anchorage off this harbour is not permitted.

PASSAGE ILE REVELLATA

Ile Revellata is a pointed rock (27m) lying just off Punta Revellata. A passage only 15m wide and 2m deep lies between them. This passage should only be used by experienced navigators in calm conditions, with great care and a careful lookout.

PUNTA REVELLATA 42°35′.05N 08°43′.5E

A conspicuous and prominent headland with a large white square tower on a house with corners and top picked out in black and a radio mast on top. The light is Fl(2)10s97m21M and is obscured when bearing less than 060°. The point and island are steep-to. (See photo page 104)

⚓ **PORTO VECCHIO** 42°34′.07N 08°42′.7E

A narrow V-shaped bay offering good protection but open to S–SW–W. Anchor in 5m to 3m, sand and rock, near its head in front of small stony beach. There is a rocky island (16m) in the mouth of the bay. Deserted.

⚓ **PORT D'AGRO** 42°32′.7N 08°43′.1E

A narrow inlet with a stony beach at its head and high sloping rocks on each side, with a track to the coast road above. Anchor in 6m, sand and rock, open to S–SW–W–NW. Deserted. It was here that Nelson landed his guns for the attack on Calvi in 1794.

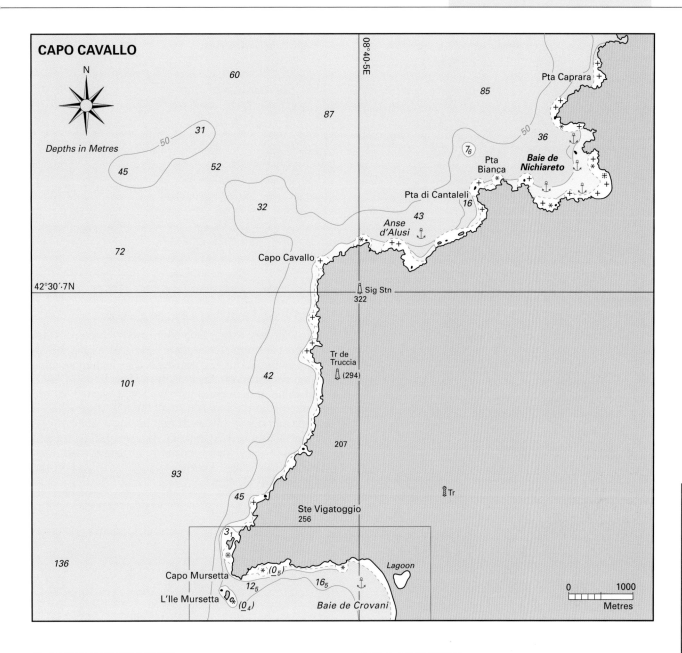

CAPO CAVALLO

N

Depths in Metres

60

87

31

50

52

45

32

72

42°30'.7N

Capo Cavallo +

08°40'.5E

85

50

36

Pta Caprara +

7₆

Pta Bianca

Baie de Nichiareto

Pta di Cantaleli

16

43

Anse d'Alusi

Sig Stn
322

Tr de Truccia
(294)

42

101

207

93

Tr

45

Ste Vigatoggio
256

3₁

136

Lagoon

Capo Mursetta

(0₅)

12₅

16₅

L'Ile Mursetta

(0₄)

Baie de Crovani

0   1000
Metres

BAIE DE NICHIARETO 42°31'.6N 08°42'.75E

This is a large bay with four small sub-bays and a long white sand and stone beach. Anchor off the beach in 4m, sand and rock, or in one of the sub-bays in 6m, rock. Open to W–NW. There is a track to the coast road.

CAPO CAVALLO 42°30'.9N 08°40'E

This major headland has rocky cliffs and a round shape. Although appearing steep-to it has a shallowish (30m) reef running some 2 miles to the northwest which in strong northwest or west winds kicks up a very nasty breaking steep sea. In strong onshore winds both this headland and Capo Mursetta, 2½ miles to the south, should be given a wide berth. It has a conspicuous disused signal station (322m) on the summit.

CAPO MURSETTA 42°28'.45N 08°39'E

Situated about 2½M south of Capo Cavallo and still part of the same extended coastline, Capo Mursetta has a more irregular outline and a group of islets extending 500m to the south. Halfway between these two capes is the conspicuous ruined Tour de Truccia (294m).

L'ILE MURSETTA AND PASSAGE

This islet lies 300m to the S of Capo Mursetta and is 16m high and 150m long. It has awash and just covered rocks on E–SE and N–NW sides. An easy passage 100m wide with a least depth 17m lies between the isle and the cape. This passage should be taken in ESE or WNW directions equidistant between the two sides.

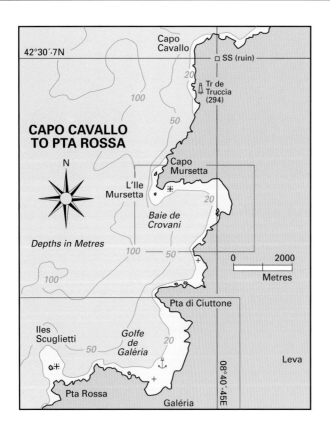

CAPO CAVALLO TO PTA ROSSA

Depths in Metres

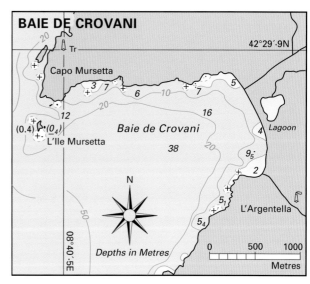

BAIE DE CROVANI

Baie de Crovani

Depths in Metres

⚓ **BAIE DE CROVANI** 42°28′.3N 08°40′.4E

This wide bay with a long white sandy beach provides plenty of room to anchor, and there are beach restaurants ashore. It is surrounded by high mountains in the background. Anchor off the beach in 4m, sand and stone. It is open to SW–W–NW. Deserted. At the south end of the bay is a small landing stage with an overhead railway (disused) running via a small village and a factory at L'Argentella (1km inland) to the old silver and lead mines inland. The coast road runs through this valley. Another factory lies inland off the north end of the beach.

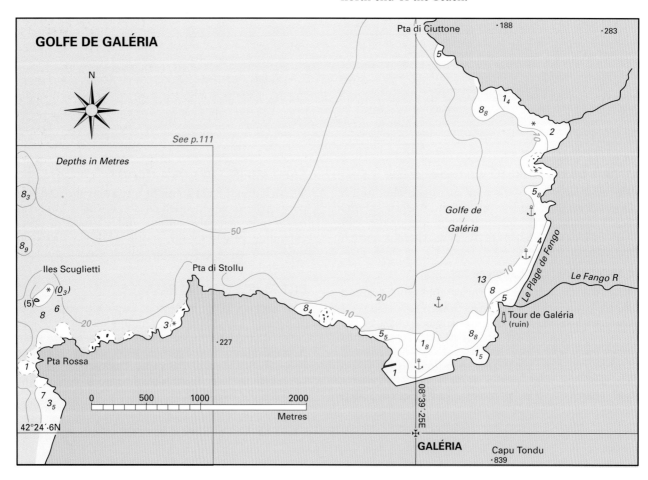

GOLFE DE GALÉRIA

Depths in Metres

See p.111

PUNTA DI CIUTTONE 42°26′.54N 08°38′.9E

This high prominent headland with red rocky cliffs has one close inshore islet but is otherwise steep-to. Inland the point rises to 200m with a stony pyramid half way up the slope.

⚓ GOLFE DE GALÉRIA 42°25′.5N 08°39′E

This wide deep gulf has one long, one medium and several small sandy beaches. The northern anchorage is off the north end of the long beach, Le Plage de Fango, in 4m sand open to W–NW–N. The area is backed by a wide river valley and the ruined Tour de Galéria stands on a hillock at the south end of this beach and close to the river mouth. There is a conspicuous cemetery and caravan site inland and track to the beach.

To the southeast of the tower there is another beach and the village of Galéria itself, which has a hotel, some shops and many houses standing behind the beach. There is also a caravan site. The road runs to the main coast road and a fuel station 3M inland. Anchor in 3m, sand, mud and rock, off the beach and clear of moorings. Pay attention in the approach to a 1.8m shallow patch off the centre of the beach. Open to W–NW–N. At the west end of the beach there is a new pier with 6 or 7 berths for shallow-draught craft only. There is a bar, restaurant and telephone 300m to the south of the pier.

ILES SCUGLIETTI AND PASSAGE
42°25′.23N 08°36′.34E

Iles Scuglietti is a dangerous shoal area of islets, awash and covered rocks stretching up to 600m to NNW of Punta Rossa. The Ile Scuglietti is 5m high. A passage 200m wide and 8m deep exists between a group of islets lying off the north side of Punta Rossa and a second group lying near Ile Scuglietti. Take the passage in NE–SW directions in calm conditions only.

PUNTA ROSSA 42°24′.9N 08°36′.3E

A broken, rocky-cliffed point with offlying dangers (see above), sloping up to 100m high inland.

PUNTA BIANCA 42°24′.5N 08°36′E

This headland is similar to Punta Rossa, steep-to but sloping up to 408m.

⚓ ANSE D'ELPA NERA 42°24′.25N 08°36′.2E

This small rocky-cliffed bay lies just south of the Punta Bianca. Anchor in 6m rock near head of bay, high land behind. Deserted. Fishing and diving are forbidden. Open to SW–W–NW.

⚓ BAIE DE FOCOLARA 42°23′.4N 08°36′.3E

A wide deep bay surrounded by high rocky cliffs and a range of high, tree-covered hills. It is most attractive. Anchor near the centre of the bay just north of a projecting rock in 4m, rocks, open to W–NW–N. Deserted. There is a small stream ashore.

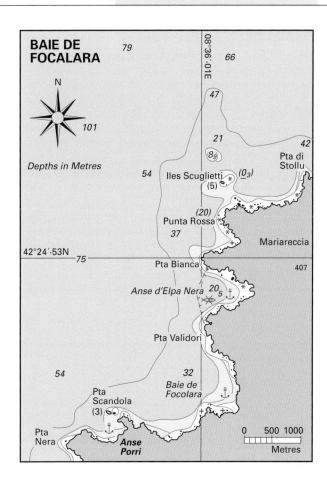

PUNTA SCANDOLA 42°23′.14N 08°36′.1E

A narrow rocky projecting point with Écueils de Porri (31m) lying 200m to NW of the point.

ÉCUEILS DE PORRI AND PASSAGE
42°23′.17N 08°34′.93E

Écueils de Porri (31m) lies 200m northwest of Punta Scandola and it has a small exposed rock 100m to its east. Punta Scandola has two exposed rocks close inshore. A passage 50m wide lies between the rocks close to Punta Scandola and the rock off Écueils de Porri with a minimum depth of 16m. Take the passage in NE–SW directions with great care and in calm conditions.

⚓ ANSE PORRI 42°23′.17N 08°34′.80E

A small rocky bay with an anchorage in 6m, rocks at its head, open to W–NW–N. Deserted.

PUNTA NERA 42°22′.9N 08°34′.4E

This square-shaped rocky headland has an islet close inshore. The land behind slopes up to 303m.

7. CALVI TO PUNTA DI U PUNTIGLIONE

⚓ BAIE D'ELBO 42°22'.5N 08°34'E

Baie d'Elbo is probably the most fantastic and beautiful area in this very attractive section of coast that stretches from here as far south as Cap Rossu. The cliffs, islands and islets are of dark red rock and their shapes are extraordinary. The sea is clear, dark blue and most of the land is covered with light and dark green vegetation. The area is a marine reserve. Fishing, diving and camping are forbidden, as are landing on the islands or the mainland, and craft must not anchor in the area between sunset and sunrise. In another smaller area, the *reserve integrale* around Ile de Gargalu (including the passage), the mooring of craft is prohibited at all times. See plan page 16 for the marine reserve boundaries. In addition to the anchorage in the Marine d'Elbo, there are many creeks, caves and fissures to explore in the area. Some have vertical sides, an ideal place for fantastic photographs. Open to NW–N–NE.

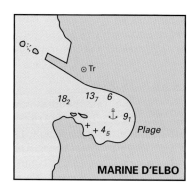

MARINE D'ELBO

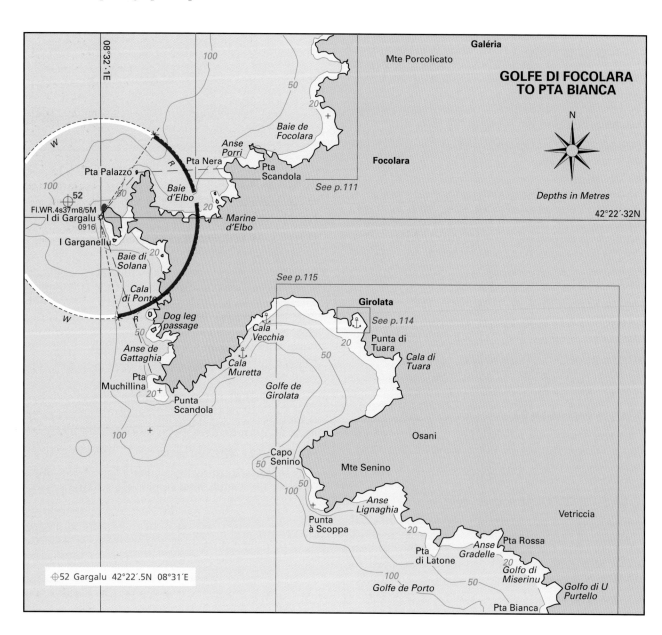

Marine d'Elbo is a small creek with a sand and stone beach used by fishermen. A line of rocky islets and awash rocks terminate at the rocky Ile d'Elbo to the north. The Tour d'Elbo on the east side of the harbour is conspicuous. A lone awash rock lies 200m northwest of the western side of the entrance. Anchor in 4m, sand and weed, in the centre of the creek, open to NW–N–NE. Mooring to two anchors (fore and aft) is advised. Track found inland and a ruined hut near the beach. Deserted. Winds from SE–S–SW sometimes funnel strongly down the valley behind the anchorage.

PUNTA PALAZZU 42°22'.8N 08°32'.9E

This high, steep-sided point has a very jagged aspect, with vertical striations. It is steep-to with Ilot Palazzu (57m) off its NW corner and a smaller *îlot* off its northern side.

ILOT PALAZZU AND PASSAGE

This is a simple little passage 45m wide and 22m deep between an almost vertical red rocky point and a steep-sided *îlot* 58m high. Take it in NE–SW directions in calm conditions. There is a smaller nameless *îlot* to the east of Ilot Palazzu with a narrow passage which can be used with great care by experienced navigators.

ILE DI GARGALU AND PASSAGE

The largish red rocky Ile di Gargalu is 750m long and 450m wide, with a highest point of 127m, where there is a tower. There is an inconspicuous lighthouse on a neck of rocks that stretches out to the northwest (Fl.WR.4s37m8/5M white column black top). There is a 140m long passage, 10m wide and 2–5m deep, to be taken in N–S directions, between the Ile and the mainland. This passage should only be attempted in good conditions. The approach from the N is easy and 16m can be carried into the passage. From the south it is necessary to approach the entrance on a NW course carrying 16m into the passage. However, three large rocks in mid-passage reduce the depth to 2.5m and the width

to 10m. Care is necessary here and a good forward lookout is advised; however, the water is crystal clear and the bottom can easily be seen. Even so, proceed slowly.

⚓ BAIE DI SOLANA 42°21'.85N 08°33'.2E

A deep anchorage in a small rocky-cliffed bay in 16m rock, open to S–SW–W. Use only in good conditions. Deserted.

'Dog Leg' passage 42°20'.7N 08°33'E

A passage with fantastic scenery around a small unnamed island in a creek. Both the sides of the creek and the island have near-vertical red rock cliffs. The water is very deep: 11–27m. This passage is just to the north of the Anse de Gattaghia and there is a pyramid-shaped rocky islet on the south side of the southern entrance. Keep a look out for tourist boats from Calvi. (A second passage has been reported to the south of Dog Leg.)

PUNTA MUCHILLINA 42°20'N 08°33'.15E

This is a prominent red rocky-cliffed point with awash and covered rocks extending 100m off shore. Proceeding east from the point, en route for Girolata, you pass an unnamed point and then Punta Scandola, where you enter the Golfe de Girolata. Some 1,000m northeast of the point there is a small islet and just beyond this there are a number of small bays, which offer reasonable shelter with the wind in the north or northwest quadrant and are a possible alternative to Girolata, if the latter is full. The first bay past the islet is Cala Muretta with rocks off the western side of the entrance. On the beach there is a smoke-blackened barbecue chimney. Anchor in 3 to 4m off the beach. There are two rings let into the rocks to the east of the beach to which a shore line can be taken, if required.

CALA VECCHIA 42°20'.8N 08°35'E

Another small, deep cala which can be used if Girolata is full. No facilities whatever and open to the S.

Ile di Gargalu and passage from N

Cala Vecchia beneath red mountain cliffs W of Girolata   *MW*

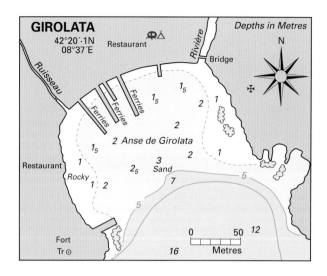

GIROLATA 42°20'·1N 08°37'E — Depths in Metres — Restaurant — Ruisseau — Rivière — Bridge — N — Ferries — Anse de Girolata — Restaurant — Rocky — Sand — Fort Tr⊙ — 0 50 — Metres — 12 — 16

⚓ LA GIROLATA 42°20'.7N 08°36'.8E

Girolata is a superb anchorage in a beautiful setting and is the only anchorage that gives reasonable shelter to the prevailing winds between Calvi and Ajaccio for a small number of yachts drawing less than 2m. The shelter for deeper-draught craft is not good because they must anchor near the entrance and might have to leave in heavy SW winds. Approach and entrance are easy as there is a conspicuous ruined fort with tower on the pyramid-shaped headland at the west end of the anchorage. To enter this anchorage, round the point at some 50m and steer north into the bay. There are a number of pontoons off the beach, which are solely for the use of ferries that run to and from the major towns. Unfortunately this anchorage becomes dangerously crowded in the season. Yachtsmen are advised not to use it during the months of July and August when there can be over 100 yachts at anchor each evening and only the first 10 or so yachts will find good shelter. Late arrivals have to anchor at the mouth of the *cala*, fully exposed to S–SW–W. Motor boats run daily trips from Calvi, Porto and Ajaccio

Girolata looking N

and other harbours for tourists to this anchorage. The only facilities are several restaurants, cafés and bars with a small shop ashore in summer season only. Note that it is forbidden to take garbage ashore here.

⚓ CALA DI TUARA 42°20'.3N 08°37'.4E

This is small bay at the foot of a valley at the mouth of a small river with a beach of sand and stone at its head just south of Girolata. Anchor in 5m, sand and weed, off the beach which is open to S–SW–W with some rocks on the south side of the entrance. Track to Girolata and also to coast road. A useful alternative to Girolata in settled weather.

CAPO SENINO 42°19'.1N 08°35'.9E

A red rocky headland, rounded and facing NW, steep-to backed by the high pyramid-shaped Mont Senino (618m).

PUNTA A SCOPPA 42°18'.35N 08°36'.3E

This is a similar headland to Capo Senino above. There is a shallow area northwest of this point.

Golfe de Porto 42°16'.7N 08°39'E

A wide-mouthed deep bay surrounded by high hills and mountains mostly of red rock. Some of the cliffs on the south side of the gulf are especially spectacular. There are anchorages on both sides of the gulf and one at its head. These anchorages should be used with caution because the gulf is funnel-shaped with high sides, and this configuration is carried on inland up a valley at the head of the gulf. Because of this shape any SW–W–NW wind is speeded up as it passes up the gulf and the seas become very rough. Yachts will find it very difficult to leave the area and are, on occasion, driven ashore. With strong or gale force winds from the IVth quadrant, yachts should never attempt to enter this gulf but should keep well clear of the coast and eventually seek shelter in Calvi to the north or Ajaccio to the south. In poor visibility or at a distance it is easy to mistake the Golfe de Porto for the Golfe de Girolata. Careful navigation is advised.

⚓ ANSE GRADELLE 42°18'N 08°39'.5E

This small bay has rocky cliffs and a beach of sand and stone at its head. A track leads up the valley. Some houses behind the beach. Anchor off the beach in 5m, sand, avoiding an awash rock on the eastern side. Open to SE–S–SW. Another little beach to the east can also be used to anchor off and there are two restaurants ashore in season.

PUNTA BIANCA 42°17'N 08°40'.4E

This is a high rocky-cliffed point with rocky dangers extending 150m offshore. The land behind slopes up to 262m and a coast road runs across it.

⚓ MARINE DE BUSSAGGHIA 42°16'.87N 08°41'.15E

A large bay, just south of Pta Bianca, with a long sand and stone beach. A river valley runs inland

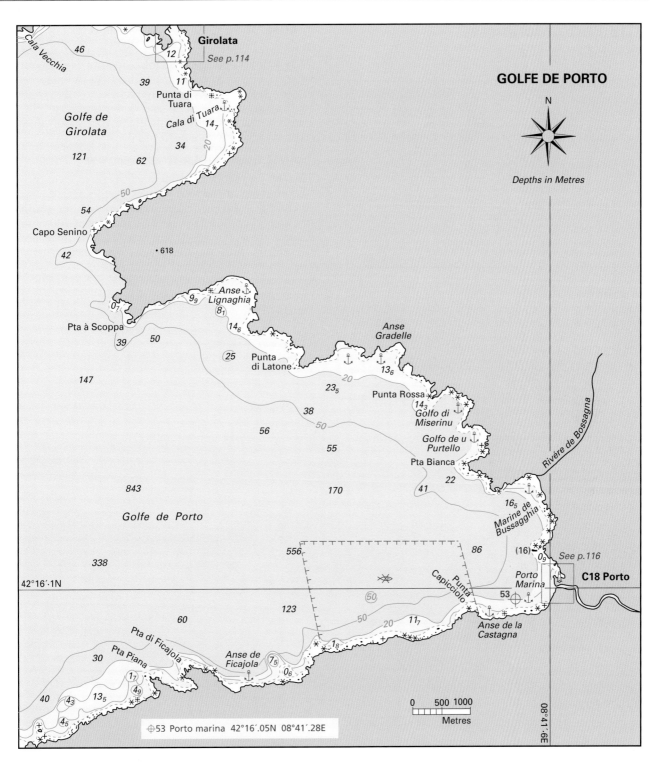

Girolata
See p.114

Cala Vecchia
Cala di Tuara
Golfe de Girolata
Punta di Tuara
Capo Senino
Pta à Scoppa
Anse Lignaghia
Punta di Latone
Anse Gradelle
Punta Rossa
Golfo di Miserinu
Golfo de u Purtello
Pta Bianca
Golfe de Porto
Rivère de Bossagna
Marine de Bussagghia
See p.116
C18 Porto
Porto Marina
Punta Capicciolo
Anse de la Castagna
Pta di Ficajola
Pta Piana
Anse de Ficajola

42°16′·1N

08°41′·6E

0   500   1000
Metres

⊕53 Porto marina 42°16′.05N 08°41′.28E

7. CALVI TO PUNTA DI U PUNTIGLIONE

where there are a number of houses, small hotels and restaurants. A road joins the main coast road. There are beach restaurants and cafés. An awash rock is located just offshore in the middle of the beach. Anchor in the north corner in 5m on sand. Open to S–SW–W.

Porto

This small fishing village in magnificent surroundings is being rapidly spoiled by the construction of low-cost apartment blocks and hotels for holidaymakers and by the daily arrival of hundreds of cars and coaches disgorging day-trippers. There is a quay with 1.5m alongside on the north side of a pinnacle rock with a small square fort on top. This is in frequent use by tourist boats from Calvi and sometimes by local fishermen. There are many restaurants and cafés. Everyday requirements can be obtained from the village and there is also a marine engineer and chandlers ashore. A restricted area lies to west of Porto between Punta Capicciolo and an unnamed headland 1½M to the west, where subaqua fishing is forbidden. See section 2 – Marine Reserves for further details. (See photo page viii)

C18 Porto Marina

⊕53 42°16′.05N 08°41′.28E

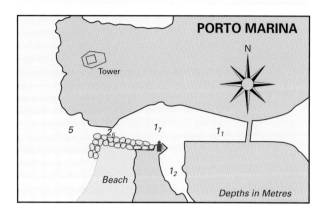

A small yacht harbour has been constructed at the mouth of the river south of the village. It has 5m depth at the entrance but only 1–2m inside. There are 120 berths with 49 for visitors (maximum length 14m). Contact the *capitainerie* on VHF Ch 9 or ☎ 06 88 16 93 38, *Fax* 04 95 26 14 12 (June to September only 0830-1830)

There are some facilities (fuel, showers (300m), water and electricity) but little else.

⚓ ANSE DE LA CASTAGNA 42°15′.8N 08°40′.65E

A minute, deserted anchorage in 5m sand tucked away behind Pointe Capicciolo, open to N–NE and where some protection from the NW–W may be found. Two anchors are advised due to the wind swirling around the point and down the steep hills. The bay has steep sides and there is a small quay (2m) alongside with a road to Porto.

⚓ ANSE DE FICAJOLA 42°15′.2N 08°37′.6E

This is yet another small anchorage in beautiful surroundings at the foot of the Côte des Calanques. Anchorages and moorings are situated to the south of a small beach in 10m sand. A restaurant 400m up a rocky path is open in the season, and there are fishermen's huts on the beach. The anchorage is open to NW–N–NE but is still subject to a swell from the west. At the top of the hill after a tremendous climb to the northwest lies the town of Piana, where everyday supplies can be bought.

Porto Marina

Porto from the E

PUNTA DI FICAJOLA 42°15′.3N 08°37′E

This red rocky-cliffed promontory, lying at 045° to the coast, points NW. There is a 2.8m shallow patch to the north of the point, otherwise it is steep-to.

Ilot Vardiola 42°14′.5N 08°34.34′E

This is a conspicuous islet (30m high) of red rock which stands 200m off the coast.

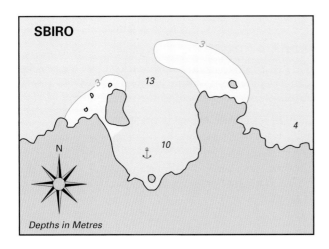

⚓ SBIRO 42°14′.5N 08°32′.9E

500m to the east of Cap Rossu there is the Sbiro rock and you can anchor to the southeast of this rock in 10m depth on rock and sand. It is quite a tricky entrance but slow speed and a good lookout at the bow should enable you to anchor in this tiny landlocked bay. If you are put off by the narrowness of the entrance you can anchor in 4m off an un-named beach some 500m to the southeast. The approach is straightforward but a careful lookout is required as there are numerous isolated rocks close in.

CAP ROSSU 42°14′.2N 08°32′.4E

This prominent peninsular headland has the conspicuous Tour de Turghio on top of a pointed hill (340m). The point is of high broken reddish rocky cliffs with an islet 100m to W and some rocky heads and shallows 200m to the northeast.

CAP ROSSU PASSAGE

A passage 250m long, 3m deep and 75m wide at the N end between the 18m high and 200m long islet off the W point of Cap Rossu. It is recommended to pass through from S to N for the first time because the entrance is obvious from the southern end. Navigate with care at slow speed with a bow lookout, in calm weather.

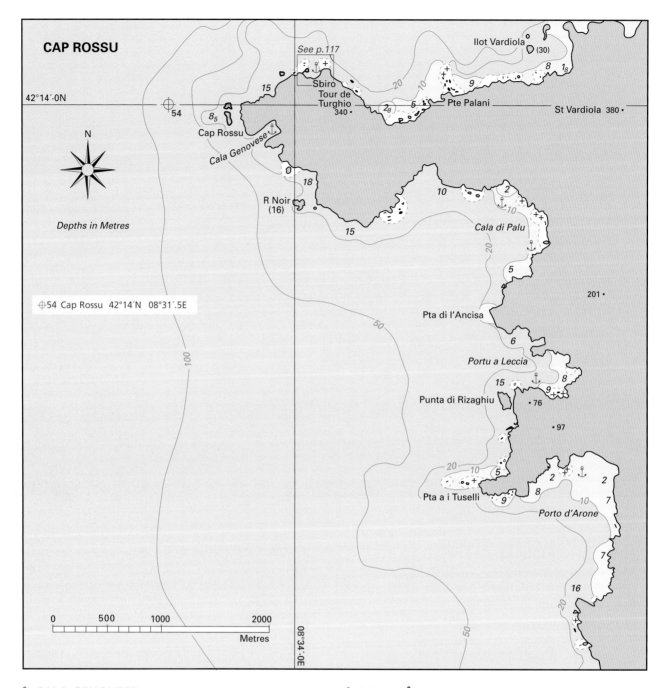

CAP ROSSU

42°14′·0N

⊕54 Cap Rossu 42°14′N 08°31′·5E

Depths in Metres

See p.117

Ilot Vardiola (30)

Sbiro
Tour de
Turghio
340 ·

Pte Palani

St Vardiola 380 ·

Cap Rossu

Cala Genovese

R Noir (16)

Cala di Palu

Pta di l'Ancisa

201 ·

Portu a Leccia

Punta di Rizaghiu

· 76

· 97

Pta a i Tuselli

Porto d'Arone

0   500   1000   2000
Metres

08°34′·0E

⟓ **CALA GENOVESE** 42°14′·05N 08°32′·5E

This is another spectacular anchorage for the
experienced navigator in calm weather. The entrance
is close to the west side of Cap Rossu and is 200m
south of its offlying islet. It has high steep red cliffs
and is narrow. There is a small white sand and stone
beach at the head of the bay. Anchor off this beach
in 5m, sand and rock, open to S–SW–W. Deserted.

⟓ **CALA DI PALU** 42°13′·7N 08°34′E

Anchorages can be found in this large bay
surrounded by rocky cliffs above which are high
hills. Anchor in the northern corner in 5m sand with
care because of rocky heads close inshore. Open to
S–SW. Another anchorage in 5m on sand and weed
lies 700m to the southeast of the above anchorage.
Deserted.

⟓ **PORTU Â LECCIA** 42°12′·9N 08°34′·3E

A small anchorage in 6–10m, rock and sand, open to
SW–W–NW. There is a road inland.

PUNTA A I TUSELLI 42°12′·3N 08°34′E

This is a hooked point with rocky cliffs and rocky
dangers extending 400m westward from the point.
A hill (97m) stands behind the point.

⟓ **PORTO D'ARONE** 42°12′·3N 08°34′·7E

This large bay with black rocky-cliffed sides has a
large sandy beach at the head. Some houses, a
caravan site and a road inland stand behind the
beach. The anchorage is off the beach in 4m, sand.
It is open to S–SW–W.

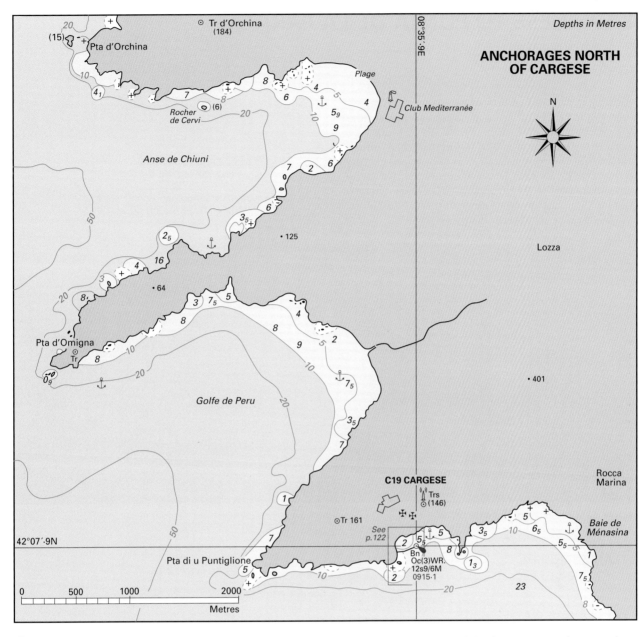

⚓ GOLFE DE TOPIDI 42°10′.9N 08°34′.9E

A deep bay sheltered from the south and southwest by the mass of Punta d'Orchina, with rocky cliffs around it. At its head are some small sand and stone beaches and an open valley. Anchor at the head of the bay in 5m, sand, open to W–NW–N. Pay attention to some rocky heads near the shore.

PUNTA D'ORCHINA 42°10′.3N 08°33′.7E

This large prominent point has a 184m high hill inland on which stands a conspicuous tower. It is a rounded point with an islet and rocky dangers extending west some 200m.

⚓ ANSE DE CHIUNI 42°10′N 08°35′.2E

A wide deep bay with sandy beach at its head and behind it a conspicuous Club Méditerranée site with buildings that look like sails. The coast road runs just inland. Anchor off beach in 5m, sand, open to SW–W–NW. A small bay on the south side of the bay provides a useful alternative calm weather anchorage in 6m, rock.

PUNTA D'OMIGNA 42°08′.8N 08°33′.46E

This long, low, narrow, rocky promontory has a conspicuous tower near its point. A small rock and 0.9m shallows lie 75m off its point.

⚓ GOLFE DE PERU 42°08′.8N 08°35′E

This is a wide, deep bay with sandy beach, behind which are sand dunes, with a housing estate in the N corner. Houses of Cargèse can be seen to the south. Anchor off the beach in 4m, sand. Open to S–SW–W.

PUNTA DI U PUNTIGLIONE 42°07′.75N 08°34′.8E

This is a pointed promontory with rocky cliffs and a conspicuous tower standing on a hill behind the point 161m high. The houses of Cargèse to NE of the tower are easily seen.

8 CARGÈSE TO PUNTA DE LA PARATA

Although the coast of this section is less spectacular than the last, it is still quite impressive, consisting of the very wide and deep Golfe de Sagone, the northeast side of which is populated to a limited extent, but the southeast side and the relatively high coast south to the Iles Sanguinaires are again virtually deserted. From this extraordinary chain of islands the coast becomes more and more populated as the distance to Ajaccio decreases.

⊕55 Cargese   42°07′.7N   08°36′.0E
⊕56 Sagone   42°06′.0N   08°41′.5E
⊕2   Iles Sanguinaires   41°52′.0N   08°33′.0E

0915.2 **Cargese S jetty** Oc(3)WR.12s7m9/6M
     White tower, red top 7m
     025°-R-325°-W-025°
0902 **Iles Sanguinaires** Fl(3)15s98m24M White
     tower, black top on house 18m

Pointe de St Joseph in centre with Cargese and Pointe di u Puntiglione at far left

PLANNING GUIDE

Headlands	Ports & anchorages	Open to winds
	C19 ⚓ **Port de Cargèse page 122**	SE–S
	⚓ *Baie de Cargèse*	SE–S–W
Punta di Molendinu		
Rocher Marifaja		
	⚓ *Baie de Menasina*	SE–S–W
Pointe de Triu		
Pointe Albellu		
	C20 ⚓ **Port de Sagone page 124**	S–SW–W
	⚓ *Baie de Sagone*	SE–S–SW
Pointe de St-Joseph		
Recif de St-Joseph and passage		
Pointe Capigliolu		
	⚓ *Baie de Liscia*	SW–W–NW
Pointe Palmentoju		
Iles de Pointe Palmentoju and passage		
	⚓ *Anse d'Ancone*	SW–W–NW
Pointe Paliagi		
Recif de Paliagi and passage		
Pointe Parragiola and Pointe Pellusella		
	⚓ *Portu Provençale*	SW–W–NW
Petra Piombata and passage		
Cap de Feno		
Écueil de Fica		
	⚓ *Anse de Fica*	S–SW–W
La Botte		
	⚓ *Anse de Minaccia*	S–SW–W
	⚓ *Anse d'Alta*	SW–W–NW
Pointe de la Corba		

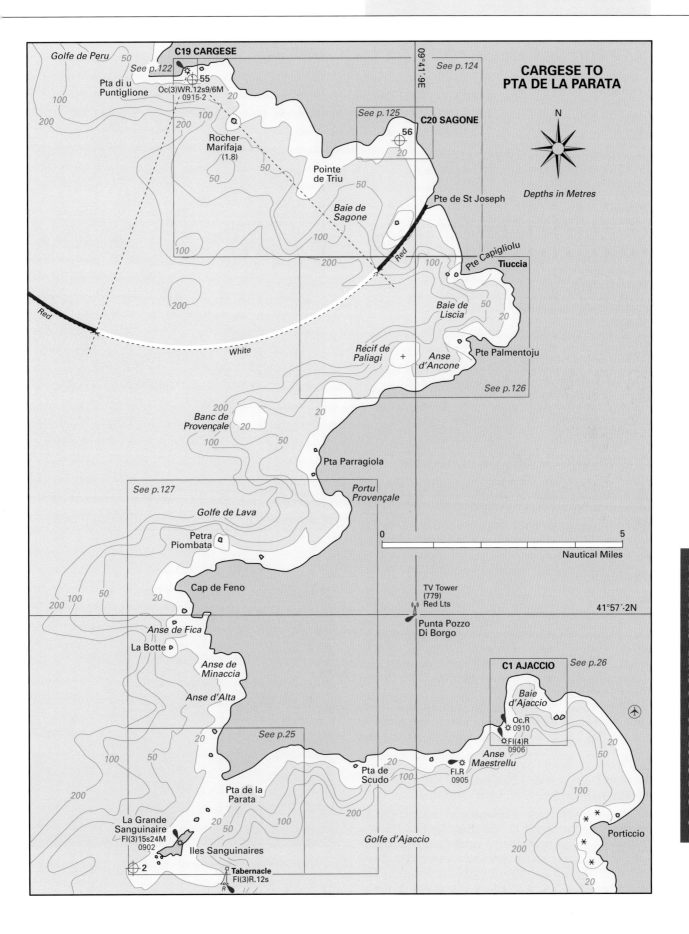

CARGESE TO
PTA DE LA PARATA

N

Depths in Metres

C19 CARGESE

Golfe de Peru   50
See p.122

Pta di u
Puntiglione
Oc(3)WR.12s9/6M
0915·2

See p.124

C20 SAGONE
See p.125
56
20

Rocher
Marifaja
(1.8)

Pointe
de Triu

Baie de
Sagone

Pte de St Joseph

Red

Pte Capigliolu
Tiuccia

Baie de
Liscia

Red

White

Récif de
Paliagi

Anse
d'Ancone

Pte Palmentoju

See p.126

Banc de
Provençale

Pta Parragiola

See p.127

Portu
Provençale

0   5

Nautical Miles

Golfe de Lava

Petra
Piombata

TV Tower
(779)
Red Lts

41°57'·2N

Cap de Feno

Punta Pozzo
Di Borgo

Anse de Fica

La Botte

Anse de
Minaccia

C1 AJACCIO   See p.26

Baie
d'Ajaccio

Anse d'Alta

Oc.R
0910
Fl(4)R
0906

See p.25

Anse
Maestrellu
Fl.R
0905

Pta de
Scudo

Pta de la
Parata

Golfe d'Ajaccio

Porticcio

La Grande
Sanguinaire
Fl(3)15s24M
0902

2

Iles Sanguinaires

Tabernacle
Fl(3)R.12s

8. CARGESE TO ROCHER CITADELLE

C19 Port de Cargèse

⊕55 42°07'.7N 08°36'.0E

Charts
Admiralty *1985*
French *7050*

Depth
2.5m

Number of berths
215 of which 35 are allocated to visitors

Maximum LOA
16m

Lights
0915.2 Jetée Sud head 42°07'.9N 8°35'.9E
Oc(3)WR.12s7m9/6M 025°-R-325°-W-025° White tower, red top 7m
0915.4 Jetée Nord head Fl(3)G.12s4m3M White pole, green top 4m

Port communications
VHF Ch 9 ☎ 04 95 26 47 24 *Fax* 04 95 26 41 47
(0800–2000 1 May–1 October only)

Warnings
There is a dangerous rocky shallow patch to the SW of the heel of the south jetty which should be avoided when approaching from the west, whilst the Rocher Marifaja (2.9M 140° from jetty head) must be avoided when coming from the south. Note that the harbour should be approached in daylight hours only. When full, a *Complet* notice is shown at the jetty head. It is dangerous to enter the harbour when a strong SW wind is blowing

A small but friendly yacht harbour

Cargèse has a small yacht harbour with a 200m long jetty pointing northeastwards, which gives good shelter in almost any conditions. Although the harbour has lights on the jetty, it is only permitted to enter and leave in daylight hours and the *capitainerie* operates only from 1st May to 1st October.

Approach

By day

From the north The sloping, reddish, rocky promontory of Cap Rossu and the four points to its south: Puntas Tuselli, Orchino, d'Omigna (which has a conspicuous tower) and Puntiglione, also with a conspicuous tower, are easily identified. Punta di u Puntiglione has the town of Cargèse on a saddle just to the northeast of the tower. All of these points have offlying islands and rocks and should be given at least 300m berth. An easterly course for 1M from half a mile south of Punta di u Puntiglione brings this harbour abeam and the rocky breakwater will be seen. Keep at least 150m south of the root of the breakwater, as there are awash rocks there.

From the south Cross the wide and deep Golfe de Sagone on a northerly course from Cap de Feno, a low rocky-cliffed point with a ruined tower, towards the far side of the gulf where the points listed above will be seen, with Cap Rossu in the far distance. The nearest, Punta di u Puntiglione, has a tower on its summit and the town of Cargèse shows on the skyline just to the east of it. Below the town lies the harbour. The two church towers are conspicuous.

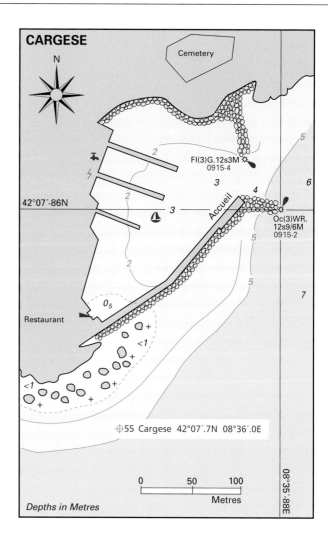

Cargese marina looking E by S

Cargese looking NE (see also photo page 2)

By night

Although lights are in place, it is not permitted to enter at night.

By GPS

Steer for ⊕55 from the SW quadrant and then shape a course to pass 20m from the jetty head.

Entrance

Round the south jetty end at 20m and proceed at very slow speed on a westerly course. When past the north jetty head, turn to port and berth near the fuel station to get berthing instructions.

Berths

Berth only on the instructions of the *capitainerie*.

Formalities

Capitainerie only between May and October. All other authorities, Customs, etc. are at Ajaccio.

Facilities

All unavailable except divers, and although the village has everyday stores it is not recommended to stock up here.

History

The history of this harbour is of particular interest in view of the present disharmony between the French Algerian settlers and the native Corsicans. In 1676 a group of Greeks from the Gulf of Colokythia in the Peloponnesus appealed to Genoa because they were being tyrannised by the Turks. The Genoese senate (who were having difficulties themselves in crushing the Corsican resistance to their occupation of Corsica) offered them the territories of Paomia, Reonda and Salogno, located inland from Cargèse. In March 1676 some 730 Greeks arrived, settled in, and within a few years, due to their hard work, were becoming prosperous. Troubles commenced about three years later in 1679 when the Corsicans of Vice and Niolo, knowing the Greeks to be allies of Genoa and envying them their prosperity, murdered one of the Greeks. From this time on there was constant friction between the two groups, ending in 1731 with the Greeks being driven out to take refuge in Ajaccio, and their villages being burnt to the ground. In 1768, when France annexed Corsica, a new village, Cargèse, was built for the Greeks, complete with their own church. The 110 remaining families, who spoke only Greek and had kept their own religion, costume and customs, moved in and have remained there ever since. Over the ages they have intermarried with the native Corsicans and, except for their religion and capacity for hard work, there is little to distinguish them from the native Corsican.

⚓ BAIE DE CARGÈSE 42°07′.8N 08°36′E

In fact there are two bays with a small rocky point and an offlying 1.8m shallows dividing them. Anchor in the northeast corner of either bay in 4m, sand and rock, open to SE–S–SW–W. The road runs above low rocky cliffs. A few houses. Landing is very difficult due to the rocky foreshore.

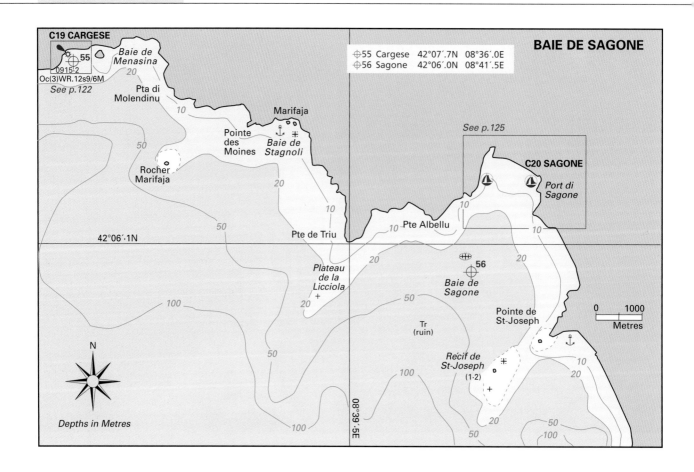

⊕55 Cargese   42°07′.7N 08°36′.0E
⊕56 Sagone   42°06′.0N 08°41′.5E

BAIE DE SAGONE

C19 CARGESE

Baie de Menasina

Pta di Molendinu

55
0915·2
Oc(3)WR.12s9/6M
See p.122

Marifaja

Pointe des Moines

Baie de Stagnoli

Rocher Marifaja

Pte de Triu

42°06′.1N

Plateau de la Licciola

Tr (ruin)

Récif de St-Joseph (1·2)

See p.125

C20 SAGONE

Port di Sagone

Pte Albellu

56

Baie de Sagone

Pointe de St-Joseph

0   1000
Metres

N

Depths in Metres

08°39′.5E

⚓ BAIE DE MENASINA 42°07′.9N 08°36′.6E

This large open bay has a big sandy beach at its head and low rocky cliffs at each side with offlying rocks. A single awash rock lies 100m off the north end of the beach. Anchor off the centre of the beach in 3m, sand, open to SE–S–SW–W. The coast road runs behind the beach where there are a few houses.

PUNTA DI MOLENDINU 42°07′.33N 08°37′.46E

This small rocky-cliffed point has three small islets off the point, but is otherwise steep-to.

Rocher Marifaja 42°06′.8N 08°37′.08E

This is a 1.8m-high isolated rock with a 1.7m shallows and some awash rocks close in. This rock lies 1,000m SSW of Punta di Molendinu and 2.9 miles on 140° from Cargèse jetty head.

POINTE DE TRIU 42°06′N 08°39′.5E

This prominent pointed rocky-cliffed headland has a 56m hill and coast road behind it, a few rocky heads close in and a 2.7m rocky shallow 250m south of the point. You are advised to keep well clear (more than 300m) of this point in all but very calm weather.

POINTE ALBELLU 42°06′.28N 08°40′.73E

This point is easy to identify due to a conspicuous tower and battery just inland standing in some trees with the coast road in front. It has many dangerous rocks close in. Again keep at least 300m off.

C20 Port de Sagone

⊕56 42°06′.0N 08°41′.5E

Sagone is a small village lying at the southeast corner of a bay at the head of the wide and deep Gulf of Sagone. A jetty and quay located on the western side of the bay offer pleasure craft a place to secure and land. Another landing is located on the eastern side of the bay and nearer the village, but this quay is reserved for local fishermen. It is an attractive area with ranges of mountains rising behind a long beach with a river mouth at its western end. The area, however, is a holiday centre and in season it is crowded with camping sites and holidaymakers and there is constant traffic on the main coast road which runs behind the area.

Approach and entry are easy as there is a conspicuous ruined tower just west of the jetty. Remember to give Pointe de Triu and Pointe Albellu a good berth if coming from the west. From the south keep outside Petra Piombata, Récif de Paliagi and Rocher de St Joseph and steer just east of north until the tower and jetty become visible. There are no lights on the jetties, so a night approach is not recommended. There are swinging moorings to the north of the jetty but even if tucked away in the western corner, any heavy swell from the SW can

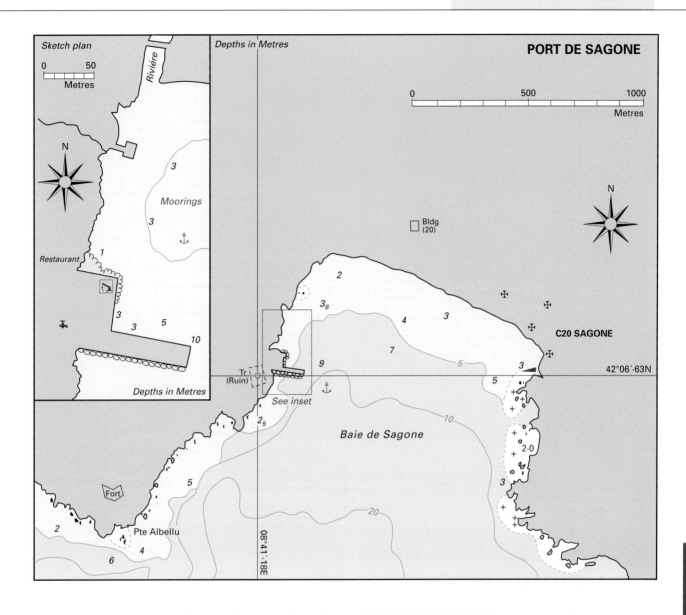

C20 SAGONE

42°06'·63N

Baie de Sagone

Pte Albellu

make it an uncomfortable anchorage (though relatively safe).

Should a strong southwest wind be forecast and no space is available in the northwestern corner of the Baie de Sagone, it is important to leave the anchorage and work out of the Golfe de Sagone. If this is not possible, some shelter can be obtained in the Baie de Liscia. Facilities are limited to everyday requirements with fuel 2km away in the village.

⚓ BAIE DE SAGONE 42°06'.5N 08°41'.5E

This large, deep, sandy-bottomed bay forms an excellent anchorage in depths of 3m up to 24m. It is open to SE–S–SW but by thoughtful choice of anchorage, the seas brought in by the southeast or southwest winds can be considerably reduced. The bay has low, rocky-cliffed sides with a long sandy beach at its head, the coast road runs around the bay and there is a road running inland. Everyday requirements can be obtained from Sagone village, (see above).

POINTE DE ST-JOSEPH
42°05'.15N 08°42'.15E (see plan page 124)

This is a sharp pointed rocky headland with an old battery on top, rocky dangers extend 300m off the point, see below.

RECIF DE ST-JOSEPH AND PASSAGE

This shallow area with one awash rock and one rocky islet (1.2m) has depths of only 1.3m to the southwest. The awash rock lies 900m WSW of Pointe St-Joseph. The reef is 400m wide, extending 900m SSW from the awash rock. The rocky islet lies near the centre of the reef. A 500m-wide passage lies between Pointe de St-Joseph and this reef with a least depth of 9m. Take the passage in NW–SE directions, equidistant between the outer awash rocks of Pointe de St-Joseph and the awash rock in the reef.

8. CARGESE TO PUNTA DE LA PARATA

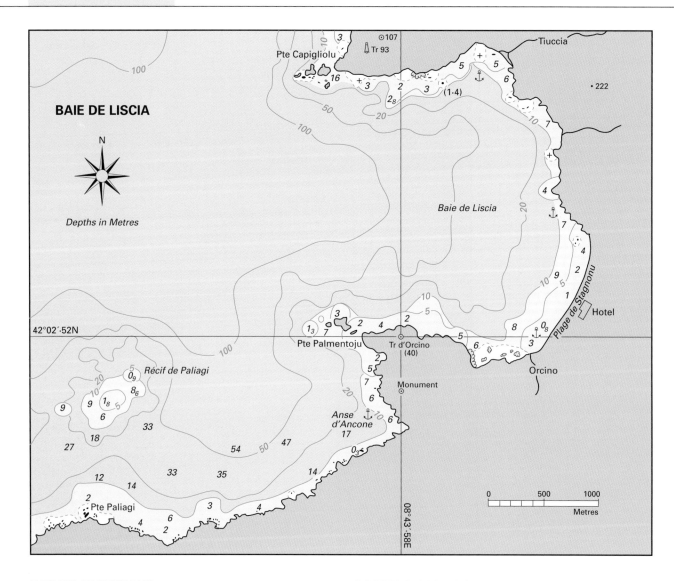

BAIE DE LISCIA

N

Depths in Metres

42°02′·52N

Baie de Liscia

Pte Capigliolu

Tiuccia

Récif de Paliagi

Pte Palmentoju

Tr d'Orcino (40)

Monument

Anse d'Ancone

Plage de Stagnonu

Hotel

Orcino

Pte Paliagi

08°43′·58E

0   500   1000
Metres

POINTE CAPIGLIOLU 42°03′.8N 08°43′.14E

A prominent, sharp, pointed rocky-cliffed headland with islet; rocks submerged and awash reaching 400m out from the point in a westerly direction. The Tour de Capigliolu on a hill 93m and an old tower 200m behind it are conspicuous.

⚓ BAIA DE LISCIA 42°03′.5N 08°44′E

Another very wide bay, which has an anchorage in a sub-bay to the northeast, with other anchorages off a long sandy beach to south. The anchorage in the northeast corner in 5m sand and weed is close to the village of Tiuccia, where everyday requirements can be bought. There are several hotels here and a mechanic at the garage. There is a small exposed rocky islet in the approach and one awash near the shore, along with some permanent moorings. This anchorage is open to SW–W–NW. The village is famous for the Capraja Castle, which belonged to the Counts of Ginarca who once ruled Corsica. This castle lies to the south of the village. The other anchorages off the sandy beach in the south of the bay are in 3m, sand, and also open to SW–WNW.

POINTE PALMENTOJU 42°02′.56N 08°43′.32E

This pointed headland has rocky cliffs, with the conspicuous Tour d'Orcino (40m) near the point with a hill sloping inland to 298m. A rocky islet and rocks, awash and covered, extend 500m westwards.

ILES DE POINTE PALMENTOJU AND PASSAGE

A short narrow passage about 50m long, 40m wide and 2.5m deep exists between the islets off the Pointe Palmentoju and the small rocks close to the point. Take a NE–SW direction with a good lookout, preferably after a reconnaissance by dinghy.

⚓ ANSE D'ANCONE 42°02′.1N 08°43′.2E

A small anchorage in 5m rock open to SW–W–NW in the east corner of a wide bay. Deserted.

POINTE PALIAGI 42°01′.67N 08°41′.48E

This is a rounded headland of rocky cliffs, with hills behind sloping up to 348m. Rocky islets extend 200m north with a 2m depth some 50m further on.

Recif de Paliagi

This reef is centred 1,200m to NNE of Pointe Paliagi. It has rocks covered 1m, 2m, 6m and 9m.

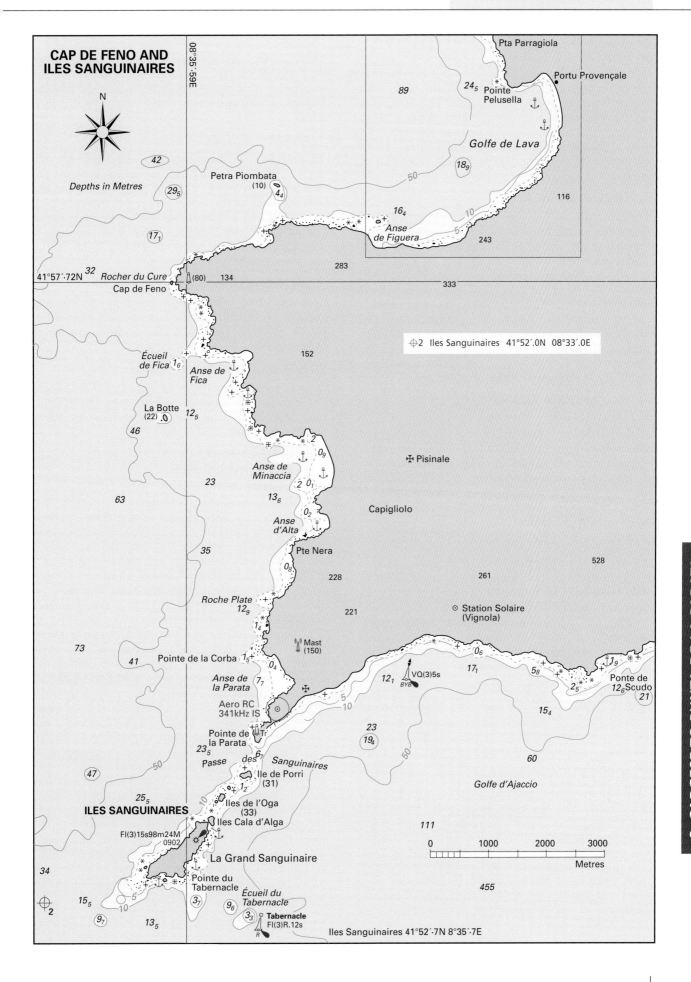

CAP DE FENO AND ILES SANGUINAIRES

N

Depths in Metres

08°35′·59E

42

29₅

17₁

41°57′·72N 32 Rocher du Cure
Cap de Feno (80) 134

Petra Piombata
(10) 4₄

283

Pta Parragiola
Portu Provençale
24₅ Pointe
Pelusella

89

Golfe de Lava

18₉

50

10

116

16₄

Anse
de Figuera

5

243

333

Écueil
de Fica 1₆
Anse de
Fica

La Botte
(22) ₀ 12₅

46

152

⊕2 Iles Sanguinaires 41°52′.0N 08°33′.0E

⊹ Pisinale

23

Anse de
Minaccia 2 0₁
13₆

0₉

2

Anse
d'Alta 0₂

Capigliolo

63

35

Pte Nera

0₈

228

261

528

Roche Plate
12₉

221

◉ Station Solaire
(Vignola)

73

41

Pointe de la Corba 1₅

1₄

0₄

Anse de
la Parata 7₇

Mast
(150)

12₁
BYB VQ(3)5s

17₁

0₆

5₈

1₉

Ponte de
2₅ 12₆ Scudo
21

15₄

Aero RC
341kHz IS ◉

Pointe de
la Parata T
23₅ 6₇

Passe des

Sanguinaires
Ile de Porri
(31)

23
19₄

5

10

50

60

Golfe d'Ajaccio

47

25₅

ILES SANGUINAIRES

Iles de l'Oga
(33)

1₂

10

Iles Cala d'Alga

Fl(3)15s98m24M
0902

La Grand Sanguinaire

111

34

Pointe du
Tabernacle

Écueil du
Tabernacle

3₇

9₆

⊕
2

15₅

9₇ 13₅

3₃

Tabernacle
Fl(3)R.12s
R

Iles Sanguinaires 41°52′·7N 8°35′·7E

455

0 1000 2000 3000

Metres

8. CARGESE TO PUNTA DE LA PARATA

POINTE PARRAGIOLA AND POINTE PELUSELLA
42°N 08°39′.2E

Pointe Parragiola has a high point of 152m (with a tower on top) and a small islet off the cliffs with Pointe Pelusella 800m to the south. This latter is a right-angled point with rocky cliffs, sloping up to 111m. A ruined tower stands close to the point. An awash isolated rock (0.8m deep) lies 350m northwest of Pointe Pelusella which is otherwise steep-to.

⚓ PORTU PROVENÇALE

The N corner of the Golfe de Lava is referred to as Portu Provençale but is actually only an anchorage that has many moorings laid for local fishing craft. There are good anchorages in 3m to 18m sand outside the moorings and off the sandy beach, open to SW–W–NW. There are many houses and several housing estates ashore, and the village can provide everyday supplies. Beach cafés, restaurants and hotels are also available. There is a road to the main coast road. The south and southwest coast of the Baie de Lava is foul with many rocks including a small islet, La Figuera, 300m off the coast.

PETRA PIOMBATA AND PASSAGE
41°58′.6N 08°36′.7E

A small islet lies 700m off the coast at the southern side of the entrance to the Golfe de Lava. The islet is steep-to except for a rock 2m deep off the SE end of the islet. A 7m depth lies halfway between the island and the shore. A passage 200m wide, 100m long with a minimum depth of 10m lies 150m off the coast in E–W directions.

CAP DE FENO 41°57′.7N 08°35′.46E

A very prominent point with high rocky broken cliffs and a conspicuous ruined tower standing on an 80m hill inland 200m from the point. The point has two close inshore islets on its western face and some small rocks extending 150m in a southwesterly direction, otherwise it is steep-to. In certain lights when approaching from the south, the ruined tower has the appearance of a seated cat.

Écueil de Fica 41°57′.02N 08°35′.49E

A rock (covered 1.6m) is located 1,250m south of Cap de Feno. Unless intending to go into Anse de Fica, it is recommended to go outside this rock (and La Botte – see below) on a passage south.

⚓ ANSE DE FICA 41°57′N 08°36′.1E

Two popular anchorages, the north of which is in a rocky-sided bay off a white, sandy beach in 6m sand and weed open to S–SW–W. There is a road and a track ashore, with some houses. This anchorage is the best of the two and offers the best protection. The southern anchorage is in a small bay with rocky sides and a sandy beach. Anchor off the beach in 2m, sand, also open to S–SW–W. There is a road ashore. Deserted. A rocky projection divides these two anchorages.

La Botte 41°56′.5N 08°35′.35E

This 22m-high island is just over a mile south of Cap de Feno. With the exception of an outlier to its southwest it is steep-to. There is a wide passage between it and the shore with a minimum depth of 12m.

⚓ ANSE DE MINACCIA 41°56′.2N 08°37′.1E

This large bay has a long sandy beach with anchorages at each end. Anchor in 3m sand off the beach open to S–SW–W. Sand dunes lie behind the northern end of the beach. There are tracks behind the beach and a few houses with a housing estate behind the southern end of the beach, where there is a beach café. A rock (covered 1m) lies 200m off the south end of the beach.

⚓ ANSE D'ALTA 41°55′.6N 08°37′.2E

This small bay, with a sandy beach at its head, has rocky sides. Anchor off the beach in 3m, sand, open to SW–W–NW. There is a road and housing estate behind the beach.

POINTE DE LA CORBA 41°54′.5N 08°36′.6E

A small rocky point slopes up inland to 211m. There are many small rocks extending up to 200m from the coast and an isolated rock 2m deep lies 400m WSW of the point.

POINTE DE LA PARATA 41°53′.7N 08°36′.45E
AND ILES SANGUINAIRES

An attractive headland and islands lying in a SW–NE direction which is similar to the Raz du Sein in Brittany but without the strong tidal streams. From the northeast the high (283m) hills slope down to the Presqu'île de la Parata which consists of two distinctive parts, a low flat isthmus connected to a rounded feature with a small house and radio beacon mast on the top (86m). There is a road on the southeastern side leading to a restaurant. A second very low isthmus connects the first part to the second feature which is of a pyramid shape (58m) with a conspicuous tower on top. It is essential to identify this feature if attempting the Passe des Sanguinaires, as from a distance it simply looks like two more islands.

Southwest of this pass lies Ile de Porri (two islets, Iles de l'Oga and Iles Cala d'Alga). Between these four islets it is shallow and foul with rocky heads. The largest island; Ile de la Grande Sanguinaire, is the outer island, it has a white lighthouse, black top and white dwelling (Fl(3)15s98m24M) on the crest near the northeastern end. A signal station is located near the centre of the island and a tower stands near the southwestern end. There are rocks and shallows extending 500m southwestwards from this point. The Écueil du Tabernacle, an isolated rock 3m deep, is 1,300m to southeast of the centre of this island and it is marked by a red pillar light buoy with a can topmark (Fl(3)R.12s4m3M).

Passages des Sanguinaires

The main passage is the Passe des Sanguinaires between the Pointe de la Parata and Ile de Porri. It is 200m long and 200m wide, with a minimum depth of 7m. Take the passage in E–W directions about 50m from the Pointe de la Parata and 150m from Ile de Porri. For yachts drawing 2m or less, the passage is 400m wide with a minimum depth of 2.8m. Currents of up to 3 knots can be experienced in the area and these frequently set across the passage. Under conditions of heavy seas and strong winds the use of this passage is not recommended. Instead proceed south and round the end of La Grande Sanguinaire keeping over ½M to the southwest and pass outside the Écueil du Tabernacle light buoy.

Grande Sanguinaire from the SW

⚓ LA GRANDE SANGUINAIRE 41°52´.6N 08°35´.5E

There are three small anchorages on the SE side of this island.

1. A very small anchorage in a little bay between the Ile Cala d'Alga and the northeastern end of La Grande Sanguinaire, anchor in 3m, sand and rock, open to NE–E–SE–S.
2. A large anchorage just north of the Pointe du Tabernacle which projects in a southeasterly direction from the middle of the island. There are two 3m-deep rocks and also small rocks close in along the coast. Anchor in 2m, rock, open to NE–E–SE. There is a small landing stage used by ferries bringing day tourists from Ajaccio.
3. A very small anchorage just below and to the southeast of the tower on southwestern end of La Grande Sanguinaire in 4m, rock, open to E–SE–S–SW. There is a small stony beach ashore.

8. CARGESE TO PUNTA DE LA PARATA

IV. North Sardinia

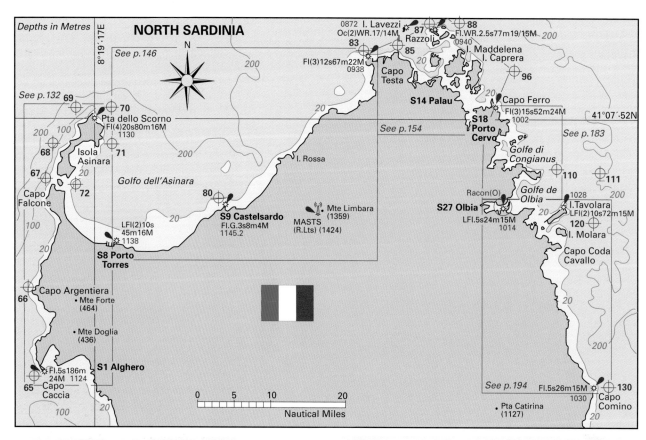

Depths in Metres

NORTH SARDINIA

8°19′.17E

See p.146

See p.132 69

See p.132

0872 I. Lavezzi
Oc(2)WR.17/14M
83
Fl(3)12s67m22M
0938

87
Razzoli
85
88
Fl.WR.2.5s77m19/15M
0940
I. Maddelena
I. Caprera
96

200

41°07′.52N

Capo
Testa

S14 Palau

Capo Ferro
Fl(3)15s52m24M
1002

See p.183

70
Pta dello Scorno
Fl(4)20s80m16M
1130

S18
Porto
Cervo

Golfe di
Congianus

68
Isola
Asinara
71

67

Capo
Falcone
72

Golfo dell'Asinara

I. Rossa

See p.154

110
111

Racon(O)
Golfe de
Olbia
1028
I.Tavolara
LFl(2)10s72m15M
120
I. Molara

200

80
Pta Vignola

S9 Castelsardo
Fl.G.3s8m4M
1145.2

Mte Limbara
(1359)
MASTS
(R.Lts) (1424)

S27 Olbia
LFl.5s24m15M
1014

LFl(2)10s
45m16M
1138

S8 Porto
Torres

Capo Argentiera
66
• Mte Forte
(464)

Capo Coda
Cavallo

20

• Mte Doglia
(436)

S1 Alghero

Fl.5s186m
24M 1124
65 Capo
Caccia

100

See p.194   Fl.5s26m15M
1030
130
Capo
Comino

• Pta Catirina
(1127)

0 5 10 20
Nautical Miles

⊕65	Capo Caccia	40°32′.5N	08°08′.5E
⊕66	C. Argentiera	40°44′.0N	08°07′.0E
⊕67	C. Falcone	40°58′.5N	08°10′.5E
⊕68	C. Tumberino	41°03′.0N	08°11′.5E
⊕69	C. dello Scorno W	41°08′.5N	08°16′.0E
⊕70	C. dello Scorno E	41°08′.5N	08°22′.0E
⊕71	C. Trabuccato	41°03′.0N	08°22′.5E
⊕72	Fornelli	40°57′.6N	08°16′.0E
⊕80	Pta. Vignola	40°56′.0N	08°41′.5E
⊕83	Capo Testa	41°15′.5N	09°08′.0E
⊕85	Pta Falcone	41°16′.5N	09°14′.5E
⊕87	N of Razzoli	41°19′.0N	09°20′.0E
⊕88	N of Maddelena	41°19′.0N	09°25′.5E
⊕96	Monaci	41°13′.0N	09°35′.0E
⊕110	Capo Figari	41°00′.0N	09°43′.0E
⊕111	Capo Figari approach	41°00′.0N	09°50′.0E
⊕120	Ile Molara	40°52′.5N	09°49′.0E
⊕130	Capo Comino	40°32′.0N	09°52′.0E

LIGHTS

1124 **Capo Caccia** 40°33′.6N 08°09′.8E Fl.5s186m24M
  White tower on 3-storey building 24m

1130 **Punta dello Scorno** (Asinara) 41°07′.1N 08°19′.1E
  Fl(4)20s80m16M
  White tower on 3-storey building 35m

1138 **Porto Torres** 40°50′.1N 08°23′.8E LFl(2)10s45m16M
  White tower on 2-storey building 20m

1145.2 **Castelsardo outer mole** Fl.G.3s8m4M Green post
  5m

0938 **Capo Testa** 41°14′.6N 09°08′.7E Fl(3)12s67m17M
  017°-vis-256°
  White tower on 2-storey building 23m

0872 **Ile Lavezzi** Oc(2) WR.6s27m17/14M White tower,
  red bands 12m

0940 **Isola Razzoli** 41°18′.4N 09°20′.4E
  Fl.WR.2.5s77m19/15M 022°-W-092°-R-137°-W-237°-R-320°
  Stone tower 12m

1002 **Capo Ferro** 41°09′.3N 09°31′.4E Fl(3)15s52m24M
  White tower on 2-storey building 18m

1014 **Isola della Bocca** (Olbia) 40°55′.2N 09°34′.0E
  LFl.5s24m15M 180°-vis-264°
  White tower on 2-storey building 22m

1028 **Punta Timone** (Tavolara) 40°55′.6N 09°44′.0E
  LFl(2)10s72m15M
  White octagonal tower 7m

1030 **Capo Comino** 40°31′.7N 09°49′.7E Fl.5s26m15M
  White tower on building 20m

Sardinia is the second largest island in the Mediterranean after Sicily. It is 260km long and 135km wide with an area of 24,093sq km. It has a coastline of 1,850km (which is almost exactly 1,000 nautical miles) long. It lies 110 miles from the Italian mainland, 7 miles from Corsica, 120 miles from Africa and 200M from the Balearic Islands. It is a mountainous island with the main range running down the east coast with the highest peak, Punta La Marmora, reaching 1,834m (6,000ft). There is another range in the southwest corner, around the mining area of Iglesias, with the high point of

1,236m (4,050ft) of Monte Linas. Sardinia has a population of around one and a half million but is quite barren for much of its area as the population is concentrated around the main towns. The mountains are covered with small bushes (*macchia* in Italian or *maquis* in French) which give out a scent in the spring which, once experienced, is never forgotten and is unmistakably the perfume of the islands.

History

The early history of Sardinia is closely linked to that of Corsica. Around 2000BC, groups of settlers arrived and possibly developed into the Nuraghi Civilisation, who built large stone-block domed towers, called *nuraghe*, similar to the towers on Corsica and the *talayots* of the Balearics. They also buried their dead in caves and tombs called 'tombs of the giants'. Then the Phoenicians occupied various parts of the island: remains can still be seen on the islands of San Pietro and Sant'Antioco off the southwest corner. The Romans arrived in 236BC and Sardinia became a Roman province with various civil, Greek and Etruscan wars, until final capitulation in about 46BC, when Caesar made Cagliari a municipality. Roman domination now lasted for 400 years, with much building going on. Cagliari, Nora and Tharros were large Roman towns with temples, spas, hot and cold water systems, etc. Over the centuries there has been a rise in sea level and areas of Tharros and Nora can be seen on calm days under the sea.

From about AD500 to 1000 the island was ravaged by the Vandals, Ostrogoths, Byzantines and finally the Saracens. In 1077 the Pope assigned Sardinia (along with Corsica) to the Pisans; this was disputed by the Genoese. Then another Pope gave it to the Aragonese who finally installed a king (around AD1430) and Spain ruled it for some years, always with local unrest.

In 1708 Cagliari surrendered to a British fleet under Admiral Lake, Sardinia was ceded to Austria and the Dukes of Savoy and it has remained Italian ever since. It is interesting to note that Nelson wanted to take the island for England (rather than Malta) and used many of the anchorages on its northeast coast during the blockade of the French in the early eighteen hundreds.

During the 1930s the Fascist Government completed great works on the island: draining of swamps, new roads and assistance with mining. It was important as an airfield during the second world war and several towns were severely damaged by the bombs of both sides. The island was granted political autonomy in 1948.

Data and warnings

From Asinara Island on the northwestern corner to Punta Coda Cavallo on the east coast there are numerous islands and each of these is bordered by even more numerous rocks and shoals. Some of these rocks are marked with posts or buoys but the majority are not. It is not recommended to sail close inshore at night. Bonifacio Straits are well known for their strong west (and east) winds. Winds, mainly the *maestrale*, can be quite strong, Force 6 or 7 even in summer, and blow for several days at a time.

Prohibited areas

1. Navigation, anchoring, fishing and landing are prohibited in the areas surrounding Isola Asinara (41°N 8°16′E) except for vessels in difficulties. (It used to be a penal colony but is now a nature reserve with the same prohibitions about landing, etc. as before). Navigation is permitted through the Fornelli passage in daylight, as is landing on Isola Piana.
2. It is prohibited to navigate or berth at the Italian naval base east of Cala Gavetta on La Maddalena.
3. It is prohibited to enter the NATO naval base on the NE corner of Santo Stefano Island.
4. The whole of the NE part of Tavolara Island is a military area and anchoring is prohibited.

As well as these, the Italians have established nature reserves on some of the small islands and more interesting coastal areas, (around the Maddalena archipelago) for example. These areas are described in more detail in Chapter II above. Visiting yachts should note any local areas and abide by the regulations set out to maintain the reserve.

Major lights

The light ranges in these waters were originally set up to ensure one could always see a light when cruising along the coast. In areas like La Maddalena, there is a plethora of street and car lights which can confuse the unwary). (In other, more remote, areas there are hardly any lights to be seen at all. The intensities of virtually all lights have been markedly reduced over the past 10-year period, therefore the given ranges are only achieved in excellent visibility, with binoculars trained on the bearing. At times, only half the given ranges are achieved.

Maritime authorities in Sardinia

The Sardinian authorities have a slightly different arrangement to that which is common in Corsica. Here there is a harbourmaster for the major ports and he may also have jurisdiction over several smaller ports in the vicinity. His main interest is in the commercial traffic of the port and, in general, he has little or no interest in pleasure craft. These are catered for by the harbourmaster delegating responsibility for the various areas set aside for pleasure craft moorings to private individuals and yacht clubs, who run their various sections as they see fit.

Thus, contacting the harbour office – *capitainerie* – may not yield direct information regarding mooring possibilities, but they should be able to give you the telephone number or VHF channel to contact for mooring details. It is difficult to give precise details of each and every firm who administer the moorings in any particular harbour as they change relatively frequently, but information given in this pilot has been gathered during a visit to the island in autumn 2005 and is as up to date as possible.

1 ALGHERO TO STINTINO

From the safety of Alghero's superb harbour the coast runs northwest with excellent beaches until Fertilia is reached. The coast then turns west and becomes more rocky with low cliffs until the large shallow inlet of Porto Conte. On the west side of this inlet the cliffs rise up to nearly 200 metres off Capo Caccia. Once round the headland the coast runs north for some 25 miles to Capo Falcone with high cliffs and no real harbours. This section of coast is open to the prevailing NW winds and if the mistral is blowing it is a dangerous place to be as the reflected waves from the cliffs can kick up a very confused sea which makes it very difficult, if not impossible to go to windward. North of Capo Falcone lies the 8 mile long island of Asinara, which although not a penal colony any more, is still a protected area and landing is only permitted with the authorities permission on the east side at the Rada della Reale. Between the island and Capo Falcone there is the Fornelli Passage which can be taken in reasonable weather and saves the 25 miles required to circumnavigate Asinara. Once through the passage Stintino is just around the low headland of Punta Negra.

1122 **I della Maddalena** Fl.R.5s10m4M
    White tower red bands 6m
1126 **Torre Nuova** Fl.3s17m10M
    White tower 8m
1124 **Capo Caccia** Fl.5s186m24M
    White tower on building 24m
1130 **Pta. dello Scorno** Fl(4)20s80m16M
    White tower on building 35m
1134.4 **Stintino outer mole head**
    Fl.G.4s6m8M Green post
1138 **Porto Torres** LFl(2)10s45m16M
    White tower on building 20m

Light 1117.2 at port hand entrance to Alghero (see page 135)

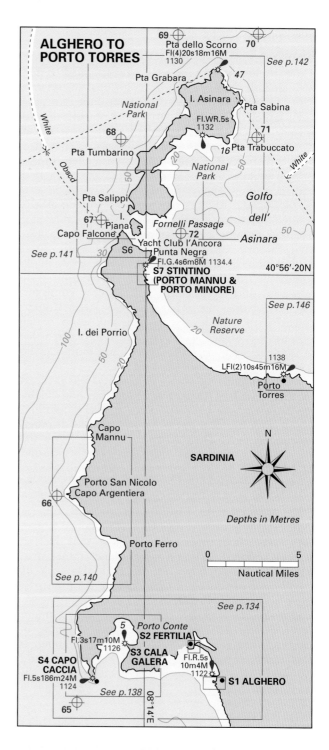

⊕65	Capo Caccia	40°32'.5N	08°08'.5E
⊕66	C. Argentiera	40°44'.0N	08°07'.0E
⊕67	C. Falcone	40°58'.5N	08°10'.5E
⊕68	C. Tumberino	41°03'.0N	08°11'.5E
⊕69	C. dello Scorno W	41°08'.5N	08°16'.0E
⊕70	C. dello Scorno E	41°08'.5N	08°22'.0E
⊕71	C. Trabuccato	41°03'.0N	08°22'.5E
⊕72	Fornelli	40°57'.6N	08°16'.0E

Above Cappo Caccia from Torre Nuova (see page 138)   *Below* Looking S/SW towards Stintino (see page 144)

PLANNING GUIDE

Headlands	Ports & anchorages		Open to winds
	S1 ⚓	**Alghero page 135**	
	S2 ⚓	**Fertilia page 137**	S–SW
	⚓	*Cala Galera*	E
Capo Galera			
	S3 ⚓	**Base Nautica Porto Conte page 138**	NW
	S4 ⚓	**Cala Tramariglio page 138**	E
	⚓	*Cala del Bollo (Neptune's Cave)*	E
Capo Caccia			
	⚓	*Porto Ferro*	S–NW
Capo Argentiera			
	⚓	*Porto San Nicolo*	SW–N
Capo Falcone			
Fornelli Passage			
Isola Asinara	**S5** ⚓	**Rada della Reale page 143**	E–SE–S
Isola Piana	**S6** ⚓	**Yacht Club l'Ancora page 143**	W–NW
Punta Negra			
	S7 ⚓	**Stintino page 144**	E
		Porto Mannu page 145	
		Porto Minore page 145	
		New development page 145	

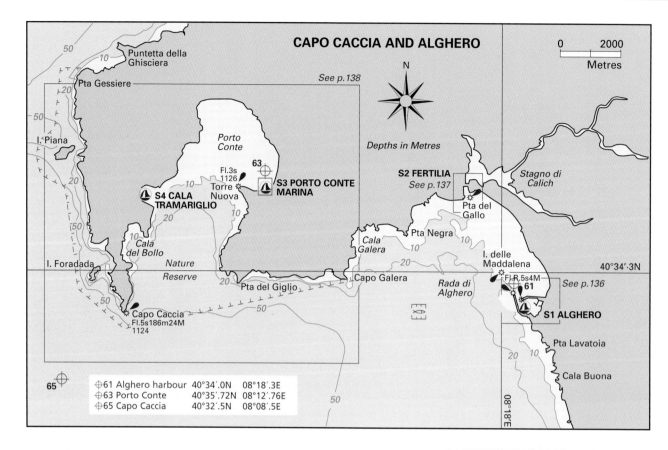

CAPO CACCIA AND ALGHERO

0 — 2000
Metres

N

Puntetta della Ghisciera

Pta Gessiere

See p.138

Depths in Metres

I. Piana

Porto Conte

Fl.3s 1126 Torre Nuova

63

S3 PORTO CONTE MARINA

S2 FERTILIA
See p.137

Pta del Gallo

Stagno di Calich

S4 CALA TRAMARIGLIO

Cala del Bollo

Nature Reserve

I. Foradada

Pta Negra

Cala Galera

Capo Galera

I. delle Maddalena

Fl.R.5s4M

40°34'.3N

61

See p.136

Rada di Alghero

S1 ALGHERO

Pta del Giglio

Capo Caccia
Fl.5s186m24M
1124

Pta Lavatoia

Cala Buona

08°18'E

65

⊕61 Alghero harbour	40°34'.0N	08°18'.3E
⊕63 Porto Conte	40°35'.72N	08°12'.76E
⊕65 Capo Caccia	40°32'.5N	08°08'.5E

1124 **Capo Caccia** Fl.5s186m24M
   White tower on building 24m
1126 **Torre Nuova** Fl.3s17m10M
   White tower 8m
1122 **I della Maddalena** Fl.R.5s10m4M
   White tower, red bands 6m

Alghero looking S

S1 Alghero

⊕61 40°34′.0N 08°18′.3E

Charts
Admiralty *1985, 1202*
Italian *48, 292, 911/05*

Depth
0.5 to 3.5m

Number of berths
In excess of 1000

Maximum LOA
70m

Lights
1122 Isolotto della Maddalena 40°34′.3N 08°18′.0E
Fl.R.5s10m4M White tower red bands 6m
1117 Molo Sud head 40°33′.9N 08°18′.4E Fl.G.3s10m8M
Green column 6m
1117.2 Molo Sottoflutto Head Fl.R.3s10m8M Red
column 6m'
1117.3 Molo Sottoflutto spur head 2F.R(vert)6m2M Red
post 5m
1119 Molo Nord head 2F.R(vert)7m3M Red post 6m
1117.6 Pontoon No.2 head 2F.GR(vert)4m3M Green and
red pole
1117.5 Pontoon No.1 head 2F.RG(vert) 4m3M Red and
green pole
1118 Banchina Sanità 2F.G(vert)7m3M Green post 6m
1119.4 New basin (left hand entrance) F.R.5m4M Red
post 4m
1119.5 Molo Furesi (right hand entrance) F.G.5m5M
Green post 4m

Port communications
Capitaneria VHF Ch 16 from 0800–2000 ☎ 079 953 174
Fax 079 984 606.
Yacht Club Alghero ☎ 079 952 074
Centro Alghermar ☎ 079 953 677
Ser-Mar di Crisafulli ☎ 347.7720544 (Frederico)
☎ 079 978 413 *Email* fecrisa@tiscali.it
Marina di S. Elmo ☎/*Fax* 079980 829/*Mobile* 333 2214342
Email info@marinadisanelmo.it
url www.marinadisanelmo.it
Aquatica ☎ 079 983 199 *Fax* 079 989 2001
Mobile 348 1303966
Email aquatica@tiscali.it *url* www.aquaticasardegna.it
Consortium of Internal Port Services ☎ 079 989 3117
Mobile 339.7329921 *Email* info@portodialghero.com
url www.portodialghero.com

A superb and safe harbour

Alghero was a delightful old walled Catalan city, with Spanish (and Gothic) style buildings and street names, set amid   groves of olive, eucalyptus and parasol pine trees but it is now becoming more and more a tourist resort with hotels taking the place of the trees. However, it is well worth a visit and the harbour authorities are making great efforts to attract the charter fleets down from Corsica by putting in many more pontoons in the harbour during the summer season. Further work is now ongoing in the west of the harbour. In October 2005 there was a dredger working, the Secca delle Murge has gone and the Molo Sud is being built up to take a promenade with berths for large yachts and motor cruisers. (See also photos on pages 11 and 132)

Approach

Both day and night approaches are straightforward, although major construction work is still continuing and pontoons are still being installed in various parts of the harbour. Also there is now a fish farm operating to the west of the entrance in approximate position 40°33′N 8°16′E. It is marked by a buoy at its centre (Fl.Y.5s2m3M with a × topmark) and there may be other buoys to the west with stroboscopic rotating lights (25 times a minute).

By day

The suburbs of large hotels and villas to the south of Alghero and the Isolotto della Maddalena to the north are conspicuous as the harbour entrance is approached. There are no particular dangers and when the southern breakwater is identified make for the outer end.

By night

Use the light on Isolotto delle Maddalena to approach on a northeasterly heading until the light on the southern breakwater is picked up.

By GPS

From the north steer to ⊕65 off Capo Caccia then alter to ⊕61. On arrival steer to leave the jetty head clear to port.

Entrance

This is quite simple, but note the course to enter between the breakwaters is just east of south.

Berths

There are now six or seven mooring areas for pleasure craft with over 1,000 berths, and craft entering are now met by representatives of the various companies touting for business. If this does not happen phone one or other of the companies to see if there are any spare berths. Unfortunately it appears that the capitano di porto, having delegated his authority to the various companies, is somewhat disinterested in pleasure craft but should be able to give telephone numbers of possible berth holders.

Formalities

All authorities are available.

Facilities

All.

Archaeology

For those interested in archaeology there are many examples of the famous Sardinian nuraghi and burial sites that abound in this part of the world. (See phootos on pages 8 and 9)

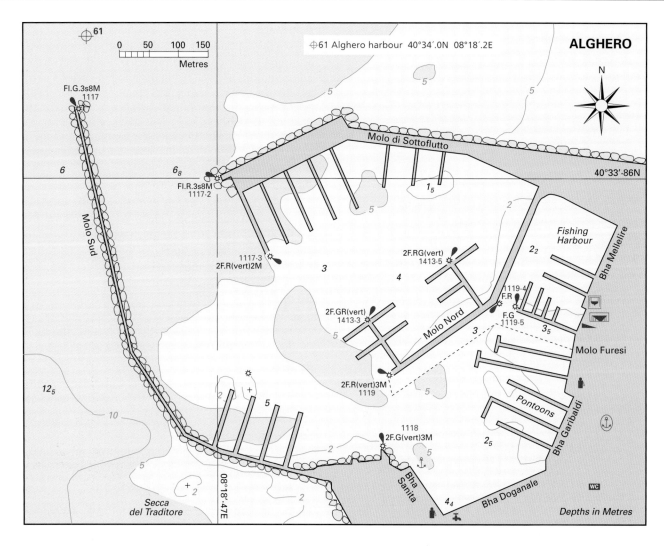

⊕61

0 50 100 150
Metres

⊕61 Alghero harbour 40°34′.0N 08°18′.2E

ALGHERO

N

Fl.G.3s8M
1117

5

5

5

Molo di Sottoflutto

40°33′.86N

6

6₈

Fl.R.3s8M
1117·2

5

2

1₅

Molo Sud

1117·3
2F.R(vert)2M

3

2F.RG(vert)
1413·5

4

2₂

*Fishing
Harbour*

Bha Melletire

2F.GR(vert)
1413·3

5

Molo Nord

3

1119·4
F.R

F.G
1119·5

3₅

Molo Furesi

2F.R(vert)3M
1119

5

12₅

10

2

5

1118
2F.G(vert)3M

5

Pontoons

Bha Garibaldi

2₅

5

2

2

*Secca
del Traditore*

08°18′.47E

Bha
Sanita

Bha Doganale

4₄

WC

Depths in Metres

Alghero

S2 Fertilia

⊕62 40°35´.4N 08°17´.6E

Depth
0.5 to 3.5m

Number of berths
250

Maximum LOA
30m

Lights
1122.5 Outer Mole Head F.R.7m3M Red pole 5m (P)
1122.6 Inner Mole Head F.G.7m3M Green pole 5m (P)

Port communications
Base Nautica Usai ☎ 079 930 233 *Fax* 079 930 088
Email basenauticausai@tiscali.it
url www.basenauticausai.it
Base Nautica CAM Mobile ☎ 338 722 2440

A small harbour

This small harbour lies at the very north of Alghero Bay on the exit canal from the Stagno di Calich. The village, to the left of the harbour, has a conspicuous steeple and there is a large, off-white, low building to the right of the harbour. The harbour consists of a long breakwater running east–west, which is rounded on the port hand to enter on a westerly course. The quay to the east is reserved for the private company moorings (Base Nautica Usai) but space may be available there for visiting yachts. Pleasure craft are also moored to the pontoons on the western side and to the inside of the southern mole, but these moorings are all privately owned and are not available for visiting yachts. Base Nautica CAM has a yard in the SW corner of the harbour and although it has no moorings available it has excellent repair facilities. The village close by can supply basic supplies and fuel.

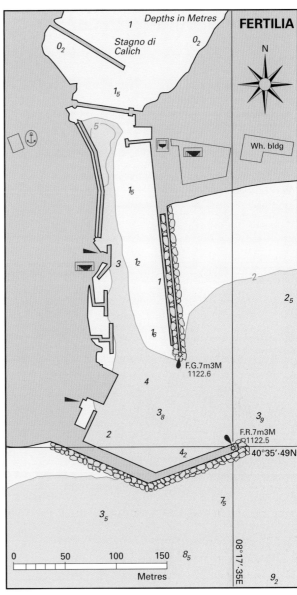

⚓ **CALA GALERA** 40°34´.75N 08°15´E

On the west side of Alghero Bay is Capo Galera. About half a mile north of the point is another small headland which has Torre Galera on it. In strong westerlies good shelter can be found in the bay just to the north of the tower where you can anchor quite close to the shore, in 5m, in sand and weed. Do not go too far north as rocks protrude from the headland at the north end of the little bay.

Fertilia looking N

S3 Base Nautica Porto Conte

⊕63 40°35′.72N 08°12′.76E

Depth
1.5 to 3m

Number of berths
300 with 10 for visitors

Maximum LOA
25m

Lights
1126 Torre Nuova Fl.3s 17m10M White tower, 8m
1127 Molo W head F.R.2m1M White pole (P)
1127.2 Molo E head F.G.2m1M White pole (P)

Port communications
Office VHF Ch 9 ☎/*Fax* 079 942 013
Email info@portocontemarina.it
url ww.portocontemarina.it

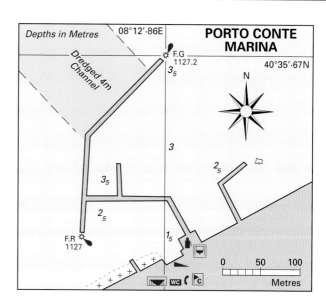

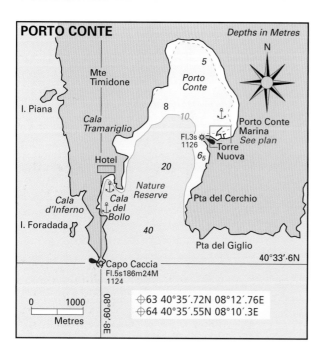

A sheltered port

Just to the east of Capo Caccia lies the large bay of Porto Conte with a headland halfway up on the eastern shore with Torre Nuova on it. About half a mile to the east of the point lies the small yacht harbour. This is a private marina with a long concrete jetty with pontoons attached, and the harbour is approached along a dredged channel (to 4m). Care must be exercised on the approach as it is very shallow outside the dredged channel. This is a very sheltered harbour with only very strong *maestrale* setting up a chop in the mooring area. All normal repair facilities are available here but food stores are limited to everyday needs and these are only available at a village 1.5kms away.

S4 Cala Tramariglio

⊕64 40°35′.55N 08°10′.3E

On the western side of the bay, opposite Torre Nuova, there is a small bay with 2 private jetties which can be used for mooring by yachts up to 10m in depths of 0.2–2m. One can also anchor off in 3–4m in sand and weed. The jetties are owned by the Club Nautico Capo Caccia which can be contacted on ☎ 079 946 638. There are very limited facilities here: showers and WCs and refuse collection but little else.

⚓ CALA DEL BOLLO 40°34′.7N 08°10′.E

In this bay just south of Tramariglio there is a large hotel complex at the north end where you can anchor off in 3–6m in sand and weed. From the south end of this *cala* it is an easy walk to the famous Grotto di Nettuno (Neptune's Cave) down the 760-odd steps of the L'Escala del Cabirol.

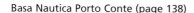
Basa Nautica Porto Conte (page 138)

Capo Caccia

Capo Caccia (see also photo page 133)

CAPO CACCIA 40°33′.6N 08°09′.8E

Capo Caccia is a very conspicuous headland, with 150m-high chalk cliffs dropping straight into the sea. There are no offlying dangers and the 2 small islets of Piana and Foradada just north of the point can be passed inside in settled weather without any concern. There is a lighthouse on the point (Fl.5s186m24M) and numbers of caves, of which the Grotto di Nettuno is the most famous.

From Capo Caccia to Capo Falcone there are 23 miles of high rocky cliffs with virtually no beaches. The prevailing westerly winds drive big seas against this forbidding coastline, with very confused reflections, and it is as well to seek calmer waters further north or south. However, in calm weather there are two possible anchorages, as follows.

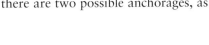

Isola Foradada N and W of Capo Caccia

Cave at Capo Caccia

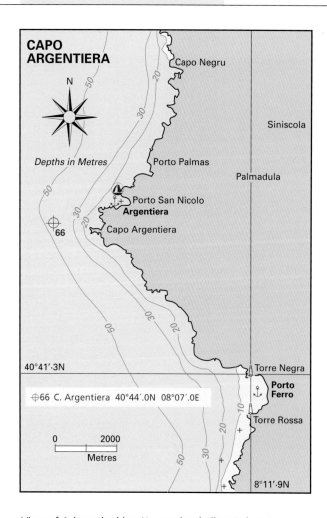

CAPO ARGENTIERA

N

Depths in Metres

Capo Negru

Siniscola

Porto Palmas

Palmadula

Porto San Nicolo

Argentiera

Capo Argentiera

⊕ 66

40°41'·3N

⊕66 C. Argentiera 40°44'.0N 08°07'.0E

Torre Negra

Porto Ferro

Torre Rossa

0   2000
Metres

8°11'·9N

View of Asinara looking N over the shallow Pelosa Passage, Isola Piana at centre right with the Fornelli passage between it and Asinara in the background

⚓ **Porto Ferro** 40°41'N 08°11'.6E

Some 8 miles north of Capo Caccia is a small bay with a beach with Torre Negra at the north end and Torre Rossa at the south. Anchor off in 4–6m in sand with excellent holding. Note that it is totally exposed to the prevailing winds and you should not stay overnight unless convinced of a stable weather pattern.

⚓ **Porto San Nicolo** 40°44'.5N 08°08'.4E

Five miles further north, just after rounding Capo Argentiera, there is a small anchorage with the remains of a 20m jetty. This was the jetty used for exporting the silver mined at Argentiera just inland and was used until the mines stopped working in the sixties. The jetty has been broken up by the seas over the last 45 years and it is now dangerous to approach it. You can anchor in the middle of the bay in 10–12m. Again, this must only be contemplated in settled weather.

San Nicolo

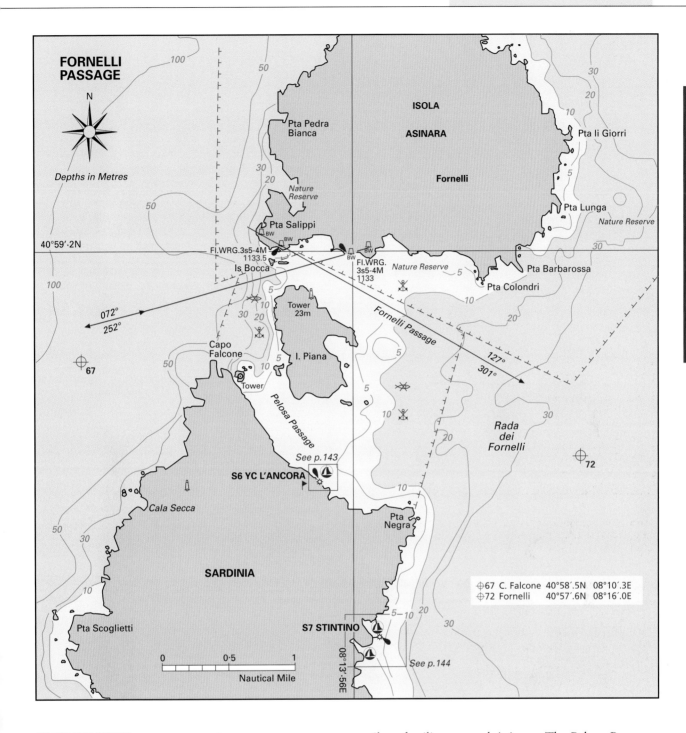

CAPO FALCONE 40°58'.35N 08°12'.1E

This is another impressive headland with 100m-high cliffs on the west side but sloping more gently down on the east side. There is a conspicuous tower on a high point (189m) one mile south of the point.

FORNELLI PASSAGE

North of Capo Falcone lies Isola Asinara, a 9-mile long fairly hilly island which was, until recently, an Italian penal colony. It is now a large nature reserve and it is still totally prohibited to land or anchor near the island. There is a shallow passage (minimum depth 3m), the Fornelli passage, between the island and Capo Falcone which saves about 25

miles of sailing around Asinara. The Pelosa Passage between Isola Piana and Capo Falcone should not be used. It has a minimum depth of less than 2m and if there is any swell, which there usually is, the depth is correspondingly less.

By day

To use the Fornelli passage from the south or west, identify the conspicuous tower 1 mile south of Capo Falcone itself at the top of a hill (183m high) and take up a position about half a mile NNW of the cape. Steer towards the north end of Isola Piana, or the tower on its north shore, until the leading marks are identified. These are on the south shore of

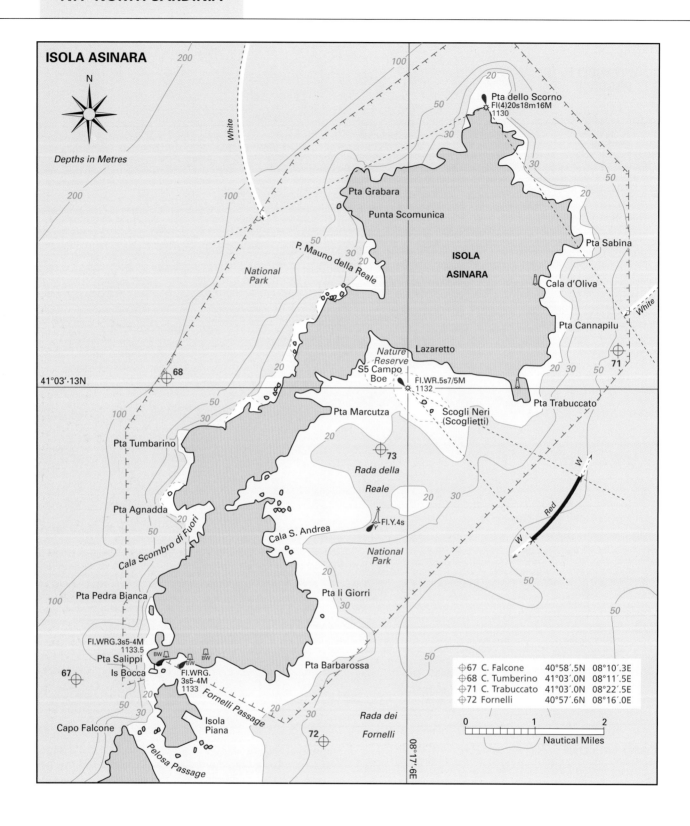

ISOLA ASINARA

N

Depths in Metres

200

200

100

White

100

50

30

20

Pta dello Scorno
Fl(4)20s18m16M
1130

20

50

30

30

20

50

White

Pta Grabara

Punta Scomunica

P. Mauno della Reale

50

30

20

National
Park

**ISOLA
ASINARA**

Pta Sabina

Cala d'Oliva

Pta Cannapilu

41°03′.13N

68

20

Nature
Reserve
S5 Campo
Boe

Lazaretto

Fl.WR.5s7/5M
1132

20 30

50

71

50

30

Pta Marcutza

Scogli Neri
(Scoglietti)

Pta Trabuccato

20

Pta Tumbarino

100

30

20

73

Rada della

Reale

20

30

Pta Agnadda

20

50

Cala Scombro di Fuori

Cala S. Andrea

Fl.Y.4s

20

*National
Park*

W

Red

W

50

100

Pta Pedra Bianca

Pta li Giorri

30

50

Fl.WRG.3s5-4M
1133.5

BW

BW

67	C. Falcone	40°58′.5N	08°10′.3E
68	C. Tumberino	41°03′.0N	08°11′.5E
71	C. Trabuccato	41°03′.0N	08°22′.5E
72	Fornelli	40°57′.6N	08°16′.0E

Pta Salippi

67

Is Bocca

Fl.WRG.
3s5-4M
1133

BW

Pta Barbarossa

50

Capo Falcone

50

30

20

Fornelli Passage

20

30

Isola
Piana

72

*Rada dei
Fornelli*

08°17′.6E

0   1   2

Nautical Miles

Pelosa Passage

Asinara and are white masonry towers with a black line. The leading line is 072° and should be kept until just past a small islet (Is Bocca) to port, when two further masonry beacons will be seen on the port beam/quarter. When these come into line alter course to 121° and steam out keeping them in line astern. The shallow 3m patch is just off the Isolotto Bocca. For the passage west simply reverse the above, i.e. steer 301° until the eastern leading markers come into line astern and then alter course to 252°.

By night

Recently two sectored lights were placed at the front marker of each leading line, which enables craft to proceed through the passage at night (previously it was a daylight-only passage) but see warning note below. These lights are:

1133 Ldg line 072° Fl.WRG.3s6m6-4M 065.2°-G-068.2°-W-076.2°-R-079.2°
1133.5 Ldg line 301° Fl.WRG.3s6m5-4M 293.3°-G-297°-W-305°-R-308.7°

Steer to a position in the white sector of one light and follow the course towards that light, keeping in the white sector until you reach the white sector of the other light. Then alter course as appropriate.

Warning note

After strong winds have been blowing in one direction for some days there may be up to a 2-knot surface current flowing through the passage, so it is advisable to use this passage in settled weather only, especially at night.

S5 Rada della Reale

⊕73 41°02′.35N 08°17′.1E

Although the Asinara marine reserve regulations prohibit navigation within 1,000 metres of the island the company Cormorano, who run the marina in Porto Torres have obtained permission to lay some mooring buoys in Rada delle Reale for visiting sailing yachts only. To use these buoys there are 15 quite stringent regulations to observe and the buoys must be booked prior to use. Booking can be made ☎ 079 512 290 and further details can be obtained from the website www. cormorano.com Interestingly, the English version of the website makes no mention of these buoys so the regulations must be read in Italian. A brief resumé is outlined below. The fees are €2.5 per metre LOA per day in August and €2per metre per day the rest of the year. It is forbidden to anchor, the maximum speed is 3 knots and engines can only be used to moor and cast off. Windsurfing and jet skis are expressly forbidden. Access to the island is by oared tender only (outboards prohibited) and only in places designated by the authorites. If the skipper or his guests disobey the regulations or exhibit bad behaviour the permission to moor can be revoked. The only

services provided are assistance to moor and cast off and there is a refuse bin available – apart from that there is nothing.

Warning – there is a shallow patch with awash rocks just to seaward of the mooring area with a light 1132 Scogli Neri Fl.WR.5s11m7/5M White tower 11m, sector 297°-R-320° indicating the rocky area.

S6 Yacht Club l'Ancora

⊕73 40°57′.57N 08°13′.2E

Lights
1134.5 W mole head F.G.Green pole (P)
1134.55 E mole head F.G.Red pole (P)

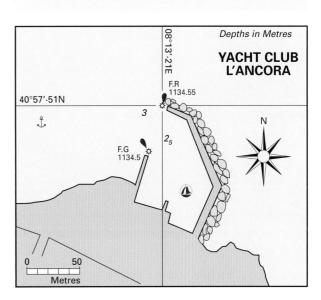

This is a private club lying just west of Punta Negra but visitors are welcome. It consists of a 110m breakwater running northwards from the shore. There are some pontoons inside but these are in depths of less than 1m and visitors moor up (stern-to) to the outer end of the jetty in 2.1m. Anchor outside in 3–5m in sand (and excellent holding) off the beach if the harbour is full. The yacht club can be reached on ☎ 079 527 085 *Fax* 079 527 087. There is electricity and water available, with showers, etc. but few other facilities.

PUNTA NEGRA 40°57′.18N 08°14′.2E

This is a low headland which has shallow reefs off to the north and the south of the point. It should be given at least a 400–500m berth to ensure clearance of these reefs. There are holiday homes built apparently randomly all over the headland.

S7 Stintino

Charts
Admiralty
Italian *910, 911, 49, 289*
Depths
0.5m to 2.5m
Number of berths
400 with about 40 for visitors
Maximum LOA
13m (in Mannu & Minore), 25m in new development
Lights
1134.4 Mole head 40°56´.1N 08°14´E Fl.G.4s6m8M
Green pole 4m.
1134 Beacon 40°56´.1N 08°13´.9E Fl.R.4s6m4M
Hexagonal stone conical tower, red and white, 5m
Porto Minore
1134.45 Mole head (right hand) Fl(2)G.6s5m3M
Green post 4m (P)

1134.46 Mole head (left hand) Fl(2)R.6s5m3M
Red post on white base 4m (P)
Porto Mannu
1134.47 Pier head (right hand) F.G.2m3M
Green post 1m (P)
1134.48 Pier head (left hand) F.R.2m3M
Red post 1m (P)
Port communications
VHF 16 or 9 gets the *capitaneria* at Porto Torres
Circolo Nautico VHF 73 ☎ 079 523 519 *Fax* 079 523 760
(N side of Mannu)
Nautilus ☎/*Fax* 079 523 721 (S side of Mannu)
Nautilus Benenati ☎ 079 523 345 (Minore Pontoon 8)
Warnings
The beacon in the centre of the harbour can be left on
either hand, but do not attempt to go between the
beacon and the shore as there is a reef of rocks running
out from the point which has a red and white striped
daymark on it.

This is a small town set on a peninsula that
separates two yacht harbours. It lies just over a mile
south of Punta Negra and is protected by a long
breakwater running south. There is a large red and
white striped beacon in the centre of the harbour
with a new development of pontoons in the
northern part.

The usual anchorage at the north end of the
harbour has now been taken up with some floating
pontoons and a lot of moorings. Unfortunately there
is very little room left for anchoring, and what space
remains is reported to be of poor holding because of
the weed. However, the harbour is still well sheltered
from the prevailing winds. (See photo 133)

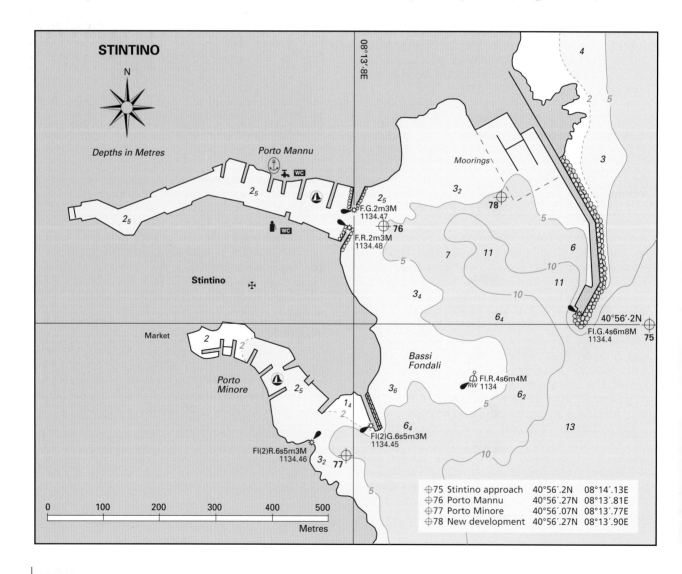

Approach

Both day and night approaches are without difficulty. The town stands out from quite a way off and the breakwater with its two green posts at the end can be seen on closing ⊕75 from the NW quadrant.

Entrance

Enter the harbour rounding the breakwater and giving it a good berth as rocks project some way south of the light. Having decided on preferred mooring site, leave the beacon to port if heading to Porto Mannu or to starboard if going to Porto Minore.

PORTO MANNU

This is the northern harbour and has been dredged to 2.5m. There are plenty of finger pontoons and quay walls for mooring, but nearly all of it is allocated to local yacht clubs and private moorings. Visitors should moor to the southern quay near the fuelling berth. Italian pilots state that there are persons available to assist with mooring but do not say how to attract their attention.

PORTO MINORE

This harbour is to the south of the town and has several jetties and pontoons but again most, if not all, are allocated to various societies. On entering, keep fairly close to the N mole end as there is a reef of rocks that runs out from the south shore opposite the mole end. Visitors should moor to No.8 pontoon (if there is room).

NEW DEVELOPMENT

There is a new development in the NE corner of the harbour with a large hard-standing and several floating pontoons. Electricity and water appear to be laid on but not operational as of September 2005. There are no shoreside facilities whatever and it is a long walk to town. There are two yellow buoys with × topmarks (usually meaning 'keep away from the works') moored off the development. It would seem that the developers ran out of money before completing the job but the pontoons are being used (it appears without paying) and a gentleman called Marco (living aboard a yacht called *Mayas*) is the resident 'helper'.

Anchorages

The above new development and some new moorings in the north of the harbour have taken up most of the room that was originally used as an anchorage. There may be still room to anchor to the SE of the pontoons but it has been reported that the holding is poor and there is quite a long dinghy ride into town.

Facilities

Most facilities are available in the town but quayside fuel is only available in Porto Mannu, although there are garages which sell fuel at the west end of town. There are no facilities whatever at the new development.

Stintino looking ENE (note isolated rock with beacon in centre of entrance)

Stintino new development (see also page 133)

2 PORTO TORRES TO CAPO TESTA

From Stintino the next 10 miles or so of coast are generally flat and marshy until the huge petrochemical and electricity generation plants west of Porto Torres which dominate the shoreside view. Offshore the sea is shallow and it is not a place to be if the strong NW winds are blowing or forecast. The land gradually rises NE of Porto Torres with only the harbours of Castelsardo and the newer Marina Isola Rossa, which can offer excellent shelter, until one reaches Santa Teresa di Gallura. Even so both these latter harbours can be difficult to enter when the prevailing mistral is blowing as the seas build up quickly and break across the entrances. (See photo page 4)

1138 **Porto Torres** LFl(2)10s45m16M White tower on building 20m
1145.2 **Castelsardo outer mole head** Fl.G.3s8m4M Green pole 5m (P)
1145.6 **Isola Rossa** Fl.R.5s6m4M Red pole 1m (P)
0938 **Capo Testa** Fl(3)12s67m22M White tower on building 23m

⊕79 Porto Torres 40°51.0N 08°24'.2E
⊕80 Pta Vignola 40°56'.0N 08°41'.5E
⊕81 Castelsardo 40°55'.0N 08°42'.26E
⊕82 Isola Rossa 41°00'.7N 08°52'.0E
⊕83 Capo Testa 41°15'.5N 09°08'.0E

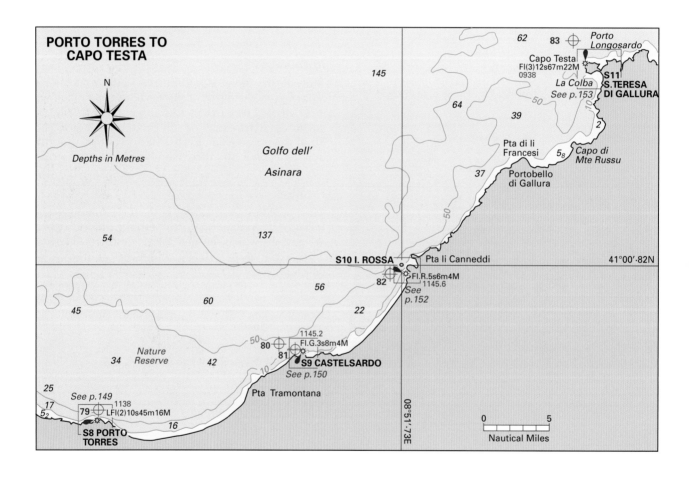

Above Castelsardo from the marina   *Below* Marina Isola Rossa

PLANNING GUIDE

Headlands	Ports & anchorages	Open to winds
	S8 ⚓ **Porto Torres page 148**	NW–N–NE
	Porto Commerciale page 148	
	S9 ⚓ **Castelsardo page 150**	
Punta Vignola		
Isola Rossa		
	S10 ⚓ **Isola Rossa marina page 152**	SW–W–NW
	⚓ *Portobello di Gallura*	
Capo Testa		
	⚓ Baia la Colba	W–S–SE
	⚓ Cala Spinosa	W–N–E
	⚓ Baia S. Reparata	N–E
Isola Municca		
	⚓ Cala	N–W–SW

S8 Porto Torres/Porto Commerciale

Porto Torres is the principal commercial port for Sassari and the north of Sardinia. It lies on a flat plain and the tall chimneys and oil storage tanks to the west of the harbour are the first objects seen. There is also a large electricity generating plant to the west of the oil terminal with a pipeline into the sea terminating in a yellow tower with a Fl.Y.3s3M light. The western harbour is for commercial traffic only and pleasure craft are prohibited from entering. In an unfortunate choice of names the harbour for pleasure craft is called Porto Commerciale and lies to the east of the industrial harbour. This is the only harbour described below. Note that a lot of construction work is going on in the western harbour, with new breakwaters being laid down and new ferry berths being made to the west of the Porto Commerciale.

A large, mainly commercial harbour

Porto Torres has been a large commercial harbour for many years and only fairly recently has opened up the smaller eastern section of the harbour to pleasure activities. Initially the activities were split between a private company and the commune, but after a few years this was abandoned and now the whole eastern harbour activities are under the private company, Cormorano.

Approach

By day

There are no problems in the approach, but do not enter the western harbour by mistake. The houses of Porto Torres behind the harbour are a good indication that you are entering the Porto Commerciale.

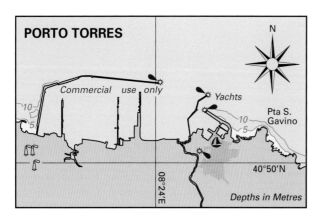

PORTO COMMERCIALE
⊕79 40°51´.0N 08°24´.2E

Charts
Admiralty *1985, 1204, 1202*
Italian *49, 289, 286*

Depth
0.5 to 3m

Number of berths
180 with 20 places for visitors

Maximum LOA
35m in Darsena Interna, 12m in Darsena Nuovo

Lights
1138 Main light 40°50´.1N 08°23´.8E LFl(2)10s45m16M White tower on building 20m
1139 Molo di Ponente head 40°50´.9N 08°24´.0E LFl.G.6s11m8M Green column on hut 9m
1140 Molo di Levante head LFl.R.6s11m8M Red column on hut, 5m
1141 Pontile del Faro head 2F.RG(vert)7m3M Red and green striped pole 5m
1142 Commercial Quay head 2F.G(vert)6m2M Green column 4m
1144 Darsena Interna left hand entrance F.R.5m3M Red pole 3m

Port communications
Capitaneria VHF Ch 16 or 12 ☎ 079 502 258.
Cormorano Marina VHF Ch 74 ☎ 079 512 290
Fax 079 515 250 *Email* cormorano@cormorano.com
url www.cormorano.com
Warnings
Keep well clear of all commercial and ferry traffic in the Avamporto.

By night

The lights of the western harbour are quite different from the eastern and the flares of the oil refinery chimneys stand out well. Make for the western mole end light and enter between the mole ends.

By GPS

Steer towards ⊕79 from the NW sector then set a course to enter between the pier heads.

Entrance

Enter on a SW course, round the eastern mole and make for the Darsena entrances.

Berth

Normal alongside/stern-to moorings are provided and assistance is available if contact with Cormorano is made on the approach.

Formalities

All authorities available.

Facilities

All.

Opposite Porto Torres Porto Commerciale looking N (not to be confused with Porto Industriale to the west where pleasure craft are not allowed)

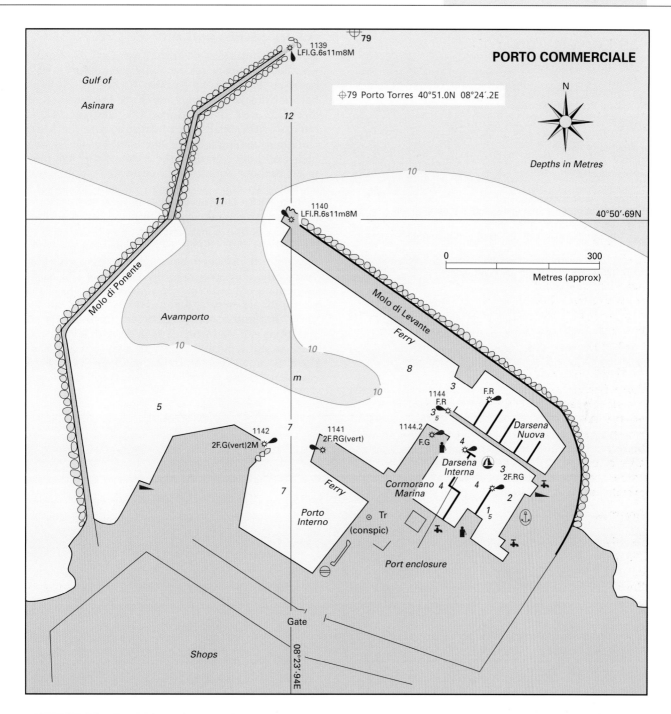

PORTO COMMERCIALE

Gulf of
Asinara

1139
LFl.G.6s11m8M

⊕79

⊕79 Porto Torres 40°51.0N 08°24′.2E

N

Depths in Metres

1140
LFl.R.6s11m8M

40°50′·69N

12

10

11

0   300

Metres (approx)

Molo di Ponente

Molo di Levante

Ferry

Avamporto

10

10

8

10

m

3

F.R

1144
F.R

3
5

Darsena
Nuova

5

1142
2F.G(vert)2M

7

1141
2F.RG(vert)

1144.2
F.G

4

4

3
2F.RG

Darsena
Interna

7

Ferry

Cormorano
Marina

4

3

4

4

2

Porto
Interno

Tr
(conspic)

1
5

Port enclosure

Gate

08°23′·94E

Shops

S9 Castelsardo

⊕81 40°55′.0N 08°42′.25E

Charts
  Admiralty *1985, 1204, 1203*
  Italian *910, 911, 49, 289*

Depth
  1 to 4m

Number of berths
  500

Maximum LOA
  28m

Lights
  1145.2 Molo Sopraflutto head 40°54′.9N 8°42′.1E
  Fl.G.3s8m4M Green pole 5m (P)
  1145 Scogliera Sottoflutto head Fl.R.3s8m4M Red pole
  5m (P)
  1145.4 Scogliera Isola Frigiano F.G.8m1M Green pole
  5m 090°-obscd-180° (P)

Port communications
  Local maritime Office ☎/*Fax* 079 470 916
  Email locamarecastelsardo@tiscali.it
  Il Cigno Soc. Coop ☎ 079 471 339 *Fax* 079 471 380
  Commune ☎ 079 470 138 *Fax* 079 471 119
  Email compmcsardo@tiscali.it

A very secure harbour

About 15 miles east of Porto Torres is Castelsardo, an attractive village set on a hilly promontory with a conspicuous belfry and castle. Closer in, the high harbour breakwater wall and Torre Frigiano can be identified west of the town. The western mole is built over the small islet of Frigiano and the Molo Curvilinio joining it to the mainland has had a very high wall built to reduce the effect of the *maestrale* in the harbour. Although the entrance is well lit, it is advisable to enter in daylight initially as there is quite a tricky chicane at the entrance. A very large development has taken place over the past few years and there is now a modern marina at the SE end of the harbour with 200 berths. The northern pontoons have been refurbished and there are now berths for 500 craft. The reef and beacon south of Isola Frigiano have been removed and water depths at the pontoons are now 2–4.5m. This is now a superb yacht harbour, totally sheltered from all wind directions and well worth a visit. As with all marinas there is still a problem with money, and although there is now fuel and all buildings have been completed there is little in the way of shore side

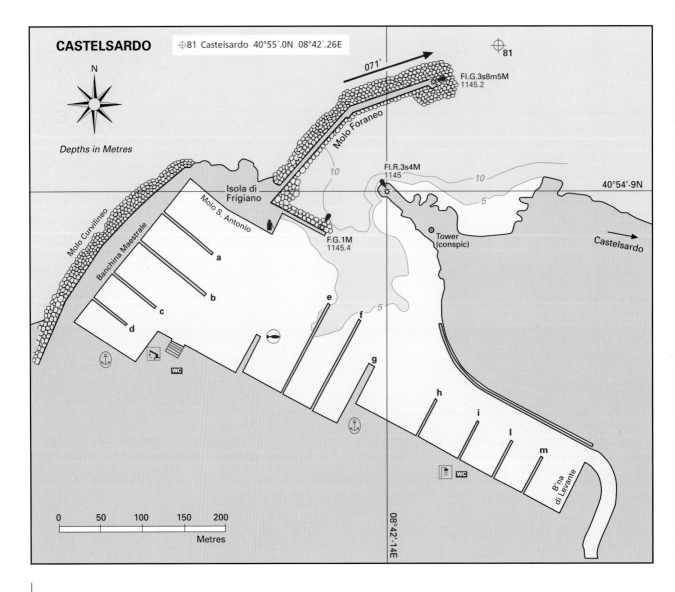

CASTELSARDO

⊕81 Castelsardo 40°55′.0N 08°42′.26E

support. In fact, some buildings are being used by the local council! There is a cafe, showers, WCs, refuse bins and good repair facilities. As in the past, food and chandlery still appear to be available in the village.

Approach

The village, set on a high hill, is conspicuous from afar. Closing the coast west of the village, the high wall of the breakwater will be seen. The end of Molo Foraneo will soon become apparent as there has been a large deposit of whitish granite at the end, which stands out clearly from the local reddish stone.

Entrance

Enter on a southwesterly course, giving the end of the Molo a reasonably wide berth. Steer slightly to port to round the point with the tower and then to starboard to enter the harbour.

Berths

Call up the Commune or the local maritime office to obtain a berth – at present there are no visitors' berths allocated. If in doubt, ask at the fuel point or report to the office.

Anchorages

Anchoring is not permitted in the harbour and there is no sheltered anchorage outside until one reaches Isola Rossa, 10 miles to the NE.

Facilities

Water and electricity on pontoons
Fuel
Reasonable repair facilities
Showers and WCs
Refuse bins
Stores and chandlery in village.

(See also photo page 4)

Above Castelsardo village and marina looking NE   *Below* Castelardo entrance

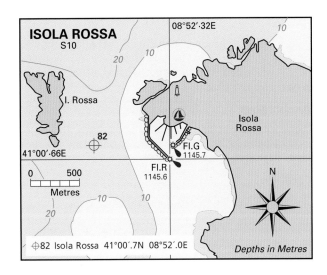

ISOLA ROSSA
S10

08°52′.32E

20

10

I. Rossa

82

41°00′.66E

0   500
Metres

10   10

20

Isola Rossa

Fl.G
1145.7

Fl.R
1145.6

N

⊕82 Isola Rossa 41°00′.7N 08°52′.0E

Depths in Metres

⚓ **ISOLA ROSSA** 41°00′.8N 08°51′.8E

Some 10 miles along the coast there is a conspicuous island (27m high) of distinctly reddish rock. In reasonable west or northwest winds excellent shelter can be found behind this island, but be careful of a 2m shallow patch 50m off the eastern coast in the northern part of the island. On the shore southeast of the island is a tourist complex and marina (confusingly, also called Isola Rossa), on a low promontory with a conspicuous round tower.

Isola Rossa town marina looking N

S10 Marina Isola Rossa

⊕82 41°00′.07N 08°52′.0E

Charts
Admiralty *1985, 1204, 1202*
Italian *911, 49, 3289*

Depths
1 to 7m

Number of berths
390 with 40 for visitors

Maximum LOA
21m

Lights
1145.6 Molo Sopraflutto head 41°00′.6N 08°52′.3E
Fl.R.5s6m4M Red pole 1m (P)
1145.7 Molo Sottoflutto head Fl.G.5s6m4M Green pole 5m (P)

Port Communication
Marina Office ☎ 079 694 184 *Fax* 079 671 400
Email cm3.marinaisolarossa@tiscali.it

A newish marina

This marina has been in operation since 2002 and it seems very keen to improve its standards. During my October 2005 visit it was one of the few open for business every day with fuel available all day as well. Certainly this will attract the out of season sailors but, unfortunately, the tourist development ashore seems to be mainly closed, with only a few restaurants and cafés open and little in the way of everyday supplies.

Approach

From almost any direction Isola Rossa is unmistakable and there is a large tower situated on the mainland about three quarters of a mile to the

east. The marina lies to the south of the tower and the island can be left on either hand, but keep a reasonable distance off, avoiding the shallow patch some 50m off the eastern coast of the island.

By GPS

Approach ⊕82 from the north or southwest, leaving Isola Rossa to starboard or port respectively.

Entrance

Follow the breakwater in a southerly direction, round the end, leaving it some 25m clear and enter on a northeasterly course. Go alongside, port side to, just inside the end of the breakwater and contact the marina office for a berth.

Berths

All pontoon berths and the breakwater have *pendillos* from them.

Anchorages

There is space to anchor south of the harbour when the tower bears about 350° in 5m on sand about 200m from the shore. Note that the bottom changes abruptly from sand to boulders and there are several awash rocks close to the shore.

Facilities

All facilities are available at the marina in season, but these may be reduced out of season.

It is understood that although the wall protecting the harbour appears robust, it is not quite high enough to allow winter usage of the marina. There are plans to extend the height of the wall but the time-scale for this is unknown at present.

⚓ PORTOBELLO DI GALLURA
41°07′.8N 09°01′.4E

A further 10 miles along the coast there is another totally private development which has constructed a small port, again for the owners' *gommones*. It is very small and visitors are not really welcome because there really is no room. It is shallow (1m) and there are no shoreside facilities at all.

CAPO TESTA 41°14′.8N 09°08′.6E

Approaching Sardinia from either the west (Bonifacio or Asinara) or the northeast (Passage de la Piantarella), this rugged promontory is easily recognisable. The lighthouse, a low white square tower on a two-storied building (67m high) is conspicuous. The cape is fringed with rocks, some above water and yachts must exercise caution close in. There are 3 anchorages round the cape.

⚓ BAIA LA COLBA 41°13′.9N 09°09′.5E

On the south side of the isthmus. Anchor in 5m on sand.

⚓ CALA SPINOSA 41°14′.8N 09°08′.9E

To the east of the lighthouse. Anchor in 10m on sand.

⚓ BAIA S REPARATA 41°14′.5N 09°09′.95E

North of the isthmus. Anchor in 4-6m on sand.

There is also a small bay, sheltered from the east only, at the south end of the small Isola Minicca off a point 2 miles east of the light on Capo Testa. It is surrounded by rocks but does offer reasonable holding, for a lunch stop, for example.

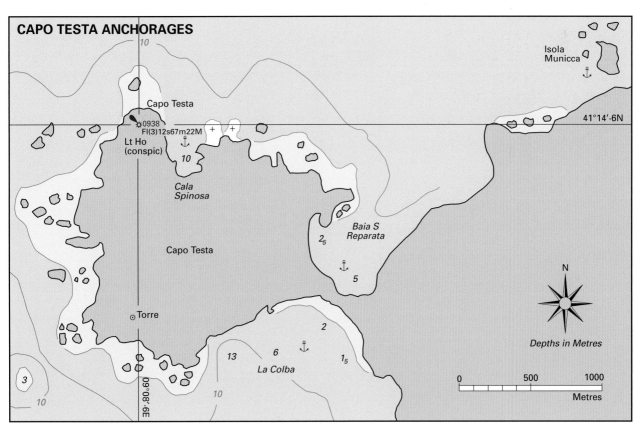

CAPO TESTA ANCHORAGES

3 SANTA TERESA DI GALLURA TO CAPO FERRO (INCLUDING LA MADDALENA ARCHIPELAGO)

From Capo Testa to Capo Ferro, just north of Porto Cervo, the coast is indented with many small harbours and even more bays with superb beaches. There are many islands with offlying rocks, which can make navigation tricky, but with up-to-date large-scale charts and GPS even the most cautious navigator should enjoy sailing in this wonderful cruising ground.

This next part of the coast forms the south side of the Bonifacio Strait. It is bordered by numerous islands which are in turn bordered by even more numerous rocks, shoals and reefs. The strait is used by large numbers of merchant vessels and ferries as well as pleasure craft and a good lookout (and giving way in ample time) is vital. It has a well deserved reputation as a rough area especially with a strong *maestrale* (west wind) or *levante* (east wind) and yachtsmen cruising in the area for the first time should exercise caution. However, it is a superb cruising ground with many attractive anchorages and safe harbours. It should not be missed.

The winds in summer blow mainly from the NW or IV quadrant, sometimes getting up to Force 5 or 6, while around the islands there are frequently southwest or southeast winds. In spring the winds are northwest or northeast, while in autumn the winds are mainly from northwest and southeast. The currents follow the prevailing wind but are diverted by the islands and headlands. They are quite variable in strength and direction but since most navigation in the vicinity of the strait is by eyeball the currents can, in general, be ignored.

0938 **Capo Testa** Fl(3)12s67m22M White tower on building 23m
0940 **Isola Razzoli** Fl.WR.2.5s77m19/15M Stone tower 12m 022°-W-092°-R-137°-W-237°-R-320°
0942 **Isola Sta Maria** Fl(4)20s17m10M Tower on white building 12m
0946 **Isola I Corcelli** Fl(2)10s22m11M Black tower, red band, 2 spheres 12m
0998 **I Monaci** Fl.WR.5s24m11/8M White tower 18m 246°-R-268°-W-317°-R-357°-W-246°
1000 **I delle Bisce** Fl.G.3s11m8M White tower, green band 9m
1002 **Capo Ferro** Fl(3)15s52m24M White tower on building 18m
0950 **Pta Sardegna** Fl.5s35m11M White house 13m
0988 **Pta Palau** Fl(2)G.10s15m4M White tower, green bands 10m
0992 **Capo d'Orso** Fl.3s12m10M White tower 10m

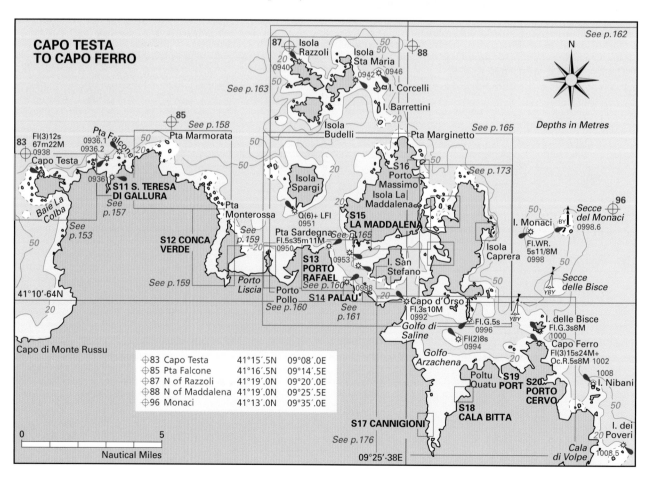

PLANNING GUIDE

Headlands	Ports & anchorages	Open to winds
	S11 ⚓ S Teresa di Gallura page 156	
	Porto Longosardo page 156	N
	⚓ *Porto Quadro*	N–NW
Punta Falcone		
Isole Marmorata		
	⚓ *S of Marmorata*	NE–E
Punta Monterosso		
(with Scoglio Pagenetto 4 cables off)		
	⚓ *Porto Pozzo*	N
	S12 ⚓ Conca Verde page 159	N
Punta delle Vacche		
	⚓ *Porto Liscia*	N–NE
Punta Cavalli (with rock 1.5 cables off)		
	⚓ *Porto Pollo (Puddu)*	N
Punta Sardinia		
	S13 ⚓ Yacht Club Porto Rafael page 160	NE–E–SE
Punta Palau		
	S14 ⚓ Palau page 161	NW–N–NE
	La Maddalena archipelago page 162	
	BOCCHE DI BONIFACIO PASSAGES	
	THE NORTHERN GROUP	
	Isola Razzoli page 163	
	⚓ *Cala Lunga*	W–SW
	⚓ *Cala Giorgio Marino*	W–S–SE
	⚓ *Cala Muro*	SW–NW
	⚓ *Cala S Maria*	E–S
	THE SOUTHERN GROUP	
	Spargi page 165	
	⚓ *Cala d'Alga*	S–W
	⚓ *Cala Corsara*	E–S
	⚓ *Cala Ferrigno (rocky)*	NE–E
	S15 ⚓ La Maddalena page 166	
	Porto Mercantile (Cala Gavetta) page 169	S
	Cala Mangiavolpe page 169	S
	Cala Camiciotto	
	Marina del Ponte page 169	S–SE
	⚓ *Cala Nido d'Aquila*	S–W
	⚓ *Cala Francese*	W
	⚓ *Stagno Torto*	N
	S16 ⚓ Porto Massimo page 171	E
	⚓ *Cala Spalmatore*	E
Isola Santa Stefano		
Isola Caprera		
	⚓ *Cala di Villamarina*	S
	⚓ Cala Stagnali	W
	⚓ Porto Palma	S
	⚓ Cala Portese	NE–E
	⚓ Cala Brigantino	NE–SE
	⚓ Cala Coticcio	S
	⚓ Porto Garibaldi	N
Capo d'Orso	⚓ Cala Capra	E
	⚓ Golfo di Saline	E
Golfo di Arzachena		
	⚓ Cala Porteddu	E
	⚓ La Conia	E
	S17 ⚓ Cannigione page 177	N
	S18 ⚓ Cala Bitta page 178	W
	⚓ North Bay	SW
	⚓ Cala south of Capo Tre Monti	W–NW
Capo Tre Monti (rocks off point)		
Secca di Tre Monti		
Punta Battistone		
	⚓ Cala Battistone	N
	S19 ⚓ Marina dell'Orso (Poltu Quatu) page 180	N
	⚓ Liscia di Vacca	N
Isola Cappucini		
Capo Ferro (with Isola delle Bisce to the N)		

S11 Santa Teresa di Gallura

PORTO LONGOSARDO

⊕84 41°15′.3N 09°11′.9E

Charts
Admiralty *1189*
Italian *325, 326*

Depth at entrance
20m, in harbour 0.5 to 3m

Number of berths
750

Maximum LOA
35m

Lights
0936.1 Beacon 41°15′.3N 09°12′.2E Fl.R.4s6m3M Port lateral, ▪ topmark
0936.2 Beacon 41°15′.2N 09°11′.8E Fl.G.4s6m3M Starboard lateral, ▲ topmark
0936 Punta Corvo 41°14′.6N 9°12′.0E Fl.WR.3s11m10/8M 030°-R-164°-W-184°-R-210° White hut 7m
0936.3 Entrance light (W) Fl.G.4s8m4M Green pole 6m
0936.4 Entrance light (E) Fl.R.4s8m4M Red pole 6m
0937 Ldg Lts 196.5° *Front* Oc.R.4s12m3M 181.5°-vis-211.5° White and green pole 10m
0937.1 *Rear* (1,280m away) Fl.R.4s45m7M 151.5°-vis-241.5° White and green pole 5m
1020.2(I) Marina entrance light F.G.6m3M on same pole as 0937

Port communications
Maritime Authorities VHF Ch 16, 9 ☎ 0789 754 602
Commune ☎ 0789 754 120
Porto Turistico ☎ 789 751 936 *Fax* 0789 753 170
url www. portosantateresa.com

Warnings
As with most commercial ports of the islands, commercial craft and ferries have right of way in restricted channels and port entrances and must not be obstructed. Anchoring is not permitted in the harbour itself.

Santa Teresa di Gallura looking N

Santa Teresa di Gallura is quite a large village on the west side of a mile-long fiord-type harbour with a yacht harbour, Porto Longosardo, at its southern end. It is a very well sheltered harbour but there is some swell effect during and after strong northerlies.

Approach

Capo Testa, 2 miles to the west of the entrance, is conspicuous on any approach.

By day

Two tall beacons marking shallow patches (3 and 5m) some half a mile north of the entrance should be identified. The conspicuous 42m high tower (Torre Longosardo) on the western entrance and the village behind it is the clearer indication of position. Go between the beacons and steer a course of 196.5° to keep in the middle of the channel (remember the need to keep clear of ferries!). The west side is clearer of rocks than the east side. On approach to the quays, steer to enter the harbour.

By night

The 2 beacons are lit and Punto Corvo light, on the east side of the entrance, has a white sector that covers the passage between the beacons. Go between the beacons and steer towards Punto Corvo light until the leading lights are in line and steer 196.5° until the quay is reached.

By GPS

Steer towards ⊕83 from the north quadrant and identify the beacons. Steer a course of 180° from the waypoint, towards the Punta Corvo light. This will take you into the middle of the channel where the leading lines can be picked up.

Entrance

The entrance itself is quite narrow (75m) but is clear from obstructions apart from a black and white striped pole floating in the middle of the entrance. Some research was needed to discover that this pole marked a bank of sand (4m minimum depth over) and it can be left on either hand.

Berths

On entering, go slightly to starboard into a large new yacht harbour and make contact by VHF to receive berthing instructions. If this fails, try calling on 0789 754 602 and there should be assistants on the pontoons to guide you to your berth.

Formalities

All authorities available.

Facilities

All.

⚓ PORTO QUADRO 41°15′.1N 09°12′.6E

A bay, to the east of Santa Teresa entrance, which has a large hotel complex on the shore. Care should be taken of the rocks at the entrance but inside, anchor in the middle of the bay in 3.5m. This bay is totally untenable in *maestrale* conditions.

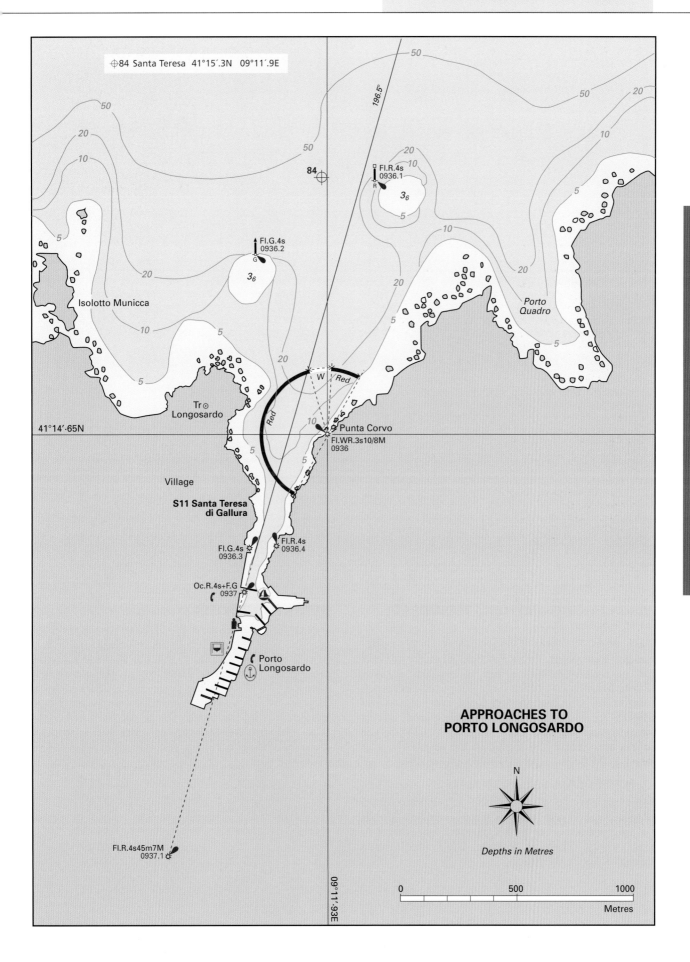

⊕84 Santa Teresa 41°15′.3N 09°11′.9E

196.5°

Fl.R.4s
0936.1

3₆

84 ⊕

Porto
Quadro

Isolotto Municca

Fl.G.4s
0936.2

3₆

W Red

Red

Tr⊙
Longosardo

41°14′-65N

Punta Corvo
Fl.WR.3s10/8M
0936

Village

**S11 Santa Teresa
di Gallura**

Fl.G.4s
0936.3

Fl.R.4s
0936.4

Oc.R.4s+F.G
0937

Porto
Longosardo

Fl.R.4s45m7M
0937.1

**APPROACHES TO
PORTO LONGOSARDO**

N

Depths in Metres

09°11′.93E

0   500   1000

Metres

3. SANTA TERESA DI GALLURA TO CAPO FERRO

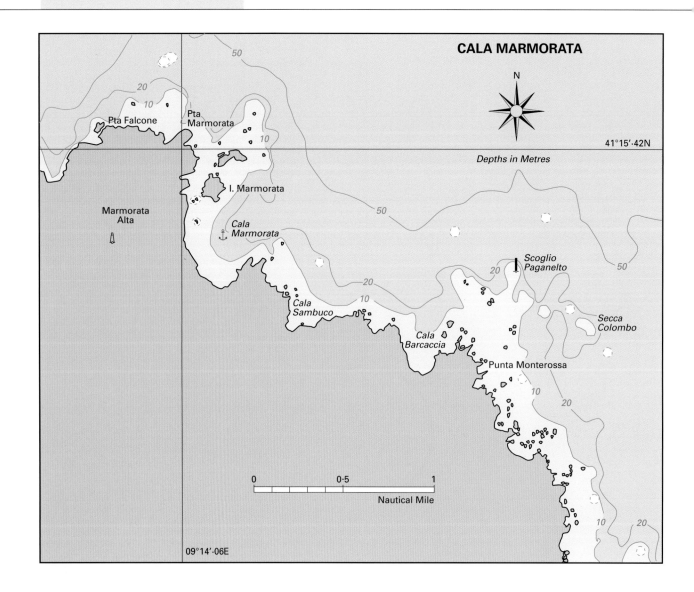

PUNTA FALCONE AND PUNTA MARMORATA
41°15′.55N 09°13′.5E

Just east of Porto Quadro there is a rather insignificant point, Punta Falcone, with a small islet off its west side. Half a mile to the east again is Punta Marmarata, which has a couple of daymarks, one on the point and another 0.4M away inland and higher up. This point has 2 sizeable islands off its eastern side and foul ground extends 0.3M to the north and nearly half a mile to the east. Give it at least a ¾M berth, especially in rough weather.

⚓ MARMORATA BAY 41°15′N 09°14′E

This bay lies about half a mile south of Marmorata Point. Anchor just south of the Marmorata islands in 5m, with excellent shelter except for northeast to east winds. There is a large Club Mediterrané complex above the beach.

PUNTA MONTEROSSA 41°14′.38N 09°16′.15E

Nearly 2 miles ESE of Punta Marmorata there is another low (26m) headland, Punta Monterossa, which has foul ground extending for 0.4M to the north and northeast. The Scoglio Paganetto lies some 0.4M NNE of the point and is marked by a beacon, which must be left well to starboard when rounding from the north. The coast south of here is also foul for some distance offshore and a prudent mariner will set a course that will be at least 0.4M from the land.

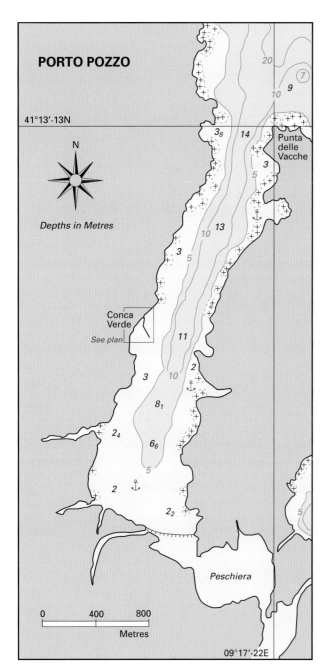

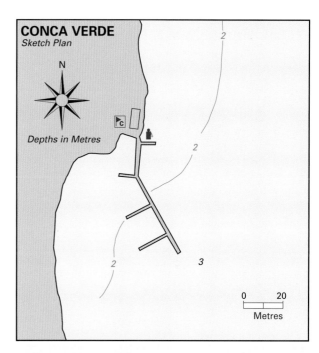

S12 Conca Verde

⊕86 41°12′.7N 09°16′.8E

There is a small wooden landing pier with some floating pontoons attached on the west side of the above inlet about 0.7M from the entrance. Depths alongside vary from 5m at the extreme end to 1.5m near the land. This is a private harbour owned by a yacht club; visitors are welcome but there are no facilities! You can also anchor off in 5+m.

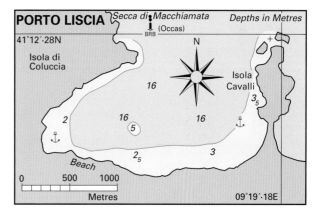

⚓ **PORTO POZZO** 41°13′.4N 09°17′.2E

This is not really a port but a long (1½M) inlet with the large Isola di Culuccia (which is not really an island as it is attached to Sardinia at its southern end) forming the east shore. Coming from the north, the beacon at the north end of the Paganetto Rocks stands out clearly and should be left to starboard. Keep to the middle of the inlet and anchor at the head in 3–5m in reasonable holding. There are 2 small bays on the east side of the inlet, that you can also anchor off in 3.5m. There are several floating pontoons at the SW corner of the inlet which appears quite shallow (1.5m, but SardaNautica mobile ☎ 0338 954 2094) has 5 pontoons with water and electricity with a crane and bar. Nautica Porto Pozzo on mobile ☎ 333 599 2241 also advertises there and these can be contacted for details of depths and berths.

⚓ **PORTO LISCIA** 41°12′N 09°18′.4E

Coming from the north, keep Punte delle Vacche (the north end of Isola di Culuccia) at least 400m clear to avoid the rocks, and watch out for the iron pole on the Secca di Macchiamata (0.8M SE of the point) [although this was reported missing in 2004), again leaving it to starboard. Anchor at the west end of the large bay in 3–5m on a good holding sandy bottom. The anchorage is exposed to winds from the NE or I quadrant but sheltered from all the rest. In calm weather there is a delightful anchorage on the east side of the bay, under Isola Cavalli. There are beaches all round the bay.

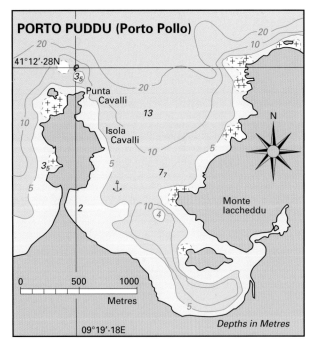

PORTO PUDDU (Porto Pollo)

41°12'·28N

Punta
Cavalli

Isola
Cavalli

Monte
Iaccheddu

0   500   1000
Metres

09°19'·18E

Depths in Metres

PUNTA SARDEGNA

Pta Sardegna
Fl.5s35m11M

41°12'·42N

Secca di
Mezzo Passo
Fl(2)6s5M
0952

BRB

Pta Stropello

YC

**S13 PORTO
RAFAEL**

Depths in Metres

Rada di
Mezzo Schifo

Fl(2)G.10s4M
0988

Punta
Palau

0   500   1000
Metres

9°21'·79E

⚓ **PORTO POLLO (OR PUDDU)** 41°12'N 09°19'.6E

Another small inlet, very sheltered from all winds. Keep well clear of Punta Cavalli, with its large rock 300m off and keep to the centre of the bay when entering to avoid extensive rocks on both shores. Anchor SE of the island in 8–10m – it shelves very quickly to 1m, so exercise caution. Rocks extend all round the island for at least 100m. There are no facilities but there are lovely beaches around the bay, with a hotel complex and campsites.

S13 Yacht Club Porto Rafael

⊕89 41°11'.75N 09°22'E

Just under 1M south of Punta Sardinia, there is a small private harbour with a quay with stern-to moorings outside and small dinghies, etc. inside. All of the moorings are usually occupied but one or two may be available if their owners are away cruising. The name now may be changed to YC Punta Sardegna but it is a most friendly club with Ottavio Pincioni as the local contact. He can be reached on ☎ 0789 700 302 or *Fax* 0789 700 231. Facilities are basic with no shops, but there is an internet point!

Note Nelson used to anchor his fleet here in the early 1800s when blockading the French fleet in Toulon. The Italian and English charts still bear the name Cala Inglese (where the YC Porto Rafael is located), Baia di Nelson (about half a mile south of the YC moorings), and the whole gulf is called Rada de Mezzo Schifo. Schifo can be translated as 'skiff' so it might be called 'Bay of Half a Skiff', but *schifo* also means 'disgusting or loathesome' and it probably takes that meaning, as the holding in the area is known to be suspect and with the anchors of Nelson's time, many a ship will have dragged.

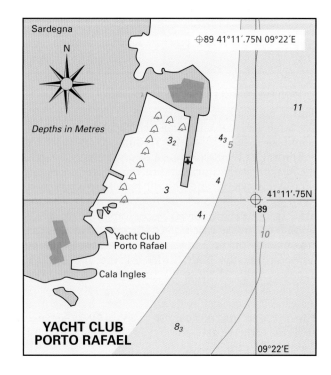

Sardegna

⊕89 41°11'.75N 09°22'E

N

Depths in Metres

Yacht Club
Porto Rafael

Cala Ingles

41°11'·75N

89

**YACHT CLUB
PORTO RAFAEL**

09°22'E

S14 Palau

⊕90 41°11′.0N 09°23′.25E (free for 2 hours)

Charts
Admiralty *1213, 1212*
Italian *42, 324, 282*

Depth
2.4m in harbour

Number of berths
380

Maximum length
18m

Lights
0988 Punta Palau 41°11′.2N 9°22′.9E Fl(2)G.10s15m4M
White tower, green band 10m
0990 Outer Mole head 41°10′.9N 9°23′.2E
2F.GR(vert)6m3M Red and green striped post
0990.6 Shelter Mole head F.G.6m3M Green post 5m
0990.4 Breakwater head F.R.6m3M Red post 5m
0990.2 Secca due Piagge 41°10′.9N 9°23′.3E
VQ(9)10s5m5M ⌀ card buoy YBY (250m at 065° from outer mole head)

Port communications
Local Maritime Authorities VHF Ch 16, 9
☎ 0789 709 419
Commune ☎ 0789 708 435
Email portoturistico@palau.it
url www.palau.it/portoturistico.asp

Warnings
There is an extensive reef of rocks, Secca due Piagge, extending over 400m from the eastern shore and marked with a ⌀ cardinal buoy. There are many ferries using the outer mole and all commercial traffic has right of way, so keep fairly close to this buoy on a southerly course to give the ferries as much room as possible.

A typical busy ferry port

At one time Palau was a small farming village. It is now a modern town which serves as an 'R and R' town for Americans stationed at the NATO base on Santo Stefano Island and as the mainland ferry port for La Maddalena. Having said that, it is still a pleasant town with reasonable shopping facilities.

Approach

By day

A straightforward approach with the town easily identified. Ferries are constantly running between Palau and the islands and are useful for locating the harbour. The ⌀ cardinal buoy is also obvious as one gets close to the mole.

By night

Use the light on Palau Point and the mole head fixed lights to approach.

By GPS

Steer to ⊕90 from the north. At the ⊕, the ⌀ cardinal buoy and ferry pier end should become obvious.

Entrance

The entrance is simple but keep closer to the northern arm as there are rocks projecting northeast from the southern arm.

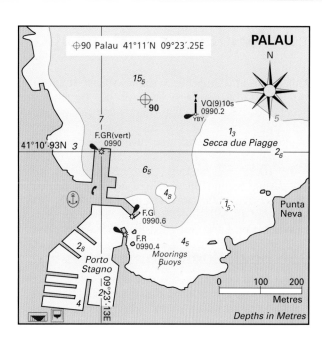

Berths

There are floating pontoons and it is possible to go alongside the quay at the south end of the harbour. It is always crowded in the harbour. About 16 mooring buoys have been laid in the bay immediately to the east of the port and these can be used for half the usual fee for a marina berth. Note that anchoring is not recommended in the waters around Palau.

Formalities

All authorities available.

Facilities

All.

Palau mooring buoys outside marina

La Maddalena archipelago

This group of islands lies to the northeast of Sardinia and forms the southern edge of the Bouches (or Bocche) di Bonifacio. The islands are composed of red granite and for the most part are bare of vegetation except for the usual Mediterranean *macchia*. They are surrounded by above- and below-water rocks and caution must be exercised when navigating around them. There are seven principal islands, three in the northern group: Razzoli, Santa Maria and Budelli and four in the southern group, La Maddalena, Caprera, Spargi and Santo Stefano.

Bocche di Bonifacio passages

The 3 main passages through the Bocche on the Corsican side are described on page 53. There are 2 further passages, one main one for those vessels going south, which simply keeps fairly close to the Sardinian coast, leaving all the islands of the Maddalena group to port. The narrowest sections (0.5 miles wide) are between Punta Sardegna and Isola La Maddalena, Isola Santo Stefano and Punta Nera (near Palau) and Capo d'Orso and Punta Fico on Caprera. From Capo d'Orso, a course of 120°should be steered for 2 miles which will take you between the south point of Caprera (Punta Rossa buoy) and the isolated Secca di Tre Monti marked with a BRB buoy with two spherical topmarks (Fl(2)8s5M). When abeam of this buoy either a course of east should be steered to pass through the Passo di Bisce (in settled weather only) or a course of 065°should be steered to take you north of Isola delle Bisce and its off-lying dangers. All isolated rock dangers are well marked in this channel and there is at least 15m depth throughout its length.

The second, less important, passage is from ⊕85 take a course just south of east and go between the islands of Budelli and Spargi (keeping closer to Budelli). When abeam of Budelli steer just north of east and go through the Passo di Barrettinelli between the north point of Isola La Maddalena and a group of rocks, Isolotti Barrettinelli, to the northwest (see plan below).

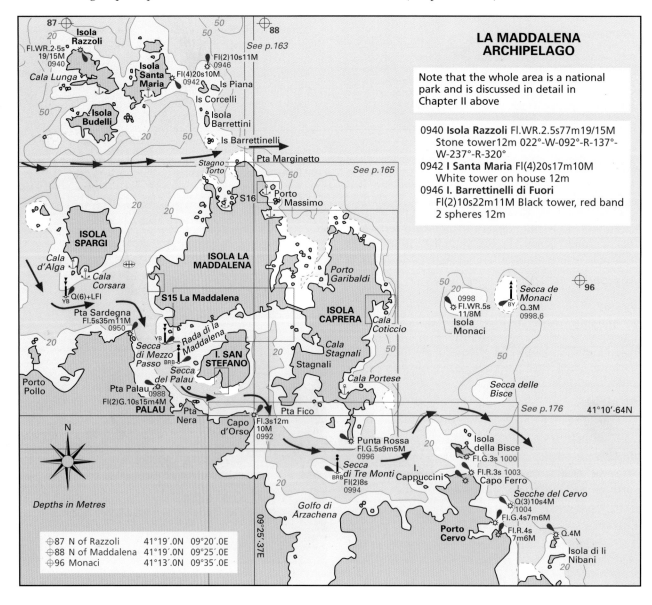

The Northern Group

This group has few inhabitants and little in the way of vegetation or water.

Isola Razzoli

The northwesternmost of the group, it is low (65m) with a distinctive square black and white striped lighthouse on its northwest point, Fl.WR.2.5s19/15M, with red sectors over the Lavezzi rocks (092°-137°) and Santa Maria (237°-320°). There are 2 anchorages.

⚓ CALA LUNGA 41°17'.9N 09°20'.2E

Care is needed to avoid the rocks on both sides of the entrance. Anchor in 3–4m on sand. It is open to the west but is otherwise well sheltered.

⚓ CALA GIORGIO MARINO 41°17'.5N 09°21'E

This is on the south side of the island but is effectively sheltered by all the islands. Anchor in 3–5m on a sandy bottom; again, it is open to the west.

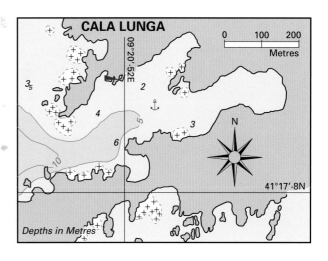

CALA LUNGA

Depths in Metres

41°17'.8N

Isola Santa Maria

Lies to the east of Razzoli, from which it is separated by Passo degli Asinelli, which is impassable for keel yachts. To the north of the island lies Isola La Presa and off the east coast a number of small islets. The passage between these latter islets and Santa Maria

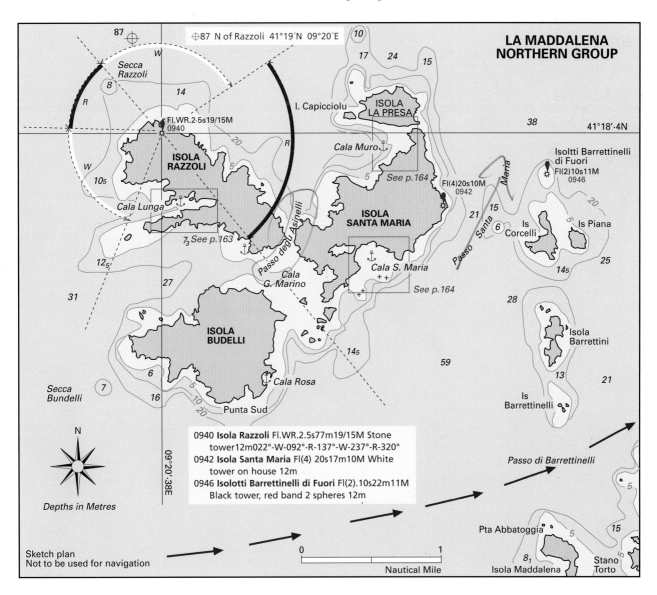

LA MADDALENA NORTHERN GROUP

⊕87 N of Razzoli 41°19'N 09°20'E

Secca Razzoli

I. Capicciolu

ISOLA LA PRESA

Cala Muro

ISOLA RAZZOLI

Fl.WR.2.5s19/15M 0940

Cala Lunga

See p.163

Passo degli Asinelli

ISOLA SANTA MARIA

Fl(4)20s10M 0942

Isoltti Barrettinelli di Fuori Fl(2)10s11M 0946

Is Corcelli

Is Piana

Passo Santa Maria

Cala G. Marino

Cala S. Maria

See p.164

ISOLA BUDELLI

Isola Barrettini

Secca Bundelli

Cala Rosa

Punta Sud

Is Barrettinelli

N

Depths in Metres

Passo di Barrettinelli

0940 Isola Razzoli Fl.WR.2.5s77m19/15M Stone tower12m022°-W-092°-R-137°-W-237°-R-320°
0942 Isola Santa Maria Fl(4) 20s17m10M White tower on house 12m
0946 Isolotti Barrettinelli di Fuori Fl(2).10s22m11M Black tower, red band 2 spheres 12m

Pta Abbatoggia

Stano Torto

Isola Maddalena

Sketch plan
Not to be used for navigation

Nautical Mile

is clear except for a 6.5m shoal. There is a distinctive lighthouse on the east coast: Fl(4)20s17m10M and a light on the northernmost islet to the east from a white stone tower on Isolotti I Corcelli (Fl(2)10s22m11M), the northernmost danger of the Barrattinelli Group. There are two bays on the island providing reasonable shelter.

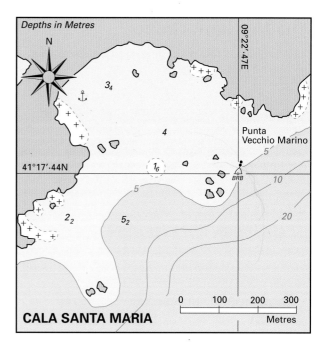

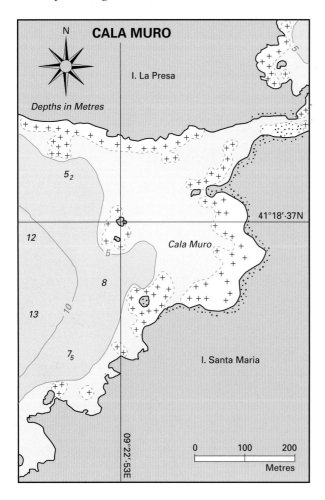

⚓ **CALA MURO** 41°18'.3N 09°22'.4E

This is near the north tip, south of the Isola La Presa. There is a rocky reef in the middle of the bay and rocks around the shores. Anchor in 6–10m on the south side of the bay. It is open to the west.

⚓ **CALA SANTA MARIA** 41°17'.45N 09°22'.6E

On the southeast side of the island; care must be taken of 2 reefs south of the entrance. There is a nondescript port-hand buoy off the northernmost reef which should be left to port on entering. Take up a position east of the buoy and, leaving it to port, steer about 300° until 4–6m is reached (keep in the clear sandy patch which is obvious from the buoy inwards). Good sandy bottom with splendid beach which is flooded with tourists in season. It is open to the south and southeast.

Budelli

This island lies to the south of Razzoli and southwest of Santa Maria. It is separated from the latter by the Passo Secca di Morto (Deadman's Rock) which has a minimum depth of 1.2m and is not recommended as a passage for a keel yacht. There was only one decent anchorage on the island which is now part of the marine reserve (see section III) and you are not allowed to enter the cove, let alone anchor there!

Spiaggia Rosa (Cala Rosa) 41°16'.7N 09°21'.48E

The cove took its name from the pink colour of the sand which came from the dead coral that grew around the islands in profusion long ago. Not only has the coral succumbed to man's harvesting (for jewellery) and pollution, but all the visitors to the beach over the centuries have taken a small sample home with them and today the beach is a normal beach colour. However do not cross the line of white buoys across the entrance of the *cala* as it is now a total no-go area (see section II).

The Southern Group

These four islands are larger and greener than the northern group. There are numerous anchorages and the sea is crystal-clear turquoise and aquamarine over a rock and sand bottom.

The group is described by individual islands as follows:

Isola Spargi

Isola La Maddalena, with S15 La Maddalena and then a clockwise description of the calas of the island

Isola Santa Stefano

Isola Caprera and an anti-clockwise description of its calas

Isola Spargi

The westernmost of this group is a rocky isle with a high point of 153m. Some 700m off its southern tip lies the Secca Corsara (3m depth) which is marked by a ⚓ cardinal light buoy (Q(6)+LFl.15s5M). A small islet, Spargiotto, lies 1,200m off the NW corner. There are 3 anchorages.

⚓ **CALA D'ALGA** 41°13′.8N 09°20′.1E

Lies on the west side of the southern tip. Anchor in 3–5m on sand and rock. It is open to the W and S but has a nice beach.

⚓ **CALA CORSARA** 41°13′.7N 09°20′.55E

Lies on the east side of the southern tip. Again anchor in 3–5m on sand and rock.

⚓ **CALA FERRIGNO** 41°14′.7N 09°21′.54E

This is a very rocky bay on the NE coast, with a white house ashore and a small pier, making identification easier. The rocks extend from the north side of the bay, but the south side is relatively clean. There is 3–4m at the end of the pier but there is little room to manoeuvre because of the rocks.

3. SANTA TERESA DI GALLURA TO CAPO FERRO

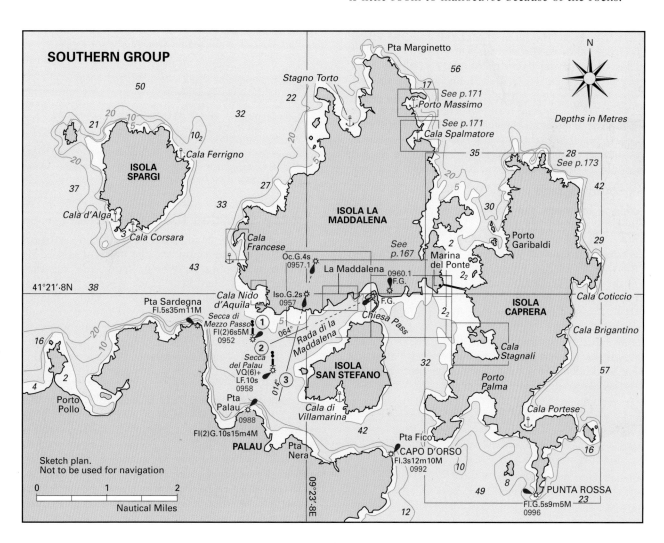

Isola La Maddalena

This is the largest island of the entire group and the only one that supports a reasonable population, mainly clustered around the town of La Maddalena itself. It is fairly hilly at the south end (153m) and at the northern end (84m), with a much indented coast and a selection of anchorages that offer good shelter in almost any wind direction. The coast is fringed with rocks and great care is needed when navigating in and around the various bays.

From the main channel between the islands and the mainland there are three passages to La Maddalena. (See plan page 165)

1. North passage

This is between Punta Tegge and Scoglio Bianco to the north and Secca di Mezzo Passo, a bank of rocks 600m south of Punta Tegge. Scoglio Bianco is painted white and has a 16m white obelisk on it. Secca di Mezzo Passo has a black and red daymark surmounted by **⁑** and is lit Fl(2)6s5M. In the channel between these two beacons is a clear 20+m depth.

2. Middle passage (Mezzo Passo)

This is between the Secca di Mezzo Passo and a large reef 0.4 miles to the SE, Secca del Palau. On the S edge of Secca del Palau there is a **⅋** cardinal buoy, yellow and black VQ(6)+LFl.10s5M. On the NE edge is a yellow cylindrical buoy with × topmark, lit Fl.Y.5s. The leading lines on Forte Camicia and Chiesa lead through the centre of this passage on a course of 064° (these are virtually impossible to make out in daylight and even at night the leading line lights of F.G.3M are not easy to see!).

3. South passage

This is between the Secca del Palau and Santa Stefano, actually Isolotto Roma, a rocky islet just off the main island. Isolotto Roma has a column on its western extremity. Shoals exist for at least 200m to the west of Isolotto Roma and the channel is nearer to the Secca. There are leading lights for this passage on the hill to the west of La Maddalena town on 014° (*Front* Iso.G.2s50m8M, *Rear* (1000m away) Oc.G.150m8M). Again these can be difficult to make out in daylight but as this passage is used mainly by the ferry traffic plying between Palau and La Maddalena, it is relatively easy to see where the ferries are going!

S15 La Maddalena

⊕91 (Porto Mercantile) 41°12′.6N 09°24′.33E
⊕92 (Cala Mangiavolpe) 41°12′.7N 09°24′.65E
⊕93 (Cala Camiciotto) 41°12′.78N 09°25′.66E
⊕94 (Marina del Ponte) 41°12′.9N 09°26′.4E

Charts
Admiralty *1212*
Italian *42, 324, 325, 281, 282*

Depth
Porto Mercantile 3–6m; Cala Mangiavolpe 1–4m; Cala Camiciotto 0.5–3.5m; Marina del Ponte 0.5–7m

Number of berths
Porto Mercantile 130; Cala Mangiavolpe 120; Cala Camiciotto 160 (60 for visitors); Marina del Ponte 120

Maximum length
Porto Mercantile 12m; Cala Mangiavolpe 14m; Cala Camiciotto 20m; Marina del Ponte 25m

Lights
0961 Porto Mercantile W mole F.R.6m3M Red pole 5m
0962 E mole F.G.7m3M Green pole 6m
0962.4 Main quay E 2F.R(hor)7m3M Red post 5m
0963 Ferry pier F.RG(vert)7m3M Red and green pole
0966 Isola Chiesa diga head F.R.7m3M Red pole 4m
0968 Rock (175m SW of 0968) F.G.6m3M Green pole 5m
0972 Hospital Pier head F.R.7m3M Red pole 6m
0974 Cala Camiciotto pier head F.R.7m3M Red pole 5m
There are other lights associated with Cala Camicia, the naval port, into which entry is forbidden.

Port communications
Port Mercantile Commune ☎ 0789 730 121
Fax 0789 790 650
Marina Office ☎ 0789 792 389
Cala Mangiavolpe VHF Ch 11 or 9 (0700–1900)
Ecomar Mobile 338 6378256
Email ecomar@yahoo.it
Cala Camiciotto ☎ 338 234 3955
Marina del Ponte ☎/*Fax* 0789 726 034
Email marinadelponte@tiscali.it

Warnings
Berthing is under the orders of the harbourmaster, who must be consulted before mooring.

A busy, crowded tourist town

The town of La Maddalena is the main centre of habitation on the island and the harbour is used by commercial, military, fishing, ferry and pleasure vessels. It is a busy little place serving the Italian Naval base and the NATO base on Santo Stefano, although it is rumoured that the Americans will shortly withdraw their forces from this base. In summer it attracts large numbers of day tourists from the hotels on the mainland. There are now four main harbours along the south coast of the island, the old Cala Gavetta, now renamed Porto Mercantile; the newer Cala Mangiavolpe just to the east; a recent addition – Cala Camiciotto – and Cala Camicia. This latter is a military installation and is strictly out of bounds for private pleasure yachts. Just to the west of Porto Mercantile is a 100m long pontoon projecting south from the Scalo di Alaggio. It is very exposed to the washes from the ferries but in settled weather it is another possible berthing position with 3–5m depth at the outer end of the pontoon. Also near the bridge over to Caprera there is a small marina, Marina del Ponte, which has one floating jetty and a buoyed mooring area.

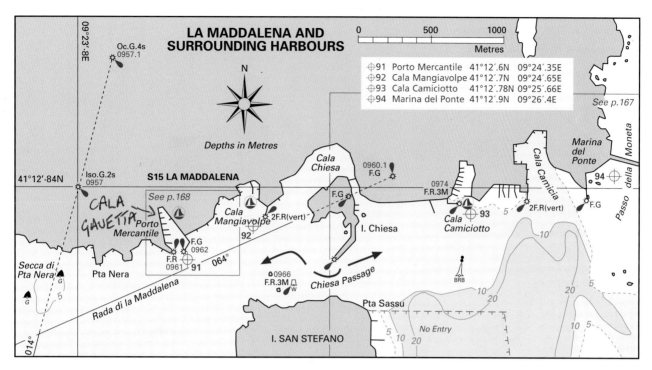

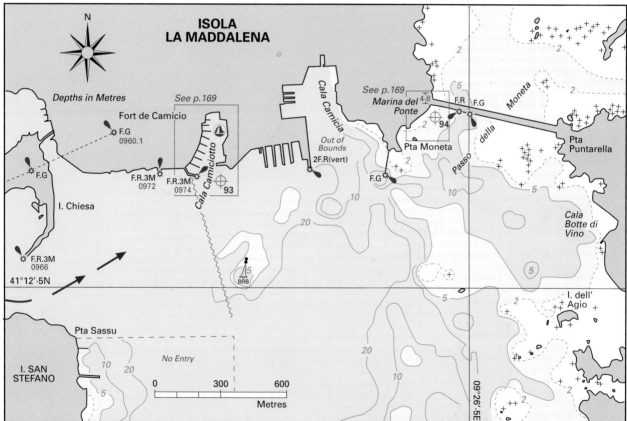

3. SANTA TERESA DI GALLURA TO CAPO FERRO

Initially visitors should contact Porto Mercantile for possible berthing instructions as it is the largest and most secure of the La Maddalena harbours. It is also closest to the shops and shoreside facilities and offers the splendid facility of mooring free for 2 hours.

Approach

By day

Despite the many rocks fringing the approaches, once inside the approach is straightforward. The leading marks below Fort Camicia (on 064°) show the way but the houses of the town are obvious and, if in any doubt, there are the many ferries to show you the way, towards the harbour.

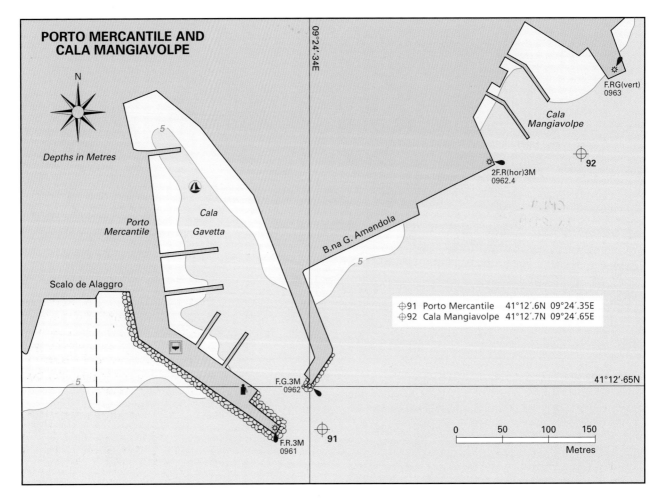

PORTO MERCANTILE AND CALA MANGIAVOLPE

N

Depths in Metres

Porto Mercantile

Cala Gavetta

Scalo de Alaggro

Cala Mangiavolpe

F.RG(vert) 0963

2F.R(hor)3M 0962.4

B.na G. Amendola

92

⊕91 Porto Mercantile 41°12′.6N 09°24′.35E
⊕92 Cala Mangiavolpe 41°12′.7N 09°24′.65E

09°24′.34E

F.G.3M 0962

F.R.3M 0961

91

41°12′·65N

0   50   100   150
Metres

By night

Follow the leading lights on the slopes to the west of the port which show the way through the south passage on 014° (*Front* Iso.G.2s8M *Rear* Oc.G.4s8M). Turn to 066° when the leading lights on Fort Camicio (two F.G.3M) come into line.

Entrance

There are no problems at any of the marinas, although care should be exercised on the approach to Marina del Ponte as it is quite shallow with rocks near the shore.

Porto Mercantile (Cala Gaveta)

Berths

Call on the VHF radio or telephone to get a berth before making fast.

Formalities

Customs and police are available.

Facilities

Small repairs can be undertaken but there is electricity and water laid on only at Porto Mercantile and Marina del Ponte. As this is a busy tourist island and all goods have to be brought in by ship, prices are high and for stocking up and major repairs use the facilities of Palau or other mainland ports.

Chiesa passage

If leaving and continuing south, or going to the eastern two marinas, one must take the Chiesa Passage north of Santo Stefano Island. There are many offlying rocks to the north of Santo Stefano and these are marked by a green buoy and a green conical beacon. To the north of this beacon a breakwater extends south from Chiesa Island. The passage is between the beacon and breakwater end and has a least depth of 3.3m. There is F.G on the beacon and F.R on the breakwater.

CALA CAMICIOTTO

⊕93 41°12′.78N 09°25′.66E

Depths
0.5 to 3m

Number of berths
160 with 60 for visitors

Maximum LOA
20m

This is a new marina in part of the naval dockyard. It has 8 floating pontoons projecting from the west side of the *cala* (it is forbidden to moor on the eastern side). There is a porta-cabin as an office and it seems to be solely for small local craft. Enquiries at the site indicated that the port operated from May until September but a call on ☎ 338 234 4955 should allow berthing there. There are no facilities at all there out of season but showers and WCs in season are apparently available (although not visible in the October 2005 visit).

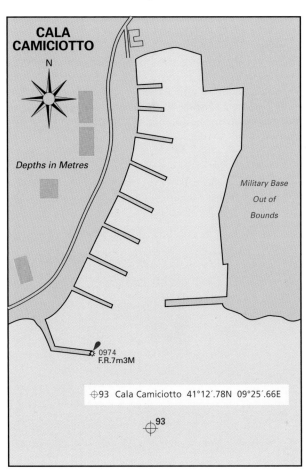

⊕93 Cala Camiciotto 41°12′.78N 09°25′.66E

PORTO MERCANTILE

⊕91 41°12′.6N 09°24′.35E

CALA MANGIAVOLPE

⊕91 41°12′.7N 09°24′.65E

MARINA DEL PONTE

⊕94 41°12′.9N 09°26′.4E

Depths
0.5 to 7m

Number of berths
120

Maximum LOA
25m

This marina had great plans for many pontoons at the outset but it has not extended much over the past few years. There is still the one floating pontoon with 80 berths and a field of 40 mooring buoys. Again there are few facilities: water and electricity on the pontoon and some repairs are possible, but there are no services whatsoever ashore.

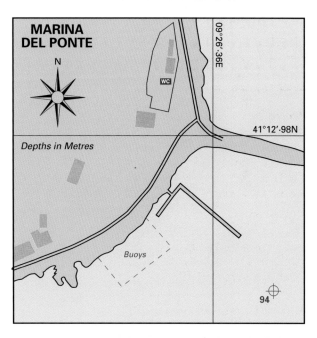

⊕94 Marina del Ponte 41°12′.9N 09°26′.4E

Anchorages around Isola La Maddalena
See plan page 165

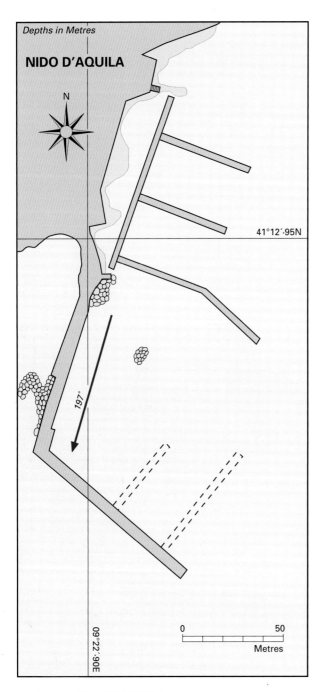

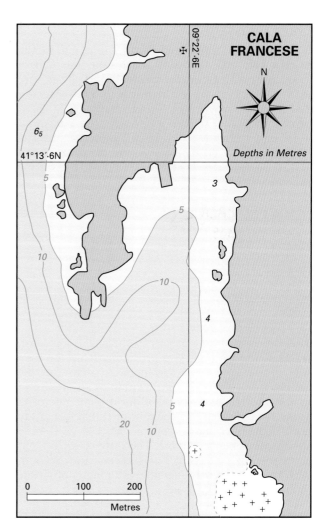

⚓ **CALA FRANCESE** 41°13′.46N 09°22′.5E

A bay on the west coast which is rocky and open at the south end but is more sheltered from the north through east to south in the northern part. Anchor in 3–5m on a sand bottom. There is a small disused military pier in the northwest corner to which a line can be taken if required.

⚓ **CALA NIDO D'AQUILA** 41°12′.8N 09°22′.8E

This *cala* lies to the north of Punta Tegge on the SW corner of La Maddalena. It is shallow and very rocky but recently a series of concrete and floating pontoons have been added with capacity for 200 craft but as the depth is 1m or less these craft are mainly *gommones* and small motor boats.

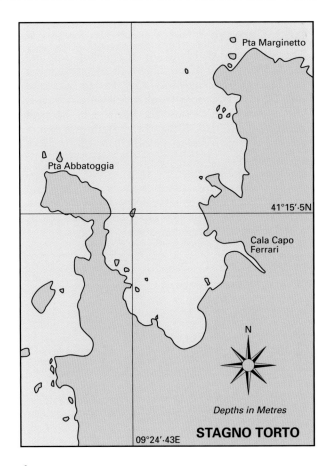

STAGNO TORTO

⚓ **STAGNO TORTO** 41°15'.45N 09°24'.5E

This is a large bay on the NW corner of the island fringed with rocks and a rocky obstruction to starboard on entering. Anchor in 6m in the centre of the bay. On the eastern shore there is Cala Capo Ferrari where there are a number of pontoons, but again these are solely for small motor boats as the depth is 1m or less. There are 2 lights at the entrance (0985 S. Jetty Fl. G.4s3M Green post 3M and 0985.2 N Jetty Fl.R.4s3M Red post 3M).

S16 Porto Massimo

⊕95 41°15'.4N 09°26'.0E

Depths
0.5m to 3.5m

Number of berths
140

Maximum LOA
25m

Port communications
☎ 0789 729 168 *Fax* 0789 721 083
www.marinadiportomassimo.com

This is a private hotel complex on the NE coast. It is difficult to see when approaching from the north but when east of the entrance the hotel complex is clear. Go stern-to inside the outer mole as the inner pier is in shallow water. There is water on the quay, a small shop, restaurant and bars. There is now a line of mooring buoys laid outside the main breakwater which can be used if vacant.

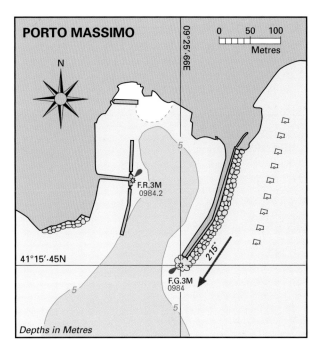

PORTO MASSIMO

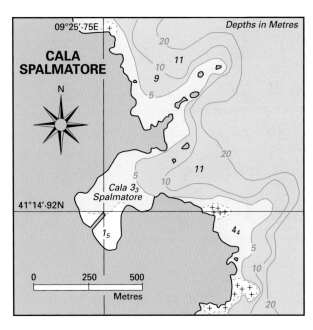

CALA SPALMATORE

⚓ **CALA SPALMATORE** 41°15'N 09°26'E

This *cala* is just south of Porto Massimo. There are a number of above-water rocks to the north of the entrance so proceed in on the south side and anchor in 3m in the southern part of the bay. The bay now has 8 buoys laid (and administered by Porto Massimo) and there are swimmers' buoys from the pier end to the land due east. All these buoys severely restrict the room to anchor: in fact, anchoring is frowned upon if not actually forbidden. There is a pier running out from the west shore that has 4m of water at its end but there are rocks inshore. Do not moor to the pier as it is part of the naval facilities. There is a bar and restaurant ashore but no other facilities.

3. SANTA TERESA DI GALLURA TO CAPO FERRO

Isola Santa Stefano

A mainly barren island with a large military area on the north and east coasts. Anchoring and landing are prohibited in this area. There is only one good anchorage on the island.

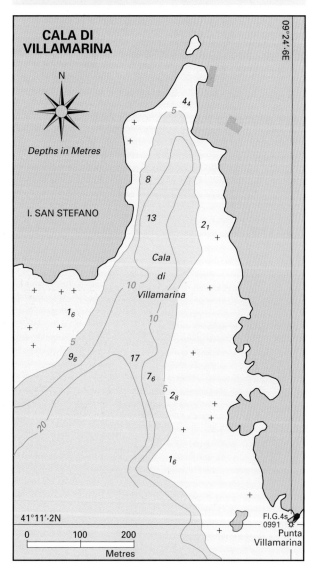

⚓ **CALA DI VILLAMARINA** 41°11′.4N 09°24′.4E

There is a green light structure (Fl.G.4s14m4M) on the eastern Punta Villamarina with an islet off. Take up a position at least 350m west of the point and steer about 020° towards the conspicuous white house near the head of the inlet. This avoids the extensive rocky outcrops on both sides of the entrance. There is excellent shelter here in all but strong southerlies. Anchor off the quay, which is now in a very bad state of repair, in 5–6m and take a line ashore if required. There are no facilities whatever. There is a path up the hill to the west which leads to a quarry where there are huge pieces of a giant statue, said to be of Garibaldi.

Isola Caprera

The easternmost island of the group is hilly (212m) and sparsely populated. It is joined to La Maddalena by a causeway with a road bridge of only 4.8m clearance (from sea level) so yachts should not expect to use the Passo della Moneta between the islands. Most of the island is a nature reserve and there are areas off the south and east coasts where it is nominally prohibited to navigate, anchor or fish. It is a very indented island, with many small bays where one can always find shelter whatever the wind direction. The six most popular are mentioned below, anticlockwise from the causeway.

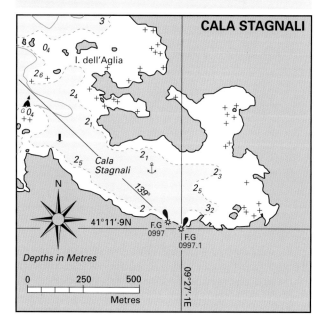

⚓ **CALA STAGNALI** 41°12′.32N 09°26′.6E

A large rocky inlet on the west coast of Caprera, just east of the north end of Santa Stefano. It has a buoy on the south side and a leading line 139° of two daymarks on the shore in front of the village (these are both lit with F.G.3M). There are 2 piers here which were reserved exclusively for military use. To enter, approach the outer buoy on an easterly course and follow the leading line into the inlet bearing to

Cala Stagnali

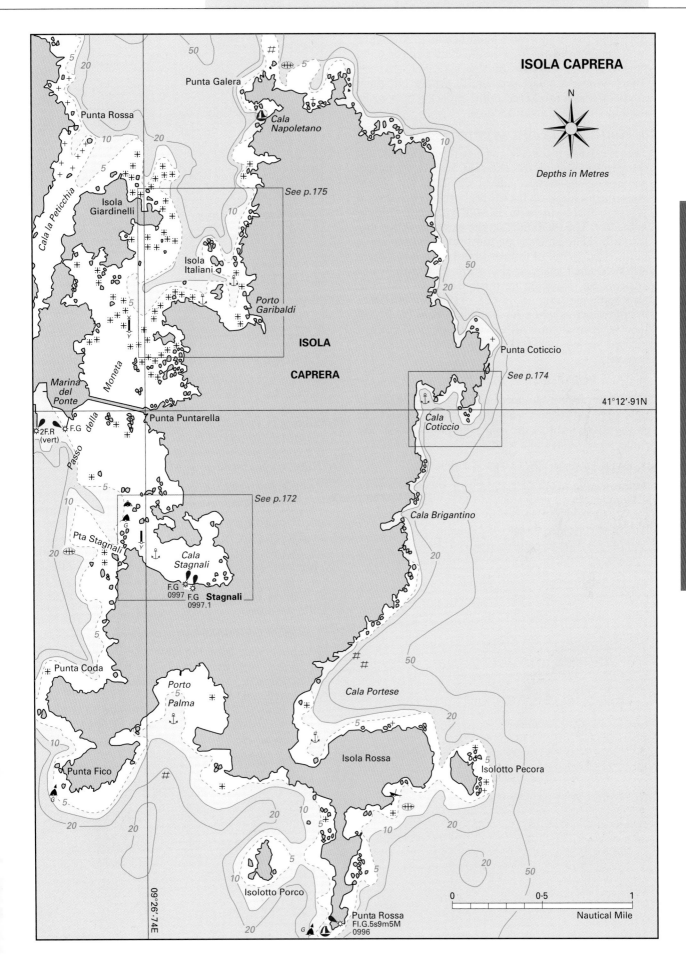

ISOLA CAPRERA

Punta Galera

Cala Napoletano

N

Depths in Metres

Punta Rossa

Cala la Peticchia

Isola Giardinelli

See p.175

10

Isola Italiani

Porto Garibaldi

50

20

ISOLA

CAPRERA

Punta Coticcio

See p.174

41°12'·91N

Moneta

Passo della

Marina del Ponte

Punta Puntarella

Cala Coticcio

2F.R (vert)

F.G

Pta Stagnali

See p.172

Cala Brigantino

See p.172

Cala Stagnali

F.G 0997

F.G 0997.1 **Stagnali**

20

Punta Coda

Porto Palma

Cala Portese

Isola Rossa

Isolotto Pecora

Punta Fico

Isolotto Porco

Punta Rossa
Fl.G.5s9m5M
0996

09°26'·74E

0   0·5   1

Nautical Mile

port after passing the port-hand headland to anchor in 2–3m on sand and rock in the middle of the inlet. Note that the inlet to the north is extremely shallow. There is now a smart promenade ashore but there are no facilities whatever and the piers appear to be used by private individuals now.

⚓ PORTO PALMA 41°11′.2N 09°27′E

This is a bay on the SW coast with many rocks on the eastern side of the entrance and two shallow patches on the eastern side of the inner bay. There are sailing schools on the shores but there are several places to anchor in 3–7m on sand with good holding in the bay. The small inlet on the west side of the bay is totally sheltered from any swell from the *maestrale* but it is fairly full of sailing school moorings. There are two small piers at the north end with water adjacent but there are no other facilities. There are now some mooring buoys laid in this bay but there is still room to anchor. Anchor where possible in 3–8 metres on sand (some areas have eel grass so you are advised to lay out two anchors if a *maestrale* is forecast).

⚓ CALA PORTESE 41°11′.2N 09°28′.1E

This is an anchorage north of Isola Rossa but it is untenable with winds from the northeast. Anchor in 3–5m at the head of the *cala* – keeping clear of the rocks on the north and west shores.

⚓ CALA BRIGANTINO 41°12′.35N 09°28′.7E

About a mile north of Portese is a small inlet with offlying rocks on both sides of the entrance, but you can go right in and anchor in 3m as long as there is hardly anyone else there!

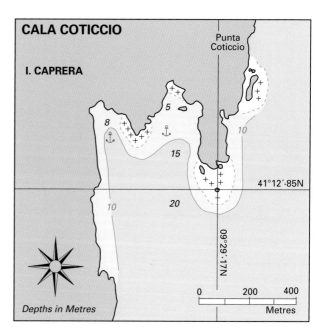

⚓ CALA COTICCIO (TAHITI BAY) 41°12′.9N 09°29′E

This anchorage is really two coves and very popular in the season. The eastern cove is the more sheltered (and thus the more crowded). It is deep (8m) and holding is suspect. With strong westerlies there are the usual gusts that sweep down from various directions and can cause confusion in the anchorage. There are no facilities at all here.

CALA NAPOLETANA 41°14′.5N 09°27′.6E

This small *cala* is situated just south of the northernmost point of Isola Caprera, Punta Galera. It is fringed by beaches but in the summer months the *cala* is closed to craft by a rope across its mouth. However, one can still anchor in 5 metres on rock and sand outside the ropes. It is open to the prevailing NW winds and should only be used in calm weather.

⚓ PORTO GARIBALDI 41°13′.5N 09°27′E

This anchorage is on the west side of Caprera, with three small islets called the Italian Isles. It is possible to anchor in 2.5–3.5m E of the southern islet. There is a small pier but with rocks off its south side, which again is for military use only, and a Club Med complex ashore. It is a short walk from here to see the house where Garibaldi spent his last years, which is now a museum to his memory.

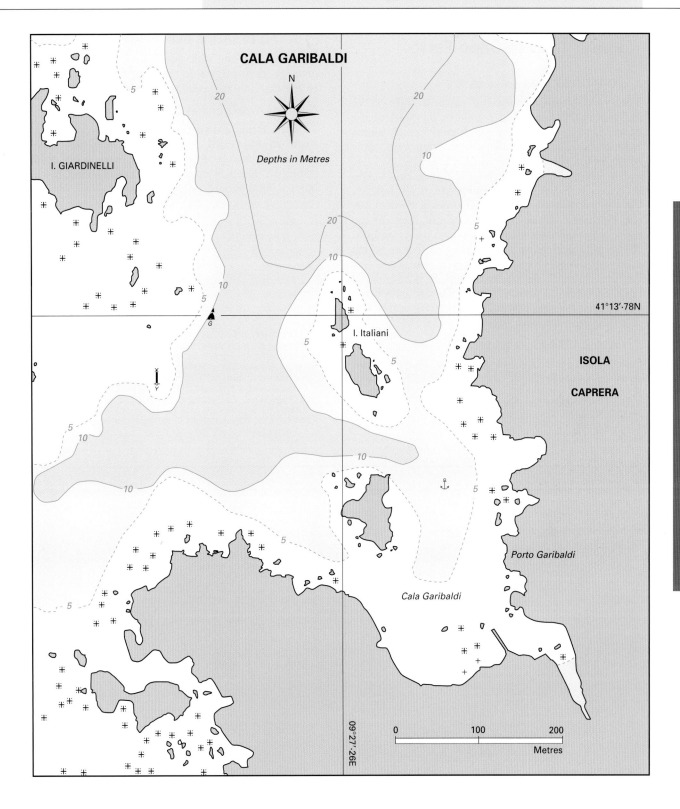

CALA GARIBALDI

N

Depths in Metres

20

20

10

10

I. GIARDINELLI

5

20

10

10

5

G

X
Y

5

I. Italiani

5

5

41°13'·78N

ISOLA

CAPRERA

10

10

5

5

5

Porto Garibaldi

Cala Garibaldi

0   100   200

Metres

09°27'·26E

Capo d'Orso to Capo Ferro

CAPO D'ORSO 41°10'.67N 09°25'.37E

This is a steep-to headland with a light 0092 Fl.3s12m10M. Some half a mile to the west of the point there is a 122 metre high peak which looks, from certain angles, just like a bear – hence the name of the point.

The channel between Isola Caprera and Capo d'Orso is half a mile wide and clear of all dangers. On the northeast side of the channel is Punta Fico, the southwest corner of Isola Caprera. Just off the point is a small islet with a black pole on its summit. A green conical buoy lies off the small islet which clears all dangers. Two miles to the southeast, just south of Punta Rossa on Isola Caprera is an isolated rock, Secca di Tre Monti. This is marked by a black pole with a red stripe with 2 spherical topmarks and it is lit in summer with 0994 Fl(2)8s5m5M.

⚓ CALA CAPRA 41°10'.06N 09°25'.3E

Just over half a mile south of Capo d'Orso there is a small cala with a couple of jetties. The northern one is lit 0993 F.G.6m4M while the southern one is partially demolished and should not be used. Anchor in 5 to 6 metres on sand if there is no room at the jetty.

⚓ GOLFO DI SALINE 41°09'.6N 09°25'E

This bay lies one mile south of Capo d'Orso and gives good protection in westerly winds but is open to the east. Anchor near the head in 5m on sand.

Golfo di Arzachena 41°08'N 09°27'.2E

This is a large, 2-mile-deep inlet. It has good shelter from all but north winds. There are two yacht harbours and a number of small bays with pontoons. Keep to the centre of the entrance of the bay to avoid shoals on both sides.

⊕97 Cannigione 41°06'.6N 09°26'.8E
⊕98 Cala Bitta 41°07'.7N 09°27'.95E

0992 **Capo d'Orso** Fl.3s12m10M White tower 10m
0994 **Secca di Tre Monti** Fl(2).8s5m5M Black beacon, red bands 2 black spheres topmark
0996 **Punta Rossa** Fl.G.5s7m4M Green post 4m
1000 **Isoal delle Bisce** Fl.G.3s11m8M White tower, green band 9m
1002 **NE Point** Fl.R.3s14m8M White tower, red band 10m
1003 **Capo Ferro** Fl(3)15s52m24M White tower on 2 storey house 18m Oc.R.5s42m8M on same tower 8m 189°-R-203°
1004 **Secche del Cervo** Q(3).10s6m4M E cardinal beacon BYB with 2 cones base-to-base 2m

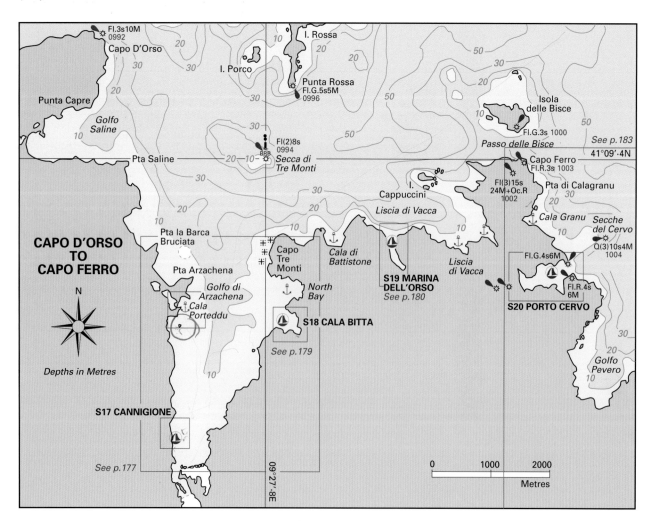

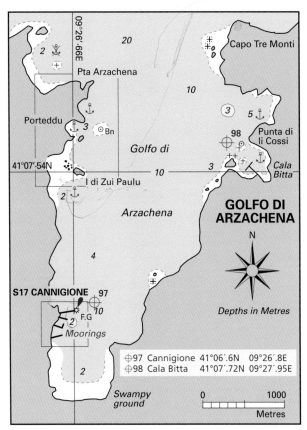

⚓ **CALA PORTEDDU** 41°07′.8N 09°26′.65E

⚓ **LA CONIA (S OF ZIU PAULU ISLET)**
41°07′.5N 09°26′.6E

There is a pier and some floating pontoons on a small bay just inshore of Isloletto di Ziu Paulu. Anchor in 3–5m at least 200m south of the islet. There is a sailing school here so it may be rather busy – especially in school holiday time!

S17 Cannigione

⊕97 41°06′.6N 09°26′.8E

Depths
0.4 to 4m
Number of berths
400
Maximum LOA
25m
Lights
0995 Pier head F.G.7m3M Green pole 5m (P)
Port communications
Sardamar Port Office VHF 11 (0700–1900)
☎ 0789 88 422 *Email* coop.sardamar@tiscali.it
Pontile dei Fiori ☎/*Fax* 0789 845 011
Mobile 339 290 4355 *Email* pontiledeifiori@libero.it

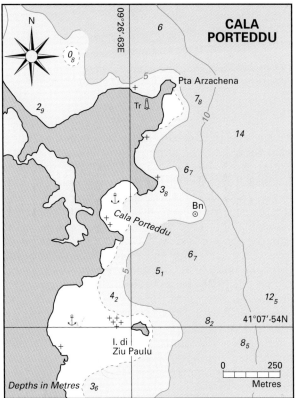

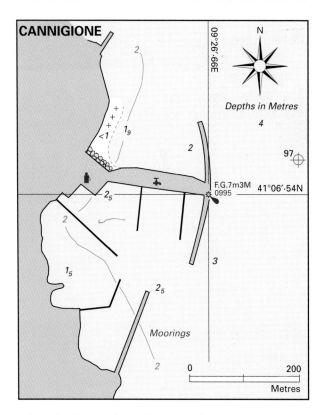

⚓ **CALA PORTEDDU** 41°07′.8N 09°26′.65E
A small bay south of the daymark on Punta Arzachena with a small pier, but it is very rocky and shallow – not recommended. There is a rock some 250m off the northern headland with a pole on it (occasionally).

This harbour has been undergoing a major redevelopment. The width of the breakwater has been greatly increased and a curved jetty some 200 metres long has been constructed at the breakwater's seaward end. However the works had come to a standstill in late 2005 but it was hoped to complete the work in 2006 or 2007.

During the season there are a number of floating pontoons available, which can be used but take care that there is adequate water as depths do go down to less than 1m in places. There are 400 berths with 50 places for visitors but a call may help to decide on a place for the night Anchoring is now forbidden south of the jetty. Electricity, water, fuel and toilets are available on the jetty and minor repairs can be undertaken. Simple everyday stores are available in the village.

S18 Cala Bitta

⊕98 41°07′.72N 09°27′.95E

Depth
1.5 to 3m

Number of berths
183

Maximum LOA
27m

Port communications
Port office ☎ 0789 99 243 *Fax* 0789 99 580
Email calabitta@tiscali.it

Old view of Cannigone and south end of Golfo di Arzachena looking NE with Cala Bitta in top left corner

This is a small harbour built as an integral part of a plan for a large hotel and tourist complex ashore. Initial work has been completed but little has happened over the past 5 years, and out of season the shoreside development appears derelict. Recently the marina has been taken over by a private company and they are making great efforts to enhance the port. Plans have been put forward to extend the jetty and the marina is now manned throughout the year. Certainly the hard standing and repair facilities have been markedly improved already. However, apart from the usual showers and WCs there is little else here out of season.

It is a difficult approach, almost impossible in strong N to NW winds, but now there are red and green buoys showing a channel of 3m minimum depth in the summer season. There is a rock to the north side of the bay which is sometimes marked with a pole, but this should not be relied on. Go stern-to inside the mole where there is excellent shelter but the place is usually completely crowded in the season. There are said to be bars and restaurants ashore in July and August.

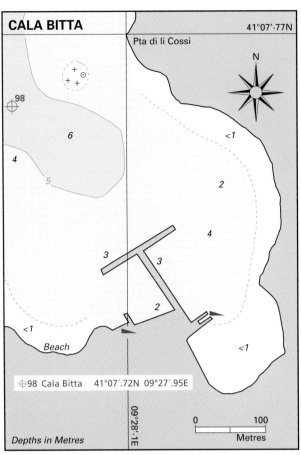

CALA BITTA

41°07′·77N

Pta di li Cossi

N

98

6

4

5

3

3

2

<1

Beach

<1

2

4

<1

⊕98 Cala Bitta   41°07′.72N 09°27′.95E

09°28′·1E

0   100
Metres

Depths in Metres

⚓ NORTH BAY 41°07′.96N 09°28′.1E

If Cala Bitta is full one can anchor in the next bay to the north, under Capo Tre Monti. Anchor in 3 to 5m on sand and weed and apart from a northwesterly swell that can roll in the anchorage has reasonable shelter.

CAPO TRE MONTI & SECCA DI TRE MONTI
41°08′.6N 09°28′.04E

Capo Tre Monti is the eastern headland of the Golfo di Arzachena. It is a broad headland which only rises to 64m high at its centre. It has extensive reefs off its west coast which extend for up to 400m and a wide berth should be given to this point.

0.8M north of the point lies the Secca di Tre Monti, a large reef of rocks marked by an isolated danger pole, BRB with ⁝ topmark, lit Fl(2)8s5M. There is a 20m deep, half-mile-wide channel both north and south of this reef.

⚓ CALA DI BATTISTONE 41°08′.6N 09°28′.8E

About 0.7 miles east of Capo Tre Monti there is a reasonably sized inlet. Again there are ropes and small buoys 100 metres off the beach in the summer months but one can anchor in 5 metres outside these buoys on rock and sand. The holding is reported to be very poor.

Cala Bitta

3. SANTA TERESA DI GALLURA TO CAPO FERRO

S19 Marina dell'Orso (Poltu Quatu)

⊕99 41°08′.63N 09°29′.7E

Depth
2 to 3.5m

Number of berths
410

Maximum LOA
35m

Lights
0995.4 LH entrance Fl.R.5s7m4M Red pole 4m
0995.42 RH entrance Fl.G.5s7m4M Green pole 4m

Port communications
Port office VHF Ch 9 ☎ 0789 99 477 *Fax* 0789 99 468
Email polquatu@tin.it *url* www.poltuquatu.com

A very sheltered marina

Rounding Capo Tre Monti and Capo Battistone, look for a narrow fiord which has been dredged and converted to a yacht harbour for 400 yachts (50 for visitors) with nearly 2,000m of pontoons. Speed must be kept below 3 knots. Call ahead before entering. The entrance is 60m wide. There is water and electricity at all berths, with some limited repair facilities ashore and fuel at the entrance. There is a small shop and a few cafés in the development but little else ashore.

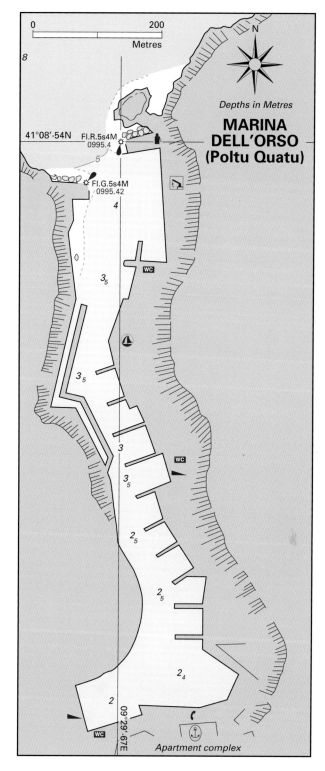

Marina dell'Orso (Poltu Quatu) looking N

⚓ LISCIA DI VACCA 41°08′.8N 09°30′.3E

This is quite a large bay just to the west of Capo Ferro. Pass to the south of Isola Cappuccini and make for the south of the bay. There is a small pier off a cluster of houses, but watch for an isolated rock marked, occasionally, by a black, red, black pole with topmarks some 250m off the western headland of the bay. The shore is ringed with rocks, so care is needed in picking a position in 4–7m. The bottom is sand and weed but holding is reputed to be reasonable. There is good shelter here in all winds except for northwesterly. Ashore there is the Pitrizza Hotel which is the most expensive in this area, if not in the whole of Italy.

Isola Cappuccini 41°09′.2N 09°30′.1E

Continuing south there is a 7m-deep passage between the mainland and Isola Cappuccini but it is not recommended if the sea is at all rough.

CAPO FERRO & ISOLA DELLE BISCE
41°09′.4N 09°31′.5E (see plan page 176)

The passage between Isola delle Bisce and Capo Ferro is deep and clear of dangers in the fairway. Capo Ferro is steep-to while the rocks to the S and SE of the island are obvious in daylight.

By night

There are lights Fl.G.3s11m8M and Fl.R.3s14m8M on the island and cape respectively. The main lighthouse of Capo Ferro is a tall white tower on a two-storied building Fl(3)15s52m24M, with a red light Oc.R.5s42m8M on the same structure covering a sector of 189°-203° over 2 shoal patches, the Secca delle Bisce and the Secca dei Monaci to the north. It is reported that there is a good lunch stop in E to SE winds in a large bay just west of the headland, due east of I. Cappuccini. The bottom is rock and sand but anchor in 5–10 metres over sand, if possible.

PUNTA DI CALAGRANU 41°09′.1N 09°31′.88E

This point lies just under half a mile south east of Capo Ferro and has many awash offliers to the north. It is recommended to keep at least 250 metres off the land to clear these rocks.

Cala Bitta looking NW

Porto Cervo old quay the next marina east (see page 184)

4 PORTO CERVO TO OLBIA APPROACH

This section of coast consists of deeply indented gulfs and bays and a profusion of artificial yacht harbours, some of which have literally been dug out of the surrounding land. There are several offshore islands and the whole coastline is dominated by Capo Figari and Isola Tavolara to the south.

Golfo Aranci in foreground; beyond is Cabo Figari with Isola de Figarolo and the SW tip of Isola Tavolara at top right (see page 193)

PLANNING GUIDE

Headlands		Ports & anchorages	Open to winds
Capo Ferro			
	⚓	Cala Granu	NE-E-SE
Punta Calagranu			
Secche del Cervo′			
	S20 ⛵	**Porto Cervo page 184**	E
	⚓	Golfo Pevero	
		Isole di li Nibani & Passo delle Galera	
	⚓	Porto Liccia	N-E
Punta Capaccia			
		Isole Poveri and Isole Mortorio and Soffi	
	⚓	Mortorio	E
Punta Capriccioli			
	⚓	Cala di Volpe	S
Punta Ligata			
		Isola Portisco	
	S21 ⛵	**Marina di Portisco page 188**	E
	⚓	Golfo di Cugnana	N
Punta Nuraghe			
	S22 ⛵	**Porto Rotondo page 189**	NW
Punta Volpe (Rocks off)			
	S23 ⛵	**Porto Oro (Palumbalza) page 191**	E
	S24 ⛵	**Punta Marana page 191**	NW-N
	⚓	Marinella (private)	N
Puntas Sabina & Canigione (Rocks off both)			
Capo Figari			
	S25 ⛵	**Golfo Aranci page 193**	W
	S26 ⛵	**Baia Caddinas page 193**	SE
	⚓	SW of Isola Porri	E

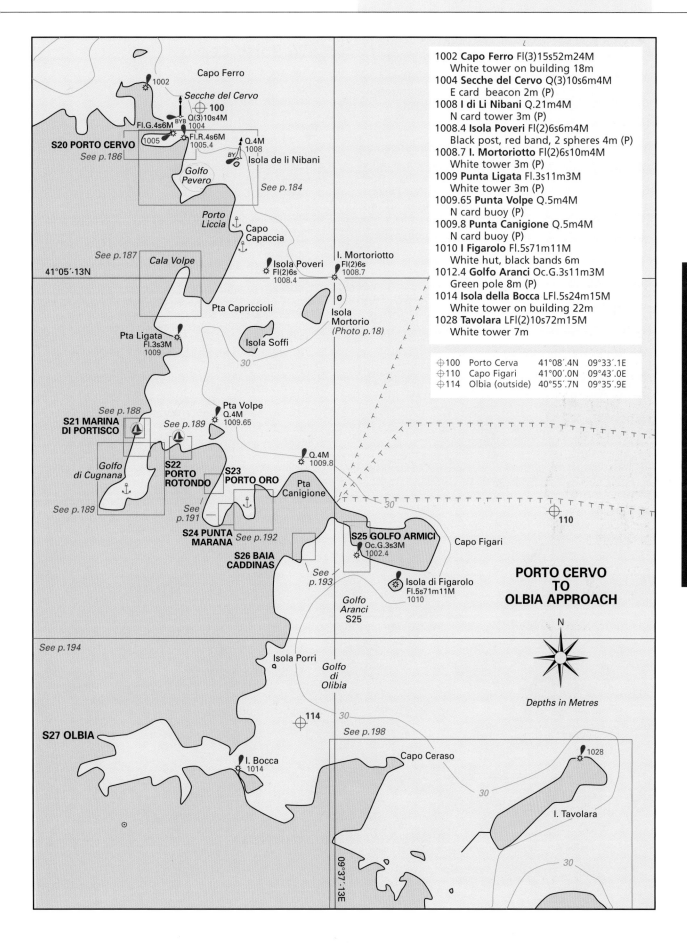

1002 **Capo Ferro** Fl(3)15s52m24M
White tower on building 18m
1004 **Secche del Cervo** Q(3)10s6m4M
E card beacon 2m (P)
1008 **I di Li Nibani** Q.21m4M
N card tower 3m (P)
1008.4 **Isola Poveri** Fl(2)6s6m4M
Black post, red band, 2 spheres 4m (P)
1008.7 **I. Mortoriotto** Fl(2)6s10m4M
White tower 3m (P)
1009 **Punta Ligata** Fl.3s11m3M
White tower 3m (P)
1009.65 **Punta Volpe** Q.5m4M
N card buoy (P)
1009.8 **Punta Canigione** Q.5m4M
N card buoy (P)
1010 **I Figarolo** Fl.5s71m11M
White hut, black bands 6m
1012.4 **Golfo Aranci** Oc.G.3s11m3M
Green pole 8m (P)
1014 **Isola della Bocca** LFl.5s24m15M
White tower on building 22m
1028 **Tavolara** LFl(2)10s72m15M
White tower 7m

⊕100 Porto Cerva 41°08′.4N 09°33′.1E
⊕110 Capo Figari 41°00′.0N 09°43′.0E
⊕114 Olbia (outside) 40°55′.7N 09°35′.9E

Capo Ferro
1002

Secche del Cervo
⊕ **100**
Q(3)10s4M
BYB 1004
Fl.G.4s6M
1005 Fl.R.4s6M
1005.4
Q.4M
BY 1008
Isola de li Nibani

S20 PORTO CERVO
See p.186

Golfo
Pevero

See p.184

Porto
Liccia
Capo
Capaccia

See p.187
Cala Volpe
41°05′.13N

I. Mortoriotto
Fl(2)6s
1008.7

Isola Poveri
Fl(2)6s
1008.4

Isola
Mortorio
(Photo p.18)

Pta Capriccioli

Pta Ligata
Fl.3s3M
1009

Isola Soffi

30

See p.188
**S21 MARINA
DI PORTISCO**

See p.189

Pta Volpe
Q.4M
1009.65

Golfo
di Cugnana

**S22
PORTO
ROTONDO**

**S23
PORTO ORO**

Pta
Canigione

Q.4M
1009.8

30

See p.189

See
p.191
**S24 PUNTA
MARANA**

See p.192

**S26 BAIA
CADDINAS**

See
p.193

S25 GOLFO ARMICI
Oc.G.3s3M
1002.4

Capo Figari

⊕**110**

Isola di Figarolo
Fl.5s71m11M
1010

Golfo
Aranci
S25

**PORTO CERVO
TO
OLBIA APPROACH**

N

See p.194

Isola Porri

Golfo
di
Olbia

Depths in Metres

⊕**114**

30

See p.198

S27 OLBIA

I. Bocca
1014

Capo Ceraso

1028

30

I. Tavolara

30

09°37′.13E

4. PORTO CERVO TO OLBIA APPROACH

⚓ CALA GRANU 41°08'.76N 09°31'.75E

A small cove, half a mile south of Capo Ferro makes a pleasant stop before entering Porto Cervo. It is very popular with the small open boat fraternity from Porto Cervo and can get very crowded.

SECCHE DEL CERVO 41°08'.7N 09°32'.76E

These rocks lie north of Porto Cervo entrance and extend for 0.6 miles from the land. There is an E cardinal buoy at their eastern extremity 1004 Q(3)10s6m4M during the summer months. There is a narrow passage inside the rocks but it is not recommended without local knowledge. The rocks should be left well to starboard when coming south.

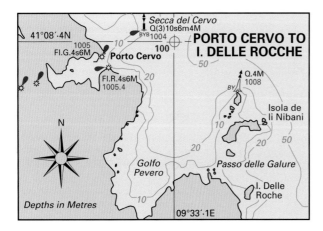

Porto Cervo looking NE with Cala Granu at top on extreme left

S20 Porto Cervo

⊕100 41°08'.4N 09°33'.1E

Charts
Admiralty *161B, 163*
Italian *42, 323, 319*

Depth
1.7 to 7m in the marina

Number of berths
720 of which 80 are for visitors

Maximum LOA
100m

Lights
1004 Secche del Cervo 41°08'.6N 9°32'.8E Q(3)10s6m4M ↟ card beacon 2m (P)
1005 North side of entrance Fl.G.4s7m6M Green tower 5m (P)
1005.4 South side of entrance Fl.R.4s7m6M Red tower 5m (P)
1006 Ldg Lts *Front* Iso.R.2s27m3M 247.4°-vis-252.4° White tower, black stripe 8m (P)
1006.1 *Rear* (270m back) Oc.R.4s47m3M 247.4°-vis-252.4° White tower, black stripe 3m (P)
1007 Diga head F.G.7m3M Green pole 5m
1007.3 On coast 80m S of 1007 F.R.7m3M Red pole 5m

Port communications
Marina office VHF Ch 16, 9 (0700-1900). ☎ 0789 905 111, *Fax* 0789 911 53
Email pcmarina@portocervomarina.it
url www.marinadiportocervo.com

Warnings
Inside the entrance there is a free anchoring zone but be wary of the 1.6m patch in this area. In season the shallow areas are sometimes marked with small buoys with Fl.R.1s lights.

Porto Cervo runs many sailing regattas and there could be buoys laid outside the entrance which are not marked on any charts. They do not indicate dangers to navigation but the racing courses should be avoided if possible.

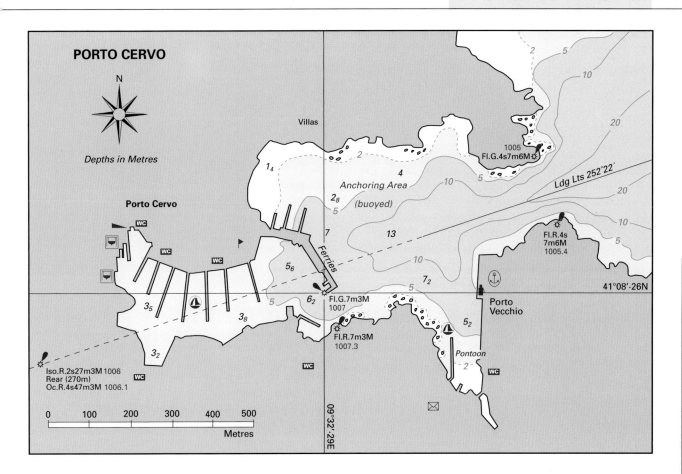

An expensive but well sheltered harbour

Porto Cervo is the yachting centre of the Consorzio Costa Smeralda and one of the first true marinas to be developed in this part of the world. It cost millions of dollars to build and is a real millionaire's playground. It has hotels, nightclubs, etc. but they are all blended in skilfully with the landscape and it is quite difficult to see the place on first approaching. In July and August it is a popular place for the jet-set but out of season it is worth the exorbitant fee just to say you have been there. (See photo page 181).

Approach

It is difficult to see the entrance to Porto Cervo when coming from the north although the passage of small vessels in and out will assist recognition.

By day

Pick out the Secche del Corvo beacon and steer south until the entrance opens up and some buildings and masts may be seen. The leading line marks are difficult to see but steer in on 252°, keeping to the middle of the entrance.

By night

The Secche del Cervo light may not be lit out of season so keep well clear until the leading lights can be picked up. Steer 252° between the red and green flashing 4s lights at the entrance.

By GPS

Steer towards ⊕100 from the NE quadrant. On arrival you are close to the leading line. Turn on to a course of 252° and pass between the entrance heads.

Entrance

There is no difficulty at the entrance except that gusts can sweep down, especially in northwest winds, and it is recommended to motor in.

Berths

The *capitaneria* is to port just inside the entrance with mooring stern-to in the Porto Vecchio, if there is space (note that mooring appears to be free out of season!). However it is also possible to contact the marina office by VHF and be allocated a berth before entering. There was a free anchoring area in the north of the harbour but it appears that this area has now been taken over by a joint venture of the Consorzio Costa Smeralda, Italgest and Siemens. Here 50 buoys have been laid and one can book a buoy on the internet and be sent a 'Seapass' – a ring which when put on the mooring rope 'talks' to the operations centre and confirms that it is at the correct buoy. The fee includes water taxi, refuse collection and 24 hours security. It is not clear how a visitor in transit can obtain a Seapass but further details can be obtained by contacting ☎ 890 100001 or website www.smartpark.it. It is still a relatively new venture and there are bound to be teething problems but it seems that anchoring is now

Porto Cervo anchorage – now buoyed (see text above)

prohibited in the buoyed area. This means anchoring is not an option in Porto Cervo anymore. Any further details on this subject will be gratefully received by the author.

Formalities

All authorities available.

Facilities

All.

⚓ GOLFO PEVERO 41°07′.5N 09°33′E

This is a large bay just south of Porto Cervo with a rock (with a black beacon with a red stripe) off the eastern headland. There is a beach at the south end but it is very rocky so anchor well off; the holding is also suspect on rock/sand/weed.

ISOLE DI LI NIBANI AND PASSO DELLE GALERA

These rocky islands have a 3m white conical structure on the northernmost islet which exhibits Q.21m4M from 1 June to 30 September. There is also a passage, the Passo delle Galera, between the islands and the mainland which had a beacon to the north and has a minimum depth of 5m. It is only recommended to use this in daylight and on calm days. On leaving this passage there are the Isole delle Rocche to the south with definitely no passage inside!

⚓ PORTO LICCIA 41°06′.3N 09°34′.2E

This is a small bay just to the north of Capo Capaccia. It is very popular with the daytime/lunch set from Cervo. There is another small anchorage just south of the cape but watch for the isolated rock, Scogli Capaccia, 200m SE of the cape, which should be left to starboard when sailing south. Both these bays are untenable in easterly winds.

ISOLA MORTORIO 41°04′.7N 09°36′.3E

Isola Mortorio has beautiful beaches on its western side and it has been very popular in the past for a lunch/beach outing. With the restrictions imposed by the Reserve Authorities (the NE corner is totally out of bounds from 1 March to 30 October, for example) it is not known what effect these may have had on the beaches to the west. It is reported that the western anchorage is still very popular, although the holding is poor and it is deep close in to the beach. (See photo page 18)

ISOLE POVERI, ISOLA MORTORIO AND ISOLA SOFFI

Isole Poveri are a group of low islands southeast of Capo Capaccia. There is a E cardinal buoy at the northern end of the islands (1008.5 Q(3)10s6m4M). At the southern end there is a black pole with a red stripe (with a topmark of 2 spheres) on an isolated rock and lit only in the summer months (1008.4 Fl(2)6s6m4M).

To seaward there are a number of larger islands with Isola Mortorio, the largest of the group, being 1 mile southeast of the Isole Poveri. To the south lies Isola Stoffi and half a mile northeast of Isola Mortorio is Isolotto Mortoriotto on which there is a small white tower with light 1008.7 Fl(2)6s10m4M, again only lit in the summer months.

Important note

The lights of Cervo, Isole Nibani, Poveri, Mortoriotto, Cala Volpe and Punta Ligata are maintained by local sources and are only lit from 1 June to 30 September. However, in some cases they may not be lit and, in fact, may not even be there because of damage etc.

⚓ CALA DI VOLPE 41°04′.8N 09°32′.35E

This is a long, shallow bay with excellent holding in sand but take care to avoid the even shallower patches. There is a pier at the north end of the bay with only 1m at the outer end and it leads to the Hotel Cala Volpe, another of the Costa Smeralda five-star hotels. The entrance lights are Fl.G.4s6m1M and Fl.R.4s7m1M. The bay is sheltered from all winds except southerlies. Note that Punta Capriccioli just east of this *cala* has foul ground to the east and south of it. Give it at least 300m berth when rounding.

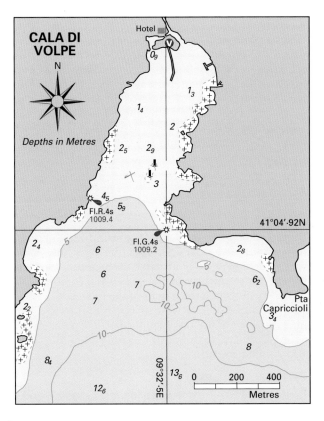

In line with the local protection of the marine environment, a large area of buoys (with data transmission capabilities) has been laid south of the *cala* and north of Punta Ligata for large yachts. It is now forbidden to anchor in the buoyed area and speed is restricted to 5 knots. This system is run by the same firm as that in Porto Cervo and it is possible to book digitally. There are water taxis, refuse disposal, laundry and weather services available. Further information and bookings can be obtained by contacting ☎ 899 100001 or the website www.smartpark.it.

Cala Di Volpe looking SE with hotel complex on left

S21 Marina di Portisco

⊕101 41°01′.96N 09°31′.7E

Charts
Admiralty *161B, 163*
Italian *910, 42, 323*

Depth
2 to 12m

Number of berths
560 with 56 for visitors

Maximum LOA
100m

Lights
1009.5 Molo Sopraflutto head 41°02′N 9°31′.6E
Fl.G.4s6m3M Tower with green pole 5m (P)
1009.52 Molo Sottoflutto elbow Fl.R.4s6m3M Red post
5m (P)
1009.51Molo Sottoflutto head F.R.3m1M Red column
1m (P)

Port communications
Marina office VHF Ch 69 ☎ 0789 33 520 *Fax* 0789 33
560 *Email* info@portisco.com *url* www.portisco.com

A well designed marina

This is one of the new marinas which have
proliferated in this part of the world and it has
recently doubled in size. In common with many
marinas, it has excellent facilities, with hotels,
restaurants and a housing development ashore.

Approach

A mile south of Cala di Volpe is Punta Ligata with
its light Fl.3s11m3M on a white conical tower.

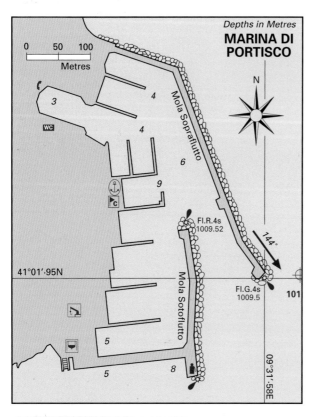

⊕101 Portisco 41°01′.96N 09°31′.7E

Another 1½ miles south of the point is an islet,
Isolotto Portisco, and just south of that is the
marina. If coming from the south give Punta Volpe
a berth of at least 500m to clear shallow areas and
make as though to enter the Golfo di Cugnana. The
harbour lies on the west side of the entrance to the
gulf, opposite Punta Nuraghe. The long Molo
Sopraflutto will easily be seen and should be
followed southwards until the entrance opens up.

By GPS

Approach ⊕101 from the NE sector and then make
for the breakwater.

Entrance

Round the end of the Molo Sopraflutto, giving it a
reasonable berth of at least 30m (during a June 2003
visit there were two awash white buoys moored
some 10m to the east of the end of the Molo which
probably indicated the extent of the mole end). Then
steer a course of just west of north and follow the
mole to port until the fuelling berth can be seen.
Moor here if a berth has not already been allocated
and contact the office.

Berths

Berth as directed by the marina staff. Most berths
have *pendillos* to the quay.

Facilities

All facilities are available, electricity and water laid
on to each berth and there is even a sewage pump-
out facility.

⚓ GOLFO DI CUGNANA 41°02′N 09°31′.6E

This natural inlet is entered between Marina di
Portisco breakwaters and Punta Nuraghe. It is very
shallow at the southern end but a yacht can find an
anchorage with good shelter and little swell. Note
there is a HT cable running across the gulf and it is
forbidden to anchor or fish for 200 metres north
and south of the cable. There is a holiday
development on the east side with some private
pontoons off Porto Asfodeli. Contact can be made
on VHF Ch 9 but the maximum LOA is 12m. At
Cugnana Verde in the southwestern corner of the
gulf there are a couple of floating pontoons with
some facilities for simple repairs but, although it
says there are 3-5m at the pontoons, it is
recommended to anchor off and row ashore and
seek advice before going alongside. Contact can be
made with Mario Mette on ☎ 3496 605 635.

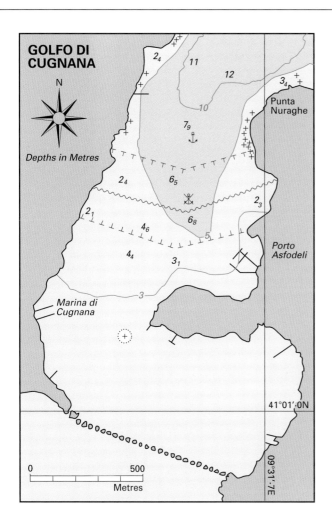

GOLFO DI CUGNANA

N

Depths in Metres

Punta Nuraghe

Porto Asfodeli

Marina di Cugnana

41°01'.0N

09°31'.7E

0   500
Metres

Rotondo looking SW

S22 Porto Rotondo

⊕102 41°01'.82N 09°32'.55E

Depth
1.5 to 6.0m

Number of berths
642 with 64 for visitors

Maximum length
70m

Lights
1009.56 Approach light 41°01'.8N 9°32'.6E
Fl.WR.5s7m7/5M White post 6m (P)
215°-R-240°-W-215° (Red sector covers the dangers
north of Punta Volpe)
1009.6 Left-hand mole head Fl.R.2s5m3M Red post 3m
(P)
1009.62 Right-hand mole head Fl.G.2s5m3M Green post
3m (P)

Port communications
Marina office VHF CH 9 ☎ 0789 34 203 *Fax* 0789 34 368
Email marinaportorotondo@tiscali.it
url www.marinadiportorotondo.it

Another modern marina with all facilities

This is a very sheltered marina complex lying a mile southwest of Punta Volpe.

Approach

The approach is relatively straightforward, with Punta Volpe 1 mile to the east. Keep well clear (at least 500m) of the offlying shallows off this point. The buildings of the development are obvious behind the port but the entrance to the harbour itself is difficult to pick out until quite close. When the approach light is identified, the entrance is just to the west.

4. PORTO CERVO TO OLBIA APPROACH

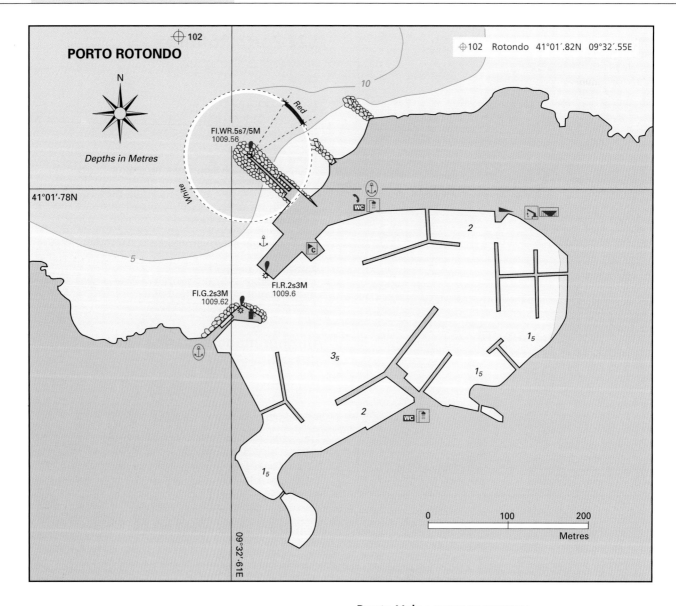

PORTO ROTONDO

N

Depths in Metres

⊕102

⊕102 Rotondo 41°01'.82N 09°32'.55E

41°01'.78N

Fl.WR.5s7/5M
1009.56

Fl.G.2s3M
1009.62

Fl.R.2s3M
1009.6

09°32'.61E

0   100   200
Metres

By GPS

Steer towards ⊕102 from the north quadrant when the approach light and entrance will be seen.

Entrance

The entrance is narrow and as sailing is forbidden in the harbour, you should lower sails and start the engine outside and motor in. Note that berths should be arranged prior to entry.

Berths

Having arranged a berth beforehand you will be met at the entrance by a RIB and taken to the berth.

Facilities

All facilities are available in the harbour.

Punta Volpe 41°02'.2N 09°33'.6E

From Porto Rotondo round Punta Volpe, keeping at least 500m clear as there are many offlying dangers to this low, unlit headland and enter the Golfo di Marinella. There is an occasional beacon on the reef of rocks 400m to the north (1009.65 Q.5m4M Cardinal N (P)). It is reported that there is a reasonable anchorage (in S to SE to E winds) on the west side of the headland in a pair of bays with beaches on 4–7 metres of sand.

S23 Porto Oro (Palumbalza)

⊕103 41°00′.64N 09°33′.24E

Port communications
VHF Ch 9 ☎ 0789 320 05 *Fax* 0789 320 09
Email palumbalza@domina.it
url www.dominapalumbalza.it

This is a small private harbour, literally dug out of the ground, on the western side of the Gulf of Marinella about 1½ miles south of Punta Volpe. There is a small rock jetty on the north side of the entrance with a F.G light. The southern side of the entrance (only 50m away) has a F.R light. Approach to the berths is up a 15m-wide, 50m-long channel 3m deep. There are 50 berths (but only 3 for visitors) but it is obligatory to call before entering. Yachts are restricted to 14m overall length and should proceed at less than 1kn. Water and electricity are available, as are minor repair facilities. There is no fixed fuel point but fuel can be delivered by tanker if required – check in the harbour office for this facility.

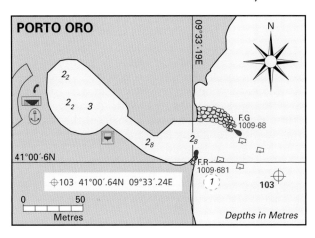

S24 Punta Marana

⊕104 41°00′.32N 09°33′.49E

Depth
1.5 to 2.5m

Number of berths
300 with 5 reserved for visitors

Maximum length
16m

Lights
1009.7 Left-hand mole head 41°00′.3N 9°33′.7E
Iso.R.6s6m3M Red pole 4m (P)
1009.72 Right-hand mole head Iso.G.6s6m3M Green pole 4m (P)

Port communications
Marina Office ☎ 0789 32088 *Fax* 0789 32089

Warnings
There is a small unlit awash rock just to the right of the entrance channel.

Another artificial marina

Punta Marana is on the opposite side of the bay from Porto Oro and it, too, has been made by digging into the land. It has a buoyed approach through rocks and shallows.

Approach

The approach from the north into Golfo de Marinella is clear of all dangers but approaching from the east, stand well offshore from Punta Canigione and Punta Sabina to close the west shore

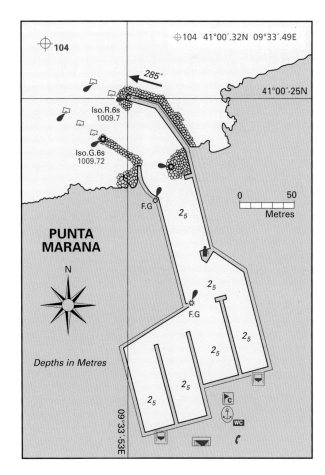

of the gulf. When the longitude of 9°33′.5E is reached, steer south and pick up the small buoys (the outer ones may be lit in season) at the start of the entrance channel.

By GPS

Steer towards ⊕104 from the NW sector and pick up the entrance buoys.

Entrance

There are port and starboard hand buoys which lead to the mole heads. Keep in the centre of the channel as there is an awash rock just to the right of the buoyed channel. On entering between the moles, watch for a pile of rocks to port: it is advisable to keep to the port side of the channel all the way into the small harbour.

Berths

It is essential to call ahead to arrange a berth.

Facilities

All facilities are available in season but there is a marked reduction in numbers of eating places and stores in winter.

⚓ MARINELLEDDA (MARINELLA)

41°00′.6N 09°34′.4E

At the southeast corner of this wide gulf there is the Isola Marinella. The whole island is a tourist complex and on the eastern side there are a number of piers and floating pontoons run by the Circolo Nautico Marinella, to which one can moor if there is space. There are 90 berths: contact the Circolo on ☎

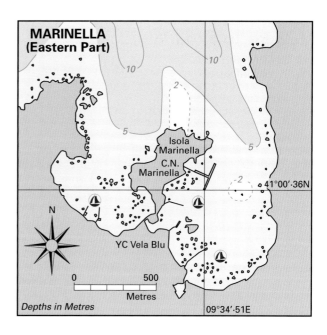

0789 32592 for details of berthing (and draught). There is water and electricity on the pontoons and there is a bar, restaurant and a small shop ashore.

To the south of the island there is a sailing school, Vela Blu, which has a floating pontoon with mooring buoys laid off. It is very rocky and shallow, 1.5–2.5m, with only limited facilities. Call on VHF Ch 9 for queries regarding berths.

It is also possible to anchor north of the island in 5m but it is a long way from the shore with reported poor holding and totally open to the NW–N winds.

SE corner of Golfo Marinella showing Isola Marinella with the T pontoon of the Circolo Nautico and the small pontoon of Yachting Club Vela Blu to the left

PUNTA SABINA AND PUNTA CANIGIONE

Exiting from Golfo di Marinella and proceeding east and south one passes Punta Sabina, a low headland with a reef of awash rocks some 400m to the north. You are advised to give this headland a berth of at least 600 metres. Three-quarters of a mile to the northeast lies the low promontory of Punta Canigione, which also has awash rocks and shallow patches extending some 400m to the north. There is an occasional beacon to the north of the offlying rocks, which may be lit in season. It is 1009.8 Punta Canigione beacon 41°01′.5N 9°35′.7E Q.5m4M ⚓ cardinal (P).

CAPO FIGARI 40°59′.73N 09°39′.88E

Capo Figari is a high (340m) rocky cape that drops straight into the sea at its eastern edge. Watch for the very fluky winds that blow around these high headlands and be prepared to motor if the wind drops completely. To the south of the headland is the Golfo di Olbia. There is a small island, Isola Figarolo, to the south of the cape with a deep water channel between it and the land. There is a light on the island Fl.5s71m11M on a white hut with black bands.

S25 Golfo Aranci

⊕112 40°59′.5N 09°37′.3E
Port Communications
Maritime Authorities ☎ 0789468 80
Email golfoaranci@guardiacostiera.it
Cooperativa Mar ☎ 0789 615 980
Gruppo Ormeggiatori ☎ 0789 468 78

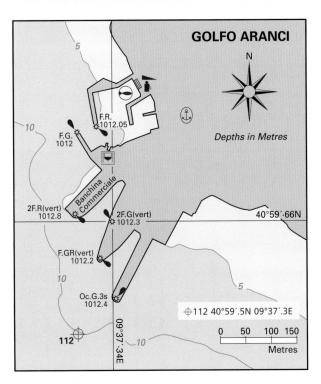

On the north shore, about 2 miles west of Capo Figari, lies Golfo Aranci. This is a commercial port with many fishing boats and ferries coming and going at all times. There are 3 large quays for this traffic and there is a small harbour for 'minor vessels' which is usually completely full of small fishing boats. There are lights on all the quays with the main light on the southeastern mole (Oc.G.3s11m3M with a foghorn). There are plans to construct a port for pleasure boats on the north side of the harbour and work has started on this project. There is fuel and water at the quay with shops, restaurants, etc. ashore and you can moor if you can find a space, but with so many other delightful spots to visit this harbour is not recommended at present. (See photo page 182)

S26 Baia Caddinas

⊕113 40°59′.67N 09°36′.24E
Port communications
☎ 0789 468 13

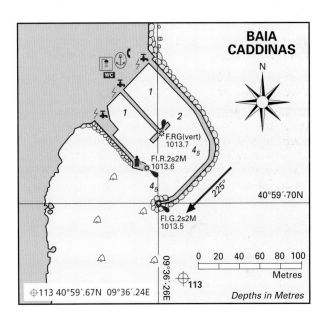

A mile west of Golfo Aranci is a small yacht harbour with red and green buoys (in season) leading into an enclosed harbour with 100 berths (5 for visitors) with depths of 1.2–5m. There are lights on the entrance (Fl.G.2s2M and Fl.R.2s2M), which appear to be in line on approaching, but as the buoys of the fairway are not lit it is not recommended to enter at night. There is another light F.RG(vert)1M on the internal quay. There is water and electricity on the pontoons, with fuel available. Repairs can be undertaken but there is little else in the way of stores, etc. These can be obtained in Golfo Aranci or Olbia.

⚓ ISOLA PORRI 40°57′.36N 09°35′.2E

Halfway down the western coast of the gulf is a small island, Isola Porri, to the west of which is an anchorage sheltered from all but southerly winds. Anchor in 5m in excellent holding of sand and rock but take care of the Secca di Porri, a shallow rock (2m) at the south end of the bay.

5 OLBIA TO CAPO COMINO

Olbia is a busy town with all supplies and facilities available and excellent communications with the rest of the world via its airport and ferry terminals. South of Olbia and down to Capo Coda Cavallo, the coast is indented with many small bays, many with a hotel complex at its head. The passages inside the islands of Tavolara and Molara are strewn with rocks and shallow patches, as the scattered rusting wrecks testify. A large-scale chart is needed but the passages are of reasonable width and, with care, should not be too daunting a prospect. South of the cape the coastal plain widens and the coast is reasonably flat with a small number of yacht harbours and more being developed each year. The area has many superb beaches – some sandy and others of pebbles – and is a favourite holiday area for local Sardinians and Italians who find the Costa Smeralda prices way above their budgets.

Note that a large marine reserve has been set up in this area stretching from Capo Ceraso out round Tavolara, then SE taking in Isola Malarotto and then SW down to nearly Porto Ottiolu. There are 10 light buoys with × topmarks and lit with flashing yellow lights around the perimeter and also enclosing the more important islands. Yachtsmen visiting this area should make themselves aware of the various zones (A, B and C) and what they can and cannot do in each zone (see section II for more details).

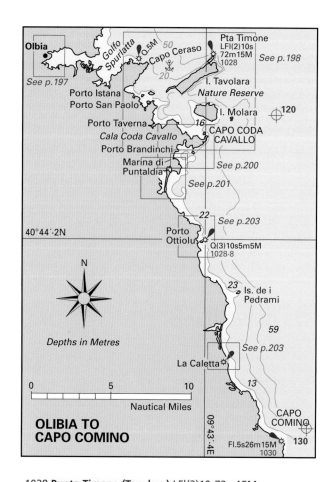

⊕120 Ile Molara 40°52′.5N 09°49′.0E
⊕130 Capo Comino 40°32′.0N 09°52′.0E

1028 **Punta Timone (Tavolara)** LFl(2)10s72m15M
White tower 7m
1028.8 **Isolotto Ottiolu** Q(3)10s5m5M
Cardinal E pole 4m
1030 **Capo Comino** Fl.5s26m15M
White tower and building 20m

Marina di Puntaldia looking S (see page 201)

Porto Ottiolu and Isolotto Ottiolu looking SW (see page 202)

PLANNING GUIDE

Headlands	Ports & anchorages		Open to winds
	S27 ⚓ **Olbia page 196**		E
	⚓ Liscia delle Saline		N
Capo Ceraso			
	⚓ Porto Istana		E
	Isola Piana		E
	⚓ Porto Spurlatta		NE
	⚓ Porto San Paolo		N
	⚓ Porto Taverna		NE
Isola Tavolara			
	⚓ Off SW beach		SE–S
Isola Molara			
	⚓ Cala Coda Cavallo		N
Capo Coda Cavallo (Isola Proratora off)			
	⚓ Porto Brandinchi (very rocky)		E–S
	S28 ⚓ **Marina di Puntaldia page 201**		NE
Punta Sabbatino			
	⚓ Porto di San Teodoro page 201		SE
Punta d'Ottiolu			
	S29 ⚓ **Porto Ottiolu page 202**		SE
Isolotto d'Ottiolu Isolotti dei Pedrami (keep to seaward)			
	S30 ⚓ **La Caletta page 203**		SE
Capo Comino (keep 1 mile offshore S of here!)			

S27 Olbia

⊕114 (outside in Golfo di Olbia) 40°55′.7N 09°35′.9E
⊕115 (just off ferry terminal) 40°55′.33N 09°31.79E

Charts.
Admiralty *1210*
Italian *43, 322, 318*

Depth
7m in channel, 1 to 3m at quay.

Number of berths
150 (all private and full) at YC, a few on quay for visitors

Maximum LOA
16m

Lights
1014 Isola della Bocca LFl.5s24m15M Two-storey white house 22m
1015 Beacon on N side of channel Fl.G.5s5m5M stbd hand ▲ topmark
1015.2 Beacon on S side of channel Fl.R.5s5m5M port hand ■ topmark
11 further beacons line the channel Fl.6s, 5s, 4s, 3s and lead S of ferry terminal
1208(I) Port hand buoy Fl.R.4s3m4M ■ topmark
1212(I) Port hand buoy Fl.R.3s 3m4M ■ topmark
1215(I) Port hand buoy Fl.R.5s 3m4M ■ topmark
1019 Isola di Mezzo S end Fl.G.3s7m4M light on green tank 5m
1020 Quay Brin head F.G.6m3M Green pole 5m

Port communications
Capitaneria VHF Ch 16, 11, ☎ 0789 21 243
Circolo Nautico Olbia ☎ 0789 26 187
Email circolonauticoolbia@tin.it
Lega Navale ☎ *Fax* 0789 26 165
Nausika ☎ 0789 57 181 *Email* info@nausika.it
url www.nausika.it
Olbia Boat Service ☎ 0789 53 060 *Email* obs.obs@tiscali.it

Warnings
This is mainly a commercial harbour and commercial vessels must not be impeded even in the approach channels, but there is ample room. Work is continually going on in the harbour and buoys and beacons may disappear or be moved at any time so care is needed at all times.

A large commercial port

Olbia is the main port for bringing commerce and tourists into Sardinia and does not really cater for yachtsmen. There is, however, a small area on the Mole Benedetto Brin, reserved for yachts, just at the root of the long jetty on the south side. There is also a yacht club with some 150 private moorings to the south where it may be possible to moor if space is available. Just north of the penultimate starboard hand beacon of the entry channel lie 2 yacht yards, Nausika and Olbia Boat Services. The former has 5 berths for visitors in 2.5–6m, while the latter is really only a repair facility but may have a spare berth. These are approached through the mussel beds with yellow buoyed channels.

Approach

From a position in the outer Gulf of Olbia, the massive Capo Figari to the north and the unmistakable granite mass of Isola Tavolara to the south make for easy recognition.

By day

Steer for the southwest corner of the gulf, but keeping well clear of Capo Ceraso which has rocks to the north (with beacon off), until the lighthouse on Isola della Bocca is identified (white square tower on a 2-storey building). Steer for that until the channel beacons are obvious then steer down the channel between the beacons on a course of 269°. When the large ferry terminal becomes obvious, veer off to the left and pick up the second set of channel buoys that lead to the yacht moorings.

By night

Identify the light on Isola della Bocca and steer for it until the ferry terminal light is clear and/or the channel beacons can be picked up. Steer in towards the ferry terminal light on 269° and when close to the end of the jetty, veer to the left and pick up the second channel buoys. Note that the lights of the yacht harbour can be difficult to pick out against the lights of the town.

By GPS

Steer for ⊕114 from the NW quadrant. On arrival steer a course of about 240° towards the Isola della Bocca light. On closing alter to starboard and pass into the channel between the beacons, steering towards ⊕115. At ⊕115 turn slightly to port and follow the latter port hand beacons and later the buoys towards Molo Brin.

Berths

Berthing for visitors is only stern-to to the quay at Molo Brin but contact should be made with the harbourmaster to make sure berths are available. The yacht club has no visitors' berths but may allow a short stay if any members are away cruising.

There are a couple of other berthing possibilities in the port. About 1 mile west of Isola della Bocca light to the north of the main channel there is a small basin protected by a breakwater run by Nausika (☎ 0789 57181/57085) with some 60 berths (5 for

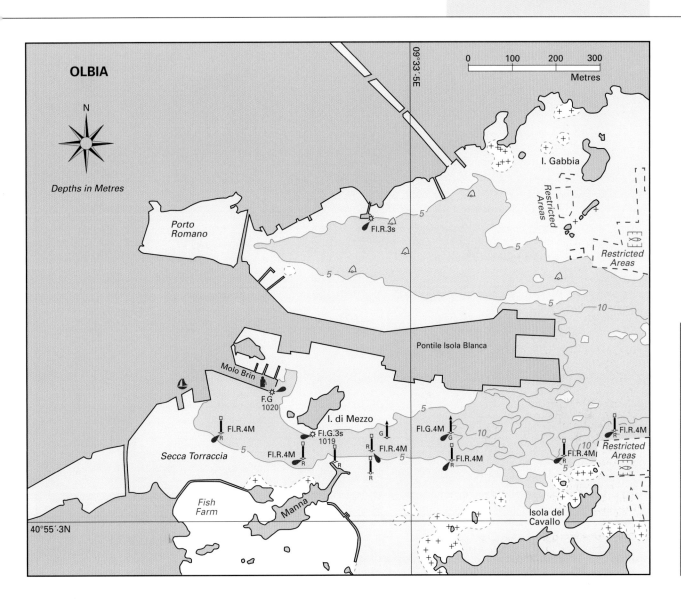

visitors) in 2.5–6 metres. There is electricity and water available but no fuel and although there are first rate repair facilities on site it is a long way to town and the shops. A further half a mile to the west there is another yard run by Olbia Boat Services (☎ 0789 53060) which is mainly a repair yard but they may have spare mooring space, but again with limited facilities. Both these latter yards are reached by threading carefully through the mussel beds which line the main channel!

Formalities

As with all big ports there are police, customs and immigration authorities who may well wish to see the ship's (and possibly the crew's) papers.

Facilities

All.

⚓ **LISCIA DELLE SALINE** 40°54′.4N 09°34′.75E

Leaving Olbia, there is a fair-sized bay just to the southeast of Isola della Bocca where you can anchor in 5m just to the west of the small island. There is just a salt marsh to the south and the anchorage is open to the north.

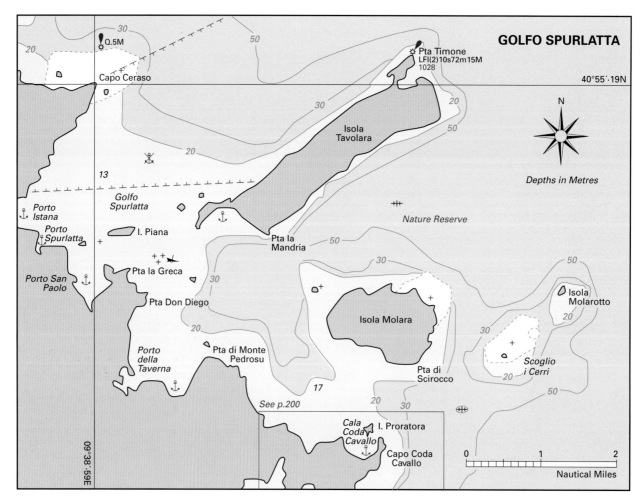

CAPO CERASO 40°55′.19N 09°38′.59E

Continuing south Capo Ceraso must be rounded. It has a large area of foul ground around it which extends for up to half a mile to the north. There is a N Cardinal buoy (1013.8 Q.6m5M) and about 1 mile ESE there is a E Cardinal buoy (1013.9 Q(3)10s6m3M) which show the extent of the foul ground. There is a tower on the point itself, but it is not lit.

⚓ PORTO ISTANA 40°53′.55N 09°37′.6E

Some 2 miles south of Cabo Ceraso at the westernmost part of Golfo Spurlatta there is a small anchorage (with its usual large hotel complex ashore). There is a reef of rocks on the north side. Anchor in 3–5m, on sand and rock but good holding.

Warning

Note that although Capo Ceraso falls steeply into the sea on its eastern side, the waters from Porto Istana to Capo Coda Cavallo have numerous unmarked shallow reefs. The passage between the mainland and Tavolara is tricky and caution must be exercised when navigating in this area. It is recommended that a large-scale chart is used to show the many dangers in these waters. Also note that the whole area is a marine reserve (described in detail in section II) and anchoring is forbidden in areas B and C except on sand and pebble seabed!

⚓ PORTO SPURLATTA (CORALLINA)
40°53′.22N 09°37′.85E

Half a mile SE of Porto Istana is a small inlet with some wooden pontoons in shallow water for hotel guests' RIBs. There are lights on the entrance piers (Fl.G.3s5m2M and Fl.R.3s5m2M) but with depths of 0.5 to 1.5m it is not recommended to enter. Contact can be made on ☎ 0789 36 680. You can anchor off in 3m on sand.

⚓ PORTO SAN PAOLO 40°52′.8N 09°38′.6E

A small bay where you can anchor in 3–5m on sand. Care is needed in the approach as there is an unmarked rock just off the beach in front of the inevitable hotel complex. There may be up to 5 pontoons extending from the shore but the depths are only 1–2m and there are said to be berths for 150 boats, but with maximum length of only 8m. A contact number for Sarda Marine is ☎ 0789 40 056.

There is a NATO pier in this cove which is lit (1028.65 Fl(2)G.6s6m3M Green post 4m). Note that this pier is not to be used by visiting craft.

⚓ PORTO TAVERNA 40°51′.64N 09°39′.9E

This bay is a mile south of Isola Reulino (inshore of which is a shipwreck!). Anchor in 5m on sand and weed but the holding is good. There is a small quay ashore for use by the military but water can be obtained from it. There are many villas on the coast around the bay but no real facilities exist ashore.

W end Tavolara

⚓ ISOLA TAVOLARA 40°53′.5N 09°40′.9E

The island is a steep-to granite plug rising to 565m (1855ft) with a low-lying spit at its western corner. At its NE point is a lighthouse 1028 Punta Timone LFl(2)10s72m15M. The NE end of the island is an American military base and used to be a prohibited area. With the Americans now rumoured to be leaving shortly there is a small porticciolo, Spalmatore di Fuori, on the north coast about a mile SW of the above light. There are two lit breakwaters:

    1028.4 Outer mole head 40°55′.2N 09°43′.6E

        F.R.7m3M Red post 1m

    1028.6 Inner mole head F.G.7m3M Green post 1m

There is a deep water anchorage inside with a rock on the northern shore. There are no facilities whatever and note that it is open to the NW winds which must make it untenable in the strong prevailing winds.

At the SW end there is a simple anchorage in a bay behind the low spit of land, Spalmatore di Terra. There is a pier lit with 1028.62 Pier head Fl.G.5s6m3M Green pole 6m. Anchor in 5 to 8 metres off the pier

Isola Molara 40°52′.1N 09°43′.5E

Another steep-to granite island lying to the south of Tavolara. There is a small bay on the north shore which affords shelter from southerlies but there is nothing else on the island whatsoever.

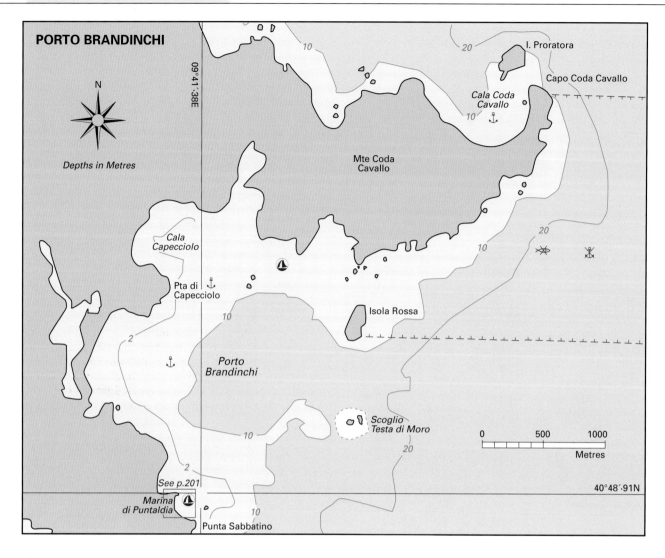

PORTO BRANDINCHI

N

Depths in Metres

09°41′.38E

10

20

I. Proratora

Capo Coda Cavallo

Cala Coda
Cavallo

10

Mte Coda
Cavallo

20

20

10

Cala
Capecciolo

10

Pta di
Capecciolo

Isola Rossa

Porto
Brandinchi

2

10

Scoglio
Testa di Moro

20

0   500   1000

Metres

See p.201

40°48′.91N

Marina
di Puntaldia

10

Punta Sabbatino

⚓ CALA CODA CAVALLO 40°50′.6N 09°43′.2E

Just to the west of the cape and south of Isola
Proratora is a pleasant beach open only to
northwesterly winds. There is some development
ashore with a concrete jetty. Anchor in 3–5m, with
the better holding ground being in the west of the
bay.

CAPO CODA CAVALLO 40°50′.7N 09°43′.5E

This is a long, low point with a hook to the north at
its end. Off the point lies Isola Proratora. Do not
attempt to pass between the island and the cape.
Sporadic development is going on over the headland.

⚓ PORTO BRANDINCHI 40°49′.4N 09°42′.3E

Immediately south of Capo Coda Cavallo is a large
bay with Isola Rossa (or Ruia) at the north end.
Approach should be made on a course of 270°,
leaving the island 100m to starboard to avoid a bank
of unmarked rocks, Scoglio Testa di Moro, situated
at the centre of the entrance to the bay. Anchor in
the bay WNW of the island in 4–8m on sand or off
some shore development WSW of the island.

Cala Coda Cavallo

S28 Marina di Puntaldia

⊕121 40°49´.2N 9°41´.55E

Depth
2.5–5m

Number of berths
400 with 32 for visitors

Maximum length
24m

Lights
1028.7 Right hand entrance 40°48´.8N 9°41´.5E
Fl.G.3s6m5M Green pole on rock 5m
1028.72 Left hand of entrance Fl.R.3s6m5M Red pole
4m
1028.74 Internal mole 2F.G(vert)5m2M Green pole 5m

Port communications
Marina Office VHF Ch 9 ☎ 0784 864 590 *Fax* 0784 864
594 *Email* info@marinadipuntaldia.it
url www.marinadipuntaldia.it

Warnings
About 1 mile at 065° from entrance there is the rock,
Scoglio Testa di Moro, which can be left on either
hand. Closer in, some 400m 085° from the entrance,
there is a large area of rocks and shallows running
south to the islets and headland, Punta Sabitino.

Another first-class modern marina

This is modern marina some 2 miles south of Capo
Coda Cavallo in the southwest corner of Porto
Brandinchi bay, just northwest of Punta Sabbatino.
As usual it is part of a shore development and all
facilities ashore are excellent.

Approach

Having passed Testa di Moro close on either side,
steer west until the longitude of 9°41´.5E is reached
then alter course to enter the marina (about 220°).
This avoids the shallow area running north from
Punta Sabatino.

Marina di Puntaldia looking NW (see also photo page 194)

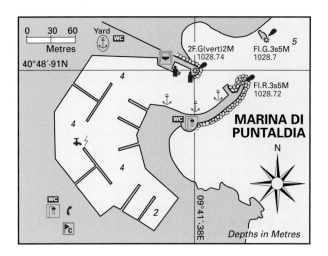

Entrance

Northeast of the entrance there may be three red
buoys which must be left to port. Pick up the green
light on a small rock and the red post on the
breakwater and steer a course to pass between them.
The visitors' berths are to port immediately on
entering. Note that, as the harbour is now well lit,
entry is no longer limited to daylight hours only.
Note that preference is given to departing craft.

Berths

Berthing details should be arranged before entering
by calling the office but if contact cannot be made,
enter and moor to the fuel berth (on starboard side
when entering) and walk to the office to arrange a
berth.

Facilities

All facilities are available.

⚓ PORTO DI SAN TEODORO

⊕122 40°46´.8N 09°41´.5E

Just south of Punta Sabatino there is a very long
(3km) beach, La Cinta, on a spit of land that
separates the Stagno di San Teodoro, an inland body
of brackish water, from the sea. At the south end of
the beach two breakwaters have been constructed.
These breakwaters were constructed back in
1999/2000, but the plan, which involves dredging
and use of several hectares of ground behind the
beach as a very sheltered marina, has been on hold
ever since while further monies are sought. Rumour
had it that work was about to start again in
November 2005, but it will be some time yet before
this marina is operational.

S29 Porto Ottiolu

⊕123 40°44′.49N 09°43′.33E

Depth
2.5 to 5m

Number of berths
400 with 32 for visitors

Maximum LOA
24m

Lights
1028.8 Isolotto Ottiolu 40°44′.2N 09°43′.4E
Q(3)10s5m5M ✦ E cardinal pole 4m
1028.85 Molo Sopraflutto head Fl.G.3s5m5M Green
pole 1m (P)
1028.9 Molo Sottoflutto head Fl.R.3s5m5M Red pole
4m (P)

Port communications
Marina office VHF Ch 9 ☎ 0784 846 211 *Fax* 0784 846
209
Email marina@ottiolu.org *url* www.ottiolu.org

Warnings
The low-lying Isolotto d'Ottiolu is connected to the
shore by a very shallow (<1m) reef which extends for at
least 200m northeast of the islet.

Another modern marina

Some 6½ miles south of Capo Coda Cavallo lies
Punta d'Ottiolu with a small island (Isolotto
d'Ottiolu) half a mile to the south again. Just west of
Isolotto lies the harbour which, has two stone moles
projecting into the sea. There are several (all
sensible) rules to be observed in this marina, such as
no fishing, no ditching of anything from the yacht, a
3-knot speed limit, etc.

Porto Ottiolu (see also photo page 195)

Approach

From the north Leave Punta Ottiolu at least half a
mile to starboard and steer south until the bearing of
the outer mole is 250°. Then it is clear to steer that
course for the harbour entrance, leaving the ✦
cardinal buoy off the island to port.

From the south Leave Punta la Batteria at least a
half a mile to port and go outside the Isola dei Pedrami
(the passage between the island and the shore is very
rocky and shallow and is not recommended). From
the island make a course for Punta d'Ottiolu. Leave
Isolotto d'Ottiolu at least half a mile to port and
continue on course until the outer mole bears
250°and follow that course to the harbour, leaving
the ✦ cardinal buoy on the port side.

By GPS

Steer to ⊕123 from the NW quadrant and then steer
towards the outer mole.

Note that at night the red and green lights appear
virtually in line on the course of 250° until you
swing to port to avoid the end of the outer mole.

Entrance

As the outer mole is approached, swing to port
leaving the mole end some 50m to starboard, then
steer a northwesterly course to enter between the
moles and turn to port on a westerly course to enter
the marina.

Berths

Again it is essential to contact the marina before
entering so that details of the craft can be passed to
the authorities. The visitors' berths are to starboard
immediately on entering.

Facilities

All.

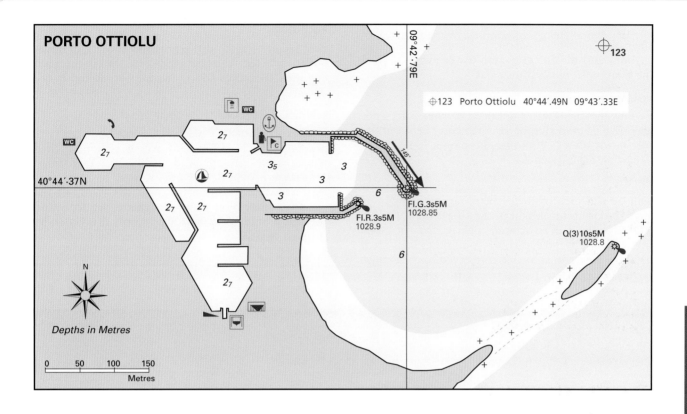

PORTO OTTIOLU

⊕123 Porto Ottiolu 40°44'.49N 09°43'.33E

Fl.G.3s5M
1028.85

Fl.R.3s5M
1028.9

Q(3)10s5M
1028.8

Depths in Metres

0   50   100   150
Metres

S30 La Caletta

⊕124 40°36'.56N 9°45'.6E

Depth
2–5m

Number of berths
450

Maximum length
15m

Lights
1029 Molo Sopraflutto head 40°36'.6N 9°45'.4E
Fl.G.3s11m1M Black and white striped pole 8m
1029.2 MoloSottoflutto head Fl.R.3s13m1M Black and
white striped pole 7m

Port communications
Circolo Nautico La Caletta VHF Ch 9 ☎/Fax 0784 810
631 *Email* Email info@circolonauticolacaletta.it
url www.circolonauticolacaletta.it

A new marina

Some 9 miles south of Ottiolu lies the yacht harbour
of La Calletta. This is a relatively new marina but
seems to have run into problems. Like Castelsardo in
the north, buildings are built but are totally empty
and there are still large-scale works going on around
the harbour. The yacht club is operational but there
are few other facilities in evidence; the fuel berth is
now operational but there are still empty buidings
around the area. The place did look as though it was
on the up, but there is some way to go to reach the
standard of the marinas further north.

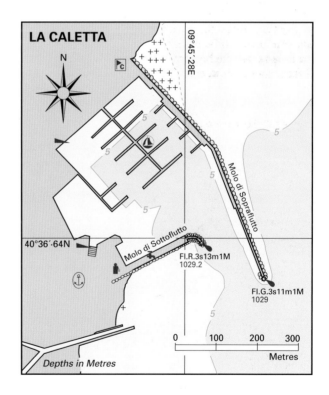

LA CALETTA

Molo di Sopraflutto

Molo di Sottoflutto

Fl.R.3s13m1M
1029.2

Fl.G.3s11m1M
1029

Depths in Metres

0   100   200   300
Metres

Approach

Keep at least a mile off shore along this coast to
avoid shallow patches inshore and the Isola dei
Pedrami. This makes La Caletta difficult to see, but

an approach towards ⊕124 on a course of 270° will clear all dangers. Closer in, the houses behind the harbour and the San Giovanni tower at the root of the long mole will become clear.

Entrance

Follow the breakwater south and round the end, leaving it 25m to starboard. Then enter between the pier heads on a NW course, keeping a lookout for departing fishing vessels.

Berths

Call up the yacht club for berthing instructions or enter, moor up to the end of the 'T' pontoon and go ashore to the club to arrange a berth. Do not moor up to the south mole as this is the fishing boat area, or in the NW corner as this is reserved for passenger ferries.

Facilities

Few facilities around the port, no shower or toilet block but use can be made of the yacht club facilities. All stores and restaurants are found in the village.

CAPO COMINO 40°31′.8N 09°49′.7E

5 miles south of La Caletta is Capo Comino, a bare headland (lit Fl.5s26m15M which is housed in a white square tower and dwelling). Yachtsmen venturing further south are advised to remain at least one mile offshore to avoid the worst of the gusts that may blow down the valleys suddenly and the many unlit rocks that abound off this generally steep-to coast.

La Caletta looking NE

Appendix

I. Waypoint list for Corsica and North Sardinia

CORSICA

1		Ajaccio landfall	41°47′.5N	08°30′.0E
2		Iles Sanguinaires	41°52′.0N	08°33′.0E
3	C1	Ajaccio approach	41°54′.0N	08°45′.0E
4	C1	Tino Rossi	41°55′.16N	08°44′.75E
5	C1	Charles Ornano	41°55′.8N	08°44′.75E
6		Cap Muro	41°44′.5N	08°38′.5E
7	C2	Porto Pollo	41°42′.41N	08°48′.0E
8	C3	Propriano approach	41°40′.9N	08°53′.9E
9	C3	Propriano marina	41°40′.7N	08°54′.4E
10		Pte Sénétosa	41°33′.5N	08°46′.0E
11		Les Moines	41°26′.0N	08°53′.0E
12		Baie de Figari	41°27′.1N	09°03′.3E
13	C4	Calderello approach	41°27′.64N	09°03′.42E
14	C4	Calderello port	41°28′.44N	09°04′.3E
15		Cap de Feno	41°23′.0N	09°05′.5E
16	C5	Bonifacio	41°23′.1N	09°08′.75E
17		Sud Lavezzi	41°17′.5N	09°15′.5E
18	C6	Port de Cavallo	41°21′.25N	09°16.06E
19		Perduto	41°21′.0N	09°20′.5E
20		La Vacca	41°33′.0N	09°26′.5E
21	C7	Porto-Vecchio landfall	41°37′.0N	09°27′.5E
22	C7	Porto-Vecchio gulf	41°36′.3N	09°22′.5E
23	C7	Porto-Vecchio buoy1	41°36′.5N	09°19′.05E
24	C7	Porto-Vecchio buoy2	41°35′.58N	09°17′.86E
25	C7	Porto-Vecchio marina	41°35′.43N	09°17′.24E
26	C8	Solenzara	41°51′.36N	09°24′.3E
27		Tavignano	42°06′.0N	09°36′.0E
28	C9	Taverna	42°20′.5N	09°32′.6E
29		Lucciana Terminal	42°34′.0N	09°35′.0E
30	C10	Bastia	42°42′.0N	09°32′.0E
31	C10	Vieux Port	42°41′.7N	09°27′.5E
32	C10	Port Toga	42°42′.65N	09°27′.5E
33		Cap Sagro	42°48′.0N	09°31′.0E
34	C11	Luri	42°53′.2N	09°28′.6E
35	C12	Macinaggio	42°57′.8N	09°27′.4E
36		Finocchiarola	43° 00′.0N	09°30′.0E
37		Giraglia N	43° 02′.3N	09°24′.2E
38		Giraglia S landfall	43° 01′.0N	09°24′.5E
39		Capo Grosso	43° 00′.0N	09°19′.4E
40	C13	Centuri	42°58′.1N	09°20′.8E
41		Pta di Canelle	42°50′.0N	09°17′.5E
42	C14	San Florent gulf	42°40′.93N	09°17′.4E
43	C14	San Florent marina	42°40′.78N	09°17′.78E
44		Pta di Mignola	42°45′.0N	09°07.5′E
45	C15	Ile Rousse approach	42°39′.0N	08°56′.5E
46	C15	Ile Rousse marina	42°38′.5N	08°56′.5E
47		Danger d'Algajola	42°37′.0N	08°50′.7E
48	C16	Sant'Ambrogio	42°36′.2N	08°49′.8E
49	C17	Calvi	42°33′.9N	08°45′.9E
50		Not allocated		
51		Pta Revellata	42°36′.0N	08°43′.0E
52		Gargalu	42°22′.5N	08°31′.0E
53	C18	Porto Marine	42°16.05N	08°41.28E
54		Cap Rossu	42°14′.0N	08°31′.5E
55	C19	Cargèse	42°07′.7N	08°36′.0E
56	C20	Sagone	42°06′.0N	08°41′.5E

SARDINIA

60	S1	Alghero landfall	40°30′.0N	08°00′.0E
61	S1	Alghero harbour	40°34′.0N	08°18′.3E
62	S2	Fertilia	40°35′.4N	08°17′.6E
63	S3	Porto Conte	40°35′.72N	08°12′.76E
64	S4	Tramariglio	40°35′.5N	08°10′.3E
65		Capo Caccia	40°32′.5N	08°08′.5E
66		C Argentiera	40°44′.0N	08°07′.0E
67		C Falcone	40°58′.5N	08°10′.5E
68		C Tumberino	41°03′.0N	08°11′.5E
69		C dello Scorno W	41°08′.5N	08°16′.0E
70		C dello Scorno E	41°08′.5N	08°22′.0E
71		C Trabuccato	41°03′.0N	08°22′.5E
72		Fornelli	40°57′.6N	08°16′.0E
73	S5	Rada della Reale	41°02′.35N	08°17′.1E
74	S6	YC l'Ancora	40°57′.57N	08°13′.2E
75	S7	Stintino approach	40°56′.2N	08°14′.13E
76	S7	Porto Mannu	40°56′.27N	08°13′.81E
77	S7	Porto Minore	40°56′.07N	08°13′.77E
78	S7	New Development	40°56′.27N	08°13.90E
79	S8	Porto Torres	40°51′.0N	08°24′.2E
80		Pta Vignola	40°56′.0N	08°41′.5E
81	S9	Castelsardo marina	40°55′.0N	08°42′.25E
82	S10	Isola Rossa	41°00′.7N	08°52′.0E
83		Capo Testa	41°15′.5N	09°08′.0E
84	S11	Sta Teresa	41°15′.3N	09°11′.9E
85		Pta Falcone	41°16′.5N	09°14′.5E
86	S12	Conca Verde	41°12′.7N	09°16′.8E
87		N of Razzoli	41°19′.0N	09°20′.0E
88		N of Maddalena	41°19′.0N	09°25′.5E
89	S13	YC Porto Rafael	41°11′.75N	09°22′.E
90	S14	Palau	41°11′.0N	09°23′.25E
91	S15	Porto Mercantile	41°12′.6N	09°24′.35E
92	S15	Cala Mangiavolpe	41°12′.7N	09°24′.65E
93	S15	Cala Camiciotto	41°12′.7N	09°25′.7E
94	S15	Marina del Ponte	41°12′.9N	09°26′.4E
95	S16	Porto Massimo	41°15′.4N	09°26′.0E
96		Monaci	41°13′.0N	09°35′.0E
97	S17	Cannigione	41°06′.6N	09°26′.8E
98	S18	Cala Bitta	41°07′.72N	09°27′.95E
99	S19	Poltu Quatu	41°08′.63N	09°29′.7E
100	S20	Porto Cervo	41°08′.4N	09°33′.1E
101	S21	Portisco	41°01′.96N	09°31′.7E
102	S22	Rotondo	41°01′.82N	09°32′.55E
103	S23	Porto Oro	41°00′.64N	09°33′.24E
104	S24	Punta Marana	41°00′.32N	09°33′.49E
110		Capo Figari	41°00′.0N	09°43′.0E
111		Not allocated		
112	S25	Golfo Aranci	40°59′.5N	09°37′.3E
113	S26	Baia Caddinas	40°59′.67N	09°36′.24E
114	S27	Olbia (outside)	40°55′.7N	09°35′.9E
115	S27	Olbia (inner)	40°55′.33N	09°31′.79E
120		Ile Molara	40°52′.5N	09°49′.0E
121	S28	Puntaldia	40°49′.2N	09°41′.55E
122		San Teodoro	40°46′.8N	09°41′.5E
123	S29	Porto Ottiolu	40°44′.49N	09°43′.33E
124	S30	La Caletta	40°36′.56N	09°45′.6E
130		Capo Comino	40°32′.0N	09°52′.0E
131		C. Bellavista landfall	39°56′.0N	09°48′.0E
132		C. Carbonara landfall	39°00′.0N	09°30′.0E
133		San Antloco landfall	39°00′.0N	08°12′.0E
134		Oristano landfall	39°46′.0N	08°11′.0E
135		Capo Teulada	38°51′N	08°39′E
136		Cagliari	39°09′N	09°07′E
137		Villasimius	39°07′.3N	09°29′.5E

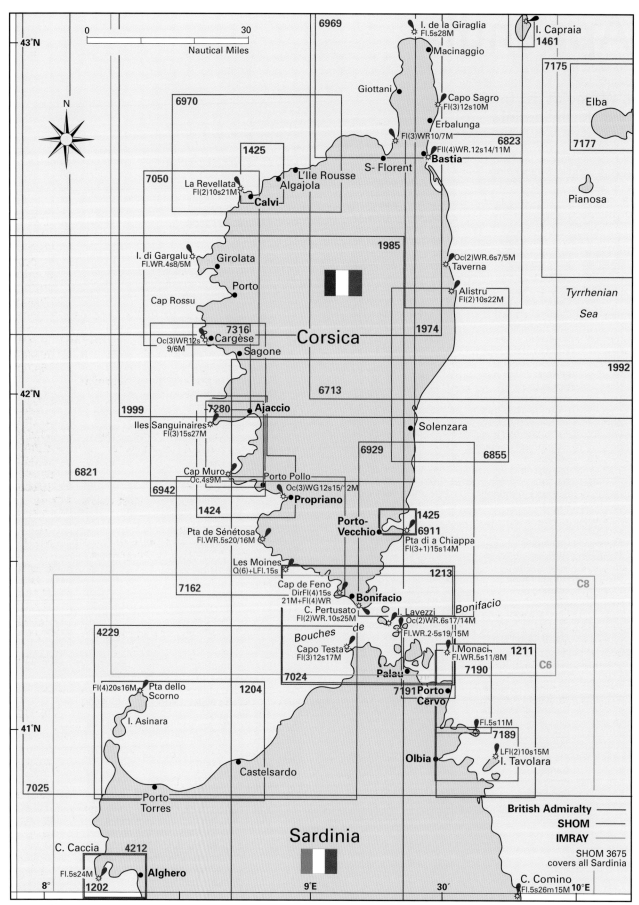

43°N

0   30
Nautical Miles

N

6969

I. de la Giraglia
Fl.5s28M

I. Capraia
1461

7175

Macinaggio

Elba

Giottani

Capo Sagro
Fl(3)12s10M

Erbalunga
Fl(3)WR10/7M

6823

7177

S- Florent

Bastia
Fll(4)WR.12s14/11M

6970

1425

7050

La Revellata
Fl(2)10s21M

L'Ile Rousse
Algajola

Calvi

Pianosa

1985

Oc(2)WR.6s7/5M
Taverna

I. di Gargalu
Fl.WR.4s8/5M

Girolata

Porto

Alistru
Fl(2)10s22M

Cap Rossu

7316
Cargèse
Oc(3)WR12s
9/6M

Sagone

Corsica

1974

Tyrrhenian

Sea

1992

42°N

6713

1999

7280

Ajaccio

Iles Sanguinaires
Fl(3)15s27M

Solenzara

6929

6855

6821

Cap Muro
Oc.4s9M

Porto Pollo

6942

Oc(3)WG12s15/12M

1424

Propriano

Porto-
Vecchio

1425
6911

Pta di a Chiappa
Fl(3+1)15s14M

Pta de Sénétosa
Fl.WR.5s20/16M

Les Moines
Q(6)+LFl.15s

1213

C8

7162

Cap de Feno
DirFl(4)15s
21M+Fl(4)WR

Bonifacio

Bonifacio

C. Pertusato
Fl(2)WR.10s25M

I. Lavezzi
Oc(2)WR.6s17/14M

4229

Bouches

de

Fl.WR.2·5s19/15M

Capo Testa
Fl(3)12s17M

Bonifacio

Palau

I. Monaci
Fl.WR.5s11/8M

1211

7190

C6

7024

7191

Porto-
Cervo

Fl(4)20s16M

Pta dello
Scorno

1204

I. Asinara

41°N

Fl.5s11M

7189

LFl(2)10s15M
I. Tavolara

Olbia

7025

Castelsardo

Porto-
Torres

Sardinia

C. Caccia

4212

Fl.5s24M

Alghero

1202

British Admiralty ——
SHOM ——
IMRAY ——

SHOM 3675
covers all Sardinia

C. Comino
Fl.5s26m15M

8°   9°E   30'   10°E

BRITISH ADMIRALTY, FRENCH (SHOM) AND IMRAY CHARTS

II. Bibliography

NAVIGATIONAL
Admiralty publications
Sailing Directions Mediterranean Pilot Vol. II (NP 46) and
supplements
List of Lights *Vol. E, Mediterranean, Black and Red Seas*
List of Radio Signals *Vol 1(1) Coast Radio Stations* NP281(1)
*Vol 2 Radio Navigation Aids, Electronic Position Fixing
Systems and Radio Time Signals* NP282
Vol3(l) *Maritime Safety Information Services* NP283(1) Vol 5
Global Maritime Distress and Safety Systems NP285 Vol 6(3)
Pilot Services, Traffic Services and Port Operations NP286(3)
Admiralty Maritime Communications NP289
French Naval publications
Instructions Nautiques Series D, Vol. II
Italian Naval Publications
Portolano del Mediterraneo Vol. 1A (Istituto Idrografico
N. 3148)
Elenco di Fan (Istituto Idrografico N. 3134)
The volumes above are all for bigger craft than are catered
for in this book, but they are useful reference works.
OTHER PILOTS AND GUIDES
Mediterranean France and Corsica Pilot Rod Heikell (Imray)
Italian Waters Pilot Rod Heikell (Imray)
Imray Mediterranean Almanac ed. Rod Heikell and Lucinda
Michell (Imray) A biennial almanac
Votre Livre de Bord A type of almanac with many plans –
published annually (Bloc Marin)
Pagine Azzurre Italian handbook/almanac, published
annually
Weather Forecasts RYA Handbook G5 (RYA) comprehensive
weather data, updated annually
Planning a Foreign Cruise Vol 2 (RYA) RYA Handbook C2,
updated annually
Plans, Pratiques des Ports (Guide Méditerranée) Produced
annually with main ports and all addresses and
telephone numbers
Further reading
The Granite Island Dorothy Carrington (Penguin Books
1984)
Green Guide Michelin – Corse. Useful detail but not up to
the usual standard
A journal of a tour to Corsica James Boswell (Turtle Point
Press, 1951)
Corsica (Lonely Planet Guides, 2004)
Corsica (Rough Guides, 2005)
Corsica Diving Guide Kurt Amsler (The Crowood Press, 2000)
Sardinia (Lonely Planet Guides, 2004)
Sardinia (Rough Guides, 2004)
Foods of Sicily and Sardinia Giuliano Bugialli (Razzoli, 2003)
Sardegna (Touring Club of Italy, 2005)
Sardinia – Ancient peoples and places Margaret Guido
(Thames and Hudson, 1964)
Diving – Sardinia Egidio Trainito (White Star Guides, 2004)

III Charts

The charts listed in this section are available from:
Imray Laurie Norie & Wilson Ltd
Wych House The Broadway St Ives
Cambridgeshire PE27 5BT England
+44(0)1480 462114 *Fax* +44(0)1480 496109
www.imray.com
Payment can be made by credit card.

British Admiralty charts

Chart Title	Scale
1202 Ports on the north and west coasts of Sardinia	
Porto di Alghero	7,500
Porto di Carloforte: Porto Vesme	12,500
Porto Torres	15,000
Approaches to Alghero	50,000
1204 Approaches to Porto Torres	60,000
1205 Oristano and approaches	40,000
Oristano	20,000
1207 Canale di San Pietro and Golfo di Palmas	50,000
Porto di Sant' Antioco (Pointe Romano)	10,000
1208 Approaches to Cagliari	30,000
Porto di Cagliari	15,000
1210 Ports on the east coast of Sardinia	
Porto di Arbatax	10,000
Porto di Olbia	12,500
Approaches to Arbatax	30,000
1211 Capo Ferro to Capo Coda Cavallo	50,000
1212 Approaches to La Maddalena	25,000
La Maddalena	10,000
1213 Bonifacio strait	50,000
Golfo di Arzachena	30,000
1424 Ports on the south and west coasts of Corse	
Bonifacio	7,500
Ajaccio: Propriano	10,000
Golfe d'Ajaccio and Golfe de Valinco	60,000
1425 Ports on the north and east coasts of Corse	
Macinaggio	10,000
Bastia	15,000
Calvi	17,500
Porto-Vecchio	25,000
Approaches to Calvi	50,000
1983 Capo Carbonara to Capo San Vito	300,000
1985 Ajaccio to Oristano including Bonifacio strait	300,000
1990 Oristano to Arbatax including Golfo di Cagliari	300,000
1992 Porto-Vecchio to Arbatax including Bonifacio Strait	300,000
1998 Nice to Livorno including Gulf of Genoa	300,000
1999 Livorno to Civitavecchia including Northern Corse	300,000

French charts (SHOM)

1461 Ile Capraja		20,000
3675 Carte générale de l'Île de Sardaigne		385,000
4212 Port Conte et Rade d'Alghero		30,000
4229 Golfe d'Asinara		94,600
Cartouches: Passage dei Fornelli		15,000
Porto Torres		25,000
6713 Côte Nord-Est de la Corse, canal de Corse		152,000
6821 Côte Ouest de Corse – Du Cap Corse au golfe d'Ajaccio		152,000

6822	Abords Nord de Bastia	50,300
6823	Abords Sud de Bastia	50,300
6850	Saint-Florent, Centuri, Macinaggio	
	Cartouches: Golfe de Saint-Florent	15,000
	Baie de Centuri	10,000
	Baies de Macinaggio et de Tamarone	10,000
6851	Ports d'Ajaccio et de Propriano	
	Cartouches: Port d'Ajaccio	7,500
	Port de Propriano	10,000
6855	Du phare d'Alistro à Solenzara	51,000
6856	Abords et Port de Bastia	15,000
6911	Golfe de Porto-Vecchio	15,000
6929	Abords de Porto-Vecchio – De l'anse de Favone aux îles Lavezzi	50,000
6942	De Punta d'Orchina au Cap Muro – Abords d'Ajaccio	50,000
6969	Du Cap Corse à la Punta di l'Acciolu – Golfe de Saint-Florent	50,300
6970	De Punta di l'Acciolu à Capo Cavallo	50,500
6980	L'Ile Rousse – Sant'Ambrogio – Calvi	
	Cartouches: Abords de l'île Rousse	15,000
	Abords de la Marine de Sant'Ambrogio	15,000
	Abords de Calvi – De Punta Spano à La Revellata	15,000
7024	Bouches de Bonifacio	50,000
	Cartoches: Golfo di Arzachena	50,000
7025	Ile de Corse	250,000
7050	De Calvi à Cargèse	50,000
7096	Baie de Figari – Port de Bonifacio	
	Cartouches: Baie de Figari	10,000
	Port de Bonifacio	5,000
7162	Du Capo Muro au Capo Feno	50,000
	Cartouches: Mouillage de Porto Pollo	10,000
	Mouillage de Campomoro	10,000
7189	Golfes d'Olbia et d'Aranci – Iles Tavolara et Molara	25,000
7190	Golfe de Congianus – De Capo Ferro à Capo Figari	25,000
7191	Archipel de la Maddelena	25,000
7280	Golfe d'Ajaccio	25,000
7316	Golfe de Sagone	25,000

Italian charts

40	Da Capo Corso ad Alistro e all'isola d'Elba	100,000
41	Da Alistro alle Bocche di Bonifacio	100,000
42	Da Castelsardo a Olbia e Bocche di Bonifacio	100,000
43	Da Olbia a Capo de Monte Santu	100,000
44	Da Capo di Monte Santu a Capo Carbonara	100,000
45	Da Capo Carbonara a Capo Spartivento	100,000
46	Da Capo Spartivento all'Isola S Pietro	100,000
47	Dall'isola S Pietro a Capo S Marco	100,000
48	Da Capo S Marco a Capo Caccia	100,000
49	Da Capo Caccia a Castel Sardo e isola Asinara	100,000
281	Rade di la Maddalena e di S Stefano	5,000
282	Ancoraggi tra La Maddalena e la costa nord della Sardegna	10,000
286	Porto Torres	10,000
289	Golfo dell'Asinara	50,000
	Passaggio del Fornelli	10,000
291	Porto di Oristano	10,000

292	Porto Conte e rada di Alghero	25,000
293	Golfo di Oristano	40,000
294	Canale di S Pietro	25,000
295	Porti di Porto Vesme e Portoscuso	5,000
296	Porto di S Antioco (Ponte Romano)	5,000
297	Porto di Carloforte	5,000
298	Golfo di Palmas	50,000
299	Litorale di Cagliari	30,000
311	Porto di Cagliari	10,000
315	Litorale di Arbatax	25,000
316	Porto di Arbatax	5,000
318	Porto di Olbia	10,000
319	Porti Minori a ancoraggi della Sardegna nord-orientale	
	Cala Volpe	5,000
	Iscia di Vacca	5,000
	Porto Cervo	5,000
322	Golfi di Oblia e degli Aranci – Isole Tavolara e Molara	25,000
	Porto di Golfo Aranci	5,000
323	Golfo di Congianus e Passo delle Bisce	25,000
324	Arcipelago di La Maddalena – Foglio est	25,000
325	Arcipelago di La Maddalena – Foglio ovest	25,000
326	Bocche di Bonifacio	50,000
	Golfo di Arzachena	50,000
911/05	Porto di Alghero	4,000
911/06	Porto di Bosa Marina	4,000
912/01	Porto di Santa Teresa di Gallura (Longosardo)	5,000
2140	Litorale e porto di Bastia	15,000
2143	Golfo di Porto Vecchio	15,000
2145	Baia di Figari – Porto de Bonifacio	
	Baia de Figari	10,000
	Porto de Bonifacio	5,000
2147	Porti de Ajaccio e di Propriano	
	Porto di Ajaccio	7,500
	Porto di Propriano	10,000
2150	Da Cap Corse a Punta di l'Acciolu – Golfo di Saint-Florent	50,300
2152	Da Punta di l'Acciolu a Capo Cavallo	50,500
2154	Da Calvi a Cargese	50,000
2156	Da Punta d'Orchina a Capo Muro – Paraggi di Ajaccio	50,000
2158	Da Cap Muro a Cap de Feno	50,000
	Ancoraggi di Porto Pollo	10,000
	Ancoraggi di Campomoro	10,000
2160	Litorale di Porto-Vecchio – Dall'anse de Favone alle Iles Lavezzi	50,000
2162	Dal faro d'Alistro a Solenzara	51,000
2164	Litorale a sud di Bastia	50,600
2166	Litorale a nord di Bastia	50,300

Imray Charts

M6	La Corse	255,000
	Plans Macinaggio, Bastia, Calvi, Ajaccio, Bonifacio, Propriano	
M8	Sardegna (north)	250,000
	Plans Porto Brandinghi, Alghero, Porto Cervo, Palau, La Caletta, Porto Torres, Stintino, Passaggio del Fornelli, Castelsardo	
M9	Sardegna (south)	250,000
	Plans Cagliari, Arbatax, Torre Grande, Carloforte, Calasetta, Capitana, Porto Seuso, Villasimius, Marina Piccola, Porto Carallo	

Index

LIFE-SAVING SIGNALS

SOLAS CHAPTER V REGULATION 29

To be used by Ships, Aircraft or Persons in Distress when communicating with life-saving stations, maritime rescue units and aircraft engaged in search and rescue operations.

Note: All Morse Code signals by light (below).

1. SEARCH AND RESCUE UNIT REPLIES

YOU HAVE BEEN SEEN, ASSISTANCE WILL BE GIVEN AS SOON AS POSSIBLE

Orange smoke flare

Three white star signals or three light and sound rockets fired at approximately 1 minute intervals

2. SURFACE TO AIR SIGNALS

Note: Use International Code of Signals by means of light or flags or by laying out the symbol on the deck or ground with items that have a high contrast background.

MESSAGE	ICAO/IMO VISUAL SIGNALS	
REQUIRE ASSISTANCE	V • • • —	⊠
REQUIRE MEDICAL ASSISTANCE	X — • • —	⊞
NO or NEGATIVE	N — •	▦
YES or AFFIRMATIVE	Y — • — —	▨
PROCEEDING IN THIS DIRECTION	↑	

3. AIR TO SURFACE REPLIES

Note: Use signals most appropriate to prevailing conditions.

MESSAGE UNDERSTOOD

Drop a message. OR Rocking wings. OR Flashing landing or navigation lights on and off twice. OR T — OR R • — •

MESSAGE NOT UNDERSTOOD

Straight and level flight. ← OR Circling. OR R • —   P • — — •   T —

4. AIR TO SURFACE DIRECTION SIGNALS

SEQUENCE OF 3 MANOEUVRES MEANING PROCEED IN THIS DIRECTION

Circle vessel at least once.   Cross low, ahead of vessel rocking wings.   Overfly vessel and head in required direction.

YOUR ASSISTANCE IS NO LONGER REQUIRED

Cross low, astern of vessel rocking wings.   Note: As a non prefererred alternative to rocking wings, varying engine tone or volume may be used.

5. SURFACE TO AIR REPLIES

MESSAGE UNDERSTOOD - I WILL COMPLY

Change course to required direction.   OR   T —   OR   Code & answering pendant "Close Up".

I AM UNABLE TO COMPLY

International flag "N".   OR   N — •

6. SHORE TO SHIP SIGNALS

SAFE TO LAND HERE

Vertical waving of both arms, white flag, light or flare

OR

K — • —

LANDING HERE IS DANGEROUS ADDITIONAL SIGNALS MEAN SAFER LANDING IN DIRECTION INDICATED

OR

Horizontal waving white flag, light or flare. Putting one flare/ flag on ground and moving off with a second indicates direction of safer landing.

S • • • Landing here is dangerous.

R • — • Land to right of your current heading.

L • — • • Land to left of your current heading.